phil
9,27

D0630569

180
C816f

FROM RELIGION TO PHILOSOPHY

A Study in the Origins
of Western Speculation

F. M. Cornford

Dover Publications, Inc.
Mineola, New York

To

FRANCIS DARWIN

Bibliographical Note

This Dover edition, first published in 2004, is an unabridged republication of the 1957 Harper Torchbook edition of the work originally published in 1912 by E. Arnold, London.

Library of Congress Cataloging-in-Publication Data

Cornford, Francis Macdonald, 1874–1943.
    From religion to philosophy : a study in the origins of Western speculation / F.M. Cornford.
        p. cm.
    Originally published: London : E. Arnold, 1912.
    Includes bibliographical references and indexes.
    ISBN 0-486-43372-2 (pbk.)
    1. Philosophy, Ancient. 2. Greece—Religion. I. Title.

B188.C6 2004
180—dc22

2004041428

Manufactured in the United States of America
Dover Publications, Inc., 31 East 2nd Street, Mineola, N.Y. 11501

PREFACE

THE words, Religion and Philosophy, perhaps suggest to most people two distinct provinces of thought, between which, if (like the Greeks) we include Science under Philosophy, there is commonly held to be some sort of border warfare. It is, however, also possible to think of them as two successive phases, or modes, of the expression of man's feelings and beliefs about the world ; and the title of this book implies that our attention will be fixed on that period, in the history of the western mind, which marks the passage from the one to the other. It is generally agreed that the decisive step was taken by the Greeks about six centuries before our era. At that moment, a new spirit of rational inquiry asserted its claim to pronounce upon ultimate things which had hitherto been objects of traditional belief. What I wish to prove, however, is that the advent of this spirit did not mean a sudden and complete breach with the older ways of thought.

There is a real continuity between the earliest rational speculation and the religious representation that lay behind it ; and this is no mere matter of superficial analogies, such as the allegorical equation of the elements with the Gods of popular belief. Philosophy inherited from religion certain great conceptions—for instance, the ideas of ' God,' ' Soul,' ' Destiny,' ' Law '—which continued to circumscribe the movements of rational thought and to determine their main directions. Religion expresses itself in poetical symbols and in terms of mythical personalities ; Philosophy prefers the language of dry abstraction, and speaks of *substance, cause, matter*, and so forth. But the outward difference only disguises an inward and substantial affinity between these two successive products of the same consciousness. The modes of thought that attain to clear definition and explicit statement in philosophy were already implicit in the unreasoned intuitions of mythology.

v

Diogenes Laertius groups the philosophers in two successions, Ionian and Italiote, headed by Anaximander and Pythagoras, as if the Greeks themselves had divined that two tendencies had been at work in shaping their systems of thought. This instinct, as I shall try to show, was right : there were, in fact, two traditions, which may be called ' scientific ' and ' mystical,' moved by two distinguishable impulses along lines diverging, more and more widely, towards opposite conclusions. These impulses are still operative in our own speculation, for the simple reason that they correspond to two permanent needs of human nature, and characterise two familiar types of human temperament.

In our own time, the scientific tendency has been the more easily understood and interpreted, because it falls in with the habit of thought of a scientific age. Driven by a deep-lying need to master the world by understanding it, science works steadily towards its goal—a perfectly clear conceptual model of reality, adapted to explain all phenomena by the simplest formula that can be found. *Malheur au vague ; mieux vaut le faux* ! In the Ionian schools of Eastern Greece, science comes to its fulfilment in Atomism. When we contemplate the finished result, we see that, in banishing ' the vague,' it has swept away everything in which another type of mind finds all the value and significance of the world. The Gods have disappeared ; the Soul is reduced to a dust of material particles ; in a word, Life has gone out of Nature. Such is the predestined conclusion of a science inspired by the ideal lucidity of geometry, and neglectful of biology. Admirable as a tool of research into inorganic nature, it strikes a chill of horror into men of an opposite temperament, who will not seek the living among the dead.

The mystical spirit, prompted by a different need, works along other lines. To Pythagoras, philosophy was not an engine of curiosity, but a way of life and death. The Western schools, overshadowed by Pythagoreanism, are rooted in certain beliefs about the nature of the divine and the destiny of the human soul. Upon those beliefs their philosophy of nature is built. Holding, no less strongly than the scientific tradition, to the characteristically Greek conviction that the world must be rational, these western philosophies present themselves as a series of attempts to justify faith to reason. Parmenides boldly condemns the sensible world to unreality, when it seems to conflict with the logical consequences of religious preconception. Empedocles expends a wealth of ingenuity in devising a reconciliation with science. Plato sinks in the Titanic effort to stand with feet on earth and uphold the sky. What most concerns all three is summed up in the words ' God ' and ' Soul '—those very terms which science so complacently dispensed with.

Now, the two tendencies, or temperaments, which, in the series of philosophical systems, have left so plain a record of their characteristic aspirations and visions of life and nature, did not suddenly spring into being in the century of Anaximander and Pythagoras. The philosophic Muse is not a motherless Athena : if the individual intellect is her father, her older and more august parent is Religion. Behind Anaximander stands the Ionian Homer, with his troop of luminous Olympians ; behind Pythagoras we discern the troubled shapes of Orpheus and Dionysus. It is natural to suppose that the two philosophic traditions are severally related to the types of Greek religion— Olympian and Dionysian—in which the same contrasted temperaments had framed mythical symbols, to express what they felt towards the life of nature and the life of man.

Beginning with the scientific tradition, I shall try to prove that a real thread of continuity can be traced back from the final achievement of science—the representation of a world of individual atoms, governed by Necessity or Chance—to the final achievement of Olympianism, mirrored in Homer's supernatural world of individual Gods, subordinate to Destiny (*Moira*). This subjection of all individual powers, divine and human, to *Moira* is the profoundest, and (at first sight) the most baffling, dogma in this type of religion. In the first chapter, I shall attempt an analysis of *Moira*, working backwards from Anaximander to Homer and Hesiod, with a view to establishing the persistence of this conception, right on through the course of Greek science, in which it holds the place now occupied by Natural Law.

When we have gone back to Homer, most scholars will think that we have touched the pillars of Hercules, and that we had better not pry into the prehistoric darkness, which the accidents

of tradition have left blank. But the problem, why the Greeks
believed that the Gods themselves were subject to the moral,
and yet impersonal and purposeless, ordinance of Destiny, is
too fascinating to be abandoned, and lures us to push out into
the misty ocean of hypothesis. The second chapter is the record
of this rash excursion. For our guide we take the theorem,
maintained by the new French school of sociologists, that the
key to religious representation lies in the social structure of the
community which elaborates it. To Professor Emile Durkheim
and his colleagues of the *Année Sociologique* [1] I owe the solution
offered of this fundamental problem of Olympian religion. I
seem to myself, also, to have here found light thrown upon
certain singularly abstract schemes of conception, which persist
throughout ancient philosophy—for instance, the grouping of
the four elements, and the separation and reunion of pairs of
contrary qualities. These particular applications of the main
theorem are put forward, not as results established with any
certainty, but rather as illustrations that may suggest to
students with a fuller ethnological and psychological equipment
a line of research hitherto neglected.

One great philosophico-religious concept remains, and that
the most fundamental of all—the concept of the ' nature of
things,' *Physis*. The object called by this name in Greek philosophy is concrete : it is a material continuum, which is also
alive and divine, Soul and God—a substance, therefore, invested
with mythical properties. This substance, rather than the
manifold phenomena which Nature presents to us through our
senses, is the primary object of early speculation ; and from
its inherent properties, as material, living, and divine, the
various systems can be deduced, according as one or another
interpretation is put upon what those properties imply. I have

---

[1] In particular, Professor Durkheim, 'Représentations individuelles et
représentations collectives,' *Revue de Metaph. et de Morale*, vi. (1898),
p. 273 ; 'Sociologie religieuse et théorie de la connaissance,' *ibid.* xvii.
(1909) ; *De la division du travail social*, ed. 3 (1911) ; MM. Durkheim
and Mauss, 'Classifications primitives,' *Année Sociologique*, vi. ; MM.
Hubert and Mauss, 'Théorie générale de la magie,' *Ann. Soc.* vii.   A
convenient account of Professor Durkheim's work is given by G. Davy, ' La
sociologie de M. Durkheim,' *Revue Philosophique*, xxxvi. (1911), pp. 42-71
and 160-195. I am also indebted to Professor L. Lévy-Bruhl's *Les
fonctions mentales dans les sociétés inférieures*, 1910.

called it the Datum of Philosophy, to mark that it was not invented by the philosophers, but derived from a representation which underlies all the shapes and symbols of religious thought. The third chapter traces its origin from a magical stage, older than religion itself, and follows out the process of its differentiation into the several categories of Greek polytheism, especially the contrasted figures of the Mystery God and the Olympian. The significance of that contrast, between the religion whose most illustrious symbol was Apollo, and the mystic faith of the suffering Dionysus, was, by sheer power of imagination, divined by Friedrich Nietzsche, from a direct study of the phenomenon of Greek Tragedy. From him we learnt, in the sphere of art, why it is that Dionysus and Apollo shared the heights of Parnassus ; but, since his day, fresh knowledge has been gained, with respect to the problems of historical genesis. A clear advance in the study of the earlier phases, not only of Greek religion, but of religion in general, is marked by the publication of Miss Jane Harrison's *Themis* (Cambridge, 1912). I have had the great advantage of going over all the main points with the author, and I have adopted many of her conclusions. It is thus possible for me to treat very briefly a number of points connected with the development of Greek religion, referring the reader to the source from which my own knowledge is derived. Miss Harrison's help has also been of much value in the revision of this book, which may be regarded as carrying on the same principles of interpretation into the domain of philosophy.

From the standpoint reached in the third chapter, we seem able to make out that Philosophy, when she puts aside the finished products of religion and returns to the ' nature of things,' really goes back to that original representation out of which mythology itself had gathered shape. If we now call it ' metaphysical,' instead of ' supernatural,' the thing itself has not essentially changed its character. What has changed is, rather, man's attitude towards it, which, from being active and emotional, has become intellectual and speculative. His earlier, emotional reaction gave birth to the symbols of myth, to objects of faith ; his new procedure of critical analysis dissects it into concepts, from which it deduces various types of systematic theory. But in shaping these systems, the standards of value characteristic of the two opposed temperaments continue to exercise their unconscious influence, dividing the stream of thought into those two channels whose cause we shall trace in the two concluding chapters.

For the convenience of the English reader, I have frequently referred to the second edition of Professor Burnet's *Early Greek Philosophy* (*E.G.P.*[2]); and I have freely borrowed from the excellent translation of the fragments which it contains. For the fragments themselves references are given to Diels' *Fragmente der Vorsokratiker*, ed. 2, Berlin, 1906 (*D.F.V.*[2]).

This book is dedicated to a man of science, with the hope that he may find in it some saving touch of the spirit associated with the name he worthily bears.

F. M. CORNFORD

Trinity College,
Cambridge,
April 1912.

CONTENTS

I

DESTINY AND LAW

1. *The Problem*

THE origin of Greek philosophy is a problem which not only is of extraordinary interest, but seems at first sight peculiarly hopeful of solution. In the case of most questions of origins, history fails us ; the earlier links of the tradition we seek to account for are hidden in prehistoric darkness. The Homeric Epos, for instance, comes before us as a finished product, and not a single scrap of documentary evidence records the stages which preceded the earliest parts of the *Iliad*. But it is generally acknowledged that the beginnings of philosophy lie well within the field of history. Ever since the school of Aristotle set about compiling the first histories of philosophy, it has been agreed to date systematic speculation of a scientific character from the Milesian school, whose activity about covers the sixth century B.C.[1] Of the work of the philosophers in the two centuries from Thales to Plato we have some direct knowledge from the surviving fragments of their writings ; we have also a doxographic tradition, derived from the Peripatetics, which records their ' opinions ' on what were held to be the most important topics of speculation. It is thus possible to construct some sort of history, based on documents, of Greek philosophy from its beginning to its end ; and when we take it as a phenomenon to be accounted for and set in relation to other activities and products of the Greek mind, we start at least with the great advantage of knowing something, however little, of the first stages of its career.

In spite of this advantage, the question how this speculation

---

[1] The first certain date is given by an eclipse of the sun in the year 585, which Thales, the founder of that school, is said to have predicted.

arose, and why it took its peculiar course, has not been satis-
factorily answered. Inquiry has failed in some measure because,
when the problem was first formulated, it was set in the wrong
light. The sources of Greek philosophy were supposed to be a
matter of 'borrowing' and of 'influence.' More than one
attempt was made in the nineteenth century to show that the
Greeks 'borrowed' the wisdom of the East; but, when it was
seen that this fascinating theory led its advocates beyond all
bounds of historic possibility, the Orientalists were crushed in a
sort of antisemite reaction, and they are only now beginning to
lift their heads again.[1] The notion of 'borrowing' having been
dismissed, there remained the view that philosophy was 'influenced' by religious doctrines; but against this account it
was rightly urged that the current forms of religion could
hardly be said to have any 'doctrines' at all; and it was
certainly difficult to point to any definite dogma of theology
which was actually built into the systems known to us. So
students fell back into thinking of the early philosophers as
singularly isolated and independent.

The most recent historian, Professor Deussen,[2] in his opening
remarks upon the general characteristics of Greek thought,
repeats an observation which, in one form or another, figures
in all books upon this subject. As the fundamental trait of
Hellenism he takes that peculiar freedom, both in thought and
action, which the Greek enjoyed, standing in the presence of
Nature. The Greek, he says, was not encumbered by any early
implanted delusion, nor constrained by any close dogmatic
system, but could take in the nature of things with untroubled
eyes and with senses open to accept its revelations.

Now, it is true that the Greek philosophers were exceptionally
untrammelled by dogmatic prejudice and priestly persecution;
they were fortunate enough to be born into a state of society
which was satisfied, in the main, with an outward conformity,
and allowed reason to pursue her inward task of seeking the
truth which makes us free. But, when we dwell upon this
liberty of thought, we must not be misled into putting another

[1] See Eisler, *Weltenmantel und Himmelszelt*, Munich, 1910.
[2] *Allgemeine Geschichte d. Philos.*, II. i. (1911) p. 3.

construction upon it, and imagining that Thales or Anaximander
was like Adam on the day of his creation, with no tradition
behind him, no inherited scheme of things, opening his innocent
eyes on a world of pure sense impressions not as yet co-ordinated
into any conceptual structure. It is very easy to fall into an
error of this sort, especially if we begin our history of Greek
thought, as Professor Deussen does, by dividing the sources of
human knowledge into two classes : the outer experience,
which, by means of the senses, comes to us from the material
world in space ; and the inner experience of our own thoughts
and will and feelings. The object of outer experience is evidently
Nature ; the most remarkable object of inner experience is 'the
moral phenomenon '—our feeling of freedom, our consciousness
of responsibility, our impulse to do or to avoid what we have
learnt to regard as right or wrong. We then proceed to consider
what construction the earlier consciousness of Greece has put
upon these two classes of object in pre-scientific representation—
the cosmogonies which account for outer Nature, and the ethical
reflection which has dealt with the inner self and its relation to
the world outside. When we approach the subject in this way,
the surviving fragments of cosmogony and ethical reflection
will soon be dismissed, because they do not, upon examination,
seem to throw much light on the work of the philosophers.
So, with a sense of relief, we dismiss the obscure question of
origins, and embark upon the descriptive history, based on
extant documents, of the several systems. We try to recon-
struct each in turn, and to trace its dependence on those that
went before and its influence on those that came after. But the
whole concatenation, so reconstructed and interrelated, is left,
as a whole, an unexplained, and even portentous, phenomenon.

The primary error in this method of procedure is the pre-
supposition that the first objects of speculation, the materials
upon which it sets to work, are the inner and outer experience
of the individual standing in presence of Nature. At first sight
this seems a truism ; for what other materials can there be,
what else is there to speculate about ? We picture the philosopher in his study. Inside him there is his consciousness,
his thoughts and feelings, awaiting his introspective analysis.

Outside, there is the world, the data of sense-perception, lying ready to be observed and explained. It seems as if he had only to make his choice between psychology on the one side and natural science on the other, and set to work.

That this picture is not complete, the following pages are intended to show. If it were complete, the course taken by Greek speculation would have been utterly different. We should find the first philosophers attempting to analyse their own consciousness, and to draw some rude distinctions between thought and perception, or feeling and will. Or, if they turned to the outer world, we should find them taking the elementary— and, as it seems to us, obvious—precaution of looking at Nature, and trying to observe and record her ways, before they ventured upon generalisation and hypothesis. They would, in fact, have begun by occupying the more accessible fields of natural science, and feeling their way towards the laws of psychology, biology, or what not. But every one knows that they did nothing of the sort. The father of western philosophy, Thales of Miletus, immediately announces that the ultimate 'nature' of all things is water, and that the universe is alive—'has soul in it' (ἔμψυχον)—and is full of spirits or Gods. A little reflection will convince us that these propositions do not simply formulate the data of Thales' inward experience or of his outward observation of natural phenomena. They are not results likely to be reached, at the outset, by our imaginary philosopher sitting alone with himself and the sensible world.

These doctrines of Thales, which are almost all that survives to us of his opinions about the general nature of the world, contain three conceptions which are the principal subject of the following pages : the 'nature' of things [1]—physis, rerum natura (declared by Thales to be water) ; 'God' or 'Spirit'; and 'Soul.' Here at once, in the very first utterance of philosophy, we encounter conceptions which have a long history, as religious representations, before philosophy begins. Unless we have some grasp of that history we are not likely to understand the speculation,

---

[1] Professor Burnet, *Early Greek Philos.*², p. 12, points out that φύσις was used in this sense by the early cosmologists. He holds that ἀρχή is only an Aristotelian term, not used by the earlier writers to mean 'primary substance.'

which, however scientific its spirit may be, constantly operates with these religious ideas, and is to a large extent confined in its movement within the limits already traced by them.

Besides the notions of God and Soul, we shall find that philosophy also inherits from religion the governing conception of a certain order of Nature, variously regarded as a dominion of Destiny, of Justice, or of Law. The character and origin of this order, within which the life of Nature is confined, will be one of the main subjects of our inquiry. It will soon appear that the reign of Necessity is also and equally a moral rule, a kingdom of Justice.

The first religious poet of Greece, Hesiod,[1] states in simple form his conviction that the course of Nature is anything but careless of right and wrong. He tells us that when men do justice, and do not go aside from the straight path of right, their city flourishes and they are free from war and famine. ' For them the earth brings forth food in plenty, and on the hills the oak tree bears acorns at the top and bees in the middle ; their sheep have heavy fleeces, their wives bear children that are like their parents,'[2] and so on. This is a clear statement that there is (as it were) a sympathetic relation between human conduct and the behaviour of Nature : if man keeps straight upon his path of right, then her orderly processes of seed-time and harvest will go forward too, and reward justice with the fruits of the earth.

So, on the other hand, when a sin has been committed—such as the unconscious incest of Oedipus[3]—all Nature is poisoned by the offence of man. The land of Thebes

> ' Wasteth in the fruitless buds of earth,
> In parchèd herds, and travail without birth
> Of dying women.'

How did this belief arise : that *Nature is moral*, so that her order is disturbed by the sins of man ? It is obviously not a result of direct, unbiassed observation. When a king or a

---

[1] Hes. *Erga*, 225.

[2] *I.e.* not monstrous births (τέρατα); cf. Aeschin. *in Ctes.* 111, μήτε γῆν καρποὺς φέρειν μήτε γυναῖκας τέκνα τίκτειν γονεῦσιν ἐοικότα, ἀλλὰ τέρατα, μήτε βοσκήματα κατὰ φύσιν γονὰς ποιεῖσθαι.

[3] Soph. *Oed. Rex*, trans. G. Murray. Jebb compares Herod. vi. 139.

nation commits an act of wrong, it is *not* true that the harvest
is blighted and famine and plague follow. We have here to
do with one of those ancient, traditional beliefs which defy the
constant refutation of experience. As we shall see in a moment,
the earliest Greek philosophers express this conviction—that the
order of Nature is a moral order—as an obvious, unchallengeable
truth, and, indeed, the most important truth about the world.
It governs their conception of the process by which the world
came into being and will perish again. And, once established in
philosophy, it influences and colours the whole course of speculation both about Nature and about morals and politics. Thus
the problem, how this belief first arose, and through what forms
it passed before it became the heritage of rational speculation,
is one of the central problems of the history of human thought.
It is the main subject of our first two chapters.

In the third chapter the investigation of the concept of
' Nature ' (*physis*) will lead us on to the other two conceptions
we found in Thales' saying, ' the All has *soul* in it and is full
of *spirits.*' We shall try to show how the ideas of Spirit or God
and of Soul grew up out of ' Nature,' and passed into the inherit-
ance of philosophic, as well as religious, thought. The argument
cannot be anticipated here. The point that now concerns us is
simply this : that these three conceptions—Nature, God, and
Soul—had all of them a long history which lay behind the first
utterance of philosophy, and of which we must form some idea
before we can place ourselves at the point from which philosophy
starts. The last three chapters will contain a sketch of the
course of Greek philosophy, designed to show that, if we take the
starting-point so defined, the development of thought can be
better understood.

We shall begin with an explicit statement, made by Anaximander of Miletus, about the nature and order of the world.
We shall see that, considered as a result of innocent and unbiassed observation of Nature, this statement is paradoxical,
absurd, even unintelligible. Then we shall try to show that,
when we take it as a restatement in rational terms of a pre-
scientific view of the world, and trace that view again back to
its origin, it becomes simple, natural, intelligible. The view in

question is of fundamental importance for all Greek cosmology, and it pervades political and ethical speculation as well. The train of thought, whose earlier links we hope to reconstitute, leads on into Plato and Aristotle, and through them into the main current of European philosophy.

2. *The Cosmology of Anaximander*

Anaximander was the second and greatest of the three Milesians who presided in succession over the first school of Greek philosophers. The chief object of speculation for all of them was, not man or human society, but ' Nature ' (*physis*). Philosophical writings of the sixth and fifth centuries were commonly entitled *Concerning Nature* (Περὶ Φύσεως).

' Nature '—the nature of things—was the name they gave to the one ultimate stuff, from which, as they held, the world of things we see has arisen and into which it will perish again. It is at once apparent that we have no satisfactory rendering for *physis*. ' Primary substance ' is charged with Aristotelian and scholastic associations ; ' matter ' suggests something contrasted with mind or life, whereas the primary meaning of *physis* is ' growth,' and its first associations are of life and motion, not of stillness and death. The mere use of this term already implies the famous doctrine which has earned for the Milesian school the designation ' Hylozoist '— the doctrine that ' the All is alive.' The universe ' has soul in it,' in the same sense (whatever that may be) that there is a ' soul ' in the animal body. We must not forget that the meaning of *physis*, at this stage, is nearer to ' life ' than to ' matter ' ; it is quite as much ' moving' as ' material'—self-moving, because alive.

Into the earlier, pre-scientific history of this living source of all things we must inquire later.[1] For the present we shall be more concerned with the forms or limits imposed upon its spontaneous activity—the twin conceptions of Destiny and Law.

Thales, the first of the school, identified the living and self-changing world-stuff with water. Anaximenes, the third, held that it was ' air ' or mist. Anaximander called it the ' indefinite ' or ' limitless thing ' (τὸ ἄπειρον). Anaximander it was who

---

[1] Chap. III.

first stated a systematic theory of the Nature of the world—
not only of the stuff it is made of, but also of the process of its
growth out of the ' limitless thing ' into the manifold of definite
things. We are not concerned with the details, but only with
the most general conception of this process of growth, as it is
described in what is almost the sole surviving fragment of
Anaximander's writings :

*' Things perish into those things out of which they have their
birth, according to that which is ordained ; for they give reparation
to one another and pay the penalty of their injustice according to
the disposition of time.'* [1]

Otto Gilbert [2] has explained this utterance as follows. We
have to do with three grades of existence.

First, there are ' things ' (ὄντα)—the multiplicity of individual
things we see around us. These are declared to perish into those
things out of which they came into existence. What, then, are
these secondary things, out of which natural objects came into
being ?

They are the primitive elements [3] of which all bodies are
composed—earth, air, water, fire. These elements were recognised long before philosophy began. The visible world groups
itself into masses of comparatively homogeneous stuffs, each
occupying a region of its own. There is first the great lump of
earth ; above it, and perhaps beneath it also, the waters ; then
the space of wind and mist and cloud ; and beyond that, the
blazing fire of heaven, the *aether*. These elements are the
secondary stuffs out of which individual things were born and
into which they are resolved again.

But the elements themselves are not everlasting ; nor is the
separation of them into distinct regions more than a transient

---

[1] *D. F. V²*., i. p. 13 : ἐξ ὧν δὲ ἡ γένεσίς ἐστι τοῖς οὖσι καὶ τὴν φθορὰν εἰς
ταῦτα γίνεσθαι κατὰ τὸ χρεών· διδόναι γὰρ αὐτὰ δίκην καὶ τίσιν ἀλλήλοις τῆς ἀδικίας
κατὰ τὴν τοῦ χρόνου τάξιν.

[2] In a valuable article, ' Spekulation u. Volksglaube in d. ionischen Philosophie,' *Arch. f. Religionswiss.*, xiii. 306 ff.

[3] I use the term ' elements ' in a vague sense to denote earth, air, water,
and fire, which were popularly recognised (as Gilbert has shown, *Meteorologische Theorien d. griech. Altertums*, chap. i.) long before they were
introduced into science. The conception of 'elements' (στοιχεῖα) in the
narrower sense of primary and unalterable bodies dates from Empedocles
(cf. Burnet, *E. G. P.²*, p. 56).

arrangement. They themselves are destined to return into that from which they came—the third and ultimate stage of existence, the 'limitless thing,' which alone is called by Anaximander 'incorruptible and undying.'[1]

To sum up the process of growth : the formless indefinite stuff separates first into the elemental forms, distributed in their appointed regions ; and then these again give birth to things, and, when they die, receive them back again.

The first important fact about the elements is that they are limited ; the second is that they are grouped in pairs of opposites or 'contraries' : air is cold, fire hot, water moist, earth dry. These contraries are at perpetual war with one another, each seeking to encroach upon the domain of its antagonist. This fact itself seems to have been used by Anaximander as a proof that the elements must each be limited, for ' if any one of them were infinite, the rest would have ceased to be by this time,' for they would have been eaten up and destroyed.[2]

The separation of the elements into their several regions was caused by the 'eternal motion'—which perhaps we should conceive as a 'whirling' motion (δίνη) of the whole universe, which sifts out the opposites from the primary, indiscriminate or 'limitless' mixture, in which they will again be all merged and confused when they perish into that from which they arose.[3]

This cosmology thus contains three main factors or representations : (1) a primary stuff (*physis*) ; (2) an order, disposition, or structure into which this stuff is distributed ; (3) the process by which this order arose. In the present chapter we shall be chiefly concerned with the second of these representations—the scheme of order, which includes all the universe in a simple primary classification. The point we hope to bring out is that this scheme was not invented by Anaximander, but taken over by him from pre-scientific representation, and that this fact

---

[1] Arist. *Phys.* γ4, 203*b* 6 ff. : καὶ τοῦτ' εἶναι τὸ θεῖον· ἀθάνατον γὰρ καὶ ἀνώλεθρον, ὥς φησιν ὁ Ἀναξίμανδρος.

[2] Arist. *Phys.* γ5, 204*b* 22 ; see Burnet, *E. G. P.*[2], p. 55.

[3] On this subject see Heidel, 'Qualitative Change in Pre-Socratic Philosophy,' *Arch. f. Gesch. d. Philos.*, xix. 313 ff. I am unconvinced by Professor Burnet's objection to this view of the 'eternal motion' (*E. G. P.*[2], p. 61). But the question will be further discussed below, p. 146.

explains those of its characteristics which seem most obscure and gratuitous.

3. *The Provinces of the Elements*

What especially strikes us in Anaximander's statement is that the secular process of birth and perishing is described in *moral* language. The passing away of things into the elements is called ' making reparation,' ' paying the penalty of injustice.' The words imply that injustice was committed in the very fact of their birth into separate existence. The manifold world, in Anaximander's view, can arise only by robbery and misappropriation.

Consider, for instance, the animal body. Its proper substance is earth; [1] but for its formation it misappropriates portions of the other elements : water for its blood, air for its breath, fire for warmth. The dissolution of death repays these robberies : each stolen portion rejoins its like—water to water, air to air, fire to fire. Or take the clouds. To shape them, air draws water to itself and plunders the rivers and seas. Then the clouds dissolve in rain, which returns to the place of the waters.

We see, then, that the general scheme of the growth of the world is this : the one primary stuff, called ' Nature,' is segregated into provinces, each the domain of one element. And this is a *moral* order, in the sense that transgression of its boundaries, the plundering of one element by another to make an individual thing, is injustice, unrighteousness. The penalty is death and dissolution. No single thing can begin to exist without an infraction of this destined order. Birth is a crime, and growth an aggravated robbery.

This is a strange, and to us a paradoxical, view of individual existence. We are disposed to think of the ever-increasing complexity of the world as an intricate order formed out of primitive disorder or chaos. Anaximander may almost be said to reverse this conception. To him order comes into being not last, but first—the order, namely, which is established when the four elements are sifted by the eternal motion into their

---

[1] See O. Gilbert, 'Spekulation u. Volksglaube,' *Arch. f. Rel.*, xiii. 306 ff. ; and *Meteorologische Theorien d. griech. Altertums*, p. 22.

distinct regions. If this separation were ever complete, there would be perfect order, and no individual things would exist at all. Every step from that simple disposition of elemental provinces towards the multiplicity of particular things, is a breaking of bounds, an advance towards disorder, a declension into the welter of injustice, rapine, and war.

And every step of this pilgrimage of wrong must be retraced ' according to what is ordained' ($\kappa\alpha\tau\grave{\alpha}$ $\tau\grave{o}$ $\chi\rho\epsilon\acute{\omega}\nu$). In this word are united the conceptions of Fate and of Right; it means a power which ordains both what *must* be and what *ought* to be. This principle of Destiny and Justice has set the bounds of the original elemental order, and it waits to exact the penalty of every transgression. The power which presides over the physical order is moral.

Like Anaximander, most of the early philosophers, as we shall see later, regard the order of the world as moral or just. We have called Anaximander's conception strange and paradoxical. The more we think about it, the more preposterous it seems. But, it must be remembered that Anaximander was not a paradox-monger. He was a man of a very sane and bold scientific imagination, trying to state the most reasonable theory of the origin and structure of the world, in straightforward terms that would recommend it to the enlightened intellects of his time. As a reasonable theory, and not as an absurd paradox, it was received (we may conclude) by those enlightened intellects. Yet the conception is one that could never occur to innocent scientific curiosity, looking out with uncoloured vision upon the world our senses show us. It is certain that both Anaximander and his readers had already in their minds some traditional representation of the order of Nature, as familiar to them as it is strange to us, which the new theory only restated in rational terms.

That traditional representation it will be our next business to discover and explain. What especially calls for explanation is that moral character of the cosmos, upon which we have insisted. The actual grouping of the four elements is an apparent fact; but why is this fact, of all others, taken as the key to the making of the world, and why should it be associated with justice? Neither its peculiar significance nor its moral character is a sense-datum. The emphasis thrown upon it can only be accounted for by showing that it was already emphasised in religious representation; and when that point is established, we shall still have to look for the causes which led to its importance in religion.

4. *Moira above the Gods*

We turn, then, from the first philosophers back to the eldest poets of Greece, Homer and Hesiod, in the expectation of finding some representation of the order of the world corresponding to that which we have seen in Anaximander. We are not disappointed. For Anaximander, as we saw, the elements are ordered and assigned to their provinces 'according to what is ordained' (κατὰ τὸ χρεών)—a conception in which Necessity and Right are united. So in Homer the Gods are subordinate to a remote power, which is both primary—older than the Gods themselves—and moral. It is called *Moira*, Destiny.

The subjection of the Gods to Fate is a belief that has passed out of modern thought, or at least taken a quite different form. With the origin of the conception of Destiny we shall be concerned in the next chapter; our present business is to define the notion at the stage at which we meet with it in Homer.

The Gods of Homer are limited.[1] They are indeed exempt from age and death; but they are not eternal. They are younger than the world, into which they were born. Nor are they almighty, though man is powerless against them. What limits their power, however, is not what we call natural law: on the contrary, miracles are their peculiar function. They are limited by Destiny (*Moira*), which they did not make and against which they cannot stand.

The Gods cannot save even a man whom they love when the 'dread fate of death' lays hold upon him.[2] Zeus himself laments that it is 'fate' that his son, Sarpedon, dearest to him of all men, must die at the hands of Patroclus.[3] He 'does not venture to undo what fate decrees.'[4] 'It is impossible even

---

[1] On this subject see Gruppe, *Gr. Myth. u. Rel.*, p. 989 ff.

[2] *Od.* iii. 236: οὐδὲ θεοί περ | καὶ φίλῳ ἀνδρὶ δύνανται ἀλαλκέμεν, ὁππότε κεν δὴ | μοῖρ᾽ ὀλοὴ καθέλῃσι τανηλεγέος θανάτοιο.

[3] *Il.* xvi. 433: ὤ μοι ἐγών, ὅ τέ μοι Σαρπηδόνα, φίλτατον ἀνδρῶν, | μοῖρ᾽ ὑπὸ Πατρόκλοιο Μενοιτιάδαο δαμῆναι.

[4] Pind. *Paean.* vi. 94: μόρσιμ᾽ ἀναλύεν Ζεὺς ὁ θεῶν σκοπὸς οὐ τόλμα.

for a God to avoid the fate that is ordained.'[1] 'What is ordained,' says Athena in Euripides,[2] using Anaximander's word
(τὸ χρεών), 'is master of the Gods and thee.' Prometheus tells
the Okeanids that the Moirai and Erinyes hold the tiller of
Necessity, and that Zeus, if not weaker than they, cannot escape
what is decreed by fate.[3]

5. *Moira as moral*

Further, as in the Ionian philosopher, so in Homer, the
ordinance of Fate is not a mere blind and senseless barrier of
impossibility : it is a moral decree—the boundary of right and
wrong. We may even say that the two notions of Destiny and
Right are hardly distinguished. This comes out in the phrase
'beyond what is ordained,' 'beyond fate' (ὑπὲρ μόρον, ὑπὲρ
αἶσαν), which in Homer halts between the two meanings :
'beyond what is destined, and so *must* be,' and ' beyond what
is right, and so *ought* to be.'

Thus, when the first sense—destiny—is uppermost, it is
denied that God or man can make anything happen ' beyond
fate.'[4] But elsewhere we find on the contrary that things do
happen ' beyond fate.' In the *Iliad*[5] the Achaeans prevail for
a time in battle ὑπὲρ αἶσαν. ' Alack,' cries Zeus in the *Odyssey*,[6]

---

[1] Herod. i. 91 : τὴν πεπρωμένην μοῖραν ἀδύνατον ἐστὶ ἀποφεύγειν καὶ θεῷ.
This passage is of great interest, as apparently stating the view of Delphic
theology. The Pythia explains that Apollo tried to persuade the Moirai
to postpone the vengeance hanging over Croesus' house till after Croesus'
death. The Moirai would not concede more than a delay of three years
later than was ordained (ὕστερον τῆς πεπρωμένης).

[2] *I. T.*, 1486 : αἰνῶ· τὸ γὰρ χρεὼν σοῦ τε καὶ θεῶν κρατεῖ.

[3] Aesch. *P. V.*, 531 : Χο. τίς οὖν ἀνάγκης ἐστὶν οἰακοστρόφος ;
　　　　Πρ. Μοῖραι τρίμορφοι μνήμονές τ' Ἐρινύες.
　　　　Χο. τούτων ἄρα Ζεύς ἐστιν ἀσθενέστερος ;
　　　　Πρ. οὔκουν ἂν ἐκφύγοι γε τὴν πεπρωμένην.

[4] For instance, *Il.* vi. 487 : οὐ γάρ τίς μ' ὑπὲρ αἶσαν ἀνὴρ Ἄιδι προϊάψει·
μοῖραν δ' οὔ τινά φημι πεφυγμένον ἔμμεναι ἀνδρῶν, | οὐ κακόν, οὐδὲ μὲν ἐσθλόν,
ἐπὴν τὰ πρῶτα γένηται. Cf. Pind. *Pyth.* xii. 30 : τὸ μόρσιμον οὐ παρφυκτόν.
frag. 232 (256), τὸ πεπρωμένον οὐ πῦρ, οὐ σιδάρεον σχήσει τεῖχος.

[5] xvi. 780 : καὶ τότε δή ῥ' ὑπὲρ αἶσαν Ἀχαιοὶ φέρτεροι ἦσαν.

[6] 　　　i. 32 : ὢ πόποι, οἷον δή νυ θεοὺς βροτοὶ αἰτιόωνται.
ἐξ ἡμέων γάρ φασι κάκ' ἔμμεναι· οἱ δὲ καὶ αὐτοὶ
σφῇσιν ἀτασθαλίῃσιν ὑπὲρ μόρον ἄλγε' ἔχουσιν,
ὡς καὶ νῦν Αἴγισθος ὑπὲρ μόρον Ἀτρείδαο
γῆμ' ἄλοχον μνηστήν.

' see now how mortal men lay blame upon the Gods ! For they
say it is from us that evil comes ; and all the while they themselves, by their own naughtiness, have trouble *beyond what is
ordained*, even as now Aegisthus, *beyond what is ordained*, has
married the wedded wife of the son of Atreus.' Here, it is evident, the moral sense is uppermost. The offenders went beyond,
not their fate, but the bounds of morality. Hence in such cases
the balance is redressed by swiftly following vengeance, which
itself is ' beyond what is ordained ' in the sense that the sinners
brought it upon themselves by their own wickedness, so that
they, and not Fate, are responsible (αἴτιοι).[1]

The truest account, perhaps, is that the clear notion of absolute
impossibility is wanting in Homer. The ἀδύνατον, which we
render ' the impossible,' is rather that which lies beyond one's
power (δύναμις); it may lie beyond the power even of a God,
for, as we have seen, no God is all-powerful. But it is not absolutely and strictly impossible ; power may be stretched for a
moment beyond its due and normal limits, so that Gods, and even
men, may achieve the impossible. But there is a strong sense
that such feats are undesirable and dangerous. For Gods and
men alike there are certain destined bounds which normally
and rightly circumscribe their power. It is just possible to
exceed them; but only at the cost of provoking an instant *nemesis*.

Thus in Homer, and in Ionian thought generally, we find a
profound belief in Destiny (*Moira*) as an ordinance which limits
all individual powers, whether human or divine ; and we see,
moreover, that this ordinance is even more a decree of moral
obligation than a barrier of sheer physical impossibility.

Our next question must be : How came this power called
Moira to be supreme above both men and Gods ? What does
Moira mean ? The conception and the view of the world
which it carries with it were no more the invention of ' Homer '
than they were of Anaximander. When we have succeeded in
defining *Moira* more clearly, we shall be in a position to recon-
struct the still earlier history of the idea.

[1] Compare the Croesus passage (Herod. i. 91 above, p. 13, n. 1), in which
Apollo ends by throwing the responsibility on Croesus' pride (ἑωυτὸν αἴτιον
ἀποφαινέτω), and Croesus acknowledges it.

6. *Moira as a system of provinces*

Some scholars[1] ask us to believe that *Moira* is a personification generalised from the individual lot or fate attached to each man from the cradle to the grave. Against this view a single consideration is decisive. It is inconceivable that an abstraction generalised from the fates of individual men, and *inapplicable to the Gods*, should ever have been erected into a power superior to the Gods themselves. The notion of the individual lot or fate, as we shall try to show later, comes last, not first, in the order of development. We must seek the original meaning of *Moira* elsewhere.

In the fifteenth *Iliad* Zeus awakes one day to find the Trojans hard pressed in battle by the Achaeans, assisted by Poseidon. After a sordid outburst against Hera, who, however, swears by Styx that Poseidon is acting of his own will and not upon her instigation, Zeus sends Iris with a threatening message, commanding Poseidon to cease from war and battle, and to withdraw among the tribes of the gods or into the bright sea. Poseidon is very angry and protests (1. 186). 'Alack,' he says, ' strong though he be, these words are past all bearing, if he will constrain me by violence against my will, though I am his equal in rank ($\delta\mu\acute{o}\tau\iota\mu\sigma$). For we are three brothers, born of Kronos and Rhea, Zeus, and I, and Hades is the third, the lord of the dead. And *in three lots are all things divided, and each took his appointed domain* (or privilege, status).[2] When we shook the lots, to me fell the hoary sea, that I should dwell therein for ever ; and Hades drew the misty darkness, and Zeus the broad heaven among the aether and the clouds : the earth and high Olympus are yet common to all. Therefore never will I live according to the mind of Zeus ; no, masterful though he be, *let him stay quiet in his own third part* ($\check{\epsilon}\kappa\eta\lambda\sigma$ . . . $\mu\epsilon\nu\acute{\epsilon}\tau\omega$ $\tau\rho\iota\tau\acute{a}\tau\eta$ $\grave{\epsilon}\nu\grave{\iota}$ $\mu\sigma\iota\rho\eta$).' Zeus may give orders to his own sons and daughters, who, as inferiors, are bound to obey him.

Iris recommends submission, reminding Poseidon that the spirits of vengeance, the Erinyes, are always in attendance upon the elder-born. Poseidon gives way ; but declares that it is a bitter pain ' when any one chides with angry words one to whom

---

[1] For instance, Weizsäcker in Roscher's *Lexicon*, s.v. 'Moira,' col. 3084.

[2] l. 189 : $\tau\rho\iota\chi\theta\grave{a}$ $\delta\grave{\epsilon}$ $\pi\acute{a}\nu\tau a$ $\delta\acute{\epsilon}\delta a\sigma\tau a\iota$, $\check{\epsilon}\kappa a\sigma\tau\sigma\varsigma$ δ' $\check{\epsilon}\mu\mu\sigma\rho\epsilon$ $\tau\iota\mu\hat{\eta}\varsigma$.

an equal portion and a like lot are ordained.' [1] However, though
he feels resentment (*nemesis*), he yields, and retires to the sea,
his own undisputed element.[2]

In this curious passage the original sense of *Moira* is clearly
apparent. *Moira* simply means ' part,' ' allotted portion ';
from that primary meaning it is agreed that the meaning
' destiny ' is derived. Poseidon's protestation shows how it is
that the Gods, as well as men, have *moirai*. Each God has his
own allotted portion or province—a certain department of nature
or field of activity. This may also be regarded as his *status*
($τιμή$) ; it gives him a determined position in a social system.
Sometimes it is called his ' privilege ' ($γέρας$). Within his own
domain his supremacy is not to be challenged ; but he must not
transgress its frontiers, and he will feel resentment (*nemesis*) at
any encroachment by another.

It is this conception, not that of the individual human fate,
that is generalised in Destiny, *Moira*. She represents the
apportionment to each God of his province, status, or privilege.
It is at once plain why she is above any or all of the Gods, and
how the limits she sets to their powers can be thought of as moral
limits. Hesiod definitely says that the Moirai, daughters of
Night, pursue the transgressions, not only of men, but of Gods.[3]

The original conception of *Moira* thus turns out to be spatial,

---

[1] l. 209 : ὁππότ' ἂν ἰσόμορον καὶ ὁμῇ πεπρωμένον αἴσῃ
νεικείειν ἐθέλῃσι χολωτοῖσιν ἐπέεσσι.

[2] For the three divisions, Earth, Sea, Sky, cf. *Il.* xviii. 483 : Hephaestos,
making the Shield, ἐν μὲν γαῖαν ἔτευξ', ἐν δ' οὐρανόν, ἐν δὲ θάλασσαν ; *Od.* xii.
315 : γαῖαν—πόντον—οὐρανόθεν ; *Hymn to Dem.* 13 : οὐρανὸς εὐρὺς ὕπερθε γαῖά
τε πᾶσα καὶ ἀλμυρὸν οἶδμα θαλάσσης. See O. Gilbert, *Met. Theor.*, 27².
Poseidon in the above passage takes a somewhat different view, according
to which Heaven (Olympos) and Earth, as parents of *all* the gods (see
below, p. 18), are 'common to all'; the three divisions included in the
δασμός are Aether (the fiery οὐρανός), Sea, and Darkness (Air)—a conception
which is nearer to the 'elements' (see below, p. 116).

[3] *Theog.* 220: αἵ τ' ἀνδρῶν τε θεῶν τε παραιβασίας ἐφέπουσιν. After
writing the above, I discovered that Walter Headlam had clearly stated
this view of Moira in his edition of Aesch. *Agam.* p. 234, note on v. 1007.
He says : 'The Μοῖραι are personifications of these μοῖραι or διανομαι (*Eum.*
726), apportionments or dispensations, provinces allotted to the various
divinities and severally administered by them. . . .' 'There exist in the
system over which Zeus presides certain "vested interests" or "spheres
of influence" assigned by Dispensation (Μοῖρα).' Headlam adduces some
interesting evidence.

rather than temporal. We are to think of a system of provinces, coexisting side by side, with clearly marked boundaries. The conception has been obscured by the—in our opinion, later—mode of conceiving the three Fates as corresponding to divisions of time—Past, Present, and Future. The spatial character of *Moira* will turn out in the sequel to be of fundamental importance, as a representation which, persisting into Ionian science, governs its whole course.

7. *The Division of the World in Hesiod*

If we turn now to the cosmogony of Hesiod, we shall find there that very division of the world into provinces to which we have traced back the original sense of *Moira*. Further, the supremacy of *Moira* over the Gods is there reflected in a temporal form ; that is to say, the separation of the world into elemental provinces is older in time than the birth of the Gods.

The cosmogony begins (*Theog.* 116) with the coming into being of ' Chaos,' Earth, and Eros ; then out of Chaos arose Darkness and Night, and of them were born blazing Fire ($ai\theta\acute{\eta}\rho$) and Daylight. This opening act we shall discuss later. Next follows (l. 124) the division of the world into three parts—Earth, Sky, and Sea.

' Earth (*Gaia*) first of all gave being to one equal to herself, the starry Heaven (*Ouranos*), that he might enfold her all round, that there might be for the blessed Gods a seat secure for ever. And she brought forth the high mountains wherein the Gods delight to inhabit. And she gave birth also to the waste Ocean, swelling with rage, the Sea ' (*Pontos*).

Here, then, we find, as a distinct stage in cosmogony, a division of the world into three portions (*moirai*), just as in Homer ' all things were divided in three,' and the three provinces were assigned to Zeus, Poseidon, and Hades. The starry Heaven is for Zeus, the Sea for Poseidon ; for Hades remains either the ' misty darkness '—that is, the Air—or the Earth, according as it is believed that the dead, whose lord he is, dwell in the western darkness beyond the sunset, or underground.

This triple division into the Sky, the dry Earth, and the Sea, takes place, be it noted, ' without love or the attraction of

desire' (ἄτερ φιλότητος ἐφιμέρου, l. 132). It was not, that is
to say, an act of marriage and consequent birth, but of division,
repulsion, 'strife' (Νεῖκος), as Empedocles would say. Only
afterwards the sundered Sky and Earth were reunited in marriage
by Eros, and of that marriage the eldest Gods were born. So
Hesiod, by making the triple division older in time than the Gods
—cosmogony older than theogony—marks by temporal sequence
the supremacy of *Moira*—the dimly personified principle of that
division—over the later-born divinities.

In Hesiod's view the Gods arose out of the several provinces
of Nature—the four elements and those other features of the
world, such as mountains and rivers, in which mysterious
powers and forces are felt to reside. His prelude [1] ends with an
invocation of the Muses, who are to sing of the race of the
immortals, ' born of Earth and of the starry Heaven, of murky
Night and of the salt Sea.' ' Say, how first the Gods and Earth
came into being, and the rivers and the limitless Sea, swelling
with rage, and the shining stars and the wide Heaven above, and
*the Gods that were born out of these, the givers of blessing; how
they parted among them their wealth and distributed their honours,*[2]
and how first they took possession of Olympus.'

In Earth and the fiery Heaven, Night and the Sea, we
recognise the four elements. Three of them speak for themselves; the fourth, ' murky Night,' evidently represents the
Air, which the Greeks regularly regarded as dark.[3] Accordingly,
when some of the sixth-century thinkers—Pherekydes, for instance, or Theagenes of Rhegium—equated the elements with
the Gods,[4] this was no mere play of allegorising fancy. Some at
least of the provinces assigned by *Moira* to the Gods were nothing

[1] *Theog.* 104.

[2] v. 112: ὥς τ' ἄφενος δάσσαντο καὶ ὡς τιμὰς διέλοντο. This *dasmos*, held by
the Gods themselves, will be discussed below, § 9.

[3] Cf. Plut. de primo frigido, 948 Ε: ὅτι δ' ἀὴρ τὸ πρώτως σκοτεινόν ἐστιν,
οὐδὲ τοὺς ποιητὰς λέληθεν· ἀέρα γὰρ τὸ σκότος καλοῦσιν· ' ἀὴρ γὰρ παρὰ νηυσὶ βαθεῖ'
ἦν οὐδὲ σελήνη οὐρανόθεν προὔφαινε' (Od. x. 143). καὶ πάλιν ' ἠέρα ἐσσάμενοι
πᾶσαν φοιτῶσιν ἐπ' αἶαν' (Hes. *Erga*, 255), κ.τ.λ. Cf. Plut. Is. et Os. 384 Β, C,
and Il. xv. 191 (above quoted, p. 15), where Hades takes the 'misty darkness' (ζόφον ἠερόεντα).

[4] See O. Gilbert, 'Spekulation und Volksglaube,' u.s.w., *Arch. f. Relig.*
xiii. p. 317.   For Theagenes see D.F.V.², p. 511 ; Pherekydes, *ibid.* p. 507.
Note especially Pherekydes' use of μοῖρα: κείνης δὲ τῆς μοίρας ἔνερθέν ἐστιν ἡ
ταρταρίη μοῖρα (frag. 5).

but these elements, and out of them, as Hesiod very truly says, the Gods themselves had come into being. The status of the elements in cosmogony is precisely parallel to the status of the Gods in Homeric theology. Both have their appointed regions and departments ; both are subject to *Moira*.

Thus we have found a departmental ordering of the world established in religious representation long before it is affirmed by philosophy. Further, in religion and philosophy alike, this disposition is both primary and moral. The physical order is guarded by the same powers that punish moral transgression— those ministers of Justice or Erinyes, the *Moirai* in their darkest aspect, who, ' if the sun should overstep his measures, would find him out.' [1] This conception of the primary world-order is taken over by Anaximander with its main outline unchanged ; and, above all, its moral character unquestioningly retained. The mutual aggression of the elements in their perpetual strife is an ' injustice '—an infringement of moral boundaries.[2] So far the philosophic representation is identical with the religious ; where Anaximander innovates is in making the primary order partly the effect of a mechanical cause—the ' eternal motion,' and in eliminating the Gods, whose place is taken by the elements, out of which, according to Hesiod, the Gods had arisen. The significance of these innovations will become clear to us later.

Meanwhile, we have to examine the religious representation more closely. As presented by Hesiod, it is not a simple and consistent scheme ; we can detect in it several layers superimposed on one another, which correspond to distinct stages of religious development. We must accordingly attempt an analysis which will bring out the successive phases.

8. *Moira is impersonal, without intelligence or design*

Let us note, in the first place, that a thoroughgoing polytheism has the singular merit of allowing the order of the world, the *cosmos*, to come into being without the intervention of any

---

[1] Heracleitus, frag. 94 (Diels): ἥλιος γὰρ οὐχ ὑπερβήσεται μέτρα· εἰ δὲ μή, Ἐρινύες μιν Δίκης ἐπίκουροι ἐξευρήσουσιν.

[2] Theagenes of Rhegium emphasised exactly this point, allegorising the battles of the Gods in Homer as the ἐναντίωσις of the elements (Gilbert, *loc. cit.*). Cf. Pherekydes, frag. 4 (*D.F.V.*[2], p. 508).

purposeful intelligence. All the Gods being merely departmental powers, no one of them can at first claim to have designed and created the whole disposition of things by an arbitrary, if benevolent, act of will. Such a claim will only gradually come to be advanced on behalf of a supreme God, as polytheism gives way to monotheism. In Greek religion this was fortunately a very late development, partly owing to the fact that in the oldest writers the tradition was firmly established that Zeus, the God who reigns supreme in the present age of the world, was not even one of the eldest-born divinities, but head of a later dynasty. Behind him lay the age of Kronos and those vague Titanic deities whose reign filled an interval of indefinite length separating the birth of the world from the birth of Zeus in the island of Crete. This representation was too clear and fixed to be overridden until the religious consciousness had become so thoroughly uncomfortable about the less edifying aspects of polytheism that a monarchical revolution in the divine world was felt as an imperative necessity. But this movement did not triumph till a time when philosophy or science had already secured an independent foothold. The spirited satire of Xenophanes is later than the foundation of the Milesian School; and, besides, philosophic monotheism tended at first rather to declare that the universe itself was the one God, than to make it the work of a creator distinct from itself. If we are to dwell on the freedom of Greek thought from dogmatic prejudice, we cannot be too grateful for the absence of this particular belief in a divine creator. No hypothesis is more facile and supine; nothing is so likely to stupefy and lull to slumber that wonder which is the parent of philosophy, than an explanation which will account with equal readiness for every feature of the world, whether good or bad, ascribing what is good to the transparent benevolence, and what is bad to the inscrutable wisdom, of omnipotence. *Moira*, it is true, was a moral power; but no one had to pretend that she was exclusively benevolent, or that she had any respect for the parochial interests and wishes of mankind. Further— and this is the most important point—she was not credited with foresight, purpose, design; these belong to man and to the humanised Gods. *Moira* is the blind, automatic force which leaves their subordinate purposes and wills free play within their own legitimate spheres, but recoils in certain vengeance upon them the moment that they cross her boundaries.

Moira, then, though we speak of her as a 'personification,' has not the most important element of personality—individual purpose. She stands for the provincial ordering of the world ; but she is not a deity who by an act of will designed and created that order. She is a representation which states a truth about the disposition of Nature, and to the statement of that truth adds nothing except that the disposition is both necessary and just. Considered in abstraction from the natural fact itself, *Moira* is a representation of the Necessity and Justice (*Must* and *Ought*) of the elemental disposition. That is the whole content of the notion of Destiny.

Such, then, was the ultimate power in the universe as conceived by Greek polytheism. But for its moral character, it could hardly be said to be religious rather than scientific ; it would be a conception of the same order as the notion of Natural Law, which has taken its place in modern thought. That is partly the reason why it is reinstated by nascent science in the system of Anaximander. But what now concerns us is to realise that this *was* a reinstatement—the restoration to *Moira* of a supremacy which, as religion developed, had been impaired, and almost overthrown, by the growing power of the Gods.

9. *The* Dasmos *of the Gods*

Just because *Moira* was at first an impersonal power, an opening was left for advancing theology to reverse the position, and ascribe her ordinance of necessity and right to the will of personal Gods, which formerly had been overridden by it. Thus the Gods, who at first were younger than *Moira* and subject to her, might now set up a claim to be the originators of the world-order, substituting their individual will for her impersonal decree. Hesiod himself shows us the stages of this process, and combines, in his simple religious way, the two inconsistent representations. On the one hand, as we have seen, the order of Hesiod's cosmogony implies that the departmental division of the world was older in time than the Gods, and he also declares that the Gods took shape within its several provinces and arose out of the elements themselves. On the other hand, in the same breath he calls upon his Muse to describe how the Gods ' parted among them their wealth and distributed their honours '—as if this disposition were not, after all, the work of Destiny, but a distribution (δασμός) voluntarily carried out by the Gods themselves. The will of the Gods is beginning to assert its claims against the inevitable appointment of Fate.

It is, however, curious to observe how the two views are reconciled in the only possible compromise. In the fifteenth *Iliad*, as we saw above (p. 15), the Gods, confronted by the problem of distribution, acknowledge the supremacy of Fate exactly as men would do on a similar occasion. They arrange the matter by drawing lots. In other words, the three sons of Kronos voluntarily surrender their volition, and abide by the appointment of *Moira*, as the Lady of the Lots, *Lachesis*.

In this Homeric passage Lachesis is not mentioned; but in Pindar's description [1] of the division of the earth among the Gods she presides in person. ' The ancient legends tell how that, when Zeus and the immortals were dividing (δατέοντο) among them the earth, Rhodes had not yet appeared upon the surface of the ocean, but the island lay hidden in the salt depths. Helios was not there, so that no one designated a lot for him, and they left the holy God without an allotted land. When Zeus was reminded, he was about to order a fresh drawing of lots ; but Helios would not suffer him, because he said that his own eye saw within the grey sea, growing up from the bottom, a land that would feed a multitude of men and be kindly to flocks. And immediately he bade Lachesis of the golden frontlet hold up her hands and not gainsay the Great Oath of the Gods, but rather with the son of Kronos affirm,[2] that when the island should be sent up into the open light of day, it should be a seat reserved to him (γέρας) for the time to come.'

Here, in spite of the polite deference to the son of Kronos, it

---

[1] *Ol.* vii. 54. This *dasmos* of the surface of the earth into seats of worship is, as we shall see later (p. 38), an older representation, on which the *dasmos* of the elemental provinces between the three sons of Kronos is modelled.

[2] l. 64 :

Ἐκέλευσεν δ' αὐτίκα χρυσάμπυκα μὲν Λάχεσιν
χεῖρας ἀντεῖναι, θεῶν δ' ὅρκον μέγαν
μὴ παρφάμεν, ἀλλὰ Κρόνου σὺν παιδὶ νεῦσαι. . . .

is evident that Lachesis herself presides, and that Zeus can do no more than confirm her decision with his nod.

10. *The Great Oath of the Gods*

Besides the appointment of Lachesis and the confirmatory nod of Zeus, the distribution in this Pindaric passage is also sanctioned by the Great Oath of the Gods (θεῶν ὅρκος μέγας). The importance of this conception is that it opens another avenue by which the will of the Gods can assert its claim to supersede Destiny. An oath may come to be regarded as a contract voluntarily entered upon ; and through this notion of contractual obligation we may pass to conceiving the departmental ordering of the universe as a system of constitutional law—an aspect under which we shall presently consider it.[1] But meanwhile we must dwell for a moment on this notion of the Great Oath and its connection with the *dasmos*.[2]

The regular formula of the Great Oath will be found, for instance, at the beginning of the fifteenth *Iliad*, where Hera swears to Zeus that she has not been instigating Poseidon to go beyond his *moira*. She swears by ' Earth and the broad Heaven above and the dripping water of Styx, which is the greatest and most dreadful Oath for the blessed Gods.' In the same form—by Gaia, Ouranos, and Styx—Leto, in the Homeric Hymn to Apollo (83), swears to Delos that her island shall always be the seat of Apollo's worship—another case where the Oath confirms the assignment of a divine province. In the Great Oath, then, the Gods swear by the two great primary divisions of the universe, Earth and Heaven, and by Styx. What is the significance of Styx ?

[1] It must be remembered, however, that originally the oath which sanctions law is not a contract, but a curse. This may be visibly embodied in a substance, such as the blood of a ' sacred ' animal, which is charged with sanctity, and so with that dangerous force which recoils upon a breach of taboo. Cf. the oath-ritual in Plato's Atlantis (*Kritias*, 119D), where the bull was to be killed ' against the top of the column ' on which the laws were engraved, so that his blood ran down over the inscription. On the column was also a Ὅρκος invoking maledictions on the disobedient. See J. E. Harrison, *Themis*, 1912, p. 163 ff.

[2] We shall see later that the Great Oath reappears in a curious way in the system of Empedocles (p. 237).

In the *Theogony* Hesiod describes in detail how the cold water of Styx is administered to the Gods as an ordeal for perjury and lying. When one of the Olympians is suspected of falsehood, Zeus sends Iris to bring, in a golden phial, some of this freezing stream, which falls from a black precipice of rock. The God convicted of perjury lies for a Great Year breathless, dumb, and paralysed by the chill draught of this ancient river, which ' traverses that desolate place where are the sources and limits of the Earth and Tartarus, of the Sea and of the starry Heaven.' [1] Styx is one of ten branches of the heaven-stream, Okeanos ; the other nine roll round the earth and the sea, but Styx falls from its rock to be the great penalty of the Gods.[2]

It is impossible to get from Hesiod's account any clear idea of the position of Styx ; but it seems that this river is vaguely conceived as a barrier which either encloses the world or separates one division of it from another. It is placed in Tartarus, where are the ' roots and fountains ' of the four elemental provinces— earth, misty Tartarus, sea, and sky—and those ' limits whose dankness strikes a shuddering chill even into Gods.' [3]

Now, when we remember that *Horkos*, Oath, is the same word as *herkos*, ' fence,' [4] we can understand why Styx is the Great Oath of the Gods. An oath is a fence which can be visibly symbolised in ritual, when he who takes an oath stands between the pieces of the divided victim, surrounding himself on all sides by the sacred thing, charged with the dangerous, inviolable power of sanctity. Styx is the ' shuddering chill,' the awful horror which is the negative, forbidding aspect of Power. Zeus, on the eve of that quarrel with Poseidon we have already noticed, concludes his angry message to his brother thus : [5] ' I declare that I am much greater than he in might ($\beta i\eta$) and his elder in birth : but his heart fears not to call himself equal to me whom the other Gods hold in shuddering awe ($\sigma\tau\upsilon\gamma\acute{\epsilon}o\upsilon\sigma\iota$).' This

---

[1] l. 736.

[2] l. 790. The tenth branch is simply invented in order to reconcile the two views that Styx is a ninefold stream running all round the world (*noviens* Styx interfusa coercet, Verg. *Georg.* iv. 480) and also an actual stream which does run down a black rock in Arcadia. The Great Oath is evidently not this stream, but the ninefold barrier.

[3] πείρατα ἀργαλέ᾽ εὐρώεντα, τά τε στυγέουσι θεοί περ, *Theog.* 738.

[4] G. Murray, *Rise of the Greek Epic* [2], p. 338.

[5] *Il.* xv. 165.

phrase makes it clear why it is that Styx is specially associated with the *dasmos*—the apportionment of provinces, each the domain of some God's ' mastery ' ($\kappa\rho\acute{a}\tau o\varsigma$) and limited by a frontier of inviolable sanctity. Styx is a representation of Taboo.[1]

11. *The supremacy of Zeus conferred by Styx*

When Zeus declares that the other Gods hold him in shuddering awe ($\sigma\tau\nu\gamma\acute{e}ov\sigma\iota$), he means that his might has the effect which the waters of Styx used to produce upon the Gods who violated the Oath. When we understand that Styx, the shuddering chill of taboo, is nothing but the recoil, or negative aspect, of power, we see in a new light that strange passage in the *Theogony*, where it is said that the supreme power or mastery ($\kappa\rho\acute{a}\tau o\varsigma$) of Zeus came to him, after his conquest of the Titans, ' by the counsel of Styx.' [2] The whole passage is instructive, because it seems to describe how the supremacy passed from an impersonal power to the will of the personal God.

Styx and Pallas had four children, *Zelos, Nike, Kratos*, and *Bia*. ' No house nor seat of Zeus is without these ; no path is there, upon which the God does not lead them, but they are established for ever beside Zeus, the Thunderer. For such was the counsel of Styx, the immortal daughter of Ocean.' This endowment of Zeus with supreme power occurred on that day when, summoning all the Gods to Olympus, Zeus declared that no God who had fought on his side against the Titans should be deprived of his privileges ($\gamma\epsilon\rho\acute{a}\omega\nu$), but each should keep that status ($\tau\iota\mu\acute{\eta}\nu$) which he had before enjoyed. Further, all who had no privilege or status under the rule of Kronos should now enter into possession of them. Then it was that Styx, with her children, was the first to arrive at Olympus ; and Zeus honoured her with gifts above all else. He ordained that she should be the Great Oath of the Gods, and that her children should dwell with him for ever. In the same way he fulfilled his promises to all the rest in turn ; but the supreme power and lordship are his own.

[1] This view of Styx in relation to Kratos and Bia (§ 11) is due to Miss J. E. Harrison (*Themis*, p. 72). For taboo as negative *mana*, see R. R. Marett, *Threshold of Religion*, chap. iii. The notion will become clearer as we go on.

[2] Hesiod, *Theog.* 383 ff. See J. E. Harrison, *loc. cit.*

This passage shows the same inconsistency that we have before noted. At the beginning it is Styx who confers on Zeus his newly won power; she is only another form of *Moira*, who apportions to each God his province. At the end the situation is reversed : it is Zeus who confers on Styx her privilege, that she should be the Great Oath of the Gods. It is he who ordains that her children, Mastery and Force, shall dwell with him for ever ; and in fact he becomes the power which authorises the whole distribution of divine provinces. These are no longer apportioned by all the Gods among themselves, according to the fall of the lots, but Zeus distributes them, keeping the supreme sovereignty for himself. Thus, at this third and last stage, the distribution which was originally an ultimate fact in the constitution of Nature—the fact represented as *Moira*—comes to be thought of as enacted by the sole will of a supreme personal God. In other words, it becomes an act of *legislation* (νομοθεσία).

In Homer, again, this same transition is marked by the odd phrases, ' fate of Zeus,' ' destiny of God ' (Διὸς αἶσα, θεοῦ μοῖρα etc.), where the original sense of ' apportionment ' or ' destiny,' not personal will (βουλή), is still the primary conception, and ' of Zeus,' ' of God,' is at first hardly more than a pious addition. Thus in the seventeenth *Iliad* (321) the Argives would have prevailed by their own might and strength, ' even beyond the apportionment of Zeus ' (καὶ ὑπὲρ Διὸς αἶσαν), had not Apollo gone to rouse Aeneas and tell him that Zeus ' wills ' (βούλεται) the victory of the Trojans. Here we find exactly the same conception as before—the might (κράτος) of men going ' beyond what is ordained ' (ὑπὲρ αἶσαν): but Διός is slipped in, as if Zeus, and not *Moira*, were the source of this apportionment.[1]

12. *Zeus as Lawgiver*

Zeus, then, comes at last to be regarded as the dispenser of fate and the upholder of that system of provinces in which at

---

[1] Cf. also Pindar, *Nem.* iv. 61, τὸ μόρσιμον Διόθεν πεπρωμένον, as contrasted with *Paean.* vi. 94, μόρσιμ' ἀναλύεν Ζεὺς οὐ τόλμα. Oldenberg (*Die Relig. des Veda*, p. 199) points out that the same phenomenon occurs in Vedic theology. The world-order called Ṛta, at first supreme over the Gods, comes to be represented as the ordinance of Varuna and the Adityas. The notion of Ṛta will be further discussed below, p. 175. Aesch. *Sept.* 485 : Ζεὺς Νεμέτωρ.

one time he had had only a third part for his domain. As Nausikaa says to Odysseus : [1] 'It is Olympian Zeus himself who distributes prosperity to mankind, good or bad, to each one according as he wills'; and similarly it is Zeus who apportions to the Gods their wealth and honours.[2] Prometheus [3] describes the first act of Zeus upon his accession in terms similar to Hesiod's. 'As soon as ever he had taken his seat upon his father's throne, at once he dispensed to the deities their several privileges, and ordained the hierarchy of his kingdom.' This dispensation involved, as we saw in Hesiod, the confirmation of old rights and honours which had formed the constitutional system of Kronos, and the supplementing of this system by the granting of new privileges to those deities who had previously had none. The word used for this act by Aeschylus is *nemein*, to 'dispense' —the word from which *Nomos*, Law, is derived. Zeus was doing precisely the office of a lawgiver, *nomothetes*, one who 'establishes *nomoi*.'

Lawgiving, to the Greek mind, was not the progressive occupation of a deliberative assembly, but the work, done once for all, of a single person of extraordinary wisdom, a Solon or a Lycurgus. The *nomoi* of a state are its written constitution—a thing sacrosanct, to be touched or altered only with the gravest precaution. It appears, too, that the act of lawgiving was especially conceived as a redistribution of provinces and powers, a fresh assignment of portions, whether of land or of political status. We may take, for instance, Dionysius' description of Numa's lawgiving at Rome. Quarrels had arisen among the patricians 'about fairness and inequality' (περὶ τοῦ πλείονός

[1] *Od.* vi. 188 :
    Ζεὺς δ' αὐτὸς νέμει ὄλβον 'Ολύμπιος ἀνθρώποισι
    ἐσθλοῖς ἠδὲ κακοῖσιν, ὅπως ἐθέλῃσιν, ἑκάστῳ.

[2] Hesiod, *Theog.* 71 :   ὁ δ' οὐρανῷ ἐμβασιλεύει
    αὐτὸς ἔχων βροντὴν ἠδ' αἰθαλόεντα κεραυνόν,
    κάρτεϊ νικήσας πατέρα Κρόνον· εὖ δὲ ἕκαστα
    ἀθανάτοις διέταξεν ὁμῶς καὶ ἐπέφραδε τιμάς.

    885 :   ὁ δὲ τοῖσιν ἑὰς διεδάσσατο τιμάς.

[3] Aesch. *P. V.* 244 :
    ὅπως τάχιστα τὸν πατρῷον ἐς θρόνον
    καθέζετ', εὐθὺς δαίμοσιν νέμει γέρα
    ἄλλοισιν ἄλλα καὶ διεστοιχίζετο
    ἀρχήν . . .

τε καὶ ἴσου). Some of the plebeians were unsettled, 'having received no portion of land (γῆς μοῖραν) nor other advantages.' Numa, by distributing (διανείμας) land to them, and giving a new status (τιμάς) to settlers, put an end to dissension.[1]

Now, in this redistribution the Gods, quite as much as men, had their share. There was also an 'ordering of sacred things' (ἡ περὶ τὰ θεῖα διακόσμησις). Exactly as Zeus in Hesiod accepted the constitution of Kronos and only supplied its deficiencies, so we are told that Numa 'took over all the arrangements of Romulus in respect of customs and laws, and left them untouched'; but he made good the omissions, 'in many cases appointing precincts for those Gods who had not yet obtained a recognised position (τοῖς μήπω τιμῶν τυγχάνουσι θεοῖς); in other cases founding altars and temples, assigning (ἀπονέμων) to each his festival, and legislating (νομοθετῶν) about their services and honours (τιμάς).'[2]

The parallel could not be more exact. If we are right in thinking that *Moira* ultimately meant the division of the universe into distinct provinces, it is clear that this division, as soon as it comes to be the work of a personal God, can be conceived as a *nomothesia*—a laying down or fixing of *nomoi*; and that this process is simply a redistribution to Gods and men of their domains, privileges, and honours.[3] Like other such redistributions, the lawgiving of Zeus for a long time wore the aspect of an act of usurpation. It was not soon forgotten that the cosmic order had not really been initiated by Zeus. Throughout the *Eumenides* of Aeschylus,[4] until the final scene of reconciliation, rises the protest of the ancient *Moirai* against the younger Gods who have 'ridden down the old laws,' and taken from them their status and functions (τιμαί). They are only appeased when Athena promises them a new 'seat' and 'function,'

[1] Dion. H. *Ant.* ii. 62.

[2] Cf. also the language used by Plato in describing the division of the territory of the State in *Laws*, 745 B ff.

[3] Cf. *Ath. Pol.* 11: ὁ μὲν γὰρ δῆμος ᾤετο πάντ' ἀνάδαστα ποιήσειν αὐτόν (Σόλωνα).

E.g. 1. 781 : ἰὼ θεοὶ νεώτεροι παλαιοὺς νόμους

καθιππάσασθε—κἀκ χερῶν εἵλεσθέ μου . . .

ἐγὼ δ' ἄτιμος, κ.τ.λ.

καθιππάζεσθαι, 'to overrun territory with horse' (τὴν χώρην καθιππ., Herod. ix. 14), revives the old spatial sense of νόμος presently to be considered.

and makes them ' portioners in the land, with honours all entire.' [1]

13. *Law as a Dispensation*

The connection of *Nomos* (Law) with the verb *nemein*, to ' distribute ' or ' dispense,' was clearly felt by the Greeks. Take, for instance, the following passage in the pseudo-Platonic dialogue *Minos*, which discusses the notion of law (317 D) :

' Who is it that knows how to dispense (διανεῖμαι) the seed over the soil ?

' The farmer.

' And the farmer dispenses (διανέμει) to each soil the seed it deserves ?

' Yes.

' The farmer, then, is a good dispenser (νομεύς) of these things, and for these matters his *laws and dispensations* (νόμοι καὶ διανομαί) are right.'

In this passage ' laws ' and ' dispensings ' are clearly synonymous. We find the same conjunction in the *Eumenides*. In one place [2] the Chorus accuse Apollo of ' abolishing ancient *dispensations* ' (διανομάς), when he tricked the *Moirai* into releasing a mortal from death ; in another and parallel passage [3] the same God is accused of ' breaking the *law* (νόμον) of the Gods, by respecting the cause of man and abolishing the ancient *apportionments* (μοίρας).' These passages show that the notion of ' dispensation ' links together *Moira* and *Nomos*, with either of

---

[1] 1. 891 :   ΑΘ. ἔξεστι γάρ σοι τῆσδε γαμόρῳ[1] χθονὸς
                          εἶναι δικαίως ἐς τὸ πᾶν τιμωμένῃ.
                      ΧΟ. ἄνασσ' 'Αθάνα, τίνα με φῂς ἔξειν ἕδραν ;
                      ΑΘ. πάσης ἀπήμον' οἰζύος· δέχου δὲ σύ.
                      ΧΟ. καὶ δὴ δέδεγμαι· τίς δέ μοι τιμὴ μένει ;
                      ΑΘ. ὡς μή τιν' οἶκον εὐθενεῖν ἄνευ σέθεν.

[2] 1. 730 :   σύ τοι παλαιὰς διανομὰς καταφθίσας
                          οἴνῳ παρηπάτησας ἀρχαίας θεάς.

[3] 1. 172 :   παρὰ νόμον θεῶν βρότεα μὲν τίων,
                          παλαιγενεῖς δὲ μοίρας φθίσας.

See W. Headlam on *Agam*. 1007 ; and cf. Joh. Diac., εἰς Ἡσιοδ. Θεογ. ἀλλη-γορίαι 886 ἔτι δὲ καὶ τὰς Μοίρας ἀπὸ τῆς Θέμιδος Ζεὺς γεννᾷ, παρόσον ἐν ταῖς θεμιστείαις διανομαί τινες καὶ μερισμοὶ προσήκοντες γίνονται. Schol. ad Plat. *Legg*. 625 A, πολιτείας τῆς μιᾶς ζωῆς τῆς ὅλης πόλεως, νόμων δὲ τῶν διανεμόντων τὰ μέρη ἐξ ὧν ἡ πόλις. Aesch. *Supp*. 403, Ζεὺς νέμων ἄδικα μὲν κακοῖς, ὅσια δ' ἐννόμοις.

---

[1] So Dobree ; Τῆδεγ' ἀμοίρου codd. ἔμμοιρον, ἐμμοίρῳ are also conjectured.

which the word διανομή is synonymous. In Pindar,[1] again, the word *nomos* itself denotes the act of dispensing: Cheiron, the wise centaur, taught Asclepios ' the *dispensing* of medicines with gentle hand '—φαρμάκων ἐδίδαξε μαλακόχειρα νόμον.

Another derivative, νομεύς, which in the extract from the *Minos* means ' dispenser,' is of course more commonly used of shepherds who take their flock to feed on their allotted pasture—their νομός or νομή, both of which substantives denote both ' pasturage ' or ' feeding-place ' and secondarily ' dwelling-place,' ' quarters.' Perhaps the nearest equivalent is ' range.' [2]

Hence the compound adjective ἔννομος, which later means ' keeping within the law,' ' law-abiding,' has the older sense of ' quartered ' or ' dwelling ' in a country, which is, as it were, the legitimate range of its inhabitants.[3]

We have dwelt upon these details in order to bring out the fact that behind the familiar sense of *Nomos*, ' custom,' ' use,' ' law,' lie traces of an older spatial significance—the notion of a range or province, within which defined powers may be legitimately exercised—what the Romans meant by a *provincia*.[4] This aspect of the idea has become obscured to us owing to the prevalence of the scientific notion of Law, which has become associated with causal sequences in time and has lost its old connection with space. For the understanding of the Greek word, it is necessary to grasp that *Nomos* does not suggest uniformity of temporal sequence, but exercise of power within spatial or departmental boundaries. We must think of Law as a dispensation or system of provinces, within which all the activities of a community are parcelled out and coordinated. The plural *nomoi* can mean a social order so constituted ; as when, for instance, Pindar [5] speaks of the monstrous child of Ixion and the Cloud as ' having no status among men, nor yet in the *social*

---

[1] *Nem.* iii. 55.

[2] νομός is early used metaphorically : ' Wide is the *range* of words '—ἐπέων πολὺς νομὸς ἔνθα καὶ ἔνθα, *Il.* xx. 249 ; cf. Hesiod, *Erga*, 403 : ἀχρήιος δ' ἔσται ἐπέων νομός. Procl. in Plat. *Tim.* 21 E, p. 30 C, ὁ μὲν νομός (Egyptian *nome*) ἀπὸ τοῦ νενεμῆσθαι τὴν γῆν.

[3] Aesch. *Suppl.* 565 : βροτοὶ οἳ γᾶς τότ' ἦσαν ἔννομοι. Pind. *P.* ix. 69 : ἵνα οἱ χθονὸς αἶσαν . . . ἔννομον δωρήσεται.

[4] Cf. J. L. Myres, ' Herodotus and Anthropology' in *Anthropology and the Classics* (Oxford, 1908), p. 157. I owe much to this valuable essay, and especially to Professor Myres' remarks on φύσις and νόμος.   [5] *Pyth.* ii. 43.

order of the Gods '—οὔτ' ἐν ἀνδράσι γερασφόρον, οὔτ' ἐν θεῶν νόμοις. The portentous thing had no proper province in the divine or the human order : it was an ' outlaw ' from the classified structure of Nature and of society. Or again when the same poet [1] speaks of the spirit of power of the infant Herakles, strangling the snakes in his cradle, the word he uses is ἐκνόμιος, where we should say ' preternatural.' The half-divine child outranged the normal sphere of an infant's strength.

14. *Nemos and Nemesis*

With this conception clearly before us, we may find that it throws some light on two other cognates of *Nomos* and νέμειν : *nemos* and *Nemesis*. *Nemos* (the Latin *nemus*) is commonly translated by ' grove '; but the word has no etymological connection with trees, and to account for it we must suppose that it did not at first mean simply a natural stretch of woodland. There is reason to believe that a *nemos* was at first rather a sacred enclosure or clearing in a wood, perhaps a clearing round a sacred tree.

Dr. Frazer,[2] dwelling on the practice of tree-worship by all the Aryan races of Europe, says : ' From an examination of the Teutonic words for " temple " Grimm has made it probable that amongst the Germans the oldest sanctuaries were natural woods. However this may be, tree-worship is well attested for all the great European families of the Aryan stock. Amongst the Celts the oak-worship of the Druids is familiar to every one, and their old word for sanctuary seems to be identical in origin and meaning with the Latin *nemus*, a grove or woodland glade, which still survives in the name of Nemi. . . . Proofs of the prevalence of tree-worship in ancient Greece and Italy are abundant.'

Varro,[3] in his interesting discussion of the meaning of *templum*,

---

[1] *Nem.* i. 56.

[2] *Golden Bough*[3], part I. vol. ii. p. 8. Cf. Plin. *Nat. Hist.* xii. 1 : ' Haec (*i.e.* trees) fuere numinum templa, priscoque ritu simplicia rura etiam nunc deo praecellentem arborem dicant, nec magis auro fulgentia atque ebore simulacra quam lucos et in iis silentia ipsa adoramus.' Νηός (temple) has been derived from the same root (ναϜ-o) as ναῦs (ship): both seem to have been hollow trees. Cf. O. Kern, ' Zwei Kultinschr. aus Kleinasien' in *Beitr. z. Gesch. d. gr. Phil. u. Relig*, p. 88. Berlin, 1895.

[3] *Ling. Lat.* vii. 6.

brings out the fact that the two essentials of the augural *templum* are its fixed and oriented boundaries and the marking of these boundaries by trees. ' A *templum* is a place whose limits are defined with a set formula for purposes of augury and auspices.' He quotes the archaic formula for the *templum* in the *Arx* :

Templa tescaque me (*i.e. mi*) *ita sunto quoad ego caste lingua nuncupauero.*

Olla ueter arbos, quirquir est, quam me sentio dixisse, templum tescumque finito in sinistrum.

Olla ueter arbos, quirquir est, quam me sentio dixisse, templum tescumque finito in dextrum.

Inter ea conregione, conspicione, cortumione, utque ea rectissime sensi.

' In the making of this *templum*,' Varro concludes, ' it is clear that trees are taken as its boundaries.' The ancient word *tesca*, he tells us, is applied ' to certain wild places which belong to some God.' The augur also marked out with his official staff (*lituus*) a certain limited region of the sky, within which the desired sign was to appear.[1] In this augural *templum*, bounded by trees, we seem to have a survival of the sacred clearing in a grove, the ancient *nemos* sanctuary. It is a ' range ' assigned for the peculiar working of a divine power.[2]

What makes a place ' sacred ' ? The presence in it of a dangerous power which makes it, as the Greeks said, ' not to be entered,' ' not to be set foot on ' (ἄδυτον, ἄβατον) by the profane—by persons, that is to say, who are not themselves sacred, sanctified, ceremonially brought into a state in which contact with the mysterious power is no longer dangerous.

Now, one ancient title of the sacred presence inhabiting a grove or *nemos* is none other than *Nemesis*.[3] Nemesis has commonly been held to be a mere abstraction, ' Vengeance ' or the Anger which avenges transgression. Mr. Cook, however, points out that her worship is not late (as we should expect with

[1] See the description of the augury taken to determine whether Numa should be king of Rome (Livy, i. xviii. 6).

[2] Compare also Pindar's description of Herakles founding Olympia (*Ol.* x. (xi.) 45). Herakles begins by ' measuring out a grove ' (σταθμᾶτο ἄλσος and ' staking it round ' (περιπάξαις Ἄλτιν διέκρινε).

[3] I owe this interpretation of Nemesis entirely to Mr. A. B. Cook, who kindly allows me to anticipate its publication in his forthcoming *Zeus*.

a mere abstraction), but early, going back at least to the fifth
and sixth centuries at Rhamnus and Smyrna. Further, her
attributes are not such as might be implements of vengeance.
She is figured holding an *apple-branch* or an apple, and with
miniature *stags* as ornaments in her hair. She is the Woodland
Goddess, identical with Diana Nemorensis, Diana of the Woods.
Her name Nemesis is derived from *nemos*, precisely as Lachesis is
derived from *lachos* (lot).

How came the Woodland Goddess to be regarded as the
abstraction ' Avenging Anger ' ? [1] It is of course possible that
the identity of the two names is a coincidence ; that Nemesis
meaning vengeance is derived from *nemein* by a different channel,
and stands for ' retribution '—the dispensing of penalties. But
it seems not impossible that the Goddess of the Grove might
wear this aspect. She was a Goddess of fertility, closely allied
with Fortuna, the lady who ' bears,' ' brings forth ' (*ferre*, φέρειν)
the fruits of the earth. But she who dispenses good things can
withhold them, or dispense blights instead of blessings. The
awful power which haunts the *nemos* may blast the profane
invader of her sanctuary. In the far-off times, when a *nemos* was
the typical sacred place, Nemesis might well have been the
typical Avenger of trespass. In the same way figures of a fertility
spirit, Priapus, were set up as boundary marks to scare tres-
passers. And when the woodland enclosures fell into disuse,
Nemesis might become the guardian of law, of *nomos* instead of
nemos, losing all her ancient gift of fruitfulness—all but the apple-
branch, which, in her character of Vengeance, she so inappropri-
ately retains.

It is perhaps something more than an odd coincidence that the
great Roman lawgiver, Numa, before he gave his *nomoi*, sought
inspiration and counsel from the Goddess of the Woodland
Nemus. And Rome herself, the centre from which law spread
to the furthest bounds of Europe, had her beginning in a place
of refuge which was nothing but a sacred grove, a woodland
sanctuary for desperadoes and outlaws. [2]

---

[1] Mr. Cook is not responsible for the answer I suggest to this question.

[2] Livy, i. 8 : 'locum, qui nunc *saeptus* descendentibus *inter duos lucos* est,
asylum aperit.' Dion. H. *Ant.* ii. 15 : μεθόριον δυοῖν δρυμῶν. See Frazer,
Totemism, i. 96, and *Golden Bough*[3], part i. vol. ii. p. 176.

Pindar, at any rate, does not forget that Nemesis, the Dispenser, may give good things as well as harm. He ends the eighth *Olympian* [1] with a prayer for the victor's family : ' that Zeus may make Nemesis not to be of two minds in the apportionment of blessings. Rather may he guide their life clear of harm, and give increase to them and to their city.' The apportionment of blessings, the giving of increase, is the positive aspect of the dispensing power ; while its negative side is the vengeance which recoils upon trespass across its defined boundaries. Corresponding to these two aspects, *Nomos* and *Moira*, which, so long as we considered their purely spatial associations, seemed almost indistinguishable, tend to diverge. *Moira*, always static, a system rather than a force, leans toward the negative side : she limits and forbids. *Nomos*, on the contrary, is dynamic and inclines to the positive. Though implying the fixed limitation of a range or province, the word perhaps always meant also the *normal behaviour* prescribed and enjoined within a given province, and so *custom*. The word *ethea* seems to have a similar history. Its older sense is ' *haunts*,' the country within which you range ; later it means ' *customs*, established behaviour, habits.' [2] Thus *Moira* stands for the limit of what you may do, and for what will happen if you exceed your limit. [3] *Nomos* rather means what you must do within your limits, the regular and rightful functions you must exercise or ' wield '—another sense of *nemein*, as in *nemein kratos*, ' to wield authority,' ' to dispense power.'

But we may bear in mind that the positive and negative aspects are only the two sides of one power or force. The power which holds a certain field and is lawfully exercised within it

---

[1] *Ol.* viii. 86 : εὔχομαι ἀμφὶ καλῶν μοίρᾳ Νέμεσιν διχόβουλον μὴ θέμεν· ἀλλ' ἀπήμαντον ἄγων βίοτον αὐτούς τ' ἀέξοι καὶ πόλιν. ἀπήμαντον, because πῆμα is the more frequent gift of Νέμεσις : Hes. *Theog.* 223 : τίκτε δὲ καὶ Νέμεσιν, πῆμα θνητοῖσι βρότοισι. Cf. *Theol. Arith.* p. 32 (of Pythagoreans): Νέμεσιν καλοῦσι τὴν πεντάδα· νέμει γοῦν προσηκόντως τά τε οὐράνια καὶ θεῖα καὶ φυσικὰ στοιχεῖα τοῖς πέντε.

[2] The old sense of ἦθος seems to survive in Empedocles, frag. 17, l. 27, who says of the elements :

ταῦτα γὰρ ἰσά τε πάντα καὶ ἥλικα γένναν ἔασι,
τιμῆς δ' ἄλλης ἄλλο μέδει, πάρα δ' ἦθος ἑκάστῳ.

[3] μοῖρα means 'limit' in *Od.* xix. 592 (one cannot always go without sleep), ἐπὶ γάρ τοι ἑκάστῳ μοῖραν ἔθηκαν ἀθάνατοι θνητοῖσι, and is almost equivalent to *taboo* in Hesiod, *Erga*, 744 :

μηδέ ποτ' οἰνοχόην τιθέμεν κρητῆρος ὕπερθε
πινόντων· ὀλοὴ γὰρ ἐπ' αὐτῷ μοῖρα τέτυκται.

is also the power which recoils in anger upon an invading power from beyond its frontiers.

15. *The Dispensation of Reason in Plato*

This idea of a dispensation can be further illustrated from several 'mythical' passages in Plato which describe the constitutional order of divine government in the Golden Age of Kronos. In that age, according to the Stranger in the *Politicus*,[1] the revolution of the universe, under the guidance of God, went in the direction contrary to its present motion. ' All the parts of the ordered universe were divided amongst Gods appointed to rule over them, just as now Gods rule over various places. Moreover, living creatures according to their kinds were assigned to *daemons*, as it were flocks to divine shepherds (νομῆς), each *daemon* being sufficient in himself in all things for his own flock (οἷς αὐτὸς ἔνεμεν), so that there was then no savagery, no devouring of one another, no war nor strife of any sort among them.' This last trait is taken from Hesiod ; [2] it marks the dominion of Justice in the Golden Age, with which the prevalence of injustice in our own Age of Iron is in melancholy contrast. For at the end of the Golden period, the Governor of the Universe let go the tiller and left the world to the reverse impulse of Fate and its own inborn desire. Then ' all the Gods who in their several places had ruled together with the highest God, perceiving what was happening, in their turn left their divisions of the world-order without oversight.' [3]

In the above passage the division of living creatures according

---

[1] 271 D : ὡς νῦν κατὰ τόπους, ταὐτὸν τοῦτο ὑπὸ θεῶν ἀρχόντων πάντῃ τὰ τοῦ κόσμου μέρη διειλημμένα. καὶ δὴ καὶ τὰ ζῷα κατὰ γένη καὶ ἀγέλας οἷον νομῆς θεῖοι διειλήφεσαν δαίμονες, αὐταρκὴς εἰς πάντα ἕκαστος ἑκάστοις ὧν οἷς αὐτὸς ἔνεμεν, ὥστ' οὔτ' ἄγριον ἦν οὐδὲν οὔτε ἀλλήλων ἐδωδαί, πόλεμός τ' οὐκ ἐνῆν οὐδὲ στάσις τὸ παράπαν.

[2] *Erga*, 276 : τόνδε γὰρ ἀνθρώποισι νόμον διέταξε Κρονίων,
ἰχθύσι μὲν καὶ θηρσὶ καὶ οἰωνοῖς πετεηνοῖς
ἐσθέμεν ἀλλήλους, ἐπεὶ οὐ δίκη ἐστὶν ἐν αὐτοῖς·
ἀνθρώποισι δ' ἔδωκε δίκην . . .
Compare also Empedocles' Reign of Love, below, p. 236.

[3] *Pol.* 272 E. For Nemesis and the Daemons see Ps.-Timaeus, π. ψυχᾶς κόσμω 104 E : ἄπαντα δὲ ταῦτα (about the soul-wandering) ἐν δευτέρᾳ περιόδῳ ἁ Νέμεσις συνδιέκρινε σὺν δαίμοσι παλαμναίοις χθονίοις τε, τοῖς ἐπόπταις τῶν ἀνθρωπίνων, οἷς ὁ πάντων ἀγεμὼν θεὸς ἐπέτρεψε διοίκησιν κόσμω. . . .

to their natural kinds—that ' original boundary (ὅρος) and law
by which Zeus distinguished their several natures and set each
kind apart ' [1]—is compared to the local distribution among the
Gods of their several seats of worship. In the *Kritias*,[2] again, it
is declared that the Gods divided among them the whole earth,
place by place, not as the result of strife, but peacefully by drawing 'the lots of Justice' (δίκης κλήροις λαγχάνοντες); and making
themselves at home in their several countries, ' as shepherds
(νομῆς) over their flocks, they fostered us, their creatures and
nurslings,' ruling us not by violence, but by persuasive reason.
Our duty in this present age is to restore this ' dispensation of
Reason' (νοῦ διανομή), to which we shall give the name of ' Law '
(Νόμος).[3]

Thus, in his ' mythical' manner, Plato amplifies and re-
interprets the famous doctrine of Anaxagoras : ' All things were
confounded together, when Reason came and introduced distinction and order.' Reason takes the place of Zeus, as Zeus had
taken the place of *Moira*. But the function of the supreme power
remains the same—to ' introduce distinction and order,' to effect
a *diakosmesis*—the very word that Dionysius, in his description
above cited (p. 27) of the legislation of Numa, uses to denote
the re-ordering of the cults of the Gods, the redistribution of
precincts and seats of worship.

What is interesting to note here is that philosophy seems to
repeat, in its own way, the two stages we traced in pre-scientific,
religious representation. Just as there we found the will of a
personal God superseding *Moira*, and claiming to ordain by a
legislative act what had before been simply the recognised fact
of classified structure in the universe, so in philosophy the creative
Mind makes a tardy appearance and claims to have designed a
system which for Anaximander was produced by motion.

The process itself, however, throughout all these stages
remains in essence the same. It is a process of apportionment
(μοῖρα), distinction (διάκρισις), dispensation (διανομή), lawgiving
(νομοθεσία), ordering (διακόσμησις). The personal God of

---

[1] Plut. *Mor.* 964 B = Porph. *de abst.* i. 5, p. 88 : οὐδὲ φάρμακον οὐδὲ ἴαμα τῆς
ἢ τὸν βίον ἀναιρούσης ἀπορίας ἢ τὴν δικαιοσύνην ἔχομεν, ἂν μὴ τὸν ἀρχαῖον νόμον
καὶ ὅρον φυλάττωμεν, ᾧ καθ᾽ Ἡσίοδον (*loc. cit. supra*) ὁ Ζεὺς τὰς φύσεις διελὼν καὶ
θέμενος ἰδίᾳ τῶν γενῶν ἑκάτερον ᾽ἰχθύσι μέν, κ.τ.λ.   [2] 109 A ff.

[3] *Laws*, 713 D : τὴν τοῦ Νοῦ διανομὴν ἐπονομάζοντας Νόμον.

religion and the impersonal Reason of philosophy merely re-
enact as ' dispensers ' (Νομῆς) that old arrangement called *Moira*
which, as we saw, was really older than the Gods themselves,
and free from any implication of design or purpose.

16. *The primitive religious representation in Greek polytheism*

The main upshot of the foregoing analysis is that in Greek
polytheism the departmental division of the world, vaguely
represented as *Moira*, was the ultimate and primary fact—a
scheme or order whose provinces were first occupied by impersonal
powers, which later took the shape and attributes of individual
personality. We may now observe that this view agrees with
what the Greeks themselves believed about the development of
their own religion.

Herodotus [1] learnt at Dodona that the Pelasgians worshipped
nameless gods, whom they called simply *theoi*, because ' they had
set all things in order (κόσμῳ θέντες), and all *dispensations*
(νομάς) were in their hands.'

' It was only yesterday, so to speak, that they learnt of what
parentage was each God, or whether they were all from everlasting,
and what they were like in figure.[2] For, in my opinion, Homer
and Hesiod lived not more than four hundred years before my
time ; and it was they who composed a theogony for the Hellenes,
gave the Gods their titles, apportioned to them their functions
and arts, and made clear their figures.'

This is a very valuable piece of religious history. Behind the
clear-cut and highly differentiated personalities of the Olympians,
it shows us older figures far less distinct and hardly personal.

The proper term for them in Greek is not *theos*, but *daemon*.
Theos always suggests individuality, whereas these daemons had
as yet no ' figures,' and no peculiar functions or arts which
differentiated one of them from another. We must give up the

---

[1] ii. 52. For the association of κοσμεῖν and νέμειν, cf. Plato, *Protag.* 320c :
The Gods ordered Prometheus and Epimetheus κοσμῆσαι τε καὶ νεῖμαι δυνάμεις
ἑκάστοις ὡς πρέπει ; and the rest of that myth.

[2] εἴδεα. For the meaning of εἶδος, see A. E. Taylor, *Varia Socratica*,
i. 184 (Oxford, 1911), who shows that the word in current usage means
' bodily form ' or *physique*.

view, associated by Herodotus with his wrong derivation of *theos*, that these daemons ' set the universe in order.' They were not cosmic powers, but local spirits, good spirits (ἀγαθοὶ δαίμονες), each rooted to the portion of earth inhabited and cultivated by his worshippers. This was his *moira*, and within it all dispensations (νομαί) were in his hands. He was the sole guardian and saviour (φύλαξ, σωτήρ) of his people in war, and he also and above all gave them the fruits of earth in times of peace. These local spirits of fertility simply consisted of their functions ; that was all there was of them. Beyond that they had no personality ; and they were only individuals in the sense that the power residing in one *moira* of earth was numerically different from the power residing in another.[1]

We have had before us more than once two variant notions of the *dasmos* : first, the division of the elemental provinces among the three sons of Kronos ; second, the distribution of the surface of the earth into separate seats of worship. It is now apparent that the cosmic *dasmos* belongs to an advanced stage of Olympian theology. Not only is it based on a doctrine of the elements, but the Gods who take part in the division are known to have had local histories before they were generally recognised as cosmic powers. The old *daemons* of the type called Pelasgian by Herodotus can have no place in the elemental *dasmos* ; but they do fit into the other notion of a *dasmos* of earth into seats of local worship. The natural inference is that the cosmic *dasmos* is modelled upon this older one—adapted from it when a panhellenic theology was put together by the gathering of many local divinities to a common Olympus. We may therefore look back to the old *dasmos* of earth among these local spirits of earth's fertility as the earlier conception. It gives us the framework of primitive religious representation in Greek polytheism or polydaemonism. This is a *system of departments (moirai) clearly marked off from one another by boundaries of inviolable taboo, and each the seat of a potency which pervades that department, dispenses its power within it, and resists encroachment from without.*

[1] The origin and nature of these local *daemons*, some of whom become personal Gods and acquire elemental provinces, will be further discussed in chap. iii. See also J. E. Harrison, *Themis*, chap. ix, From Daimon to Olympian.

We find, in fact, that the basis and framework of Greek polytheism is an older form of that very order of Destiny and Justice which is reaffirmed by nascent science in the cosmology of Anaximander. Out of the provinces of that dispensation, the personal powers which had taken shape within them have disappeared again. The Gods have faded, and we are left with the elements from which Hesiod tells us that the Gods arose. Seen against the background of the destined order, the life of the Gods from first to last shows up as a mere episode. Nature— the living and self-moving stuff of all things that exist—and the primary forms in which her upspringing life is confined by the appointment of Destiny and Justice—these are older than the Gods and they outlast them. The course of philosophy starts from the same point from which, centuries earlier, religion took its departure on the way that led to the last and fatal absurdities of complete anthropomorphism. The history of this episode, called Olympian religion, we shall try to trace in the third chapter. Meanwhile, what we have called the primitive religious representation, to which our analysis has led us back, still remains to be accounted for. Our task in the next chapter will be to trace its yet remoter origin.

II

THE ORIGIN OF *MOIRA*

17. *How did the representation of Moira arise?*

OUR inquiry in the last chapter led us from an apparently
paradoxical statement of the first systematic cosmologist,
through an analysis of Destiny and Law, to the conclusion that
for Greek religious representation, no less than for early philosophy, the most significant truth about the universe is that it is
portioned out into a general scheme of allotted provinces or
spheres of power. The elements came into possession of their
fixed regions when the first limits were set up by the eternal
motion within the primary undifferentiated mass, called by
Anaximander ' the limitless thing.' The Gods had their provinces by the impersonal appointment of *Lachesis* or *Moira*.
The world, in fact, was from very early times regarded as the
kingdom of Destiny and (in the sense we have defined) of Law.
Necessity and Justice—' must ' and ' ought '—meet together in
this primary notion of Order—a notion which to Greek religious
representation is ultimate and unexplained.

Yet, if we reflect upon it, we shall see that some explanation is
called for. Why was it that, in Greek theology, cosmogony, and
philosophy alike, the primacy of *Moira* is so strikingly emphasised ? The departmental distribution of the four elements,
the segregation of pairs of ' contraries,' hot and cold, wet and
dry—these are not features of the universe which could instantly
present themselves to innocent speculation as obviously *the*
important guiding threads in the bewildering maze of sense-data.
And if we accept the results of the last chapter and admit
that such general conceptions are taken by philosophers from
pre-scientific thought, we have only pushed the problem back
one stage. If the departmental ordering of the elements is
only the physical transcript of the departmental ordering of the

divine powers by *Moira*, how did that representation itself arise ? No more than the cosmological application of it, is it a matter of simple common-sense, which would occur to any man who sat down, in presence of Nature, to invent a religion.

The question that now confronts us is whether we can trace the notion back to a yet earlier stage. Hitherto we have been guided by survivals in Greek thought and linguistic usage, which gave us a sufficient basis for reconstruction. But at this point we must either fold our hands and rest content, like the Greeks themselves, in the contemplation of *Moira* as a final and inexplicable fact, or we must have recourse to our knowledge of other religious systems of a type indisputably more primitive than any recorded for us in Greek sources. We must boldly enter the domain of hypothesis, taking for our guide the comparative method.

18. *The change from Religion to Philosophy*

How does the cosmology of Anaximander differ from the cosmology of Homer or of Hesiod ? We have seen that the philosopher and the poets have the same fundamental scheme in common. Why do we call Anaximander's treatment philosophic or scientific, and Hesiod's religious or mythical ?

One obvious difference is that Anaximander has expurgated the supernatural, with a boldness and completeness to which many of his successors failed to attain. To be more precise, he has expurgated those features and factors, the supernatural or mythical character of which he was able to detect. He has eliminated Zeus and his fellow Olympians, and in so doing has struck out of his scheme of things the objects on which the religious consciousness of his time was, whether in name or reality, focussed. The effect, as we have seen, is that he restores the more ancient reign of *Moira*. The primary order is still said to be ' according to what is ordained ' ; it is still a moral order in which Justice prevails; but the will of the personal God has disappeared, and its place is partly taken by a natural cause, the eternal motion. We seem to have left the supernatural behind and to have passed at one step into the shining air of reason.

The Milesian School strikes a new note, unheard before. It has a fresh sense of the meaning of truth—a feeling for what might or might not be literally and prosaically true, and for the sort of thing it is reasonable to suppose. The hypothesis it characteristically deals in is concerned with the nature of the one primary stuff; and although *we* may be able to see that about this entity there still clung much that was of mythical origin, the Milesians seem to make a great conscious effort to get at something which really does exist. They strike us as throwing off the vast symbolic visions of mythology, and waking, clear-headed, to see and touch real things. If we have a rational temperament, we feel at once a refreshment. Here at last is a statement about the world which is meant and offered as true—a *logos*, not a *mythos*.

It is perhaps the sudden pleasantness of this change of air that has caused us to draw too hard a line between religion and philosophy, and either to overlook the persistence of fundamental conceptions, or to follow the matter-of-fact Peripatetic tradition and wave them aside as poetical metaphors.[1] We may easily attach more importance than it deserves to the disappearance of the Olympians from the framework of the world, and suppose that, when they went, they took with them the whole element of the mythical or supernatural. That is by no means true. Homer's Gods had drifted so far out of touch with Nature and with the demands of human morality that any man of intellect like Anaximander could run a pen through them and leave the world and the heart of man none the poorer. They had grown so personal and individual and human that nothing but a wide freedom of allegorical interpretation could keep the old idols on their bases. But when the Gods were eliminated, a moral or sacred character still clung to the framework of the world itself, that system of provinces within which the Gods had sprung up and developed, till they were overblown and died. The stuff of the world, the *physis* portioned out into those provinces, was also, as we shall see, a conception of mythical

---

[1] Cf. Simpl. *Phys.* 24, 13, who, after quoting Anaximander's sentence about 'paying the penalty for injustice,' adds: ποιητικωτέροις οὕτως ὀνόμασιν αὐτὰ λέγων. Similarly, Aristotle dismisses Plato's technical terms παράδειγμα and μετέχειν as 'poetical metaphors' (*Met.* A 9) instead of trying to understand them.

origin. In other words, when Anaximander thought he was getting to close quarters with Nature, this Nature was not simply the outer world presented to us through our senses, but a *representation* of the world-order, actually more primitive than the Gods themselves. This representation was, moreover, of a religious character ; it was taken over by philosophy from religion, not independently deduced from observation of the world and its natural processes.

19. *The moral order of the world as a collective representation*

It would, perhaps, be generally assumed that to think of the world as moral through and through, as a kingdom of Justice, belongs to a late period of reflection. The assumption hangs together with that picture we drew at the outset, of the individual philosopher examining his inner and outer experience and drawing well-considered deductions from what he observed. It would be long indeed before anything presented to his un-biassed perceptions would lead him to suppose that Nature had any respect whatever for moral standards. Wherever and whenever a professed man of science upholds such an opinion, we may be certain that he is not formulating a description of observed facts, but turning his knowledge to the defence of a belief which he has learnt, not direct from Nature, but at his mother's knee ; in other words, a *collective representation*. And this particular representation is not the outcome of long accumulated results of science and philosophy. On the contrary, the further back we trace it, the more firmly planted it appears ; and the daily contradiction of all experience has not yet uprooted it from the popular mind.

20. *The nature of collective representations*

The term ' collective representation ' has been made familiar to us by the modern French school of sociologists. It is roughly defined by one of them as follows : [1]

' Representations called collective can be recognised by the

[1] L. Lévy-Bruhl, *Fonctions mentales dans les sociétés inférieures*, 1910, p. 1.

following marks : they are common to the members of a given social group, within which they are transmitted from generation to generation ; they are imposed upon the individuals, and awaken in them, as the case may be, feelings of respect, fear, adoration, etc., towards their objects. They do not depend for their existence upon the individual ; not that they imply a collective subject distinct from the individuals composing the social group, but in that they present themselves with characters which cannot be accounted for merely by considering the individuals as such. It is thus that a language, although, properly speaking, it exists only in the minds of the individuals who speak it, is none the less indubitably a social thing, founded on a mass of collective representations. It imposes itself on each of the individuals ; it exists before each of them and survives him.'

But, it may be objected, are we not here denying what we before admitted—that peculiar liberty of Greek thought from dogmatic imposition, which made possible the free development of ancient speculation ? To meet this objection and define our meaning, we must make the notion of a collective representation, in so far as it concerns our subject, more precise.

We do not mean that the Greek philosopher, at any rate in Ionia, was compelled by society to profess his belief that Zeus sat on a throne somewhere in the sky and controlled the course of natural events ; or that he was liable to be burnt alive if he publicly denied that the sun goes round the earth. Such persecution, though not unknown in the pre-Christian world, was in the main characteristic of later ages and of religions which claimed to be universal. It was possible for a Greek to dispense with the supernatural, and even openly to attack the morality and the existence of the Gods of popular belief. Xenophanes of Kolophon, who criticised Homeric theology with unsparing plainness, lived to a good old age. The philosopher was not in this sense trammelled by dogma ; and when we speak of collective representation, it is not dogma—a formulated creed or collection of final truths about the world and its governance— that we mean.

But, when we have eliminated all such formulas and creeds and put aside the supernatural, there remains embedded in the very substance of all our thoughts about the world and about ourselves an inalienable and ineradicable framework of conception, which is not of our own making, but given to us ready-made by society—a whole apparatus of concepts and categories, within which and by means of which all our individual thinking, however original and daring, is compelled to move. This common inherited scheme of conception, which is all around us and comes to us as naturally and unobjectionably as our native air, is none the less imposed upon us and limits our intellectual movements in countless ways—all the more surely and irresistibly because, being inherent in the very language we must use to express the simplest meaning, it is adopted and assimilated before we can so much as begin to think for ourselves at all. This mass of collective representation is, of course, constantly undergoing gradual change, largely due to the critical efforts of individual thinkers, who from time to time succeed in introducing profound modifications. It is different for every age in history, for every well-marked group in the intellectual chart of mankind, and even within such groups, in a minor degree, for every nationality. Hence the error of supposing that human nature is much the same at all times, and that, since non-human nature is much the same too, the Greek philosopher of the sixth century B.C., studying his inner and outer experience, was confronted with the same problems seen in the same light as the English philosopher of to-day. The difference—the immense difference—between the two lies in their several inheritances of collective representation. It is a difference that comes home to any one who has to ' translate ' (as it is called) from Greek into English. He will soon discover that, when once we go beyond the names of objects like tables or trees and of simple actions such as running or eating, no Greek word has an exact equivalent in English, no important abstract conception covers the same area or carries with it the same atmosphere of association. Translation from one language to another is impossible, from an ancient to a modern language grotesquely impossible, because of these profound differences of collective representation, which no ' translation ' will ever transfer.

It will now be clear in what sense Anaximander's cosmological scheme may be said to embody a religious representation. We do not mean that it is any longer obligatory [1]—imposed as a matter of faith, either by society upon the philosopher, or by the philosopher upon his readers. But the representation itself is unchanged and still bears the marks of its collective origin ; the only difference is that for Hesiod it had been a matter of faith, while for Anaximander it is a theory.

21. *How collective representations are imposed*

But when we have classed the belief in *Moira* under the head of collective representation, the question still remains open : how did humanity first come by this particular belief ? If it is not deduced by experience and observation, what is its origin ? The notion of a universal order in all Nature is strikingly general and abstract. Still more inexplicable, at first sight, seems the moral or sacred character attributed to this order. Let us first consider what we mean when we speak of it as ' moral ' or ' sacred.'

In primitive societies, as we shall presently see, the nature and order of the world, or certain specially important features of this order, are a *mystery*, in the sense of a received doctrine, revealed in many cases at the critical moment of adolescence, when the mind is most plastic and impressionable. The rites of initiation are of a terrifying character, often including protracted torture. They are well calculated to effect their object, which is to enforce these socially important representations with the strongest emotional colour and power. They are not to be pale intellectual opinions, at the option of the individual to take or leave upon his own estimate of their probability ; they are to be objects of indefeasible faith, charged with awful and tremendous feelings, fraught with associations of the most terrific experiences.[2] If ' morality touched with emotion ' is a bad definition of religion, ' custom touched with emotion ' is a good definition of morality ;

---

[1] Obligatoriness is taken by Durkheim ('Définition des phénomènes re-ligieux,' *Année Sociol.* ii. p. 1 ff.) as the essential characteristic of religious representations ; and he points out that it is a sign of collective origin, since the group is the only moral power superior to the individual, and capable of imposing beliefs and communicating to them that mysterious or ' sacred ' character which marks the articles of religious faith.

[2] See Lévy-Bruhl, *Les fonctions mentales dans les sociétés inférieures*, p. 29.

and in primitive initiation ceremonies the confirmatory touch of emotion is laid on with no light hand.

But the terrors and tortures of initiation are only an occasional and specially lively enforcement of a power which pervades with permanent and imperceptible dominance any social group of mankind. This is the power now recognised by psychologists under the name of ' herd-suggestion.' Until quite recently this factor of human psychology has been almost overlooked by students of the history of religion ; yet it has had more to do with the making of religious dogma than anything else. We only begin to understand the meaning and origin of religious belief and of morality, when we give up the fallacy of supposing that these great fabrics are the work of autonomous individual intellects, facing the facts of nature and constructing quasi-rational hypotheses to account for them. This fallacy is by no means yet abandoned ; even the scientific anthropologist some-times relapses into the assumption that his own attitude in the study of religion is the attitude of the social groups in whose consciousness religion took shape. We still are apt to take at least half seriously the ' savage philosopher,' imagined as pro-pounding hypotheses in much the same spirit as a Newton—hypotheses which have the misfortune to be absurd only because they are based on incorrect observation. This conception of the noble savage is excusable in Rousseau, because at the end of the eighteenth century no one had cared to inquire what savages were really like ; but it must be abandoned now. Religious beliefs are not the clever inventions of individual minds, but imposed upon the individual from without. Or, to speak more strictly, we must for these purposes give up thinking of the individual as having any separate existence over against society, and rather conceive him as completely immersed in one continu-ous social mentality.

It is true, of course, that every human being, in respect of a certain part of his mental life, exists in a world that is exclusively his own—a world of inner and outer sensation, and of move-ments directly connected with these states of the organism. This is the ' primary and inalienable basis of all individuality ' and is independent of the state of society.[1] But, for all that lies

---

[1] See Durkheim, *Sur la division du travail social*[3], p. 175.

beyond the sphere of simple physical necessities on the plane of representations of a higher kind, the primitive consciousness seems to possess no individuality. Where the civilised man has private and original opinions, beliefs, and inspirations, the savage has no self-assertive individuality, no consciousness of himself in distinction from his group. To this higher plane, moreover, belongs the whole sphere of religion and morality. In respect of these, the savage has no independent beliefs—no faith or practice that are not also and equally shared by every other member of his group. Hence it is not even strictly correct to say that these beliefs and practices are ' imposed ' upon the individual. That is how it now seems to us, among whom at last individuality is beginning to lift its head and to be allowed a very restricted field of toleration. But it is not so with the savage, who in respect of this field of mentality can more truly be said not to exist as an individual at all. The social group is the compact unit ; it can no more be said to consist of individuals than the wine in a bottle can be said to consist of distinct drops. Religious and moral beliefs might be compared to the colour of this wine, pervading every part of it in continuous distribution. There is no question of this or that drop of wine holding out against the infusion, and having the colour forced upon it by other drops who have previously submitted. The liquid behaves as a continuous and undivided whole : so also does the social group.[1]

Further, we should be deluded indeed, if we fancied that we ourselves are in this respect very different from the savage. A host of notorious facts would spring up to refute us. Why is it that the religions of the world are geographically and socially distributed, so that you can point to one area in which the enormous majority are Buddhists, to another in which they are Christians, to a third in which they are Mohammedans, and so

---

[1] Cf. Durkheim, *Sur la div. du trav. soc.*[3], p. 180 : ' Si l'on a cru parfois que la contrainte avait été plus grande autrefois qu'aujourd'hui, c'est en vertu de cette illusion qui a fait attribuer à un régime coercitif la petite place faite à la liberté individuelle dans les sociétés inférieures. En réalité, la vie sociale, partout où elle est normale, est spontanée ; et si elle est anormale, elle ne peut pas durer. C'est spontanément que l'individu abdique ; et même il n'est pas juste de parler d'abdication là où il n'y a rien à abdiquer.'

on ? No one can suppose that in any one of these areas, by some miraculous dispensation, each individual has been led by an independent process of reason to accept the truth of the religion which happens to prevail. Religions and moralities are epidemic now as they have always been. They are transmitted contagiously by herd-suggestion, and each tends to spread over as wide an area as is covered by a type of mentality homogeneous enough to absorb that particular mode of belief. Hellenised Rome was easily converted to Hellenised Christianity ; easy too was the diffusion of the same religious system over Romanised Europe. Anglicanism makes some advances in Anglicised India. But missionaries best know the obstacles which stand in their way, when they have to deal with a comparatively untouched civilisation, like the Chinese. Buddhism, on the other hand, was readily absorbed in China, because its ruling conception of *Dharma* (the order of the world and of morality) was practically identical with the Chinese *Tao*, and the same consciousness that was satisfied with the one conception assimilated the other without a struggle.[1]

In our own country, perhaps the freest in the world, the heretic and the innovator in morals are no longer burnt at the stake ; but, like the Christian missionary in China, they alone are conscious of the full weight of that collective feeling which sanctions the creeds, and enforces the morality, of the herd. But even the orthodox, who is so immersed in the collective mind that he is no more aware of its pressure than a fish is aware of the pressure of the water in which it floats, can yet form some idea of what we mean, if he will attend for a moment to what he experiences in the presence of something he regards as ' sacred '—let us say, a king at his coronation in Westminster Abbey. Or, let him isolate from all rational considerations the emotional element in his state of mind, when he contemplates committing some gross breach of social custom, which he personally does not consider to be bad or harmful. He will then be able to detect in himself the emotional charge communicated to a collective representation by intense feeling diffused throughout

---

[1] De Groot, *Religion of the Chinese*, 1910, p. 2 : 'Buddhism eradicated nothing ; the religion of the Crescent is only at the beginning of its work ; that of the Cross has hardly passed the threshold of China.' See also p. 165.

his herd. Finally, let him imagine his emotion intensified a hundredfold and quite freed from rational control, and he will be in the way to understand the same force of suggestion in a primitive group, undisturbed by heresy and individualism.

Now, it is precisely this emotional charge that makes a belief or a custom religious or moral. It is the fading out of it that marks the transition from faith to speculative opinion—from religion and morals to science and ethics. We have already noted, in another context, the refreshing effect of this change of atmosphere, which comes with the Milesian School. A representation of the world-order which had once been a mystery, fraught, in its earlier days, with awful emotion and serious practical consequences, is now put forward as a rational theory, which any one who can understand it is free to take or leave. In that sense, this representation has ceased to be religious, and become scientific : it is no longer imposed as a matter of faith, but offered for intellectual acceptance. On the other hand, the representation itself—the view of the world so recommended—is still, through and through, a *moral* representation, in the sense that a moral or sacred character is ascribed to the world-order itself.

22. *The order of Nature ' sacred,' because once continuous with human society*

So, once more, we come back into presence of our problem, having learnt by the way something of what ' moral ' or ' sacred ' means. We are still faced by the question : How did it come about, in the first instance, that the disposition of the cosmos and of its parts was charged with those tremendous emotions which enforce human custom or morality ? How did it come to be a religious or moral representation at all ?

We think we understand why positive laws of conduct are still enforced by those emotions. If we were called upon to defend them, we should urge that, in the main, they correspond to practical interests at all times important for the existence or wellbeing of socialised humanity.[1] But why should the same

---

[1] I do not imply that I think this account true. I accept Durkheim's view : 'Le seul caractère commun à tous les crimes, c'est qu'ils consistent . . . en des actes universellement réprouvés par les membres de chaque société' (*Sur la div. du trav. soc.*[3], p. 39).

emotional sanction ever have become attached to beliefs about the order and structure of non-human nature; and this so firmly that, even when religion had decayed, it was long before science could vindicate them for her own domain, in which no belief is sacred, and all emotion, save curiosity, is out of place?

When the question is thrown into this shape, the answer lies near at hand. It is this:

Moira *came to be supreme in Nature over all the subordinate wills of men and Gods, because she was first supreme in human society, which was continuous with Nature. Here, too, we find the ultimate reason why Destiny is moral : she defines the limits of mores, of social custom.*

This continuity of the order of Nature with the grouping of society, foreign as it is to our modern ways of thinking, is abundantly evidenced from various parts of the world, where we shall find that the social structure is used as a framework, into which all classes of natural phenomena are fitted.

23. *Classification based on tribal structure*

Among the Zuñis, a totemistic tribe of North American Indians, we are told [1] that all natural objects, and even abstractions, are classified in one solid system, the parts of which are coordinated according to degrees of kinship. The principle, moreover, of this classification is the seven regions of space—north, south, east, west, zenith, nadir, and centre. To one or other of these seven regions everything in the universe falls. Each region, too, has a certain colour, the centre having all colours at once.[2] The social structure corresponds: three clans of the tribe are assigned to each region, except the centre, which has but one.[3] The

---

[1] Durkheim et Mauss, 'Classifications primitives,' *Ann. Sociol.* vi. p. 34. Most of my evidence and, to a large extent, the theory based on it are taken from this essay.

[2] Similarly colours are attributed to the zones by Eratosthenes, ap. Ach. Tat. and Heracl. Pont., quoted by Conington on Verg. *Georg.* i. 233: πέντε δέ οἱ ζῶναι περιειλάδες ἐσπείρηντο, αἱ δύο μὲν γλαυκοῖο κελαινοτέραι κυάνοιο, ἡ δὲ μία ψαφαρή τε καὶ ἐκ πυρὸς οἷον ἐρυθρή. . . .

[3] See also Lévy-Bruhl, *Les fonctions mentales dans les sociétés inférieures*, p. 33: 'Les régions de l'espace, les directions (points cardinaux) ont leur

two classifications are the same, in the sense that everything
belongs to some ' oriented clan,' though it is possible that the
orientation comes later, and is superimposed on an original clan
division.   There are traces of an older scheme, with six regions ;
and an older still, with only four—the cardinal points.   To this
fourfold classification is traced the belief, held by the Zuñis,
that there are *four elements*, belonging to the four regions.

It is held that orientation begins with the division of the
round tribal camp into quarters, occupied by groups of clans.
Among another tribe, the Ponkas of the Sioux Indians, we find
the camp divided into two phratries and four quarters, and
these quarters are respectively occupied by two clans of *fire*
(thunder) ; two of *water* ; two of *wind* ; two of *earth*—the four
elements.

In China there are similar schemes, some more complex, some
of a simple type, used as the basis for divination, astronomy,
geomancy, and horoscopy.   In one of them, there are five elements—earth, water, wood, metal, fire—located in five regions
of space, earth being at the centre.

The aboriginal Mexicans, again, recognised four great Gods ;
four quarters of the heavens, the four chambers of *Tlaloc*, each
with its vessel containing a different species of rain ; and four
quarters of the *pueblo* of Mexico.   Similarly in Peru we find four
elements, four principal *huacas* (the Creator, Sun, Thunder, and
Earth-mother), and the four quarters of *Cuzco*, ' a division subsequently extended to the Cuzco district between the *Apurimac*
and *Paucartampu* rivers, and later still applied to the wide-
stretching quarters of the Inca dominion.' [1]

It seems clear that, in these and similar cases, the ultimate
basis of classification is the grouping of the tribe.   The segmentation of the tribe into two, or four, or however many
subdivisions there may be, is the primary fact.   It can be
accounted for by causes such as the over-pressure of population
in a given area, leading to a fission like that which occurs in the

signification mystique.   Quand les indigènes se rassemblent en grand nombre
en Australie, chaque tribu, et, dans chaque tribu, chaque groupe totémique,
a une place qui lui est assignée par son affinité mystique avec telle ou telle
région de l'espace.   Des faits du même genre sont signalés dans l'Amérique
du Nord.'

[1] Payne, *History of the New World*, ii. p. 283.

lowest types of biological organism. This segmentary structure is then reflected outwards upon the rest of the universe. The macrocosm was at first modelled upon the microcosm; and the primitive microcosm is the tribe. We are reminded that the very word *cosmos* was a political term among the Dorians, before it was borrowed by philosophy to denote the universal order.[1] In later days the situation is reversed, and the organisation of society, or of the individual, comes to be regarded as a miniature copy, in which the majestic order of the macrocosm is to be reproduced.

The art of divination is employed to trace the area occupied for social purposes, in accordance with the outlines of the disposition of nature. Thus, the Roman *comitium* was inaugurated as a *templum*. It was square in shape, and the four sides were oriented to the four quarters of the sky.[2] Plutarch preserves a curious account of the founding of Rome, from which we learn that the boundary of the original *comitium* was actually called *mundus* — the Latin equivalent of *cosmos*. When Romulus founded the city, we are told that he sent for men of magical wisdom from Etruria. A circular trench was dug round what is now the Comitium, and in it were deposited specimen offerings (ἀπαρχαί) of all things esteemed good by custom or necessary by nature, and a portion of earth brought from the country from which each man came. ' This ditch is called *mundus*—the same name as is given to the firmament (Ὄλυμπος).' Then, taking this *mundus* as the centre, they marked out the circuit of the walls with a plough drawn by a bull and a cow. Where they planned to have a gate, they lifted the ploughshare to make a break in the furrow; so that the whole wall is sacred (or ' taboo,' ἱερόν), except the gates. But for this precaution, they could not without fear of spirits (ἄνευ δεισιδαιμονίας) have carried in or out necessaries which were not pure.[3]

---

[1] It is a curious circumstance that Pindar (*Ol.* vii.) clearly suggests a parallel between the triple political division of Dorian Rhodes (which was settled 'according to tribes,' τριχθὰ δὲ ᾤκηθεν καταφυλαδόν, *Il.* ii. 668) and the division of the world among the Gods, which he describes in the context. Kameiros, Ialysos, and Lindos ἀπάτερθε ἔχον, διὰ γαῖαν τρίχα δασσά-μενοι πατρωίαν, ἀστέων μοῖραν, κέκληνται δέ σφιν ἕδραι. Cf. above, § 9.

[2] Pauly-Wissowa, *Real-Encycl.* s.v. 'Comitium.' [3] Plut. *Vit. Rom.* xi.

24. *Moira a projection of Nomos*

Now if, in various widely sundered parts of the world, the separation of the four or more elements into the regions of space was based on the quartering of the tribal camp among the divisions of the social group, we here have tangible evidence of that social, and therefore moral and religious, emphasis which our hypothesis demanded to account for the prominence of this representation in the historic religion and philosophy of Greece. We can hardly resist the conclusion that it came down to Homer and Hesiod and Anaximander from a primitive stratum of thought, which we could never have reconstructed, had it not lain fossilised to this day, in the beliefs and institutions of existing races of mankind.

Here we touch at last the bedrock. Behind philosophy lay religion; behind religion, as we now see, lies social custom— the structure and institutions of the human group. In the first chapter, we divined that *Moira*, the supreme power in the universe, was very closely allied to *Nomos*, in the sense of constitutional order. Now it appears that *Moira* is simply a projection, or extension, of *Nomos* from the tribal group to the elemental grouping of the cosmos. We can read a new sense into the apophthegm ascribed to Pythagoras,[1] that ' *Themis* in the realm of Zeus, and *Dike* in the world below, hold the same place and rank as *Nomos* in the cities of men; so that he who does not justly perform his appointed duty, may appear as a violator of the whole order of the universe.' The eternal laws, of which Antigone said that no one knew from whence they were proclaimed, can now be seen to have been projected, as a sort of Brocken spectre, from those very laws of the state with which she contrasts them.[2]

---

[1] Iambl. *Vit. Pyth.* ix. 46: τοὺς γὰρ ἀνθρώπους εἰδότας ὅτι τόπος ἅπας προσδεῖται δικαιοσύνης μυθοποιεῖν τὴν αὐτὴν τάξιν ἔχειν παρὰ τῷ Διὶ τὴν Θέμιν καὶ παρὰ τῷ Πλούτωνι τὴν Δίκην καὶ κατὰ τὰς πόλεις τὸν Νόμον, ἵνα ὁ μὴ δικαίως ἐφ᾽ ἃ τέτακται ποιῶν ἅμα φαίνηται πάντα τὸν κόσμον συναδικῶν. The conception of *Dike* will be further discussed below in chap. vi.

[2] Soph. *Ant.* 449:

> ΚΡ. καὶ δῆτ᾽ ἐτόλμας τούσδ᾽ ὑπερβαίνειν νόμους;
> ΑΝ. οὐ γάρ τί μοι Ζεὺς ἦν ὁ κηρύξας τάδε,
> οὐδ᾽ ἡ ξύνοικος τῶν κάτω θεῶν Δίκη
> τοιούσδ᾽ ἐν ἀνθρώποισιν ὥρισεν νόμους·

We are now in a position to formulate the answer to our main question, as follows :

Primitive beliefs about the nature of the world were sacred (religious or moral) beliefs, and the structure of the world was itself a moral or sacred order, because, in certain early phases of social development, the structure and behaviour of the world were held to be continuous with—a mere extension or projection of—the structure and behaviour of human society. The human group and the departments of Nature surrounding it were unified in one solid fabric of moirai—*one comprehensive system of custom and taboo. The divisions of Nature were limited by moral boundaries, because they were actually the same as the divisions of society.*

25. *Totemism*

To make this point clearer, we shall examine certain features of the well-known early phase of social development called Totemism. The reason for selecting this phase is partly that a great mass of evidence has lately been put together in convenient shape by the magnificent industry of Dr. Frazer.[1] But it especially suits our purpose because, as we shall see, its essential principle involves an extension of the structure and classification of human society to include the departments of the non-human universe. In this phase, in fact, we shall find *Moira* and *Nomos* established in undisputed sway over regions from which, in the later ages of theology and philosophy, they were very slowly driven out.

To guard against misapprehension, it must be clearly stated that we do not mean either to assert, or to assume, that totemism, in any complete form, ever prevailed among the remoter ancestors

οὐδὲ σθένειν τοσοῦτον ᾠόμην τὰ σὰ
κηρύγμαθ', ὥστ' ἄγραπτα κἀσφαλῆ θεῶν
νόμιμα δύνασθαι θνητὸν ὄνθ' ὑπερδραμεῖν, κ.τ.λ.

The significance of the view above put forward for the origin of the notion of the unwritten Law of Nature (cf. Arist. *Rhet.* i. 13. 2) will be apparent, but it cannot here be followed out. We shall find, as we go on, the same conception pervading philosophic thought. Another instance of the idea in Sophocles is *Oed. Tyr.* 863 ; where note that the Chorus invoke *Moira* to be with them in the observance of these heavenly laws, and say that an evil *moira* will overtake him who breaks them and fears not *Dike*.

[1] *Totemism and Exogamy*, in four vols. Macmillan, 1910.

of the Greeks. It may have been so; certain facts seem to point in that direction; but the question is open, and lies outside our argument. No one denies that the races who peopled Greece and Italy were, both in historic and in prehistoric times, given to the practice of magic. It will appear later that a great part of magical practice is essentially based on a certain relation of continuity between a human and a non-human group—a continuity which is said to amount to identity. This is all our thesis demands. Totemism is merely a social system in which this fundamental representation has hardened into a permanent framework, still extant for our observation. It is, therefore, convenient to describe its institutions, just in so far as they embody the principle under consideration—a principle which appears to have been, at one time or another, the property of every division of mankind.

26. *Solidarity of the Totemic Group*

The first point to be noted about a society in the totemic stage is that it is an aggregate, not of independent individuals, but of groups. As we have already said, it is the group, not the individual, that must be taken as unitary. These groups are externally marked off from one another by the sharpest distinction, and internally united by the strongest solidarity. The bond which unites the group, however, is not family relationship, nor even blood-kinship (in our sense) at all.

The totem-clan is defined by a peculiar relation, possessed in common by all its members and by them alone, to its particular totem. A totem is not an individual thing, but, like the clan, a group—a whole class of objects, ' generally a species of animals or of plants, more rarely a class of inanimate natural objects, very rarely a class of artificial objects.' [1] It must be remembered that the distinctions between these three classes of object, important as they may seem to us, are much less obvious to the savage. ' Animate and inanimate ' are not familiar categories to him; ' natural and artificial ' is probably a distinction of little significance. Far more important than these distinctions which interest us, is the property which all these objects have in common, and which qualifies them to be totems. They must all

---

[1] Frazer, *Totemism*, i. 4.

alike be of some social importance, in a sufficiently high degree
to focus attention upon them.. They are, all of them, things
whose existence and behaviour in some way *matters* to society.
A great majority of them are connected with one of our most
fundamental interests—food : they are either eatable species,
or phenomena (such as wind, rain, sun) on which the food supply
depends, or tools used in procuring food.

The nature of the relation which unites the human clan and
its totem-species perhaps defies exact analysis in our civilised
terminology. It is certainly an exceedingly close relation, which
some observers declare amounts to identity—or, since negative
terms are safer, to the absence of any sense of distinction. The
word *totem* itself is said to mean simply ' tribe '; and this fact
marks that the totem rather *is* the social group, embracing
human and non-human members alike, than an external badge,
or attribute, or anything of that sort. We must, therefore,
think of the totem-clan and its totem-species as forming one
continuous social group, with the highest degree of solidarity ;
and the less we distinguish between the clan and the species,
the nearer we shall keep to the true point of view.

The members of a totem-clan normally believe themselves
to be descended from a totem-ancestor, who is often half human
and half plant or animal—a mythical representation which
significantly symbolises the identity of the clan and its totem-
species. By virtue of this descent, they are of one blood ; and
we may conceive the blood as a continuous medium running
through the whole group, as it were the material substrate of
its solidarity. Through it, every part of the group is in vital
sympathy with every other, so that in the blood-feud the group
is collectively responsible, and in some cases a man cannot cut
his own finger with his own knife without paying blood-money
to his mother's family. ' Being of their blood, he is not allowed
to spill it without paying for it.' [1] Or, the blood may be thought
of as the life of the totem—the one life derived from the common
ancestor and immanent throughout the clan.

Possibly derived from this continuity of the blood are two
great taboos which go with totemic social classification. The

[1] Frazer, *Totemism*, i. 53.

full member of a totem-clan may not, in ordinary circumstances, eat his totem animal or plant; and he may not marry a woman of the same clan with himself.[1] The latter prohibition normally involves the division of the tribe into two (or some multiple of two) phratries, within each of which all marriage is incestuous. This exogamous classification is combined with classification into totem-clans in various complex schemes—an exogamous group (phratry) often including several totem-clans, none of which may intermarry.

27. *The primacy of the group*

We have dwelt on these details with a view to making it clear that, in a society so organised, the unit is the group, not the individual; and, whether or no the ancestors of the Greeks had a developed totemic system, we may be certain that, the further we go back into the prehistoric past of any race of mankind, the less the individual will count, and the more his social group, however it may be defined, will be the unitary factor. As evidence of this, survivals are not wanting among the Greeks. Pindar makes us familiar with the daemon, or genius, of a clan, to whom, rather than to the individual competitor, the glory of success in the Great Games is ascribed in so many of his Odes of Victory.[2] In the tragedians, especially Aeschylus,[3] we encounter the notion of hereditary guilt—of those ' taints and troubles which, arising from some ancient wrath, existed in certain families,' [4] and were transmitted with the blood to the ruin of one descendant after another, who, in the view of a later individualistic morality, were personally innocent. These and

---

[1] The view that endogamy is taboo because marriage involves the shedding of blood is disputed; but see Durkheim, 'La prohibition de l'inceste,' *Année Sociologique,* i. p. 1 ff.

[2] See my chapter on the Olympic Games in J. E. Harrison, *Themis,* p. 257.

[3] The *Agamemnon,* 1451-1576 (Clytaemnestra and Chorus), brings out most of the important aspects of this deep-seated belief. In the course of it, Clytaemnestra successfully diverts the attention of the Chorus from her personal motive, sexual jealousy, to the δαίμων γέννης of the house of Tantalus. By representing herself as an incarnation of this, she shifts responsibility from her individual self on to the collective soul of her clan.

[4] Plato, *Phaedrus,* 244 D : νόσων καὶ πόνων τῶν μεγίστων, ἃ δὴ παλαιῶν ἐκ μηνιμάτων ποθὲν ἔν τισι τῶν γενῶν ἦν.

other such representations illustrate the persistence of the moral solidarity of the group. We may note, too, the implication of this solidarity : namely, that the circumference of the group is, so to say, the moral frontier. Inside that frontier, the group as a whole has its proper duties, exercised in common, and its collective rights, diffused over the whole area. Outside the frontier are other groups, equally coherent and internally undistinguished. And this frontier is the surface at which moral friction occurs.

Society, in a word, is a system of *moirai* ; and the boundaries of its groups are also the boundaries of morality. Within them lies *Nomos*—all that you *ought* to do and *must* do—the exercise of the group functions, the expression of its peculiar magical powers. Beyond them lies all you must *not* do—all that is taboo.[1] The sentinel at the frontier is Death. It may be significant that *moira* is the counterpart of *moros*, death ; and that the word *moira* itself easily passes from its sense of allotted portion to mean *doom*—'the grievous doom of death' (μοῖρ' ὀλόη θανάτοιο).

28. *The social structure projected to include the order of Nature*

Now, the totemic social system, involving as it does the identity of each human clan with a non-human species, rests, in its essential principle, on an extension of the structure of human society beyond what seem to us its natural limits, so as to include in one solid system the departments of Nature with which the clans are severally united. In the more advanced cases, the social system is thus projected until it becomes conterminous with the visible universe, and every kind of natural object belongs to some social group.[2] Thus, the whole universe

---

[1] I am of course speaking of a very early stage. Later, when individuality begins to assert itself in the moral area, repression of the individual by his own group becomes necessary. But at first all taboos are imposed upon classes as such, not on individuals.

[2] Frazer, *Totemism*, i. 118 : 'There is something impressive, and almost grandiose, in the comprehensiveness, the completeness, the vaulting ambition of this scheme, the creation of a crude and barbarous philosophy. All nature has been mapped out into departments ; all men have been distributed into corresponding groups ; and to each group of men has been assigned, with astounding audacity, the duty of controlling some one depart-

is brought within the bounds of human morality, and portioned out into its provinces; for each department of nature must be subject to the same taboos, and bound to the observance of the same customs, as the human group with which it is identified. The positive side—observance of custom—we shall consider later, when we turn to magic. But on the negative side—the side of taboo—we find at last the explanation of our problem—the supremacy of *Moira* in the universe, human and non-human alike. The moral character of the physical order is finally accounted for, when we see that the primitive boundaries of Right are not the limits of the individual as against society, nor yet those of society as against nature, but radiate in unbroken lines from the centre of society to the circumference of the cosmos. This, in the last resort, is the reason why the disposition of the elemental provinces persists, right into the age of rational speculation, as *the* important feature of the universe. The moral, or socially important, or sacred, force and colour, with which in earlier ages it had been charged, have not yet faded out of the imperious figures of *Moira* and *Nomos*.

29. Survivals in Greek cosmology

There are two outstanding features of the Greek philosophic cosmologies which seem to become intelligible in the light of our hypothesis. They are (*a*) the recognition of *four elements*, (*b*) the grouping of qualities in *pairs of contraries*. We will briefly consider them in turn.

But first, to guard against misconception: our hypothesis does not imply that Homer and Hesiod, any more than Anaximander, had ever heard of totemism and its peculiar institutions. All it comes to is this. In every age of mankind certain aspects of the world, certain features of the infinite manifold our senses show us, are specially significant, attended to, emphasised, studied. Further, the aspects and features dwelt upon by the early philo-

ment of nature for the common good.' Cf. *ibid.* p. 134. The 'audacity' involved, however, is only apparent, if we recognise that the whole process was unconsciously and spontaneously effected by the collective mind, which took it all as the most obvious and simple representation of nature, and indeed did the whole thing, as we shall later see, before it felt the need of conceiving the 'philosophy' implicit in it. See also Lévy-Bruhl, *Fonct. ment.* p. 284.

sophers often strike us as by no means superficially obvious ; and—what is also important—they are remarkable for their generality and abstract character. Physical science, neglecting the task of accumulating detailed knowledge by observation, immediately on its first appearance, attacks the problem of the ultimate ' nature ' of all things. Or again, it assumes, as an admitted *a priori* truth, a maxim so general as ' Like can only act on like.' What we seek is the cause of this curious phenomenon ; and we hold that the reason why the early philosophers attended to these ultimate problems, and presumed such universal maxims, is that they were already emphasised in religious and popular representation. To take our present instance : the disposition of the elemental provinces—the importance attached to this can only be explained by supposing that it had once been of religious significance ; and we saw in the last chapter that such, in fact, was the case. In the present chapter we have taken a further step, and made out that its religious significance probably points back to a stage when it was continuous with the moral and social structure of the human group. What we suggest is that this line of investigation gives the clue to the early philosophers' choice of objects to speculate about. They, one and all, constructed theories about the arrangement of the universe, and again about meteoric phenomena—sun and moon, shooting stars, thunder, earthquakes, etc.—because these were objects on which religion and magic had concentrated attention for uncounted ages.[1]

30. (a) *The Four Elements*

The totemistic organisation of society is complex, involving, as it does, the division of the tribe into a number of subordinate groups, each with specialised functions. We cannot suppose that a system which entails such a nicely adjusted division of labour is the primitive form of human society. Rather, there are good grounds for holding that the original society was a single

[1] Tannery, *Pour l'histoire de la science hellène*, p. 20, enumerates the headings under which, in an order regularly observed, the doxographic tradition, derived from Theophrastus, records the ' opinions ' of the various philosophers. They are : Principle, God, Universe, earth, sea, rivers, Nile, stars, sun, moon, milky way, meteors, wind, rain, hail, snow, thunder, rainbow, earthquakes, animals.

group or tribe—a human herd, as yet undifferentiated and un-specialised. The breaking up of this group may have been, as biological analogy suggests, a simple process of segmentation, due to the mere mechanical cause of the increase of population in a given area. The primary homogeneous group was held together by a solidarity of a low mechanical type, which has much less binding force than the higher organic solidarity in-volved in the mutual dependence of specialised groups. As population grows, that mechanical solidarity is diffused over a continually widening area, and grows thinner and thinner until a trifling cause may make it snap. The tribe is like a pool of mercury : the larger it is, the slighter the shock that will scatter it into separate drops. Each of the new groups resulting from this segmentation, being smaller, will be more strongly united.[1]

Such a process, however, would give only an aggregate of separate groups, each internally coherent, but not united to its neighbours. In the totemic system (however it may be caused) we find a structure of the higher type—an organism. Besides the strong solidarity of specialised function which holds together each clan, there is a looser, but very real, bond linking all the clans into one tribe. The older structure thus survives in the new, the organic groups being superimposed upon, but not altogether superseding, the primitive inorganic group.

Now, if we take the cosmological scheme of Anaximander, and consider the relation of his one primary 'nature' ($\tau\grave{o}$ $\ddot{a}\pi\epsilon\iota\rho\sigma\nu$) to the four subordinate elements with their allotted *moirai*, we observe that this type of cosmic structure corresponds to that of a totemic tribe containing four clans. The 'limitless thing,' like the primitive herd, is continuous, homogeneous, undifferen-tiated, and so loosely united that a mechanical cause—the ' eternal motion '—can make it fall asunder into smaller groups. The four elements, like the subordinate totemic clans, are differentiated and specialised, and each is drawn together into a coherent mass by the attraction of like to like—the solidarity of affinity. The elements, moreover, are not utterly distinct or indifferent to one another : there is also a repulsion between unlikes, a war and feud, to which, as we saw, all individual

---

[1] For this theory of the two kinds of solidarity and the cause of segmen-tation, see E. Durkheim, *Sur la division du travail social*.

existence was due. The cosmology is a transcript in representation of an organic structure, such as we find in a totemic tribe, in which the primitive unitary tribal group and the organic nexus of clans reappear as two separate stages—the primary *physis* and the four elements separated out from it.

31. *The Philia and Neikos of Empedocles*

In the system of Empedocles, we find the two opposed principles of solidarity and repulsion actually distinguished as two 'elements,' over and above the four fundamental forms of matter—earth, air, water, and fire—recognised in earlier systems. Empedocles made these four elements ultimate irreducible forms, the 'roots of all things,' and reasserted their 'equality.' [1] Their complete mixture in a 'sphere' is one pole, their complete separation in four homogeneous masses is the other pole, of his two alternating hemicycles of existence.[2]

If we press our analogy with the processes and factors of tribal organisation, the Love which draws all the elements into the indiscriminate mass, called the Sphere, corresponds to the solidarity of the whole tribe. Strife, or feud, is the disintegrating force, which causes segmentation into minor groups. Each group, like a clan, has a solidarity of its own, and an internal consistency. The separation of unlikes is the same fact as the coming together of likes—earth to earth, water to water, and so forth ; so that the action of *Neikos* can also be interpreted as the attraction of like by like—the cause of the differentiated, organic solidarity of groups within a larger group, of clans within a tribe.[3]

32. (b) *The segregation of pairs of Contraries*

We turn next to the process by which the elements come into possession of their provinces. In Anaximander's scheme, this process is conceived as the 'separating out' (ἔκκρισις, ἀπόκρισις) from the indeterminate One, of 'contraries' (ἐναντία). Two

---

[1] Arist. *de Gen. et Corr.* β 6, 333a 16.

[2] The details of the system are discussed below, pp. 224 ff.

[3] This interpretation of the Philia and Neikos of Empedocles was first suggested to me by Miss Harrison. It will be shown later how these principles were inherent in what we shall call the datum of philosophy.

pairs of contraries appear to be primary—the hot and the cold, the wet and the dry—and these are naturally identified with fire and air, water and earth. The elements are thus not merely separated into four distinct regions, but grouped in pairs. Two contraries must be conceived as equal in nature and power, neither of them the mere negation or absence of the other.[1] They are, like the three Homeric Gods,[2] equal in status or in lot (ἰσότιμοι or ἰσόμοροι). Empedocles [3] states this equality of the elements in very distinct terms :

' For all of them are equal, and of equal birth. Each is lord of a different function, each has its wonted range,[4] and in turn they gain the mastery, as the cycle of time comes round.'

Between the two members of each pair of contraries there is antagonism, strife, feud. Each seeks to invade the province of the other, to overmaster it and usurp part of its domain. Out of this strife, as we have seen (§ 3), arises, according to Anaximander, all individual existence, which is the offspring of aggression and injustice. And, since the moral order of Nature demands that every injustice shall be atoned, every individual thing must ' pay the penalty ' and ' perish into that out of which it came into being.'

This war of antagonistic principles, on the other hand, though unjust, is not purely destructive ; in fact, it generates the whole world of things we see. In other systems we shall encounter the idea that not only all existence, but all goodness and perfection in the visible world, involve a balance or harmony of opposed powers—a reconciliation in which the claims of both are, if only temporarily, adjusted. Besides War, there is also Peace ; besides Hatred and Feud (Neikos, Eris, etc.), there is also Love and Agreement (Philia, Harmonia, etc.). This general scheme of conception runs through all ancient physical

---

[1] For all this subject, see O. Gilbert, Met. Theor. p. 28 ff.

[2] See above, p. 15.

[3] Frag. 17. 27 :

> ταῦτα γὰρ ἶσα τε πάντα καὶ ἥλικα γένναν ἔασι,
> τιμῆς δ' ἄλλης ἄλλο μέδει, πάρα δ' ἦθος ἑκάστῳ,
> ἐν δὲ μέρει κρατέουσι περιπλομένοιο χρόνοιο.

Sophocles, El. 86, follows Empedocles (Gilbert, Met. Theor. 35) : ὦ φάος ἁγνὸν καὶ γῆς ἰσόμοιρ' ἀήρ.

[4] For this meaning of ἦθος, see above, p. 34.

speculation, and, after all that has gone before, we shall not be surprised to find it dominant in ethical speculation also. Its moral and social colour is no mere trapping of superficial metaphor ; it is ingrained and essential.

But—to go back to Anaximander's scheme of cosmology—it is not only with the birth and perishing of individual things that we are concerned, but also with the previous stage, in which the ' contraries' were sifted out by the eternal motion into their distinct regions—the first appearance of distinction within the limitless One. An examination of the pre-scientific cosmogonies will show that this extremely general and abstract conception can be traced further back to a very primitive social origin.

33. *Sex the prototype of Contrariety*

If we look more closely into this conception of pairs of contraries, we find that Anaximander is more purely rational than many of his successors. In later systems—notably in those of Parmenides and Empedocles—mythical associations and implications, which he has expurgated, emerge again. In particular, we can discern that the prototype of all opposition or contrariety is the contrariety of *sex*.

The Eleatic Stranger in Plato's *Sophist* notes this feature, in reviewing the early physical philosophers. He complains that they treat us like children, and put us off with fairy tales. One will tell us that there are three Beings, which ' sometimes carry on a sort of warfare with one another, and then again become friends and go in for *marriages and child-bearing and nursing up of their offspring.*' Another speaks of a pair—Wet and Dry, or Hot and Cold—whom he ' *marries off and makes them set up house together.*' [1] The Eleatics base their wondrous tale on the doctrine that all things are really One. Then, certain inspired sources in Ionia (Heracleitus), and later in Sicily (Empedocles), saw that it was safest to combine both views and say that ' Being is both many and one, and is held together by Hatred and Love ' ; the sterner sort (Heracleitus) declaring that, ' being

---

[1] 242 C : ὁ μὲν ὡς τρία τὰ ὄντα, πολεμεῖ δὲ ἀλλήλοις ἐνίοτε αὐτῶν ἄττα πῃ, τότε δὲ καὶ φίλα γιγνόμενα γάμους τε καὶ τόκους καὶ τροφὰς τῶν ἐκγόνων παρέχεται· δύο δὲ ἕτερος εἰπών, ὑγρὸν καὶ ξηρὸν ἢ θερμὸν καὶ ψυχρόν, συνοικίζει τε αὐτὰ καὶ ἐκδίδωσι.

drawn asunder always, it is always being drawn together ' ;[1]
the softer (Empedocles) relaxing this ' always,' and saying that
the All is one and many *in turn*, now in a state of Love through
the power of Aphrodite, now at war with itself owing to a certain
' Feud.'

Before cosmology were cosmo*gony* and theo*gony*. Becoming
(γένεσις) was conceived as birth, and birth is the result of marriage. The primal marriage in the early cosmogonies is the
union of Sky and Earth, represented in the anthropomorphic
religion of historic times by the ritual marriage of Zeus, or
Jupiter, and his female partner.

34. *The Separation of Sky and Earth*

But Sky and Earth cannot meet in fruitful marriage till they
have first been sundered from their original unity of form. The
cosmogonies open, not with the marriage, but with the *separation*
of Earth and Sky.

' First of all,' says Hesiod,[2] ' Chaos came into being ; then,
Earth with her broad breast, for all things a seat secure for
ever, and misty Tartarus in the hollow of the wide-wayed Earth,
and Love, the fairest of the immortal Gods.'

' First of all, Chaos came into being '—what does that mean ?
' Chaos ' was not at first, as we conceive it, formless disorder.
The word means simply the ' yawning gap '—the gap we now
see, with its lower part filled with air and mist and cloud,
between earth and the dome of heaven.[3] Originally Earth

---

[1] Cf. [Arist.] de *Mundo*, 5: ἴσως δὲ τῶν ἐναντίων ἡ φύσις γλίχεται καὶ ἐκ
τούτων ἀποτελεῖ τὸ σύμφωνον . . . ὥσπερ ἀμέλει τὸ ἄρρεν συνήγαγε πρὸς τὸ θῆλυ
καὶ οὐχ ἑκάτερον πρὸς τὸ ὁμόφυλον. Heracl. frag. 10 (Diels), 59 (Byw.),
διαφερόμενον συμφέρεται κ.τ.λ., is quoted in illustration.

[2] *Theog.* 116 : ἦ τοι μὲν πρώτιστα Χάος γένετ', αὐτὰρ ἔπειτα
Γαῖ' εὐρύστερνος, πάντων ἕδος ἀσφαλὲς αἰεί,
Τάρταρά τ' ἠερόεντα μυχῷ χθονὸς εὐρυοδείης
ἠδ' Ἔρος. . . .

[3] It is this gap that is filled with heat when Zeus makes his thunder-
storm, *Theog.* 700 : καῦμα δὲ θεσπέσιον κάτεχεν χάος. Schol. ad v. 116 : οἱ
δὲ εἰρῆσθαι φασὶ χάος παρὰ τὸ χεῖσθαι, ὅ ἐστι χέεσθαι· οἱ δὲ φασὶν ἀπὸ τοῦ χαδεῖν,
ὅ ἐστι χωρεῖν . . . ἡ οὖν εἰς τὰ στοιχεῖα διάκρισις καὶ διαχώρησις, χάος. . . .
ΑΛΛΩΣ. χάος λέγει τὸν κεχυμένον ἀέρα, καὶ γὰρ Ζηνόδοτος οὕτως φησί. Βακχυλίδης
δὲ χάος τὸν ἀέρα ὠνόμασε, λέγων περὶ τοῦ ἀετοῦ· ' Νωμᾶται δ' ἐν ἀτρυγέτῳ χάει '
(ἀτρύτῳ is the true reading, Bacch. v. 26). Cf. Ibycus, frag. 28 : ποτᾶται δ'
ἐν ἀλλοτρίῳ χάει.

and Heaven were one, as Melanippe the Wise, in Euripides,[1]
had learnt from her half-divine mother:

> ' It is not my word, but my mother's word,
> How Heaven and Earth were once one form; but stirred,
> And strove, and dwelt asunder far away:
> And then, re-wedding, bore unto the day
> And light of life all things that are, the trees,
> Flowers, birds, and beasts, and them that breathe the seas,
> And mortal man, each in his kind and law.'

The Orphic cosmogony used by Apollonius Rhodius [2] tells
the same tale. Orpheus sang ' how earth and sky and sea were
at first joined together in one form, and then disparted, each
from each, by grievous strife.'

This account of the beginning of the world is of enormous
antiquity. A hymn in the *Rig-Veda* (vii. 86) says of Varuna,
whom some scholars identify with Ouranos:

> ' Wise truly and great is his own nature,
> Who held asunder spacious Earth and Heaven.
> He pressed the sky, the broad and lofty, upward,
> Ay, spread the stars and spread the Earth out broadly.'[3]

In the Babylonian cosmogony, from which that of *Genesis* is
derived, Marduk cut in two pieces the monstrous Tihamat, and
' one half of her he set in place, he spread out as heaven.' The
primitive Egyptians, likewise, described *Shu* as separating the
sky (*Nut*) from the earth (*Seb*). In the Taoism of China, an
original ' Chaos ' splits of its own accord into the two opposed
moieties called *Yang* and *Yin*, the regions of light and darkness
associated with heaven and earth.[4]

---

[1] Frag. 484 N², ap. Diod. Sic. i. 7, trans. Professor Murray.

[2] i. 496 (Diels, *Frag. d. Vors.* ii. p. 479):

> ἤειδεν δ' ὡς γαῖα καὶ οὐρανὸς ἠδὲ θάλασσα
> τὸ πρὶν ἐπ' ἀλλήλοισι μιῆι συναρηρότα μορφῆι
> νείκεος ἐξ ὀλοοῖο διέκριθεν ἀμφὶς ἕκαστα.

[3] Bloomfield, *Religion of the Veda*, p. 124.

[4] De Groot, *Religion of the Chinese*, New York, 1910, p. 152. It may be
noted that in this system there is no creator or God superior to the Tao or
order of the universe (pp. 102, 135); cf. the position of Moira as described
above, § 8.

35. *Social origin of this representation*

We ought not to allow the familiarity of this conception of the world's origin to blind us to the fact that it is not a simple and obvious belief, which the mere appearance of the universe would readily suggest to many independent observers. It is, on the contrary, a commonplace that the dome of the sky, with its apparently unchanging stars, seems, of all things in nature, the most permanent, and indeed eternal. Why suppose that it was ever ' joined in one form with the earth,' and then lifted up to its present place ? How are we to account for such a representation ?

The question is not commonly raised, and I do not know how it would generally be answered. One thing seems clear : the conception is not an extravagant flight of some individual mind, gifted with a specially wild and grotesque imagination. If it had been so, it is hard to believe that it would have been accepted and perpetuated, as an article of faith, even among one people ; it is quite out of the question that it could have been independently invented by several grotesquely imaginative individuals in various parts of the world, and in each case accepted. The conception must have been elaborated, not by any singular imagination, but by the collective mind ; and its wide diffusion in independent centres could be explained, if we could point to some actual fact capable of suggesting it.

The representation is this : the world began as an undifferentiated mass, without internal boundaries or limits—an *ἄπειρον*. This mass separated into two parts, which were opposed or ' contrary '—male and female. Finally, the male and female were united by Eros, the contraries were combined, and gave birth to individual existence—to Gods, or to things.

Is it a mere coincidence that this description of the origin of the cosmos reflects a social institution already mentioned, of great importance in totemic societies—the division of the tribe into two exogamous phratries ? The principle of this division (from whatever cause it may arise) is sex. In a sense, the two exogamous segments are opposed as male and female, since the male belonging to one phratry must marry a female from the other. This contrariety is reconciled in marriage—the union of opposites. This exogamous principle, as we have seen, is of equal importance with the totemic classification with which it is combined. It is the focus of intense religious and moral emotions, and guarded by impassable taboo. Moreover, the continuity between human society and Nature on which we have already dwelt, the actual identity of their structural grouping, makes it inevitable that the same conception should be extended to the divisions of the universe.

In support of this hypothesis, we have the express evidence of an Omaha Indian, Francis Laflesche, who delivered in 1905 an address at the unveiling of a statue of the Medicine Man.[1] He described, as follows, the structure of his tribal camp. ' The plan, or order, which was carried out when all the people camped together, was that of a wide circle. This tribal circle was called Hu-dhu-ga, and typified the cosmos. . . . The circle was divided into two great divisions or halves ' (the exogamous phratries). ' The one called In-shta-sun-da represented the Heavens ; and the other, the Hun-ga-she-nu, denoted the Earth. . . . Each of the two great divisions was subdivided into clans, and each of the ten clans had its particular symbol ' (totem) ' representing a cosmic force, one of the various forms of life on the Earth.'

It is true that Francis Laflesche is a sophisticated person, and that on this occasion he was talking up to his white brothers ; but any one who reads the authentic descriptions of the Omaha rites of initiation, in which the child is introduced successively to the various parts and provinces of the universe,[2] will not doubt that in this particular statement he is telling the truth. It gives us exactly the proof we need, that the heavens and the earth were identified with the two contrary phratries, by whose fission the exogamous grouping of society first came into being.

36. *The Pythagorean Table of Contraries*

The Pythagorean community, as we shall see later, preserved, more than any other ancient society, the characteristic traits of

[1] F. Laflesche, *Who was the Medicine Man?* 1905, p. 8. I did not meet with this tract till the theory above put forward was already written down.

[2] For an account of these rites, taken from Miss Alice Fletcher, see J. E. Harrison, *Themis*, p. 69.

primitive social groups. In their earlier speculation an important place is given to the table of Contraries, the two columns (συστοιχίαι) of opposites, in which, exactly as if in two exogamous phratries, they grouped ten pairs of principles, like so many clans.[1] At the head of the two columns stood ' the Even and the Uneven, one of which is unlimited, the other limited,' the pair which were the elements of all number, and so of all the world.[2] And the Even and the Uneven they held to be, respectively, female and male; while the undivided monad, the One, was bisexed. Thus the Pythagorean cosmology, once more, starts with the separation, out of an undifferentiated unity, of a male and female principle.

37. *Eros and the Marriage of Opposites*

The coming into existence of individual things is variously attributed by the early cosmologists to love or harmony, and to feud, strife, or war. The two representations are, as Heracleitus insisted,[3] not so irreconcilable as they seem to be at first sight. They are only two ways of conceiving the meeting of contraries. The two contraries are antagonistic, at perpetual war with each other. It is a war of mutual aggression—each seeking to invade the province of the other. But this very invasion involves a mixing of the two elements—a reconciliation, or marriage,[4] in which both combine to produce a compound, the individual thing. Earth and Heaven are essentially the female and male principles in Greek cosmology. In the ' gap ' between their sundered forms appears the winged figure of the cosmic Eros, whose function is to reunite them. In the more primitive cosmogonies, which make the world begin with the hatching of an egg, whose two halves form Sky and Earth, Eros is the bird with golden feathers who comes out of the egg.[5]

When we come to the detailed discussion of the pre-Socratic systems, we shall see how the war and marriage of opposites is worked out. As late as Plato we shall find that a sexual char-

---

[1] *D. F. V.*[2], i. p. 271.   [2] Arist. *Met.* A 5, 986a 15.
[3] See below, p. 190.
[4] μίξις, μίσγεσθαι φιλότητι, is perhaps the commonest metaphor for marriage in Greek.
[5] Ar. *Birds*, 693. For the world-egg see Eisler, *Weltenmantel*, ii. 410 ff.

acter still clings to the great contraries, Form and Matter. ' We must conceive three kinds : first, that which comes into being ; second, that in which the first comes to be ; third, that from which the first is copied, when it is born into existence. And we may fittingly compare the recipient to the mother, the model to the father, and that which springs into life between them to the offspring.' [1] Even in the desiccated terminology of Aristotle the same representation persists, where he says that, whereas one piece of matter can contain only one form, the cause which imposes the form can generate many. ' So is it with the female and the male.' [2]

38. *Summary*

At the outset of our inquiry, we called attention to three factors in Anaximander's cosmology which needed explanation : (1) the primary *physis*, (2) the disposition or structure into which this living stuff is distributed, (3) the process by which the order arose. We have now, by tracing back the conceptions of *Moira* and *Nomos* to primitive social structure, thrown some light on the second factor, and incidentally on the third.

We have seen how the social group is the original type on which all other schemes of classification—at first magical, and later scientific—are modelled. At a very early stage, the whole of the visible world was parcelled out into an ordered structure, or cosmos, reflecting, or continuous with, the tribal microcosm, and so informed with types of representation which are of social origin. To this fact the order of nature owes its sacred or moral character. It is regarded as not only necessary but right or just, because it is a projection of the social constraint imposed by the group upon the individual, and in that constraint ' must ' and ' ought ' are identical. Such we believe to have been the process by which *Moira* came to rule supreme over the Gods, and Justice to ordain the boundaries of the elements in Anaximander's philosophy.

We must now turn to the consideration of *physis*—that homogeneous living fluid which is parcelled out by Destiny or Justice into the elemental provinces. It has already been hinted that

[1] *Timaeus*, 50 c.   [2] *Met.* A 6, 988 a 3.

this primary world-stuff is the material out of which daemons, Gods, and souls were made. We have now to trace the process of their making, and first of all to make out what was the primitive representation which, as we believe, re-emerges at the threshold of philosophy under the name of *physis*. We shall seek for this conception also a social origin.

III

NATURE, GOD, AND SOUL

39. *Nature and Custom in the dynamic sense*

THE term 'Nature' (*physis*, *natura*) has had a long and varied history, which we cannot here attempt to trace even in outline. No philosophical term is more dangerously ambiguous. We seem able to distinguish, however, two main heads under which its shifting senses may be grouped : [1] the static and the dynamic. Statically conceived, Nature means the system of all phenomena in time and space, the total of all existing things ; and the 'nature' of a thing is its constitution, structure, essence. But it has never lost its other, 'dynamic, side—the connotation of force, of primordial, active, upspringing energy—a sense which, as its derivation shows, is original.[2]

Hitherto, in our study of the three great conceptions, Destiny, Law, and Nature, we have been mainly concerned with their static or spatial aspect. The first of them, *Moira*, leans, as we have already seen, towards this side—a process hastened by the emergence of personal Gods, who, as they absorb the positive functions, leave to Destiny the negative attitude of prohibitive necessity and limiting taboo. Though it is not altogether forgotten that the *Moirai* preside at the three transitional crises in the curve of life, at two of them—birth and marriage—they fade into the background behind the newer and more definite figures of Artemis and Aphrodite ; and only the third moment, where life passes into the darkness of death, is left undisputed by the deathless ones to the daughters of Night.

In the case of Law, again, the negative aspect has some

---

[1] Cf. J. Dewey in Baldwin's *Dictionary of Philos. and Psychol.* s.v. 'Nature.'

[2] Thus, by the 'nature' of a thing the Scholastics understood its essence specially 'considered as the active source (or principle) of the operations by which the being realised its end' (Dewey, *loc. cit.*).

tendency to prevail. When laws come to be written down, ' thou shalt not ' occurs much more frequently than ' thou shalt.' A customary action is performed unconsciously, and attracts no attention ; we only come to think of it as a duty, and to feel the binding obligation (τὸ δέον) to perform it, when some natural impulse prompts us to do something else. But the mere mention of ' custom ' (τὰ νόμιμα, τὰ νομιζόμενα) reminds us of the active content of *Nomos*, which, before it means a prohibitive- enactment, stands for *behaving* in a certain way, behaviour that is standardised, moralised, socialised—in a word, group-behaviour. Against this, sometimes intolerable, imposition of herd usage, our individual ' nature ' occasionally cries out and denounces convention as ' unnatural.' Custom and Nature are set at variance.[1] But this outcry marks an age of individualism and self-consciousness.[2] In earlier days, when the unitary moral and religious consciousness was coextensive, not with the individual, but with his group, no such conflict could arise : custom and nature were at one.

40. *Primitive identity of Nature and Custom*

We may go a step further and say that custom and nature were, not merely harmonious, but identical. If we recur to our illustration of the totemic clan, our meaning will be clear. This social group, consisting of its human members and their totem-species, is defined by the collective function it exercises as a continuous whole. If the nature or essence of a class of things is something which all of them have, and which nothing else has, in an early stage, when practical interests are paramount and disinterested speculation is unknown, the essential ' nature '

---

[1] Thus at the end of the fifth century φύσις is used in the sense of *natural instincts* as opposed to the restraint of morality. The Adikos Logos in Aristophanes' *Clouds*, 1078, says : ἐμοὶ δ' ὁμιλῶν χρῶ τῇ φύσει, σκίρτα, γέλα, νόμιζε μηδὲν αἰσχρόν. Isocr., *Areop.* 38, says that, in presence of the august Areopagus, you may see people who in other circumstances are unbearable ὀκνοῦντας τῇ φύσει χρῆσθαι καὶ μᾶλλον τοῖς ἐκεῖ νομίμοις ἢ ταῖς αὐτῶν κακίαις ἐμμένοντας.

[2] Cf. J. L. Myres, ' Herod. and Anthrop.' (*Anthropology and the Classics*, Oxford, 1908), p. 158, who points out that the opposition of νόμος and φύσις is not primitive. It does not become prominent in Greece until the age of the Sophists.

will be nothing but the social importance of the group—all that is expected of that division of society. It *is*, in fact, what it collectively *feels* and *does* : all that matters about it, all that is (as we say) ' essential,' is its behaving as it ought, fulfilling its function, performing its customs. It is, probably, in the light of this idea that we should interpret the alleged ' identity ' of the human clansmen with their totem-species.[1] They are, in the literal sense, *practically* identical. The superficial differences of appearance between (say) an emu-man and an emu-bird are ignored, and if necessary denied, because they are of no practical interest. The religious emphasis is entirely upon the group-behaviour, the group-functions ; and these, as we shall presently see, are identical for all ' emus,' whether they happen to look like men or birds. It may, indeed, be doubtful how much meaning this last phrase will have. The universals ' man ' and ' bird ' are conceptions which will not be formed at all, until some practical interest calls for them. The Andamanese are said to have no word in their language for ' tree ' or ' animal ' ; they have only a name for every species. They have no word for ' fish ' : they call it simply ' food,' because that expresses the essential importance of fish in their economy.[2] Thus the ' nature' or ' essence ' *is* the social function : the *physis is* the *nomoi*; and both words denote the active, socially organised force expressed by a group, or *moira*.

41. *Primary Sympathetic Magic*

Seen in this light, the mystic identity of nature or consubstantiality with the totem resolves itself into a set of common duties and magical observances, centred on the totem ; the unity of the *moira* is the unity of its *nomoi*. The whole collective function of the human members, we are told, is to control and influence their non-human kindred of the same group. When the totem is an edible species, their business is to multiply this food for the common use of the tribe ; where it is a phenomenon like rain, wind, or sun, they have to make the rain fall or cease

---

[1] Cf. Lévy-Bruhl, *Fonctions mentales*, p. 77, for illustrations, and p. 135.
[2] I learnt these facts from Mr. A. R. Brown. Further evidence to the same effect is collected by Lévy-Bruhl, *Fonct. ment.* p. 187 ff.

from falling, to raise or lay the wind, to regulate the sunshine. The means employed are commonly mimetic dances, in which men are disguised as impersonations of the totem, and which are representations of the functions of a group.

When, however, we speak of these operations as ' controlling ' or ' influencing ' the natural species, we are wrongly anticipating a later phase of magic. In a pure system of totemism, the human and non-human members, as we have insisted, are not distinguished, but considered as identical; hence neither can be said to ' control ' the other. Their magical ceremonies are essentially *co-operative* and *sympathetic*—the common function of the group as an undivided whole. So, too, when we speak of the dances as *mimetic*, we must beware of interpreting that term from our own civilised conceptions. ' Imitation ' suggests to us the act of deliberately copying or mimicking the external appearance of something unlike oneself, with the object of creating an illusion in the spectator. The mimetic magical dance is not imitative in this sense; the focus of attention is not centred on an unlikeness which has to be overcome, or on any impression to be imposed on the onlooker. The disguise is rather an incidental means of helping out the emotion and desire of the actors themselves. If they want to feel with religious intensity what they at all times believe—that they *are* emus or kangaroos, it is obviously helpful to paint themselves so as to resemble the animal, and to put themselves into contact with parts of it, whether real or symbolically represented. But the chief and overmastering desire of the performers is not to produce an illusion, even in themselves; it is to *behave* in the characteristic way, to represent, or rather *pre*-present,[1] the group-behaviour—actually to produce, there and then, with more or less realism, the action required of their totem, that is to say, of themselves and their species in co-operation. The circumstances of the performance exalt the sense of identity of nature by producing identity of behaviour—the practical expression of the common nature.

The whole magical process, in this primary stage, is not to be conceived as a mock ceremonial, mimicking a real process, and designed to cause that real process to happen some time

---

[1] For magic as pre-presentation, see J. E. Harrison, *Themis*, p. 44.

afterwards. That is how it may present itself to us, and perhaps to the magician of a decadent age, when the faith of magic has grown fainter. But, in the early stage now under consideration, magical action consists in actually *doing what you want done*. The rainmakers believe themselves simply to be ' making rain,' not to be imitating rain, so as to cause real rain to fall later. If we are right in insisting on the identity and continuity of the whole group—rainmakers and rain—and of their functions, then rainmaking and rainfall are, to the magicians, one and the same, not distinct events related as cause and effect.

42. *Collective emotion and desire*

What is actually experienced is sympathetic or collective emotion and desire. The emotion expresses itself in action, which, being necessarily co-operative, is of a customary and ritual kind, the rhythm of a dance or the prescribed gesture of a pantomime, motions which both enhance the feeling and give it vent. The desire is realised in the representation of its end. When the totem-clan meets to hold its peculiar dance, to work itself up till it feels the pulsing of its common life through all its members, such nascent sense of individuality as a savage may have—it is always very faint [1]—is merged and lost; his consciousness is filled with the sense of sympathetic activity. The group is now feeling and acting as one soul, with a total force much greater than any of its members could exercise in isolation. The individual is lost, ' beside himself,' in one of those states of contagious enthusiasm in which it is well known that men become capable of feats which far outrange their normal powers. Yet here again we are inclined to misuse the language of later phases of development. ' Ecstasy,' ' getting outside oneself,' implies that one ordinarily has a self, and can only get outside it under the exceptional stimulus of excitement, deliberately induced to that end. ' Enthusiasm ' means being possessed by a power other than oneself which enters one at privileged moments. Both these conceptions belong to mystical religion, which must have recourse to ritual stimulants precisely because it has lost the primitive sense of constant and

[1] See P. Beck, *Die Nachahmung*, Leipzig, 1904, p. 84 ff.

continuous identity. The Australian savage, in whom that sense
is hardly, if at all, disturbed, goes about his magical operations
in a singularly businesslike way. His belief that he is a kangaroo is so unquestioned that he has no need to pretend that
he is one, or to induce a kangaroo to enter into him and possess
him for the nonce ; all he has to do is to be a kangaroo by
behaving as one.

43. *Primary Magic needs no representation, and is pre-religious*

It appears, then, that the primitive magical fact is intense
emotional activity, collectively experienced by a group. We
shall presently have to inquire under what form this experience
is expressed in conception—how it is represented. But in the
first stage of magic, at present under consideration, there is not,
as yet, any need for a representation at all. The collective
life pervades the whole group in undisturbed continuity ; the
collective emotion is felt, the customary actions are performed,
in sympathetic co-operation, by the group as a whole. Now,
so long as it is thus lived and immediately experienced, and the
distinction between my own power and the collective power has
not broken out, there will be no image, or idea, or conception
either of myself in contrast with it, or of it in contrast with
myself. There is nothing but the actually existing natural facts
of collective emotion, desire, and action.[1]

In this primary stage we find a pre-religious condition of
mankind ; for in the definition of religion we include some representation of a power which is in some sense ' not ourselves,'
and at the level we have now reached, although there exists
such a power—namely, the collective emotion and activity of the
group—we may infer that it will not be represented, because no
need for representation will have arisen.

Even among societies which have passed beyond this primary
stage into a developed totemic system, there are some which
have advanced so little from the pre-religious condition that they
are reported to have no religion whatever (in the common sense
of the word). Messrs. Spencer and Gillen expressly declare that

[1] Cf. Lévy-Bruhl, *Fonct. ment.* p. 283 ff.

'the Central Australian natives . . . have no idea whatever of the existence of any supreme being who is pleased if they follow a certain line of what we call moral conduct, and displeased if they do not do so. They have not the vaguest idea of a personal individual other than an actual living member of the tribe, who approves or disapproves of their conduct, so far as anything like what we call morality is concerned.' At initiation a boy is instructed in his moral duties, but he is not taught to believe in any supreme being. 'In fact, he then learns that the spirit creature whom up to that time, as a boy, he has regarded as all-powerful, is merely a myth, and that such a being does not really exist, and is only an invention of the men to frighten the women and children.' [1]

Apart from these and similar reports from direct observers of savage tribes comparatively untouched by white civilisation, if we consider our primitive magical complex, we shall see that it is perfectly self-contained and complete without any kind of God. The sympathetic and continuous force which animates the unitary group fully suffices, at first, to express the collective emotion and to realise the desired end, involved in magical practice. There is no need for a God outside this complex, no room for him within it. Given that the object of a clan ceremony is to multiply the totem-species and promote its right behaviour, this object is immediately effected in mimetic representation. The thing desired is felt as actually performed ; and that not by way of influence or compulsion, but by sympathetic co-operation of human and non-human clansmen alike. This is not religion, but pure magic. The difference between the two is seen to be this. The religious complex consists of worshippers on the one side and a spirit or God, distinct from them in kind and power, on the other. This distinction first makes it possible for the worshippers to control, influence, persuade, worship, the God ; they can offer him gifts and beg for benefits in return. But in the stage of pure magic the distinction has not yet broken out. The magical complex is one and continuous, both in kind and in power. No distinction is felt between one part of it and

---

[1] *Northern Tribes of Central Australia*, p. 491 ff. See further evidence in Frazer, *Totemism*, vol. i. p. 141 ff. In our view the 'spirit creature' above mentioned *is* a religious representation, but it is minimal.

another, because no distinction, however superficially obvious, is of any importance as against the identity of nature and functions. Hence, anything of the nature of worship is excluded by the very definition of such a group. A totem is not a God ; it is in any case (as we must never forget) a species, not an individual ; and it has at first no powers that can be called ' divine,' because it has none that its human kin do not share with it and exercise in common. All theology is the work of doubt and criticism, not of simple and childlike faith, which has at no time felt the need of it.

44. *The first representation needed*

How, then, will the need of representation first arise, and what is it that will be represented ?

If we consider our primary complex—the continuous human group—we observe that its mentality contains two distinguishable factors. The group is composed of individuals, each of whom has his own private world of inner and outer experience. But this by no means exhausts the psychology of these individuals ; otherwise, the group would be a casual aggregation of independent atoms, destitute of continuity. Over and above their individual experiences, all the members of the group alike partake of what has been called the collective consciousness of the group as a whole. Unlike their private experiences, this pervading consciousness is the same in all, consisting in those infectious or epidemic states of feeling, above described, which at times when the common functions are being exercised, invade the whole field of mentality, and submerge the individual areas. To this group-consciousness belong also, from the first moment of their appearance, all representations which are collective— a class in which all religious representations are included. These likewise are diffused over the whole mentality of the group, and identical in all its members. The psychological force which diffuses them is known as ' suggestion ' or ' herd-suggestion.'

The collective consciousness is, thus, superindividual. It resides, of course, in the individuals composing the group— there is nowhere else for it to exist—but it resides in all of them together, and not completely in any one of them. It is both in myself and yet not myself. It occupies a certain part of my mind, and yet it stretches beyond and outside me to the limits of my group. And since I am only a small part of my group, there is much more of it outside me than inside. Its force, accordingly, is much greater than any individual force, and the more primitive I am, the greater this preponderance will be. Here, then, there exists in the world a power which is greater than any individual's—superindividual, that is to say, ' superhuman.'

Because this force is continuous with my own consciousness, it is, as it were, a reservoir to which I have access, and from which I can absorb superhuman power to reinforce and enhance my own. This is its positive aspect, to which we shall return in a moment. But it will also have a negative aspect, which will concern us later, and may here be touched upon.[1] In so far as this power is not myself and greater than myself, it is a moral and restraining force, which can, and does, impose upon the individual the necessity of observing the uniform behaviour of the group.

With the first dawning of a distinction between myself and the social consciousness comes the first shadowy representation which can be called religious or moral. The characteristic of moral and religious representations is that they are *obligatory*—objects of faith which we are not allowed to question. The reason of this is now apparent. When the power of society—the only known moral power in the universe, superior to the individual—first comes to be felt as different from my own power, it is necessarily felt, in part, as a constraint, which imposes from without some sort of control over my actions. At first I shall feel myself powerless against it. Its dominance is absolute because the force is not wholly external. The collective consciousness is also immanent in the individual himself, forming within him that unreasoning impulse, called *conscience*, which, like a traitor within the gates, acknowledges from within the obligation to obey that other and much larger part of the collective consciousness which lies outside. Small wonder that obedience is absolute in primitive man, whose individuality is

---

[1] See R. R. Marett, *Threshold of Religion*, chap. iii., ' Is Taboo a Negative Magic ?' and p. 127.

still restricted to a comparatively small field, while all the higher levels of mentality are occupied by this overpowering force.

We conclude, then, that the first religious representation is a representation of the collective consciousness itself—the only moral power which can come to be felt as imposed from without, and therefore need to be represented. Considered as moral and prohibitive, it is the first ' not ourselves which makes for righteousness.' From its positive content come the two great religious conceptions of God and Soul, and—strange as it may seem—that idea of 'Nature' which lies at the root of philosophy.

The negative aspect of this superindividual moral power—its aspect as repression, imposing an external constraint—will give rise to conceptions such as Avenging Anger (*Nemesis*), Justice (*Dike*), and Destiny (*Moira*), when these are conceived as keeping individuals in their places, and asserting against arrogant egoism the self-protective instinct of the social group. These abstractions are all various ways of conceiving what the savage calls Taboo. We shall see, moreover, that when the positive content of the superhuman power is absorbed in the twin notions of God and Soul, its negative, repressive force still rises above them both, in the figure of Necessity or Destiny, *Moira*, to whom all Gods and souls are alike subordinate.

But, as we before observed, this negative aspect is only the recoil of a positive force, which we have now learnt to identify with the collective power of the group. This power is only incidentally manifested as repressive, on the rare occasions when individual aggression calls it forth ; and, although it is probably the sense of constraint that first causes it to be represented at all, the content of the representation will not be purely negative, but rather consist of the positive, dynamic properties which give it body and force. This energy is normally expressed not in the repression of individuals, but in the exercise of the group-functions. As such it really consists, as we have seen, in collective emotion and desire, manifested in magical operations. These, then, we may expect to form the content of our primary religious representation.

45. *The Sympathetic Continuum as the representation of the collective consciousness*

At this point, however, an obvious caution is required. When we speak of the savage forming a representation of the collective emotion and desire which animate a group in the performance of its ceremonies, we seem to be attributing to him our latter-day psychology and falling into the most elementary of errors. The subsequent argument will show that, if the savage had been capable of representing these facts of group-consciousness as they now appear to us, either theology and philosophy would never have existed, or their whole course would have been totally different. What we mean to affirm is that, while the real, natural fact embodied in the first religious representation was the group-consciousness in its active and emotional phase, the character of the representation formed of it by primitive man was, to our modern thinking, so unlike the real fact that we have only just come to recognise *what* it was that was represented.

In the first place, we must remember that even civilised man, right on into the age of philosophy, did not succeed in conceiving anything as immaterial, or non-spatial. The *Logos* of Heracleitus, the Being of Parmenides, the *Nous* of Anaxagoras, the Love and Hate of Empedocles, are all indubitably possessed of material and spatial properties. Even when the term ' bodiless,' ' incorporeal ' (ἀσώματον), makes its appearance in Plato, it is often doubtful how many material properties it negates. A ghost is ' bodiless,' but, even when it is invisible and intangible, it is still extended in space and perhaps endowed with some active force. We may be certain, then, that when a savage was driven to form a mental image of the collective nature or powers of his group, he would conceive them as a subtle and mobile form of matter, not distinguished from vital force.

An entity corresponding to this description does, in fact, hold a fundamental place in the philosophy of existing savages in various parts of the world. Accounts of its nature and qualities have, of course, to be received with caution. Much so-called savage philosophy and theology have been developed by contact with Christian missionaries, who have forced upon savages the need to raise their implicit beliefs to a level of consciousness at which mutual explanation can begin. The scientific inquirer is, of course, exposed to the same risk of suggesting the categories and ideas which he seeks to elicit. But when all allowances are made for these sources of error, recent students seem to have agreed to postulate a conception now familiar under the various forms of *mana, wakonda, orenda*, etc. These various forms, though it appears from the descriptions of them that they have developed in different places along diverging lines, appear to be only varieties of one conception, which, as some think, lies at the root alike of magic and of religion.[1]

The *mana* of the Melanesians is thus described by Dr. Codrington :[2] ' The Melanesian mind is entirely possessed by the belief in a supernatural power or influence, called almost universally *mana*. This is what works to effect everything which is beyond the ordinary power of man, outside the common processes of nature ; it is present in the atmosphere of life, attaches itself to persons and to things, and is manifested by results which can only be ascribed to its operation. When one has got it, he can use it and direct it, but its force may break forth at some new point; the presence of it is ascertained by proof. A man comes by chance upon a stone which takes his fancy ; its shape is singular, it is like something, it is certainly not a common stone, there must be *mana* in it. So he argues with himself, and he puts it to the proof ; he lays it at the root of a tree to the fruit of which it has a certain resemblance ; . . . an abundant crop on the tree . . . shows that he is right, the stone is *mana*, has that power in it. Having that power, it is a vehicle to convey *mana* to other stones. . . . This power, though itself impersonal, is always connected with some person who directs it ; all spirits have it, ghosts generally, some men.'

In North America, we are told by a cautious and competent

---

[1] MM. Hubert et Mauss ('Esqùisse d'une théorie générale de la magie,' *Année Sociol.* vii. p. 116), after an interesting analysis of *mana*, remark that it may be taken as universally believed in, at a certain stage of development. At later stages it is replaced by daemons and then by metaphysical entities, *e.g.* the Indian *brahman*, which ends by being an active principle immanent in the world, the *real* (as opposed to illusion) union (*yoga*) with which confers magical powers.

[2] *The Melanesians*, Oxford, 1891, p. 118.

observer, ' The Omahas regard all animate and inanimate forms, all phenomena, as pervaded by a common life which was continuous and similar to the will-power they were conscious of in themselves. This mysterious power in all things they called *Wa-kon-da*, and through it all things were related to man, and to each other. In the idea of the continuity of life, a relation was maintained between the seen and the unseen, the dead and the living, and also between the fragment of anything and its entirety.' [1]

We may note at once that these Indians, who, of course, have long been in contact with whites, and assiduously urged by monotheistic missionaries to acknowledge a single ' Great Spirit,' have generalised their conception into one common life pervading all things. This is an inevitable stage, but probably not the first stage, in its history. For reasons already touched upon, it is likely that, the further back we could go, the more we should find that every group of things, defined by its social importance, would have a specific *wakonda* or *mana* of its own. [2] Indeed, we are driven to this view by the consideration that this medium is the vehicle of sympathetic action at a distance, ensuring that persons and things related by it shall feel, act, and suffer together ; and in systems of magic we find that sympathetic interaction occurs not equally between any two objects whatever, but specially within the area of a group of objects which are related or akin. [3]

A *system* of magic thus involves a system of classification.

---

[1] A. C. Fletcher, 'The Significance of the Scalp-lock,' *Journ. of Anthrop. Studies*, xxvii. (1897-8), p. 436. For other accounts of the conceptions of *wakonda, orenda, mana*, etc., see Hewitt, *American Anthropologist*, N.S., iv. 38 ; E. S. Hartland, *Address to Anthrop. Section of the British Association*, 1906 ; R. R. Marett, *Threshold of Religion*, pp. 115 ff.; A. C. Haddon, *Magic and Fetichism*, London, 1906, chap. vii. ; Lévy-Bruhl, *Fonctions mentales*, 141 ff. ; Hubert et Mauss, 'Esquisse d'une théorie générale de la magie,' *Année Sociol.* vii. (1904), p. 108 ff. On the work of these last-named authorities, the theory put forward in this chapter is based.

[2] On the other hand, the *continuum* is prior to distinct *individuals*. Cf. Lévy-Bruhl, *Fonctions mentales*, p. 109.

[3] Thus, ' among the Wakelbura and kindred tribes of Northern Queensland we are told that everything, animate and inanimate, belongs to one or other of the two exogamous classes into which the tribes are divided. *A wizard in performing his incantations may use only things which belong to his own class.*' Frazer, *Totemism*, i. 134.

We have already seen, too, that the primitive type of all classification is the grouping of society [1]—a fact still marked in linguistic usage by the use of the words '*genus*,' '*genre*,' 'kind,'
etc., to designate any sort of class. In other words, all *likeness*
was originally represented as *kinship*. There exists, moreover,
within any group of kin a strong bond of solidarity, which finds
its characteristic expression in sympathetic emotion and collective action. The members of such a group are thus psychologically *en rapport* with one another; in literal fact they do
act and react on one another in a quite special degree. This
psychological fact is the basis of that early axiom of causality
which asserts that 'like can only act on like'—an axiom assumed
by magic and expressly formulated by early philosophy. The
mysterious action of magical power only works within the field
of a certain group of things, which are 'akin.' Our suggestion
is that the notions of *mana*, *wakonda*, etc., were at first representations of the bond of 'kinship' uniting a social group—a
supposed vehicle of sympathetic interaction. Later, they have,
at least in some cases, been generalised into the typical form of
all 'spiritual' substance.[2]

When we consider under what form such an entity would be
represented, the answer lies near at hand. Kinship is to our
minds an immaterial entity—a relation. But, as we have said,
to conceive anything as immaterial is a feat that is not achieved
till late on in the history of rational speculation. Just as, to
Empedocles, *Philia* (the solidarity of a group) was a mobile fluid
running between the particles of the denser forms of matter, so
to a savage the vehicle of kinship—the *sympathetic continuum*,
as we shall henceforth call it—can only be represented as a
fluid which takes the shape of the compartments which it fills.

Following our principle that the functions of a group define
its nature, we can see how inevitably the power resident in any
group would be identified with the material substrate of kin-

---

[1] See Durkheim et Mauss, 'Classifications primitives,' *Ann. Sociol.* vi.

[2] Cf. Lévy-Bruhl, *Fonctions mentales*, etc., p. 145: 'Wakan (Wakonda
*ne saurait mieux se comparer qu'à un fluide qui circule, qui se répand dans
tout ce qui existe, et qui est le principe mystique de la vie et de la vertu des
êtres.* Cf. also the *mulungu* of the Central African Yaos—a conception which
covers the individual soul, collective soul, and the mystic property possessed
by all 'sacred' or 'divine' things (*ibid.*, p. 141).

ship—the blood of the group-kin. This actual substance answers exactly to our description of the *continuum*, for the blood is the life—the common life, derived, not from the natural parent, but from the totem-ancestor.[1] The same fact, of kinship, is expressed statically and materially in terms of continuity of the blood, and dynamically or vitally in terms of identity of function. Both aspects are covered by the conception of ' nature ' (*physis*). The terms *mana*, *wakonda*, etc., specially emphasise its character as force—the expression of life in action.[2]

A totemic society, as we have already remarked, is complex and organic ; it is a group of groups. This complexity is of a secondary or still higher order, developed out of the unitary group, which is the primary social fact. It is now clear that this primary group, with its collective consciousness, is sufficient to give birth to the first religious representation. This, we have argued, would be nothing but a representation of that collective consciousness itself, in its emotional and active phase. But, since a savage could not conceive such a thing as we conceive it, we have suggested that it would present itself to his mind as a subtle form of matter, not distinguished from life or from the vehicle of life and sympathetic interaction—the kindred blood.

46. *Summary*

We have now defined what, at the end of Chapter I., we called the primitive religious fact, and seen in what sense it is also the primitive social fact. We find it to be a social group (*moira*), defined by its collective functions (*nomoi*) ; these functions constitute its nature (*physis*), considered as a vital force proper to that group. Religion begins with the first representation of this fact.

To resume the characteristics of this representation. (1) As collective, it is superindividual, or superhuman. (2) Being

---

[1] P. Beck, *Die Nachahmung*, p. 87 : ' Die sinnliche Vorstellung, die mit dem Kollektivbewusstsein verbunden ist, ist das Blut. Wie der Hauch des Mundes mit dem Einzelleben identifiziert wird, so das Blut mit dem Leben des Stammes.'

[2] I shall try to show later how the notions of *mana*, etc., would come to be differentiated from the kindred blood. I am only arguing that there was probably an early stage in which this differentiation had not yet arisen.

imposed on the individual by the group, its force is felt as obligatory and repressive. (3) But, on the other hand, its content is, also and mainly, dynamic—the energy of the group as expressed in collective emotion and activity, its *mana*. (4) It is necessarily conceived in a material form, as fluid charged with life. (5) And this fluid, since it takes the outline of a social group, whose ' nature ' it is, will inevitably be identified with the blood, which is common to the kin. (6) This kindred blood is, however, a mythical entity, in the sense that it may be conceived as uniting members of a group who are not really akin by blood, but may even (as in totemic clans) belong to different natural species (*e.g.* men and emus).

47. *The differentiation of ' God ' and ' Soul '*

In the following pages we shall try to show how, out of the simple and fundamental conceptions which compose this primitive social fact, arose two collective representations which are still discussed by philosophers as well as by theologians. These are the ideas which we name ' God ' and the ' Soul.' Our primary object in this inquiry will be to make out still more clearly the fact, established in the first chapter, that throughout the development of Greek polytheism, and on into rational speculation, the notion constantly persists, of a system of *moirai*, each filled by a specific living force, beneficently operative within its sphere, maleficent in its recoil upon the intruder. We have now to watch the process by which this force shapes itself into spirits, Gods, and human souls, and to realise that this process, with all its advance in clearness of conception and imagery, is as it were an overgrowth, which leaves untouched beneath it the fundamental conceptual framework within which it springs up.

The primitive complex of notions we have just defined—*moira*, *physis*, and *nomos*—was ineradicably fixed in collective representation. The reinterpretation of it into terms of personal Gods or human souls all took place inside the outlines of this formula ; it did not break them down and sweep them away. Hence, as we shall see, when the Milesian philosophers quietly left the Gods out of their scheme of things, and supposed themselves to be dealing straight with natural facts, what really happened was that they cleared away the overgrowth of theology, and disinterred what had all the time persisted underneath. Hylozoism, in a word, simply raises to the level of clear scientific assertion the primitive savage conception of a continuum of living fluid, portioned out into the distinct forms of whatever classification is taken to be important. What the Milesians called *physis* has the same origin as what the savage calls *mana*.[1]

The brief sketch, then, which follows, of the passage from magic to religion, is not a digression; it is an attempt to indicate the process of theological complication which was unravelled again at the passage from religion to philosophy. But not completely unravelled. Philosophy, in our view, tried to cut away the superstructure of theological representation, and, in so doing, unwittingly harked back to the magical representation which preceded theology; but meanwhile, in the religious age, the ideas of God and of the soul had become too firmly established. Philosophy could not sustain the effort of simply dispensing with them altogether. They perpetually haunt the philosopher, and distract speculation from the domain of observable fact to a region of metaphysics which escapes the control of scientific procedure. Hence, for the understanding of philosophy, it is essential to grasp the character of these collective representations, and to trace, if possible, their origin and growth, with just so much detail as our purpose demands. The real process of development must, it need hardly be said, be much more complicated; and in different parts of the world it must have branched off along different lines, and been arrested at different stages. All that we shall attempt is a hypothetical reconstruction, in the barest outline, of the course which would lead from the primitive fact above defined to the religion of Greece as we know it in historic times. If we are right as to the starting-point, we have both ends of the chain in our hands; and the only question is how, out of the confused, undifferentiated primary datum, the factors of Greek polytheism came to be distinguished and set up as separate classes of supernatural or supersensible beings. To construct anything like a complete history is impossible in the present state of our knowledge.

[1] This identification was, so far as I know, first put forward by MM. Hubert et Mauss, *Année Sociol.* vii. p. 116 ff.

Innumerable ethnographical and sociological changes will have to be made out before this chapter of pre-history can be written. We do not pretend to describe the causes. All that we attempt is really little more than an analysis—the drawing of certain distinctions, which must, somehow and at some time, have emerged out of the primary confused representation we have outlined, to give us the categories of Greek polytheistic religion. To define these, and to set them clearly before the reader, is our main object.

In this inquiry, the two characters of the primary religious representation which specially concern us are : (1) that it is, from the first, a representation of the collective life in its positive, dynamic expression—it is thus the *soul* of the group ; (2) that it is a superindividual or superhuman power, and so gives rise to the notion of the *divine*, of ' God.' When we look at it in this light, it appears that ' God ' is, as it were, an offshoot of ' Soul.' The notion of the group-soul is closer to the original fact of group-consciousness, of which, indeed, it is the first mythical representation. The notion of God, as distinct from Soul, arises by differentiation. Gods are projections into non-human nature of the representation of the group-soul. At the same time, Soul is only by one stage the older of the two conceptions. After that, they develop side by side in parallel courses.

Our next question must be : how the differentiation occurs in the first instance. It will soon appear that this is the same as the problem : how ' God ' was projected from society into Nature. The answer to both questions was implicitly contained in the last chapter ; we have now only to deduce some further consequences of the results there reached.

48. *From Primary Magic to Religion*

The outlines of the magical group are not, we must remember, necessarily conterminous with the limits of a genuine natural species, as recognised by our own science. In totemism, on the contrary, as we have seen, its boundaries traverse these limits, because the classification is based, not solely or primarily on biological facts, but on the social importance of its various elements. Man, for instance, is not a distinct species at all.

Even a tribe of men—the largest group of mankind that is conceived—so far from being a single species, is divided up into as many species as there are totems; and every totem-clan traverses what seems to us the natural boundary between men and other creatures, and brings a department of Nature inside a subdivision of society. The kindred blood pervading such a group is a mythical, not a natural, fact, appropriately represented by the mythical totem-ancestor.

It is only when the dim consciousness of distinction has dawned, and the nature and behaviour (say) of an emu begin to appear in some degree different from, and independent of, the nature and behaviour of Emu-men, that the first step is taken from magic on the road to religion. The intrusion of this fatal doubt, which, if it prevail, must shatter the social system, will for a long time be resisted by the whole force of herd-suggestion, instinctively protecting the moral fabric. Magical ceremonies, at first so simple and businesslike, will gather round them the apparatus of mystical rites, which at all times resort to emotional stimulants, with the very purpose of restoring the old sense of perfectly unbroken communion. If they are successful, the system may last on, as it has lasted in Australia, for an indefinite time. But, in less favourable circumstances, it may at any moment be broken down, either from without, by contact with the developed religion of some foreign people, or from within, by the growth of the intellect. Reason, whose advance is marked at every stage by the drawing of some new distinction, by some fresh attempt to 'carve reality at the joints,' may find an opening for a new classification, in which the real differences between men and emus will be too strong for their mystical identity. Then a time may come when no amount of dressing up in emu feathers and strutting about will bring back the old sense of communion and co-operation.[1]

---

[1] It is perhaps probable that the cause of this change in representation, where it is not due to foreign influence, should be sought in some change of social structure, which again may be due to mechanical causes. With that question we are not concerned, but only with the breaking down of the old faith, however caused, and its consequences.

49. *Corresponding change in representation : the two pools*

If we consider what effect this weakening of the old faith would have, in respect of the mythical continuum of magical sympathy, it is clear that this bond of union will be strained until it snaps. Or, to use a better metaphor, the mysterious fluid will part into two pools—one pool representing the magical powers and nature of the human clan, the other those of the natural species or department, formerly identified with it.

This crisis closes the first, or pure, stage of magic, and opens the second, in which the magical energy of the human group is directed upon a natural force *other than itself*, which it seeks to control, to set in action, or to restrain. The threshold of this second stage of magic is also the birthplace of what is currently called religion. Here, for the first time, we encounter recognition of a power ' not ourselves,' towards which the cult-attitude is possible. There is something in Nature which we can woo, flatter, cajole, intimidate, bribe. In proportion as this something ceases to be human and familiar, it becomes divine and mysterious. Its ways are no longer just the same as our ways; it has begun to be incalculable, and acquired the rudiments of a will of its own. In some departments, moreover, such as the winds, the thunder, or the sea, the physical force now slipping from control is enormous and terrific. The making of a God has begun : where it will end, depends upon the genius and development of the race. The liberated force may acquire, one after another, any or all of the attributes of personality, by an advance which moves, step for step, with the advance of self-consciousness in its worshippers. At whatever point the worshippers stop, the God will be arrested too. He may crystallise as the vague, impersonal genius or daemon of his *moira*—a power resident in some department and strictly confined to it. Or, like the Greek Gods, he may travel the whole road to completely self-conscious personality, and become a figure so distinct that, if he would visit mankind unrecognised, he is forced to assume a disguise, since any one who met him in the street would instantly know him by sight ; as men took the tall and bearded Barnabas for Zeus and the eloquent Paul for Hermes. Probably no other race of mankind has ever developed its Gods to this pitch of individual distinctness. For the moment, our point is that the process implies and reflects a corresponding development on the human side—a passage from group-consciousness to individual consciousness in the history of the human mind.

The parting of the magical continuum into the two pools of human and non-human force must be accompanied—whether as cause or effect, we need not consider—by the dissolution of any social structure of a totemic type. Such structures imply the identity of human groups with natural species ; when this basis is weakened and destroyed, the elaborate departmentalism must break down on the human side. On the natural side, on the contrary, it may persist, because there the lines of division to a large extent separate real biological species, or classes of phenomena which really have a specific behaviour. Thus, in Nature, the old provinces of *Moira* can remain undisturbed ; but in the social organism the lines of demarcation, which were once continuous with their boundaries, may be obliterated, and superseded by a new grouping. This means, of course, a new system of human kinship—a change such as occurs, for instance, when the natural fact of paternity is for the first time recognised. Whatever it may be that causes a change of this kind, it is clear that, when the outline of a group of kindred is determined by real affinity of blood, the correspondence between clan and natural department is doomed to break down.[1]

50. *Blood-kin and Magical Society differentiated*

Such a regrouping of society will, moreover, be reflected by a corresponding change in representation. In the present case, we shall now have two types of group, where before there was only one. The magical group will, henceforth, no longer coincide with the group of blood-kin. Over and above the structure based on consanguinity, there will accordingly emerge the magical fraternity, not held together by any ties of blood or supposed

[1] Of course, various changes in the mode of life will also profoundly modify social structure and religious custom. A wandering pastoral tribe will be focused on its herds ; a stationary society of agriculturalists will be mainly interested in the behaviour of the weather, the round of the seasons, the fertilising genius of its fixed portion of earth.

descent from a common totem-ancestor, but only by the common possession of magical powers. The magical society will differ from the groups of kindred in the same sort of way as the Church differs from the family.

, This differentiation of the two types of group will cause a distinction in representation between the two types of bond which severally unite them. The magical society is united by its magical powers—its *mana*; the group of kindred by its common blood. In the original sympathetic continuum we supposed that these two notions were both contained in undistinguished union. Henceforth, they are in some degree separate; *mana* ceases to be a visible substance, but retains the properties of a material fluid; while the blood, though losing some of its magical power, remains the vehicle of life, which is, as it were, its specialised *mana*.

51. *Magical Societies*

A magical society, then, is a group held together by the possession of exceptional and secret powers, reserved to an initiated order. These powers, moreover, being no longer limited to one totem-species, naturally claim a wider control over Nature, especially over the weather and the elements—the hot and the cold, the wet and the dry, rain and sun and thunder—on whose behaviour all life depends.

Now, whether or not the remote ancestors of the Greeks ever passed through a phase of developed totemism, there certainly existed among them magical fraternities of the type we have just described. They were remembered in legend under the names of *Kouretes, Telchines, Idaean Daktyls, Korybantes, Satyrs*, etc., and in some cases actually survived as secret cult-societies far into historic times.[1]

52. *The Group-Soul*

A fraternity of this type has its existence as a whole; its 'nature,' as before, consists of its collective functions. The individual, when he is initiated into the order, becomes just a

---

For these societies see J. E. Harrison, *Themis*, where they are so fully treated that further discussion of them here is unnecessary.

Koures or a *Daktyl,* an undistinguished part of the whole. So, to-day, the first question to be asked about a monk is whether he is a Dominican or a Franciscan, not whether he is Brother This or Brother That. His personality is merged when he assumes the uniform dress, behaviour, and beliefs of his order.

When we say of a man, ' He has the soul of a Jesuit,' we convey in a condensed form a large amount of information (true or false) about the sort of behaviour that may be expected of him. Now, as applied to a member of a magical fraternity, a phrase of this type may be taken quite literally. The only ' soul ' a *Koures* has is the group-soul of his order, and this consists of nothing beside the group-functions, the behaviour expected of the group. This is what Aristotle would call ' the being what it really is to be a *Koures.*' The ' soul ' is the collective ' nature.' Rites of initiation are regularly regarded as new births ; and this implies that the admission of a candidate to the exercise of the new functions is the same fact as his being born again and receiving a new ' soul.' The soul is thus, at this stage, simply a pool of *mana,* which takes the outline of a group distinguished by specific functions and behaviour.[1]

53. *The Daemon of the Magical Society*

Another point to be noted is that a secret society of this sort, claiming as it does exceptional powers not possessed by all

---

[1] Cf. Lévy-Bruhl, *Fonctions mentales,* etc., p. 92 : '*Originairement (dans la mesure où l'usage de ce terme est permis), l'idée d'âme ne se trouve pas chez les primitifs. Ce qui en tient la place, c'est la représentation en général très émotionelle, d'une ou de plusieurs participations qui coexistent et qui s'entre-croisent, sans se fondre encore dans la conscience nette d'une individualité vraiment une. Le membre d'une tribu, d'un totem, d'un clan, se sent mystique-ment uni à son groupe social, mystiquement uni à l'espèce animale ou végétale qui est son totem, etc. . . . Ces communions, dont l'intensité se renouvelle et s'accroît à des moments déterminés (cérémonies sacrées, rites d'initiation et autres), ne s'empêchent nullement les unes les autres. Elles n'ont pas besoin de s'exprimer par des concepts définis pour être profondément senties, et pour être senties par tous les membres du groupe. Plus tard, quand ces cérémonies et ces rites auront peu à peu cessé d'être compris, puis d'être pratiqués, ces participations conservées dans les usages et dans les mythes précipiteront, pour ainsi dire, sous forme d' " âmes multiples " . . . et plus tard enfin, tout près de nous, comme le montre l'exemple des Grecs, ces âmes multiples cristalliseront à leur tour en une âme unique, non sans que la distinction d'un principe vital et d'un hôte spirituel du corps reste visible.*'

humanity, is lifted to a higher plane; it is, in some peculiar sense, sacred or holy; its members are something more than ordinary mortals, they are in some degree *divine*. Thus the Kouretes are called *daemones*, and even *theoi*; the magician for Hesiod is a ' divine man ' ($\theta\epsilon\hat{\iota}o\varsigma$ $\dot{\alpha}\nu\dot{\eta}\rho$).[1] The epithet ' divine,' the term ' *daemon*,' at this stage mean nothing more than that the group embodies that magical superhuman force, withheld from the profane, which is its nature and collective soul. This collective soul is the *daemon* of the society; its members are *daemones* in so far as it resides in them and they partake of it.

54. *The Daemon of the Gens*

The second type of daemon or collective soul corresponds to the new unitary group of a society whose structure is based on real consanguinity. This is the daemon of the *gens* or house. Such an entity was probably at first impersonal; the process by which it acquired personality and even individuality will be discussed later.

The Spirit, Fortune, or Genius of a *gens* is the common factor of a group united by kinship—as it were their collective personality, all that the family of kin have in common, underlying their separate individualities, and making them different from any other clan or house. It survives the death of any individual or generation. It is the transmitted vehicle of hereditary qualities, including the taint of hereditary guilt. It is also a continuum, identified with the blood, which entails collective responsibility : any kinsman may be held accountable for any action of the whole group or of any other kinsman. Hence the blood-feud or vendetta.[2]

55. *Daemons of natural departments*

If we turn now from the human side to external nature, we can trace a parallel development.

---

[1] For the suggested derivation of *theos* from *thes-* which appears in $\pi o\lambda\acute{\upsilon}\theta\epsilon\sigma\tau o\varsigma$ $\theta\acute{\epsilon}\sigma\sigma\alpha\sigma\theta\alpha\iota$, perhaps $\theta\epsilon\sigma\mu\acute{o}\varsigma$, Latin *festus* and *feriae*, see G. Murray in *Anthropology and the Classics*, p. 77. For the $\theta\epsilon\hat{\iota}o\varsigma$ $\dot{\alpha}\nu\dot{\eta}\rho$ of Hesiod, cf. J. E. Harrison, *Themis*, p. 95.

[2] For some survivals of this *daemon* of a *gens* see above, p. 54.

It was suggested that the opening of the second stage of magic, which supersedes pure totemism, might be represented as the parting of the sympathetic continuum into two pools. The human pool, as we have seen, is the reservoir of superhuman force which makes the group of magicians something more than man. Correspondingly, the natural pool is a reservoir of supernatural force which makes the department of Nature—the element, or whatever species of natural objects you please—something more than a natural object. This something more is the raw material of the elemental daemon or God. It is necessarily endowed with some of the elements of human consciousness; for (as we must never forget) it really consists of emotion and will-power projected out of human consciousness into a non-human species in the co-operative ceremonies of primary magic. It is now cut loose from its human counterpart, and is entering upon an independent existence. The power of the fire, for instance, is more than the real, natural energy of the element as known to science; it is the life and will of the fire—the will which the magician feels opposing his own, and has to deal with by means of the similar virtue in himself. The fire is, or has, a daemon in exactly the same way as the magical group possesses, or is possessed by, a daemon. Only, for reasons already pointed out, the one human group is confronted by a host of natural daemons, each specifically different, and occupying a distinct *moira*—a fire-daemon, a water-daemon, a fever-daemon, and so on indefinitely.

A nature-daemon is thus defined as the soul, or force, or *mana*, resident in some species of natural phenomena. It is, like its human counterpart, the soul of a group, not of an individual thing, except in cases where a species happens to have only one member, as, for instance, the sun. The fire-daemon is manifested in all fire; for all fire has the same specific behaviour. It is for this reason that daemons, in Greek theology as elsewhere, remain impersonal; they consist of will and force without individuality, because they are each the soul, not of an individual object, but of a species or kind (γένος), to which they are related exactly as the daemon of a human kindred (γένος) is related to his group.

With these daemons may be classed also the spirits of striking natural features—rivers, rocks, trees, mountains, wells, etc.—

which in Greek religion tended to be female (*nymphs*). They owe their existence to the same psychological causes which, among the Australians and elsewhere, make any feature of the landscape which is at all remarkable into an abode of spirits, or ' totem-centre.'

56. *Local Good Daemons of Fertility*

Besides the elemental spirits who are the counterparts and antagonists of the weather magician, Herodotus, in a passage discussed above (p. 37), describes a class of divine beings who belong to a phase of Greek religion which preceded Olympianism. The essential feature of this phase was that the Gods, or more properly daemons, were undifferentiated and local. Each daemon was a daemon-of-all-work, and we may be sure that his function mainly consisted in providing an abundant and regular supply of the fruits of earth.

When a tribe passes into the agricultural stage, the focus of its religious attention is centred on the portion of earth (its μοῖρα γῆς) which gives it sustenance. The Earth, just because it is now pre-eminently the source of life, will be pre-eminently ' sacred,' endowed with the mysterious power which feeds the force of all living things. This power, possessing the bare elements of personality, is centred, for each agricultural group, in the Good Spirit ('Αγαθὸς Δαίμων), giver of the fruits of the soil. He was worshipped sometimes beside the maternal figure of *Tyche*, *Fortuna*, the power of Earth herself, who brings all things to successful issue.[1]

We must think of Greece, in pre-Olympian days, as parcelled out among as many of these undifferentiated local fertility spirits as there were distinct agricultural communities. This view corresponds with Plato's ' mythical ' reign of the daemons in the age of Kronos. We have seen (§ 15) how he expressly compares the division of the parts of the universe among daemons to the present distribution of the earth into the seats of worship of the various Gods. He also tells us that each daemon was ' sufficient in himself in all things for his

---

[1] The importance of the Good Spirit is brought out in Miss Harrison's *Themis*, chap. viii. Sext. *Math.* ix. 40 : καθάπερ τὸ τὴν γῆν θεὸν νομίζειν, οὐ τὴν αὐλακοτομουμένην ἢ ἀνασκαπτομένην οὐσίαν, ἀλλὰ τὴν διήκουσαν ἐν αὐτῇ καὶ καρποφόρον φύσιν καὶ ὄντως δαιμονιωτάτην.

own flock.' Although Plato, for the purposes of his own philosophy, puts a mythical interpretation upon this rule of the daemons, it seems to reflect a genuine tradition of the phase described by Herodotus.

57. *Polydaemonism in China*

The system of polydaemonism, which we can thus make out in the background of the more familiar polytheism of later Greece, appears to subsist to this day in China, arrested at the stage of growth we have now reached. Taoism presents singularly clear traces of a course of development parallel to that which we have hypothetically reconstructed. We need only quote a few statements from a first-rate authority on Chinese religion.[1]

' The universe consists of two souls or breaths, called *Yang* and *Yin*, the *Yang* representing light, warmth, productivity, and life, also the heavens from which all these good things emanate ; and the *Yin* being associated with darkness, cold, death, and the earth. The *Yang* is subdivided into an indefinite number of good souls or spirits, called *shen*, the *Yin* into particles or evil spirits, called *kwei*, spectres ; it is these *shen* and *kwei* which animate every being and every thing. It is they also which constitute the soul of man ' (p. 3).

Tao is the ' universal order which manifests itself by the vicissitudes of the *Yang* and *Yin*.' ' There is no god beyond nature, no maker of it, no Jahweh, no Allah. Creation is the spontaneous work of heaven and earth, repeating itself regularly in every year, or in every revolution of time or the *Tao*, the order of the universe ' (p. 102). ' Chaos, before it split into *Yang* and *Yin* and became the *Tao*, occupies the principal place in the pantheon under the name of *Pan-ku* ' (p. 152). ' The sub-divisions of the universe, of heaven and earth, were the gods of ancient China, and are the gods of China to this day ' (p. 134). ' The gods are such *shen* as animate heaven, sun, moon, the stars, wind, rain, clouds, thunder, fire, the earth, seas, mountains, rivers, rocks, stones, animals, plants, things—in particular also the souls of deceased men ' (p. 5).

[1] De Groot, *The Religion of the Chinese*, New York, 1910.

On the human side, there is ' a *Tao* or way of man (*jen-tao*), being a system of discipline and ethics based upon observation and divination of nature, conducive to its imitation. This is a system of occult science, magic, a *Tao* of man pretending to be a copy of the great *Tao* of heaven and earth ' (p. 135). ' Men who possess the *Tao* by having assimilated themselves with nature, also possess miraculous powers, *the same as those which nature herself displays ; they are, indeed, gods or* shen *of the same kind as those who constitute the* Tao ' (p. 159). ' The human *Tao* is synonymous with virtue ; it is synonymous with classical or orthodox doctrine ; it is synonymous with *shen* or divinity, and also with harmony with the world of gods.' It is ' behaving as nature behaves ' (p. 138).

This departmental polydaemonism preserves all the main features we have described above. The undifferentiated Chaos splitting into the two contrary segments we can trace from Hesiod's cosmogony, through Anaximander, to Parmenides,[1] whose two opposing principles of heavenly light and earthly darkness are closely analogous to *Yang* and *Yin*. What especially concerns us now is the parallelism between the magical practitioners of the human *Tao* and their divine counterparts— the departmental spirits or Gods of the natural order. *Shen* is manifestly the Chinese for beneficent *mana* ; it is the substance of which Gods and the souls of ' divine ' or holy men are alike composed. Its primitive continuity survives in the doctrine that ' the universal Athmos, or *Shen*, pervades everything, and man's life is derived from an infusion of a part of it into himself. Therefore he may prevent his death by constantly absorbing Athmos from the world surrounding him ' (p. 146).[2]

58. *From Polydaemonism to Polytheism*

In the foregoing discussion of the daemonic phase of religion we distinguished four types of daemon in Greek theology. These were (1) the daemon, or genius, of the *gens*, or social group united by blood-kinship ; (2) the local *Agathos Daimon*, the Good Spirit

---

[1] For Parmenides' system, see below, §§ 115 ff.

[2] Cf. Aristotle, *de Anima*, a v. 15 : ' The account in the so-called Orphic poems asserts that the soul enters from the universe in the process of respiration, being borne upon the winds.' See further, p. 129 below.

or genius of fertility, embodying the life-giving power of the portion of earth inhabited by the social group ; (3) the daemon, or collective soul, of a magical fraternity, which consists of their collective powers or superhuman *mana*, exercised in magical control of nature ; (4) the daemon of a natural element—the non-human (or dehumanised) counterpart of (3), the supernatural *mana* of a natural department.

From these four types of daemon we have now to show by what process there emerge four types of divine beings who are *individual*—the King, the Hero, the Mystery God, and the Olympian. These are the four principal factors in Greek polytheism, as known to us in historical times.

59. *From impersonal daemon to individual soul and personal God*

When we call all these entities 'daemons,' we imply that they are still impersonal, and not individual. They retain the collective character which marks them as derived from the common consciousness of a group, not from the individual consciousness of one person. It is upon this point that we join issue with animism as popularly understood. The animistic theory of the origin of religion commonly states that *the savage* believes everything in the world to possess a soul like *his own*. Now, if we are right in supposing that individual self-consciousness is quite a late growth, that it is only after an age-long struggle that the individual soul comes to define itself in distinction from the group, it follows that animism, as so stated, must be of correspondingly recent date. At first, the individual has no soul of his own which he can proceed to attribute to other objects in nature. Before he can find his own soul, he must first become aware of a power which both is and is not himself—a moral force which at once is superior to his own and yet is participated in by him.

Now, as we have seen, the only thing in the world which answers to that description is the collective consciousness, which both is immanent in every member of the group and also lies beyond him, diffused throughout all the members in continuous distribution. This, then, is the primal source of religious representation. In proportion as it comes to be felt more and more as 'not ourselves,' it becomes increasingly superhuman and divine ; and, on the other hand, human individuality comes to be defined, hardened, and consolidated in contrast with it. The process, therefore, may be conceived as an externalisation, or projection, of the collective power which once was ourselves, into a power, at first daemonic and then personal, which is not ourselves. What we have now to do, is to form some notion of how this process takes place. How does the collective consciousness or emotional and active life of a group come to be externalised and projected into a personal daemon or God, while, on the other hand, the group-soul gives place to the individual soul ?

60. *The emergence of the Chief, or King*

The collective authority of the tribal group was, at first, vested in the group as a whole. This state of things survived in the Hebrew organisation, where we find the criminal arraigned before the whole tribe, which both gives and executes judgment. It existed also in Germany as described by Tacitus.[1] So again, under the laws of Solon, the ἡλιαία nominally consisted of all citizens above the age of thirty. The social group as a whole is the administrator, and even the source, of law, which immediately affirms the emotional reaction of the common consciousness upon crime.

The first individual embodiment of the repressive authority of the tribe is the despotic chief. ' The individuals, instead of subordinating themselves to the group, subordinate themselves to its representative ; and since the collective authority, when it was diffused, was absolute, that of the chief, which is only an organisation of it, naturally took the same character.' ' It is a general law that the pre-eminent organ of any society partakes of the nature of the collective entity which it represents. Accordingly, where society has that religious, and (so to say) superhuman, character, which we have traced to its origin in the constitution of the common consciousness, it is necessarily

---

[1] *Germ.* 11, 12. Cf. E. Durkheim, *Sur la div. du trav. soc.*[3], p. 42, from whom these instances are taken.

transferred to the chief who directs it, and who is thus elevated
high above the rest of men. Where the individuals are simply
dependent on the collective type, they quite naturally become
dependent on the central authority in which that type is
incarnated.' [1]

Thus, out of the collective life of the many, emerges the One.
But this one is not an independent individual. However absolute his power may be, he is not a tyrant claiming to be the
original source of all authority. He does not rule by his own
right, but solely as the representative of society. The authority
he wields is drawn from the group, and only temporarily deposited in him. He is an externalised group-soul—a daemon,
not yet a God. This representative character explains the
curious phenomenon of temporary kingships, upon which
Dr. Frazer's work has thrown so much light. This frequent
phenomenon shows how the authority deposited in a king
retains its collective character and remains distinguishable from
his personality.

Just because it remains distinguishable, a third and final stage
is possible, in which the collective authority rises above the
human sovereign and becomes transcendant in the impersonal
form of *Law*. It ascends from the daemonic plane to the divine.
Such was the position of the Mosaic Law in Hebrew society.
The divinity of the Law is, of course, represented by declaring
it to be the direct utterance of God. But the sovereign in a
society which calls itself theocratic is, of course, really the divine
Law itself. Thus, the collective authority first passes upwards
to the daemonic chief, and then, through him, to the heaven
above him, whose representative and functionary he now becomes,
ruling by ' divine right.' At a much later stage of social development, a similar phenomenon occurs in the Greek democracy,
the constitutional theory of which is that the sovereign is that
impersonal and dispassionate reason, called *Nomos*.[2]

Such, too, appears to be the position of *Moira*, above and

[1] E. Durkheim, *Sur la division du travail social*[3], pp. 156, 172.

[2] Herod. vii. 104 : ἐλεύθεροι γὰρ ἐόντες οὐ πάντα ἐλεύθεροί εἰσι· ἔπεστι γάρ σφι
δεσπότης Νόμος. Arist. *Pol.* 1287a 28, ὁ μὲν οὖν τὸν νόμον κελεύων ἄρχειν δοκεῖ
κελεύειν ἄρχειν τὸν θεὸν καὶ τὸν νοῦν μόνους, ὁ δ'ἄνθρωπον κελεύων προστίθησι καὶ
θηρίον· ἥ τε γὰρ ἐπιθυμία τοιοῦτον, καὶ ὁ θυμὸς ἄρχοντας καὶ τοὺς ἀρίστους ἄνδρας
διαφθείρει· διόπερ ἄνευ ὀρέξεως νοῦς ὁ νόμος ἐστίν.

beyond the humanised polity of Olympus. She is the constitutional Law of the universe, restricting the aggression of individual egoism. When the divine community is patriarchalised
—a change which presumably reflects a corresponding transformation in human society—an attempt is made to substitute
for Destiny the *patria potestas*, the will of Father Zeus. But
the attempt is not wholly successful. It will be remembered
how in the fifteenth *Iliad*, Poseidon claims that his status and
moira are on the same level with Zeus—he is ἰσόμορος and
ἰσότιμος. Zeus, he adds, had better try to terrorise his own sons
and daughters, who must of necessity obey his commands.[1] Thus,
the *patria potestas* has its limits, and these are fixed by the social
consciousness of Olympus, which still rises, even above Father
Zeus, in the all-dominating figure of *Moira*.

61. *The King as Arch-magician*

But, as Dr. Frazer has pointed out, the functions of the
primitive king are not solely, or even chiefly, political. In the
light of what has gone before, the reason is clear. The
collective powers deposited in him were not merely repressive
and punitive; they were also magical. The king is the
arch-magician. He has to regulate the weather, to stimulate
the growth of herds and crops, to see that the sun may shine
and the rain fall.[2]

In this respect, he is the successor of the magical society, whose
appearance we described above. From such a society it is
possible that he may directly emerge, extending his scope from
magical to political power. But, here again, his position at
first is of the type we have called daemonic; he gathers to himself the force derived from the group. Only later will he become

---

[1] *Il.* xv. 197 : θυγατέρεσσιν γάρ τε καὶ υἱάσι βέλτερον εἴη
ἐκπάγλοις ἐπέεσσιν ἐνισσέμεν, οὓς τέκεν αὐτός,
οἵ ἔθεν ὀτρύνοντος ἀκούσονται καὶ ἀνάγκῃ.

[2] Lévy-Bruhl, *Fonct. ment.* p. 291. In most societies of a type slightly
higher than the Australian, the desired (magical) result is no longer assured
by the totemic group. ' *Un membre du groupe, particulièrement qualifié, est
souvent le véhicule, obligé ou choisi, de la participation qu'il s'agit d'établir.*'
The individual is sometimes designated by his birth, for a man *is* his
ancestors, or a particular ancestor reincarnated. ' *C'est ainsi que les chefs
et les rois, de par leur origine, sont souvent les intermédiaires nécessaires.*'

the priest, who poses as the representative of a higher power descending upon him from the divine region above.

Especially interesting, as marking a transitional phase, are what Dr. Frazer calls the ' departmental kings of nature.' [1]   ' In the backwoods of Cambodia live two mysterious sovereigns, known as the King of the Fire and the King of the Water.   Their royal functions are of a purely mystic or spiritual order ;   they have no political authority ;   they are simple peasants, living by the sweat of their brow and the offerings of the faithful.'   They hold office for seven years, spending their time, according to one account, in absolute solitude, shut up in a tower on a mountain.   If they fall ill, they are stabbed to death.   The offices are hereditary in certain families, because these possess talismans which would lose their virtue or disappear, if they passed out of the family.   When a vacancy occurs, the kinsmen of the dead king flee to the woods to escape the dreadful office ; the first who is hunted out is made King of the Fire or of the Water.

It is transparently clear from this strange story that these magical kings are simply human daemons—the individual depositaries of the magical power possessed by a certain clan, which power is the correlative of the daemonic power of the elements they control.

There is abundant evidence from all quarters that this magical control of nature remains as the primary function of kingships of more developed types.   Because at one time human society and nature formed one solid system, the head of society is *ipso facto* the head of nature also ;   he is the source of law, which governs the elements no less than mankind.   In this sense, he is pre-eminently ' divine.'   His judgments or ' *dooms* ' ($\theta\acute{\epsilon}\mu\iota\sigma\tau\epsilon\varsigma$) are, as Hesiod [2] tells us, inspired.   The word *Themis*, like its cognate, the English ' doom,' means both ' judgment,' ' decree of right,' and also the oracular utterance of Fate ;   once more we find what *ought* to be undistinguished from what *must* and *will* be.   The king is spokesman of the world-order, of destiny and law ;   for he is the seer, and moves in the world of supersensible, sacred things, in immediate and perpetual contact with that

---

[1] *Golden Bough* [3], part I. vol. ii. p. 1 ff.

[2] *Theog.* 80 ff.   For *Themis*, see J. E. Harrison, *Themis*, chap. xi.

power in nature which is the magnified reflex of his own august potency.

That reflex, that Brocken spectre, of the king of men will come to be none other than the king of Gods ; for the divine monarchy evolves step for step with the human institution which it reflects. Hence we are not surprised to find the human king conceived, by developed theology, as the embodiment or representative of the divine king—the Greek Zeus or the Roman Jupiter.[1]

62. *The Eponymous Hero*

Somewhat similar to the development of the king is the growth of the representation called the eponymous hero. The source of this figure is transparently revealed by the fact that his name is not an individual appellation, but merely the singular form of the tribal name. Ion, for instance, is neither more nor less than *the Ionian*—the type and genius of all Ionians. As such, the eponymous hero is not an individual, but a *persona*—a mask, a representation of the genius of a social group.

His life-history, if he has any, is, at least partly, made up out of the life-history of the tribe. Thus it has been shown conclusively that many of the duels ($\dot{a}\nu\delta\rho o\kappa\tau a\sigma\acute{\iota}a\iota$) of the warriors in the *Iliad* are simply real conflicts between the tribes, individualised into the personal achievements of the eponyms that represent them.[2] This is mainly the work of epic poets, who endow a daemon of purely mythical origin with a quasi-historic personality, so vivid and distinct that the Euhemerists of all ages will defend his historic existence.

The tribal hero may reach the final stage of individualisation, if the empty *persona* happens to be filled by an historic person- ality. This may occur if some actual chieftain of great renown, who renders exceptional services to his tribe, is looked upon as the incarnation, *par excellence*, of the tribal genius. Thus a real man may, after his death, become a patron saint ; but only because the empty frame into which he steps is already

---

[1] So in *Il.* i. 238 the sceptre is held by the kings who are δικάσπολοι, οἵ τε θέμιστας πρὸς Διὸς εἰρύαται. Their judgments are derived from Zeus.

[2] E. Bethe, ' Homer und die Heldensage,' *Neue Jahrb. klass. Alt.* 1902 ; G. Murray, *Rise of the Greek Epic*[1], p. 181.

provided in the representation of the 'hero.' The individual hero in this way resembles the individual king. He owes his position, not merely to his really exceptional character and powers, but to the fact that there already exists a representation, personalised and daemonic, of that superhuman *mana* which is recognised as embodied in his individuality. The historic circumstances of his life and character, which occasioned his canonisation, are the least important part of him, and may soon be forgotten. His actual achievements blend with the other glorious acts of tribal history in a composite memory that defies analysis.

63. *Hero-worship*

Since, as we have seen, the hero is not originally an individual man, but represents the genius, or soul, or *mana* of a tribe, he keeps, like the king, a functional character. Saints are worshipped, not for the miracles which they performed in their lifetime, but because those miracles proved that they possessed superhuman power, which may be counted upon to work more miracles in the future. The expectation of these benefits to come gives vitality to the cult. In precisely the same way, the hero who saved his country while he lived, watches over it after his death as guardian and saviour ($\phi\acute{v}\lambda\alpha\xi$, $\sigma\omega\tau\acute{\eta}\rho$), and is the object of worship.

His cult may easily blend with that of the local daemon of fertility—the Good Spirit who provides the fruits of the earth to a society dependent on agriculture.[1] He will then become a daemon-of-all-work, charged with all the main functions which contribute to the social welfare—a saviour in war, and in peace 'a giver of wealth, for that too is a kingly function.'[2]

When such a fusion has taken place, the supposed life-history of the hero will be further enriched by *ritual* myths. These myths, which were originally representations of rites performed in the service of the Good Spirit, come to be translated into historical incidents in the hero's career. The Greek hero-

---

[1] This explanation of hero-worship by the blend of Hero and Agathos Daimon is due to Miss J. E. Harrison (*Themis*, chap. viii.).

[2] Hesiod, *Erga*, 125 of the Spirits of the Golden Race:

$\pi\lambda o\upsilon\tau o\delta\acute{o}\tau\alpha\iota\cdot$ $\kappa\alpha\grave{\iota}$ $\tau o\hat{\upsilon}\tau o$ $\gamma\acute{\epsilon}\rho\alpha\varsigma$ $\beta\alpha\sigma\iota\lambda\acute{\eta}\ddot{\iota}o\nu$ $\check{\epsilon}\sigma\chi o\nu.$

legends are full of myths which have this ritual origin, and require to be carefully distinguished from those personalised exploits of tribal history which go to make another element in the legends.[1]

64. *The Individual Soul and Immortality*

In the king and the hero we have found transitional forms, which make, as it were, a bridge from the daemon of a group to the individual soul. The chief was, probably, the first individual.[2] The collective authority of the tribe, vested in him, must inevitably be confounded with his individual will, which it reinforces with superhuman power; for he will not be capable of those nice distinctions which modern officials love to draw between the various ' capacities ' in which they act. The most successful tyrants, like Napoleon, are men of childish vanity, who believe that their own will is the primary source of their power. Thus, by a curious perversion, egoism establishes itself by the absorption of force derived from the subjects of its tyranny. The sense of individuality grows strong by feeding on the collective *mana*.

On the other hand, the king is still regarded by others as a mere depositary of social authority—a temporary embodiment of a power which existed before him and will be transmitted to his successor. The same holds true of the head of the *gens* or of the patriarchal family. In other words, the soul possessed by these individuals does not begin and end with their lifetimes, but is *immortal*. The soul has been held to be immortal, primarily because it was at first impersonal and superindividual—the soul of a group, which outlives every generation of its members. Beginning as the collective and impersonal life of the group, it becomes confounded, as we have seen, with the individual personality of the chief; and there was, probably, a stage in which only chiefs or heroes had immortal souls. The tradition of such a phase seems to survive in Hesiod's Age of Bronze—a class of immortals which consists of the heroes who fought at

---

[1] In my chapter on the Olympic Games in Miss Harrison's *Themis*, I have tried to show that the Pindaric legend of Pelops consists of ritual myths of this kind.

[2] See E. Durkheim, *Sur la div. du travail social*[3], p. 172.

Ilion and Thebes, but does not include the undistinguished mass of their followers.[1]

The democratic extension of immortality to all human beings was perhaps partly helped by the rise of the patriarchal family, as the unit of a new social structure. The family differs from the original undifferentiated group, in that it is organic : the father, the mother, the son, and the daughter, have each a distinct function in the household economy, and this means a distinct ' nature,' essence, or ' soul.' [2] But, no doubt, many other causes contributed to this result.

One such cause may have been the dream-image or memory-image, in which some inquirers have sought the whole origin of the belief in immortality.[3] The point to be noted about this image (*eidolon*) is that it is from the first individual—it is the visible ' shape ' (*eidos*) or appearance, which is recognisable as belonging to one particular person whom we have seen and known. It would, therefore, be peculiarly effective in facilitating the idea that some part of every human being survives his death.

The psychology of Homer shows that this *eidolon* may remain distinct from that other kind of soul we have hitherto considered —the blood-soul, in which the vital powers or *mana* reside. Man in Homer has two souls. His *eidolon* or *psyche* escapes from his mouth at the moment of death ; it is his recognisable shape, which may, for a time, revisit his survivors in dreams. It does not exist until the moment of death ; and it does not carry with it to the world of shades any of his vital force. This resides in the other soul ($\theta \upsilon \mu \acute{o} \varsigma$), whose visible vehicle is the blood ; and it is only by drinking blood that the *eidolon* can recover its ' wits ' ($\phi \rho \acute{e} \nu \epsilon \varsigma$) or consciousness. In the mortal soul we find again the same combination of blood and *mana* which composed the sympathetic continuum of primary magic. As contrasted with the individual and recognisable *eidolon*, it is less personal—the

---

[1] *Erga*, 156 ff. They were ἀνδρῶν ἡρώων θεῖον γένος, ἡμίθεοι, and ὄλβιοι ἥρωες, for whom the earth bears fruit three times a year—so much functional fertility-*mana* have they carried with them to the Isles of the Blest.

[2] Some of the Sophists delighted in defining the *virtue* of the father, of the wife, etc., *i.e.* their specific function.

[3] Mr. A. E. Crawley (*The Idea of the Soul*, London, 1909) has defended the memory-image in a new and interesting way, as against the older dream-theory. While emphasising the importance of the group-soul, I would not seem to underrate these other factors.

same in all men alike—and thus bears the mark of its original collective character.[1]

The distinction between these two kinds of soul is important for the later course of philosophic psychology. The *eidolon* soul, the recognisable shape or image, is the soul as object (and later as subject) of *knowledge*; the blood-soul is the soul as the principle of force and *motion*. It is under these two heads that Aristotle, in the first book of his *Psychology*, groups the theories held by his predecessors, about the nature and functions of soul.[2]

So, at last, we reach the notions of the individual *ker*, *daemon*, and *moira*. The *ker* is an *eidolon*, or winged sprite, which wears a sinister aspect—is an object of fear. If it is angry and seeks vengeance, it is an *Erinys*. Considered as allotted to the individual at birth, it is his *moira*—the span or limit of his vital force, the negative and repressive aspect of his fate. Being derived from a vanished group, the *moira* is necessarily shadowy, negative, unreal. The *daemon* (*genius*) of a person, on the other hand, retains the element of beneficent power, of functional *mana*. When Heracleitus, for example, says that a man's character is his *daemon*, he means that it is the force which shapes his life from within, and makes or mars his fortunes, not a ' destiny ' allotted him from without.[3]

65. *The formation of personal Gods, Mystic and Olympian*

Such, in briefest outline, is the history of the king and of the hero, leading to the individual soul. The two other types of divine being recognised by Greek polytheism still remain to be considered—the Mystery God and the Olympian. We shall

---

[1] For Homeric psychology, see Rohde, *Psyche*, chap. i. Among the Melanesians, 'if a man has *mana* it resides in his "spiritual part" or "soul," which after death becomes a ghost. . . . Not every man has *mana*, nor every ghost ; but the soul of a man of power becomes as such a ghost of power. . . . *Mana* can come very near to meaning "soul" or "spirit," though without the connotation of wraith-like appearance' (Marett, *Threshold of Religion*, p. 134).

[2] See below, § 77.

[3] Cf. Isocrates, ix. 25, speaking of Euagoras : τοσαύτην ὁ δαίμων ἔσχεν αὐτοῦ πρόνοιαν, ὅπως καλῶς λήψεται τὴν βασίλειαν, ὥσθ' ὅσα μὲν ἀναγκαῖον ἦν παρασκευασθῆναι δι' ἀσεβείας, ταῦτα μὲν ἕτερος ἔπραξεν, ἐξ ὧν δ' οἷόν τ' ἦν ὁσίως καὶ δικαίως λαβεῖν τὴν ἀρχήν, Εὐαγόρᾳ διεφύλαξεν. For the guardian genius of the individual, see Rohde, *Psyche*[3], ii. 316.

try to exhibit their nature and origin by recurring to our conception of the two pools of *mana*, into which the original sympathetic continuum divided. The essential difference between these two types of God, which persists in spite of all reaction between them, is that the Mystery God is, from first to last, the daemon of a human group, while the Olympian God develops out of the daemon of a local department, who has become distinct from his worshippers.[1]

66. *The Mystery God*

The typical Mystery God of Greek religion is, of course, Dionysus. In his case, the cult organisation reflects the essential fact that he is the daemon of a human group. From first to last he is attended by this group, called his *thiasos*, whether it be in the idealised form of the troop of Maenads and Satyrs, or the actual band of human worshippers, of Bacchae and Bacchoi. The group, moreover, becomes a religious, not a political, unit—a church, not a state. It is a secret and mysterious society; admission to it is a matter of initiation, because Dionysus is a wandering divinity, not a fixed part of an official state religion, access to which is the birthright of every citizen. His church, accordingly, is a trans-social organisation, and essentially of the same type as the secret society of magicians, with which, indeed, it easily amalgamates, if it does not directly arise from it.[2]

It is true that Dionysus represents, not only the soul or life of a human group, but also the life of all animate nature. But we must note that this life of nature is modelled upon the cycle of human life. The seasonal round of vegetation—its death in winter and rebirth in spring—is a larger transcript of the phases of human existence, birth and death and rebirth in the wheel of reincarnation. Hence, in this type of religion the conceptual framework is temporal—the recurrent circle of the year, which ends where it began; whereas in the case of Olympian Gods

---

[1] The distinction between these two types of religion has never been better stated than by Friedrich Nietzsche in his *Geburt der Tragödie*, a work of profound imaginative insight, which left the scholarship of a generation toiling in the rear.

I do not, of course, deny that the group was originally local and tribal; I am only describing a later stage at which the religion had become delocalised.

the framework is spatial—the provincial order of *Moira*.   Hence,
too, the mystery cult gathers up those older magical ceremonies
(in which at first sexual magic was prominent), designed to
promote by sympathetic co-operation the birth and flowering
and fruitfulness of trees and plants.   The religion holds fast
to the sympathetic principle that all life is one, and conceives
Nature under that form which seems to keep her processes most
closely in touch with the phases of human experience.   Dionysus,
then, and other such Mystery Gods, are fundamentally human
daemons, however much they may be naturised ; and the course
of their development is, to that extent, the reverse of the process
by which an Olympian, from being the impersonal daemon of a
department, becomes more and more humanised, or (as we say)
anthropomorphic.

Because the province of a Mystery God is always, primarily,
the human society from which he immediately springs, it is
possible for him to remain human as well as divine.   In this lies
the secret of the vitality of mystical religions.   The characteristic rite is sacramental—an act of communion and reunion with
the daemon.   Its effect may be conceived under two comple-
mentary aspects : either as *enthusiasm*—God enters into his
group and they become ἔνθεοι ; or as *ecstasy*—man rises out
of, and above, the prison of his individuality and loses himself in
the common life of the whole, becoming ' immortal ' and ' divine.'
Thus, the God remains both human and daemonic, being perpetually, at every celebration of the rite, re-created in the collective emotion of his congregation.   Orgiastic ritual ensures that
the passage from the human plane to the divine remains open,
and is continually traversed.   God can enter into man, and man
can become God.[1]

In theology the same truth is reflected in the fact that
Dionysus, even when his worship was contaminated with Olympian cults, never became fully an Olympian.   His ritual, by perpetually renewing the bond of union with his group, prevented
him from drifting away from his province, as the Olympians
had done, and ascending to a remote and transcendental heaven.
Moreover, a mystery religion is necessarily monotheistic or

[1] Schol. Ar. *Knights*, 406 : βάκχον οὐ τὸν Διόνυσον ἐκάλουν μόνον, ἀλλὰ καὶ
πάντας τοὺς τελοῦντας τὰ ὄργια.

pantheistic. Teaching the unity of all life, it disposes of polytheism by the doctrine that all the Gods are only diverse shapes
of one divine principle, ' one nature with many names.' Dionysus, accordingly, could not, for all the grotesque attempts of
theologians, be fitted into a subordinate place in the Olympian
polity. He was the God of his church—a group not social or
organic, but defined precisely by its unique relation to its daemon-
soul. Such a group cannot have more than one God.

It is easy to see how this mystical scheme, rather than Olympianism, provides the appropriate setting for half-human and
half-divine figures like Pythagoras, Buddha, and Jesus—actual
living prophets, who, during their life or after their death, became
the daemons of religious societies. The several stages in the
deification of Jesus provide an instructive analogy to the attempted Olympianisation of Dionysus. The process shows the
same tension between opposite forces. The upward-pulling
force is the metaphysical affiliation to an already transcenden-
talised Father God : the emphasis on the divine nature threatens
to exclude the human, and to draw the daemon away from his
group into a heaven of philosophical abstraction. But this tendency is prevented from completely triumphing by those mystical
rites which perpetually reconstitute the emotional sense of
communion and realise the promise : ' Where two or three are
gathered together, there am I in the midst.' In Romanist
countries the real, human relation of Mother and Son has almost
completely eclipsed the Fatherhood, which was never more than
metaphysical.[1] The really living objects of Christian cult are
the figures of actual men and women—the Virgin, her Son, the
saints and martyrs ; not the two other Persons of the Trinity, or
the angels, in whom the Christian Fathers recognised the daemons
of paganism.

In this type of religion, then, the central fact is the human
group, with a homogeneous, inorganic type of solidarity,[2] held
together by the unique relation in which it stands to its daemon
—a relation by which man can participate in the divine, and,

---

[1] M. Jacques Raverat points out to me that for the French peasant the
human father has effaced the divine. His trinity is Jésus-Marie-Joseph.

[2] Hence the communism and equality of the Early Church and of the
Pythagoreans.

conversely, the divine can enter into man. It is the parent of mystical philosophies, of monistic and pantheistic systems, which hold that the One can pass into the Many and yet remain One. It is also idealistic in tendency, in the sense that it is other-worldly : the One is not only within, but beyond and above, the Many, and more real, because more powerful, than they. Accordingly, the Many, as such, are condemned to un-reality, to mere ' seeming ' or appearance—half-false representations of the One reality.

67. *The Olympian God*

In almost every important respect the Olympian presents a striking contrast to the Mystery God. With the progress of his worshippers towards increasing self-consciousness, he has advanced to the stage of quasi-individual personality. Like the tribal Hero, he has been endowed by the poets with a definite character, and a biographical record. He stands on his own feet, and is detached from the human group: he has no church, no *thiasos*. From this fundamental fact the chief characteristics of Olympian religion can be deduced.

Since such a God has no human congregation, whose soul or daemon he can be, the relation of worshipper to God cannot be one of communion : the worshippers cannot re-create and feed him with their own emotional experience in mystical rites. God and worshippers do not form one solid group, but con-front one another, as a social or political unit and a power of Nature—between which only an external relation, of a con-tractual or commercial type, can subsist.[1] Accordingly, the characteristic rite of Olympianism is the commercial sacrifice, regarded as a gift or bribe, in exchange for which benefits are to be returned. This ritual supersedes the attempt at direct compulsion previously made by the magician, who still believed that his own *mana* was a match for the divine *mana* of Nature. He who can no longer feel himself strong enough to compel, resorts to persuasion and the methods of commercial barter.[2]

[1] Cf. the analysis of religion in Plato's *Euthyphro*.

[2] Cf. Plato, *Rep.* 364 B, where the mendicant magician at once describes his power as ' derived from the Gods ' (δύναμις ἐκ θεῶν ποριζομένη) and claims to ' induce the Gods to *serve* him ' (τοὺς θεοὺς πείθοντές σφισιν ὑπηρετεῖν).

Further, there is not for the Olympian God that bond of union which prevents the Mystery God from drifting altogether away from his province. The Olympian God sheds his functions, and so is cut loose from his anchorage in the life of earth. In proportion as he becomes anthropomorphic, he comes to be less and less in touch with his natural region. The formation of a pan-hellenic religion meant that the Olympians left their provinces, to go and form a polity of their own on the top of a mountain. Finally, they leave the earthly Olympus, and vanish into the sky. Nature, dispeopled of Gods, is left free for science.

The grouping of the Gods into a patriarchal family involves (as we saw in the case of human society) differentiation of function. The Gods, as Herodotus says, from being an indistinct plurality of impersonal daemons, come to have separate ' arts ' and ' figures,' and to form a group of the organic type. Thus, thanks to the extraordinary definiteness of Greek imagination, they acquire very clear personalities. But, though such a God may become a person, this *persona* is not really more than an empty mask—not an individual. A God who was never a man, can never acquire individuality, for the simple reason that the indispensable basis of individuality is the unique world of inner and outer experience which every real animal being has, but nothing else can have. The Olympian God can never be more than an *eidos*, a *species*. As such, moreover, he is without any inward principle of life and growth—immortal and immutable. The only life he ever had was the daemonic and supernatural energy of his province, derived from its source in human emotion. As he recedes from this province and withdraws to his humanised Olympus, the *mana* passes out of him. Whither does it go ?

Much of it, no doubt, is retained by the local divinity, the patron of the community, Athene at Athens, Hera at Argos, and so forth. The Olympian system does not supersede and efface the worship of a local spirit, any more than Catholic theology has succeeded in universalising its divinities. The Notre Dame of one village is distinct from, and may even be at enmity with, the Notre Dame of the next.[1] But, for more intellectual minds, these

---

[1] See A. Daudet, ' La Diligence de Beaucaire' in *Lettres de mon Moulin.*

local Gods will be weakened and discredited by the mere existence of an Olympian pantheon to which they half belong. The Gods are uprooted, and what power is left to them must become not local, but cosmic.

68. *The Gods and the Elements*

We seem to discern one attempt to provide the Gods with new *moirai* in that cosmic *dasmos* of the elemental regions which we described in Chapter I. It has already been remarked that this is a late and artificial proceeding. It seems to be based on a primitive elemental complex, which includes the powers instrumental in providing man with food—the thunder (fire), the rain, the clouds, and the earth. These were at first grouped in a pair—earth and the thunder-cloud, which breaks into fire and descends in rain to fertilise the dry ground in the primal marriage of Earth and Heaven, united by Eros. In the triple *dasmos* of the sons of Kronos, the trinity of Gods divide among them the three superterrestrial factors. Zeus is the thunder-God of all light and fire and warmth, who, for political and other reasons, happened to prevail. Poseidon has in the same way come to stand for all the powers of moisture, wells and rivers and seas; Hades is lord of the dark and cold air— the clouds and the western darkness. Earth remains yet common to all; but the agriculturalist is now taught to look upwards to heaven for the powers that give increase.[1]

In the climate of the Mediterranean, with its rainless summer, the natural anxieties of the farmer, and consequently many of his religious rites, are concentrated on the powers of heat and cold, of wet and drought. The year divides itself into two well-marked periods—the θέρος and χεῖμα of Homer—in which the hot and the dry are leagued against the cold and the wet,[2] and each pair

---

[1] The battle of the Gods in Pherekydes is between the sons of Earth on the one side and the Heaven-God with spirits of fire, water, and wind on the other; see Eisler, *Weltenmantel*, ii. 660. For the *Titanomachia*, see J. E. Harrison, *Themis*, p. 453.

[2] This opposition peeps out in odd places; cf. the herald's speech in Aesch. *Agam.* 655, ξυνώμοσαν γάρ, ὄντες ἔχθιστοι τὸ πρίν, πῦρ καὶ θάλασσα, and in Eurip. *Troades*, prologue, the same unholy alliance, on the same occasion, of Athena, who contributes the thunder and fire of Zeus (80), and Poseidon who raises a storm in the waters.

of allies has its appointed moiety and 'prevails,' as Empedocles says of his elements, 'as the circle of time comes round.' For the farmer the behaviour of the universe is satisfactory when the aggression of these warring contraries is counterchecked and balanced, and he gets enough of each, and not too much of either. From their due mixture and harmony arise the individual things which interest him—the birth and blossoming and fruitage of his crops and trees.[1]

Now, already in Homer it is clear enough that Zeus and Poseidon have drifted out of touch with their elements, which they rule only as absentee proprietors. Most of the time they are occupied with quite other interests, such as the progress of the siege of Troy. This means that the elements themselves regain the divine *mana* and potency which a God who leaves his department cannot carry away with him. The Hot (thunder, fire), the Cold (mist, clouds, air), the Wet (rain, sea, water), and the Dry (earth), are left to themselves as elements endowed with daemonic, supernatural energy. They become the four primary forms of *physis*. The perpetual war of these opposed powers goes on, obviously enough, before our eyes in the processes of Nature. In the phenomena of evaporation and precipitation, we see 'the fire of the sun and stars feeding itself on the exhalation of the waters.'[2] This is taken by the early physicists as the type of 'rarefaction and condensation' by which they explained qualitative change.[3]

We can see now why Anaximander laid such stress on the departmental ordering of the four elemental opposites, and on their warfare and aggression. We must not, however, lose sight of the fundamental principle of *Moira*, as ordaining the distinction of spatial provinces. Before we leave religion for philosophy, we must bring out one more aspect of this principle, because it will show us another contrast, of vital importance, between Olympian and Mystic religion.

---

[1] Hippocr. *de Nat. Hom.* 7: ὡς γὰρ ὁ ἐνιαυτὸς μετέχει μὲν πᾶς πάντων καὶ τῶν θερμῶν καὶ τῶν ψυχρῶν καὶ τῶν ξηρῶν καὶ τῶν ὑγρῶν. . . . Plato, *Symp.* 188A, quoted below, p. 121.

[2] Aet. i. 3. 1 (Thales).

[3] See Heidel, 'Qualitative Change in Pre-Socratic Philosophy,' *Arch. f. Gesch. d. Phil.* xix. 333, and O. Gilbert, *Meteor. Theorien.* chap. i.

69. *The Olympian God cut off from man*

For lack of the mystical link of communion, the Olympian recedes from man, as well as from Nature. A cardinal principle of Olympian theology is that man cannot become a God or 'immortal,' neither can God become man. Each is confined to his own region, and the boundary of *Moira* set between them cannot, and must not, be passed. Unfed by human emotion, and shedding his own inherent life, the Olympian God is doomed to perish of inanition.

Such psychology as the Gods possess mainly consists in the old doctrine of *Moira*, reinterpreted into terms of human passion. The power which pervades a department, and formerly used, with law-abiding regularity, to dispense its benefits, is now a capricious and arbitrary will, differing from a human will only in the superiority of its strength. The negative aspect, which defends the frontier against aggression from without, is a human passion, sometimes still called *nemesis*, more familiarly known as 'grudging jealousy' ($\phi\theta\acute{o}\nu o\varsigma$). The prominence of this passion in the psychology of an Olympian God, undignified as it has often seemed, becomes intelligible when we realise that it covers half the field of the divine morality—indeed much more than half, inasmuch as the God is far more acutely conscious of the respect due to his position and privileges than of any duty towards his equals or inferiors. This is a necessary consequence of the growth of his humanised personality. The God who develops even this much of a 'self,' loses his sense of duty. He no longer consists solely of his function, which was at first his *raison d'être*: he forgets that his utility was once all that there was of him. The history of the word $\tau\iota\mu\acute{\eta}$ illustrates the transition. In Hesiod it retains much of its original sense: the $\tau\iota\mu\acute{\eta}$ of a God is the *office* which determines his *status*; it is the same as his $\gamma\acute{\epsilon}\rho\alpha\varsigma$, the privilege to *do* something, to operate in a certain department. But, when we come to developed Olympianism, the burden of $\tau\iota\mu\acute{\eta}$ shifts from the God to his worshipper: it comes to mean the *honour* which we are bound to render to him, no longer the service he is bound to render to us.

Anything he may now be pleased to do for us is an act of grace, with which he may, or may not, repay our dues of sacrifice. His *nemesis* again is no more the ' dispensation ' of good things ; it passes wholly to the sense of anger against our presumption in expecting too much of them.

Like other functionaries, he tends to withdraw into an attitude of aloofness and majestic condescension, and to insist, correspondingly, on humanity keeping its distance. Apollo's message to his worshippers was : ' Know thyself, and do not go too far.' Greek morality of the Olympian type is governed by this precept. Be conscious of yourself, realise yourself, make the most you can of it, up to the boundaries which limit its sphere; but be conscious also of those limits and keep your head—be σώ-φρων. Going too far is πλεονέξια—' having more than your equal share ' ; it is ὕβρις, ' getting above yourself ' ; or it is ὑπερβασία, ' stepping across,' invading the sphere which your neighbour claims to occupy from centre to circumference. With the instancy of an electric shock, your intrusion will be met by a discharge of φθόνος.

70. *Olympian and Mystic doctrines of Eros*

Once more Earth and Heaven are parted asunder, the Gap has come into being ; and Olympian theology is clear that this gap is not to be bridged by Eros. The space between Earth and Olympus comes to be the great moral gulf which mortals may never pass. ' Of one race, one only, are men and Gods ; both of one mother's womb we draw our breath ; but far asunder is all our power divided, and fences us apart : here there is nothingness, and there, in strength of bronze, a seat unshaken, eternal, abides the heaven above.' [1] And it is significant that the prevailing type of sinner who attempts to pass this gulf is he who seeks *marriage* with the Queen of Heaven.

' Destiny and Device, eldest of the Gods, are masters of all ; but Strength has no winged sandals. Let no man ever fly aloft to heaven, nor seek to wed Aphrodite, the Cyprian queen, or

---

[1] Pind. *Nem.* vi. 1. Cf. frag. 104c (Schröder) : τιμαὶ δὲ βροτοῖσι κεκριμέναι.

some fair daughter of Porkos, whose dwelling is in the sea.
. . . There is a vengeance of the Gods.'[1]

Ixion's two offences were that he was the first who ' imbrued
kindred blood,' and that he ' attempted the spouse of Zeus.'[2]
Tityos, another typical sinner, committed the same act of unlawful aggression.[3]   It is noteworthy that the Chorus in the
Prometheus Bound invoke the *Moirai* when they pray that they
may never share the bed of Zeus, nor approach in marriage any
of the inhabitants of heaven.[4]   To do so would be to pass from
the *moira* of men, the earth, and invade the heavenly *moira* of the
Olympians. ' Device ' (*Poros*), and his child Eros, thus come to
be conceived as symbols of unlawful and overweening ambition,

---

[1] Alkman, *Partheneion*, l. 13 :

κράτησε γὰρ Αἶσα παντῶν
[καὶ Πόρος] γεραίτατοι
[θιῶν· ἀλλ' ἀπ]έδιλος ἀλκά.
[μῆτις ἀνθ] ρώπων ἐς ὡρανὸν ποτήσθω,
[μηδὲ πει]ρήτω γαμῆν τὰν Ἀφροδίταν,
[Κυπρίαν] ἄνασσαν, ἤ τιν'
[ἠνειδ-]ῆ παῖδα Πόρκω
[εἰναλίω. Χά]ριτες δὲ Διὸς δόμον
[εἰσβαινου]σιν ἐρογλέφαροι . . .
ἔστι τις θιῶν τίσις.

This is an instructive passage. *Aisa* is a synonym of *Moira*. *Poros* is
' device,' which is lord of all that is not prohibited or prevented by *Aisa*.
(So in Thucydides γνώμη, man's foresight and decision, and Τύχη share the
world between them. See my *Thucyd. Mythistoricus*, p. 105.) In Plato's
Symposium, 203 B, Poros is father of *Eros*—the Eros which *does* pass from
earth to heaven ; and we can understand why the Scholiast on the Alkman
fragment says that Poros = Hesiod's *Chaos*: ὅτι τὸν Πόρον εἴρηκε τὸν αὐτὸν τῶι
ὑπὸ τοῦ Ἡσιόδου μεμυθευμένωι χάει. But Strength (man's *mana*) has not
winged sandals to cross 'Chaos.' 'Eros' is a bad passion. Only the
Charites (*i.e.* victory) may innocently exalt man to the Gods. (Cf. Emped.
frag. 116 : χάρις στυγέει δύστλητον Ἀνάγκην.) They are ἐρο-γλέφαροι : Eros
dwells in their eyes, and they may look up to heaven.

[2] Pind. *Pyth.* ii. 30 : αἱ δύο δ' ἀμπλακίαι | φερέπονοι τελέθοντι· τὸ μὲν ἥρως
ὅτι | ἐμφύλιον αἷμα πρώτιστος οὐκ ἀτὲρ τέχνας ἐπέμιξε θνατοῖς· | ὅτι τε . . . | Διὸς
ἄκοιτιν ἐπειρᾶτο. Χρὴ δὲ καθ' αὐτὸν αἰεὶ παντὸς ὁρᾶν μέτρον. I suspect that in
the first offence, 'the mingling of kindred blood,' we have a misunderstood
reminiscence of the introduction of patriarchal marriage within the prohibited degrees of the matriarchal system, which is known to have prevailed
among the Locrians. The two offences may be only two ways of regarding
this breach of taboo.

[3] Pind. *Pyth.* iv. 90.

[4] Aesch. *P. V.* 984 : μήποτέ μ', ὦ πότνιαι Μοῖραι, λεχέων Διὸς εὐνάτειραν ἴδοισθε
τέλουσαν· μηδὲ πλαθείην γαμέτᾳ τινὶ τῶν ἐξ οὐρανοῦ.

like the insolence and violence of the wooers of Penelope, which 'reached even to the iron heaven.' [1]

In accordance with this condemnation of Eros by Olympian theology, we shall find that the scientific tradition in philosophy, derived from that theology, lays emphasis on the justice and necessity of the separation of the elements, and regards their 'mixing' or marriage as an injustice. Such was the view of Anaximander. On the other hand, the mystical schools look back to a quite opposite view of Eros, which any reader of Plato's *Symposium*, and especially of the discourse of Diotima, will know to be characteristic of mystical religion.

One of the speakers in the *Symposium* (p. 186 ff.), Eryximachus, a pythagorising physician, sets the two conceptions of Eros—the Olympian and the mystic—in clear contrast. In opposition to the Eros that goes with insolence and excess (ὁ μετὰ τῆς ὕβρεως Ἔρως), he speaks of the Eros who is orderly (κόσμιος), and indeed is the principle which binds all things into an order, a *cosmos*, or a harmony. Both these Loves are present, he says, in the blending of the seasons of the year ; and when the hot and the cold, the dry and the wet, are regulated in their relations to one another by the Love which is orderly, and they are mixed in temperate harmony, then they bring a good year and health to men and beasts and plants, and there is no injustice. But when the disorderly and excessive Love prevails in the yearly seasons, there is much injustice and destruction done by pestilence and various diseases. Frosts and hail and mildew are caused by this aggression and want of orderly adjustment (πλεονεξίας καὶ ἀκοσμίας). Such is the physician's point of view ; he regards the whole medical art as concerned with establishing the orderly and harmonious Eros between the opposites that make war upon one another in the body, each being impelled by the bad Eros to usurp the domain of its antagonist and set up ' injustice ' and disease.[2]

As the dialogue proceeds, a deeper conception of the cosmic Eros is unfolded in the speech of Diotima. We cannot follow

---

[1] *Od.* xvii. 565 : τῶν ὕβρις τε βίη τε σιδήρεον οὐρανὸν ἵκει.

[2] Cf. Plato, *Laws*, 906c: τὴν πλεονεξίαν, ἐν μὲν σαρκίνοις σώμασι νόσημα καλούμενον, ἐν δὲ ὥραις ἐτῶν καὶ ἐνιαυτῶν λοιμόν, ἐν δὲ πόλεσι καὶ πολιτείαις τοῦτο αὖ τὸ ῥῆμα μετεσχηματισμένον ἀδικίαν.

it out in detail, but only notice the passage which directly contra-
dicts the Olympian doctrine of the impassable gulf between
Gods and men. Eros is a daemon, and intermediate between
the human world and the divine. He ' fills up the interval
between the two, so that the universe is bound together in one.' [1]
Plutarch, we believe, is unquestionably right in associating this
doctrine with the mystical cults centred round the figures of
those suffering daemons, like Adonis, Osiris, or Dionysus, whose
passion ($\pi \acute{a} \theta \eta$) and death showed them to be partakers of a
common life with all things that live, and die, and are born again
in Nature.[2] When we come to the mystic tradition in philosophy,
it will become clear how fundamental is this doctrine that God
is not cut off from the world, nor man from God ; there is no
impassable gap between earth and a brazen heaven, but all things
are bound together in harmony and linked by permeable ways.
The soul can still regain its ancient continuity with the divine.

71. *From Olympianism to Ionian Philosophy*

In competition with a form of religion which held out to man
the prospect of union with God, it is easy to see why Olympianism,
with its doctrine of divine jealousy and of the impassable gulf
of *Moira*, failed and died, while mystic religion continued to be
a source of inspiration. The Olympians had passed beyond the
reach of human needs and the touch of human emotion ; they
had even left their provinces in Nature, and it was found out that
the business of the world could go forward without them, just
as it had been found out that the magnificent traffic of cloud
and sunshine, and the daily circling of the heavens, could go on
its appointed way without the impertinent aid of magical dances
and incantation. The time had come for religion to give place
to philosophy.

---

[1] *Symp.* 202 E : ἐν μέσῳ δὲ ὂν ἀμφοτέρων συμπληροῖ, ὥστε τὸ πᾶν αὐτὸ αὑτῷ
συνδεδέσθαι. For this ξύνδεσμος, see Eisler, *Weltenmantel*, ii. p. 418 ff.

[2] Plut. *Def. Orac.* 415 A : ἐμοὶ δὲ δοκοῦσι πλείονας λῦσαι καὶ μείζονας ἀπορίας
οἱ τὸ τῶν δαιμόνων γένος ἐν μέσῳ θέντες θεῶν καὶ ἀνθρώπων καὶ τρόπον τινὰ τὴν
κοινωνίαν ἡμῶν συνάγον εἰς ταὐτὸ καὶ συνάπτον ἐξευρόντες· εἴτε μάγων τῶν περὶ
Ζωροάστρην ὁ λόγος οὗτός ἐστιν, εἴτε Θρᾳκιος ἀπ' Ὀρφέως εἴτ' Αἰγύπτιος ἢ Φρύγιος,
ὡς τεκμαιρόμεθα ταῖς ἑκατέρωθι τελεταῖς ἀναμεμιγμένα πολλὰ θνητὰ καὶ πένθιμα
τῶν ὀργιαζομένων καὶ δρωμένων ἱερῶν ὁρῶντες.

The type of philosophy to which an Olympian theology will give rise will be dominated by the conception of spatial externality, as *Moira* had dominated the Gods; and it will tend towards discontinuity and discreteness. Originating in an essentially polytheistic scheme, it will be pluralistic. It will also move steadily towards materialism, because, having no hold upon the notion of life as an inward and spontaneous principle, it will reduce life to mechanical motion, communicated by external shock from one body to another. It will level down the organic to the inorganic, and pulverise God and the Soul into material atoms.

72. *Physis*

But, when reason seemed to herself to have dispensed with the supernatural, and to be left with nothing but Nature, what was the Nature, *physis*, she was left with? Not simply the visible world as it would present itself to unbiassed sense-perception, if such a thing as sense-perception unbiassed by preconceived notions could ever exist, unless it be in a new-born baby.

The 'Nature' of which the first philosophers tell us with confident dogmatism is from the first a metaphysical entity; not merely a natural element, but an element endowed with supernatural life and powers, *a substance which is also Soul and God*.[1]

It is that very living stuff out of which daemons, Gods, and souls had slowly gathered shape. It is that same continuum of homogeneous matter, charged with vital force, which had been the vehicle of magical sympathy, that now is put forward explicitly, with the confident tone of an obvious statement, as the substrate of all things and the source of their growth.

[1] Cf. O. Gilbert, *Meteor. Theorien*, 703: *Diese Auffassung der Materie* (in Ionian monism), *nach der die anderen Elemente Erzeugte des einen sind, bedarf keiner besonderen göttlichen Kraft, die über dem Stoffe als solchem stehend, ihn ordnet und bestimmt, bewegt und leitet: der Stoff selbst, als der Grundstoff und als die abgeleiteten Einzelstoffe, lebt : und als lebend und persönlich gedachtes Wesen bewegt er sich ; der Stoff ist die Gottheit selbst, welche, in ihm waltend, eins ist mit ihm.*

IV

THE DATUM OF PHILOSOPHY

73. *Recapitulation*

IN the foregoing chapters we have tried to define the starting-point of Greek philosophy, the fundamental representation of the world which would persist, in the minds of men like Thales and Anaximander, when the personal Gods of over-developed Olympianism were put aside. Our conclusion was that the representation they called *physis*, and conceived as the ultimate living stuff out of which the world grew, could be traced back to an age of magic actually older than religion itself. In that first age, it was not as yet a representation at all, but a real fact of human experience, namely the collective consciousness of a group in its emotional and active phase, expressed in the practices of primary sympathetic magic. The need for a representation would first arise when the collective emotion and desire ceased to find complete and immediate satisfaction in mimetic rites. The tension of this deferred reaction would give an opening for a representation of that power which is no longer available at the first demand, but has to be recovered with something of an effort. Here, then, would be formed the first conception of the ' something not ourselves ' ; and this, we have argued, is precisely the collective consciousness itself. Because it is not ourselves, it wears the negative aspect of a moral power imposing constraint from without ; and this power, projected into the universe, leads to the conception of a supreme force, above Gods and men, in which Destiny and Right—*Moira* and *Dike*—are united. Its positive content, on the other hand, we identified with the sympathetic continuum, which is the vehicle of super-normal, magical power. This, as constituting the functions, and therefore the ' nature,' of a group, could be visibly embodied in the blood, which is the substrate of all kinship or

124

'likeness,' and so the medium of interaction between like and like. Out of this primitive representation arose, by differentiation, the notions of group-soul and daemon, and finally the individual soul and the personal God.

These imaginary objects, souls and Gods, are made of the same stuff; their substance is simply the old sympathetic continuum, more or less etherealised. In the case of the Gods the process has gone further than it has with souls, because Gods —or at least Olympian Gods [1]—have no visible and tangible bodies ; but it is still possible for souls, which have such bodies, to be identified with the blood. On the other hand, the analogy of the Gods helps souls to get clear of visible substances, and enables men to conceive a sort of spiritual substance, common to souls and Gods, a supersensible vital fluid, or gas, which is not to be completely identified with any visible or tangible form of body. This subtle and mobile stuff, considered as both animate and divine—endowed, that is to say, with all the properties that are held to belong to Soul and God—is what the Milesians called *physis*.

74. *Philosophy as the analysis of religious material*

In our survey of Greek speculation, we shall try to show that the various systems are deduced from the properties inherent from the outset in this primary datum of philosophy. The philosophers, one and all, speculated about the ' nature of things,' *physis* ; and the *physis* about which they speculate is nothing but this animate and divine substance. The several schools attach themselves to one or another of the attributes of the primitive complex, which they emphasise to the ultimate exclusion of the rest, or interpret in various senses, thus reaching highly diverse conclusions about the nature of things. But they hardly seem to travel outside the content of their original datum. Rather they seem merely to sift and refine the material it gives them, distinguishing factors in it which at first were confused, and, in that progress toward clearness and complexity, discovering latent contradictions and antinomies, which force

---

[1] Gods like the sun and stars have of course visible bodies, but they too are helped to get clear of them by the anthropomorphic Gods.

them to accept one alternative and reject another. The work of philosophy thus appears as the elucidation and clarifying of religious, or even pre-religious, material. It does not create its new conceptual tools ; it rather discovers them by ever subtler analysis and closer definition of the elements confused in its original datum.

From another point of view, which will be clear from what has gone before, philosophy rediscovers in the world that very scheme of representation which had, by a necessary process, been projected into the world from the structure and institutions of society in its earlier stages of development. The concepts and categories which the intellect brings with it to its task, are precisely those by which the chaos of phenomena had long ago been coordinated and organised into the significant outlines of a cosmos. No wonder that they seem to fit their object with a sort of pre-established harmony. The philosophers may be compared to the medieval scholastics, who were delighted to find that Christian theology could be reconciled with Aristotelianism, not realising that almost the whole of that theology had originally come from the schools of Plato and Aristotle. This accounts for the confident and successful tone in which the first philosophers unhesitatingly declare their vision of those ultimate things which many prophets and kings of thought, since their days, have desired to see and have not seen. It accounts, too, for the *a priori* methods of early science : in following the lines of its own concatenations of concepts, it is *ipso facto* tracing the framework of the world.

After all, when we consider what it is that is presented to the philosopher for his study, it is not the real world of things, as it may be supposed to exist in objective independence of human consciousness. It is from the first a representation, to which the subject, as well as the object, contributes its quota. And it is, of course, true that this representation does not consist of a series of uncoordinated sense-impressions—the fleeting pageant of particular colours and sounds and tastes and muscular feelings, immediately presented in the life of sensation from moment to moment. It is, on the contrary, a persistent whole, unified and organised by conception. Though each of us lives imprisoned in a world of his own, centred about his own consciousness, with sensations, feelings, and images which exist in no other brain but his, we are convinced that all these worlds somehow fit together into one and the same world, and all possibility of communication rests on the truth of that conviction. It is this common world that the philosophies seek to account for and explain ; and, as we have tried to show, what at first seems most significant in that cosmos is of religious, and therefore of social, origin—a product, not of individual invention, but of collective mentality. When the individual intellect gets to work upon it in what is called philosophic speculation, it hardly succeeds in introducing any new conceptions, but merely analyses the content of its datum, and deduces from it diverging systems.[1]

75. *Physis as Substance, Soul, Divine*

In order to establish our point, that Greek philosophy, in its theories of the ' nature of things,' does not travel outside the elementary factors contained in the primary datum which it inherited from religion, we must first try to distinguish these elementary factors by a somewhat clearer analysis. When the Ionians said that the *physis* of things was water or air or fire, what did they mean by the subject of these propositions ? What was the content of that ultimate thing which they variously identified with one or another of the sensible elements ?

The gist of the whole matter is contained in those three doctrines of Thales which we have already quoted : (1) the nature of things is water ; (2) the all is alive (has *soul* in it) ; and (3) is full of *daemons* or *Gods*.

(1) The first of these propositions has been allowed to eclipse the second and third, for no other reason than that it happened to be the one which interested Aristotle, from whose school our doxographic tradition is derived. Modern historians of Greek philosophy are, of course, aware that Aristotle's review

---

[1] It is, I hope, clear that I am speaking only of the theories put forward about the nature or ultimate constitution of the universe, not of the detailed explanations of various natural phenomena (earthquakes, thunder, meteors, etc.), which are sometimes mere guesses, sometimes deduced from *a priori* views about the structure of the world, sometimes supported by genuine observation.

of his predecessors' theories in the first book of the *Metaphysics* is based upon his own distinction of the four ' causes.' His point of view is not historical ; what interests him is to point out the process by which this distinction was reached, and so he groups the earlier thinkers according as they recognised, in his opinion, only a ' material cause,' or added to that a ' principle of motion,' and so on. Governed by this scheme, he ranks the primary substance of the Milesians under the head of ' material cause,' defined as ' that of which all things consist, from which they are originally generated, and into which they are finally dissolved, its substance persisting, though its attributes change.' The modern historians, though aware of Aristotle's unhistorical methods, generally accept the emphasis thus thrown on the ' material ' properties of *physis*, as a continuous and homogeneous stuff, filling space. We shall not further discuss this side of *physis*, because it is already overemphasised. What we have to make clear is that the other properties attributed to *physis* under the names ' Soul ' and ' God ' are of at least equal importance. It is, as we shall see, the differences of opinion as to what these properties imply that give rise to the main divergences between the various philosophic schools.

(2) The second proposition of Thales declares that the All is alive, or has Soul in it (τὸ πᾶν ἔμψυχον). This statement accounts for the mobility of *physis*. Its motion, and its power of generating things other than itself, are due to its life (ψυχή), an inward, spontaneous principle of activity.[1] So misleading is Aristotle's suggestion that the Milesians did not recognise a ' principle of motion.'

Further, this Soul in the universe is identical with *physis* itself. In other words, the materiality of *physis* is supersensible, a stuff of that attenuated sort which is attributed to all supersensible objects—souls, spirits, Gods—as well as to all sorts of *eidola*, ghosts, concepts, images, etc.[2] It is soul-substance,

---

[1] Cf. Plato, *Laws*, 892c : φύσιν βούλονται λέγειν γένεσιν τὴν περὶ τὰ πρῶτα· εἰ δὲ φανήσεται ψυχὴ πρῶτον, οὐ πῦρ οὐδὲ ἀήρ, ψυχὴ δ' ἐν πρώτοις γεγενημένη, σχεδὸν ὀρθότατα λέγοιτ' ἂν εἶναι διαφερόντως φύσει.

[2] On this subject see the valuable articles of P. Beck, ' Erkenntnisstheorie des primitiven Denkens,' *Zeitschr. f. Phil. u. phil. Kritik*, Leipzig, 1904, bd. 123, p. 172 ff. and bd. 124, p. 9 ff.

not 'body,' differing from body in being intangible and invisible. The water or air or fire in which it is recognised is related to it as body to soul; these elements are embodiments of *physis*, but *physis* itself is soul, with a supersensible substance of its own—that minimum of materiality without which nothing could be conceived. That is one reason why none of the Ionians identified the nature of things with the fourth element, earth. Earth is pre-eminently ' bodily '—tangible, heavy, immobile— and so least suited to be the vehicle of the living soul-substance. We understand also why the philosophers do not go on to investigate the natural properties of water or air or fire; these are mere gross vehicles of the primary soul-substance upon which their attention is fixed. The object of their speculation is thus from the first a supersensible, metaphysical entity, or in other words a representation, which moreover, as we have seen, is of mythical origin.

(3) Finally, this soul-substance is declared to be ' divine ' (τὸ θεῖον): the All, says Thales, is full of daemons or Gods. This predicate preserves the attribute of superhuman force or *mana*, which was contained in the notion of the magical continuum, and gave rise to the twin representations of Soul and God. We saw in the last chapter that Greek religion included two contrary notions of the divine and of its relations to man and nature—the Mystic notion and the Olympian. The divinity of *physis* thus contains the germ of a latent contradiction, the discovery of which will constitute a dilemma for philosophy.

In the following sections we shall establish in detail this summary statement about the content of *physis*.

76. *Physis as Soul*

It is a general rule that the Greek philosophers describe *physis* as standing in the same relation to the universe as soul does to body. Anaximenes,[1] the third Milesian, says : ' As

---

[1] Frag. 2: οἷον ἡ ψυχὴ ἡ ἡμετέρα ἀὴρ οὖσα συγκρατεῖ ἡμᾶς, καὶ ὅλον τὸν κόσμον πνεῦμα καὶ ἀὴρ περιέχει. Compare Pythagoras' 'boundless breath' outside the heavens, which is inhaled by the world (Arist. *Phys.* δ 6, 213b 22), and Heracleitus' 'divine reason,' which surrounds (περιέχει) us and which we draw in by means of respiration (Sext. Emp. *Adv. Math.* vii. 127). See Burnet, *E. G. P.*², pp. 79, 120, 170, and Eisler, *Weltenmantel*, ii. 749.

our soul is air and holds us together, so a breath or air embraces the whole cosmos.' Aristotle remarks that ' there are some, too, who say that soul is interspersed throughout the universe : which is perhaps why Thales supposed all things to be full of Gods. But this view presents some difficulties. For why should the soul not produce an animal, when present in air or fire, and yet do so when present in a compound of these elements ; and that too, though in the former case it is believed to be purer ? One might also inquire why the soul present in air is purer and more immortal than soul in animals. Whichever of the two suppositions open to us we adopt, is absurd and irrational. To speak of fire or air as an animal is very irrational ; and, on the other hand, not to call them animals is absurd. But it would seem that the reason why they suppose soul to be in these elements is that the whole is homogeneous with its parts. So that they cannot help regarding universal soul as also homogeneous with the parts of it in animals, since it is through something of the surrounding element (τοῦ περιέχοντος) being cut off and enclosed in animals that the animals become endowed with soul. But if the air when split up remains homogeneous, and yet soul is divisible into non-homogeneous parts, it is clear that although one part of soul may be present in the air, there is another part which is not. Either, then, soul must be homogeneous, or else it cannot be present in every part of the universe.' [1]

Through the dry and obscure argumentation of Aristotle shines the primitive conception of soul-substance, as a material continuum charged with vital force, interfused through all things, or ' cut off and enclosed ' in various living creatures.

---

[1] *De anim.* a v. 17 ff. The case of the Indian *âtman* appears to be exactly parallel to that of *physis* and the individual soul in Greece. The oldest Upanishads recognise only one soul: 'It is thy soul, which is within all.' ' He who, while dwelling in the earth, the water, the fire, in space, wind, heaven, sun, etc., is distinct from them, whose body they are, who rules them all from within, "he is thy soul, the inner guide, the immortal." . . . This *âtman* who alone exists is the knowing subject in us . . . and with the knowledge of the *âtman*, therefore, all is known. . . . The *âtman* created the universe and then entered into it as soul,' and this gives rise to the later conception of individual souls, imprisoned in the eternal round of *samsâra* and needing deliverance. See Deussen, *Relig. and Philos. of India, Upanishads*, Eng. trans. 1906, p. 257.

'Soul' and *physis* are not merely analogous, but identical. The two conceptions—Soul, and ultimate matter—are as yet fused in one, just as we found that at a certain stage *mana* and the blood-soul were fused in the magical continuum. The later differentiation of the two conceptions will bring out one of the latent contradictions which divide the philosophic schools. As the properties of life come to be distinguished from those of inanimate matter, philosophers will have to make their choice between conceiving the ultimate reality as mind or as matter, as living or as dead. Whichever choice they make, the nature of Soul will still be the same as that of *physis*.

77. *Soul as Moving*

In reviewing the psychological doctrines of the earlier schools, Aristotle remarks: 'There are two points especially wherein that which is animate is held to differ from that which is inanimate, namely motion and the act of sensation (or perception): and these are, speaking in general, the two characteristics of soul handed down to us by our predecessors' (*de anim. a* 2, 2).

The two vital functions of moving and knowing were much less clearly distinguished by the early philosophers than by Aristotle. With regard to the first of them—motion—the primitive assumption is that whatever is capable of moving itself or anything else, is alive—that the only moving force in the world is Life, or rather soul-substance.[1] The existence of motion in the universe is thus an immediate proof of Thales' doctrine: 'The All has soul in it.' Aetius [2] describes the doctrine as follows: 'There extends throughout the elemental moisture (Thales' *physis*) a divine power capable of moving it.' This divine or magical power is the same as that 'soul' which Thales ascribed to the loadstone, because it moves iron.[3] Aetius, a late writer, distinguishes more clearly than Thales could have

---

[1] Plato at the end of his life reasserts this doctrine, defining 'soul' as 'that which is capable of moving itself' (*Laws*, 896 A), and deducing the conclusion that the heavenly bodies have souls and 'all things are full of Gods' (θεῶν εἶναι πλήρη πάντα), as Thales said (899 B). Cf. Arist. *Phys.* 265*b* 32.

[2] Aet. i. 7. 11 : τὸ δὲ πᾶν ἔμψυχον ἅμα καὶ δαιμόνων πλῆρες· διήκειν δὲ διὰ τοῦ στοιχειώδους ὑγροῦ δύναμιν θείαν κινητικὴν αὐτοῦ. In Diog. L. ix. 7, πάντα ψυχῶν εἶναι καὶ δαιμόνων πλήρη is attributed to Heracleitus. Cf. also Sext. *Math.* ix. 76.   [3] Arist. *de anima*, a ii. 14.

done, between the ' elemental moisture ' and the divine power pervading it. For Thales the moving soul was the same as the ultimate element, recognised in water, which pervades all things. The same holds of the ' ever-living fire ' of Heracleitus.

At first, then, mechanical motion was not distinguished from vital activity. Once more we shall reach a parting of the ways when the distinction comes to be drawn ; and before the two are recognised as independent and coordinate facts, science will go to the opposite extreme, and, instead of interpreting all motion as the spontaneous, internal activity of *physis*, will try the expedient of levelling down life to external mechanical motion, communicated by colliding particles of dead matter.

78. *Soul as Knowing*

The second function of Soul—knowing—was not at first distinguished from motion. Aristotle [1] says, ' The soul is said to feel pain and joy, confidence and fear, and again to be angry, to perceive, and to think ; and all these states are held to be movements, which might lead one to suppose that soul itself is moved.' Sense-perception ($a \emph{i} \sigma \theta \eta \sigma \iota \varsigma$), not distinguished from thought, was taken as the type of all cognition, and this is a form of action at a distance. [2] All such action, moreover, was held to require a continuous vehicle or medium, uniting the soul which knows to the object which is known. Further, the soul and its object must not only be thus linked in physical contact, but they must be *alike* or *akin*.

The early philosophers, almost or quite unanimously, [3] assumed the maxim that ' like knows like,' which is a special case of the more general axiom : ' Like can only act on like.' [4] Here again

---

[1] *De anim.* a4, 408b 1.

[2] *De anim.* a5, 410a 25, Those who make soul consist of all the elements, and hold that like perceives and knows like, 'assume that perceiving is a sort of being acted upon or moved ($\pi \acute{a} \sigma \chi \epsilon \iota \nu \ \tau \iota \ \kappa a \grave{\iota} \ \kappa \iota \nu \epsilon \hat{\iota} \sigma \theta a \iota$), and that the same is true of thinking and knowing.'

[3] Heidel, *Arch. Gesch. Phil.* xix. 357, disputes Aristotle's and Theophrastus' exceptions to this rule.

[4] Another application of this maxim, 'Like *attracts* like,' is assumed by the philosophers down to Plato, and this assumption makes them to explain weight and lightness by the tendency of all bodies to move towards their ' *kindred*'—$\mathring{\eta} \ \pi \rho \grave{o} \varsigma \ \tau \grave{o} \ \sigma \upsilon \gamma \gamma \epsilon \nu \grave{\epsilon} \varsigma \ \acute{o} \delta \acute{o} \varsigma$, Plato, *Tim.* 63 E ; cf. Burnet, *E.G.P.*[2], p. 396.

we encounter a by no means obvious principle, which is surely not drawn from experience, but accepted from collective representation. The formula which states that this action can only take place between ' like ' objects, is derived from that old magical doctrine which grouped things into classes of kindred, united by a sympathetic continuum. This continuum is, as we have seen, a pervasive ' soul ' running through all the class. It is the vehicle and medium of motion and interaction of all kinds, and so of that special kind of action called ' knowing ' or ' perceiving,' which is an attribute of Soul. The maxim had become embedded in common sense, and was accepted without question by the philosophers.

It follows from this principle that, if the Soul is to know the world, the world must ultimately consist of the same substance as Soul. *Physis* and Soul must be homogeneous. Aristotle formulates the doctrine with great precision :

' Those who laid stress on its knowledge and perception of all that exists, identified the soul with the ultimate principles, whether they recognised a plurality of these or only one. Thus, Empedocles compounded soul out of all the elements, while at the same time regarding each one of them as a soul. His words are " With earth we see earth, with water water, with air bright air, ravaging fire by fire, love by love, and strife by gruesome strife." In the same manner Plato in the *Timaeus* constructs the soul out of the elements. Like, he there maintains, is known by like, and the things we know are composed of the ultimate principles. . . .

' Thus those thinkers who admit only one cause and one element, as fire or air, assume the soul also to be one element ; while those who admit a plurality of principles assume plurality also in the soul. . . . Those who introduce pairs of opposites among their principles make the soul also to consist of opposites ; while those who take one or other of the two opposites, hot or cold, etc., reduce the soul also to one or other of them.' [1]

So, again, Aristotle tells us elsewhere that ' Diogenes of Apollonia, like some others, identified air with soul. Air, they thought, is made up of the finest particles, and is the first principle ; and

[1] *De anima*, a 2, §§ 2, 6, 21.

this explains the fact that the soul knows and is a cause of motion, *knowing by virtue of being the primary element from which all else is derived*, and causing motion by the extreme fineness of its parts.'[1]

Aristotle himself, though he refined upon the doctrine that 'like knows like,' by maintaining that perception involves a process of assimilation, is really at one with previous thinkers. ' At the basis of his whole theory of perception there is for him, as for his predecessors, the thought that the fundamental community of elementary constitution in αἰσθητά (sense-objects) and αἰσθητήρια (sense-organs) is the cause of our being able to perceive objects. The ἀλλοίωσις (*i.e.* the process of assimilation), by which he reconciles these different views (that " like knows like," and " like knows unlike ") implies in every case a medium by, as well as through, which αἰσθητά and αἰσθητήρια are brought into correlation. For this medium has a common nature with' both.[2]

Thus, the possibility alike of motion and of knowledge is explained by the Greek philosophers by means of a conception of *physis* as soul-substance, in which all the chief characteristics of the sympathetic continuum of magic are reproduced. The main proof that the philosophic conception is lineally descended from the magical one is the otherwise gratuitous and inexplicable assumption that ' Like can only act on, or know, like.' We can understand this assumption only when we know that the sympathetic continuum was originally the substrate of kinship; that it was the vehicle of interaction only within a group of the same kin ; and that kinship is the primitive form of all ' likeness.'

79. *Physis as the Divine*

Now that we have identified *physis* with that primitive substance out of which, by processes traced in the last chapter, all the divinities of Greek religion took shape, we are prepared to find that the early philosophers call *physis* the ' divine.' The All is not only alive, but full of daemons. Thales' Water is

---

[1] Arist. *de anim.* a ii. 15, 405 a 21. Diog. Apoll. frag. 4 : ἄνθρωποι γὰρ καὶ τὰ ἄλλα ζῷα ἀναπνέοντα ζώει τῷ ἀέρι. καὶ τοῦτο αὐτοῖς καὶ ψυχή ἐστι καὶ νόησις. . . . καὶ ἐὰν τοῦτο ἀπαλλαχθῇ, ἀποθνήσκει καὶ ἡ νόησις ἐπιλείπει.

[2] I. Beare, *Greek Theories of Elementary Cognition*, p. 237.

' pervaded by a *divine* power capable of moving it ' ; in other words, the soul-substance possesses a superhuman *mana*, a daemonic energy, distinct from the natural properties of water. Of the ' limitless ' of Anaximander Aristotle [1] says that it is ' the divine (τὸ θεῖον), immortal and imperishable.' The Air of Anaximenes, similarly, is spoken of as a God. Diogenes of Apollonia says of the same element that ' what men call air is that which possesses thought, and it directs all and masters all ; for just this is, I believe, God, and it reaches everywhere and disposes all things and is in everything.' [2]

Speaking of the heavenly bodies, Aristotle [3] says : ' Our forefathers in the remote ages have handed down to us a tradition in mythical form, that these substances (the firmament and the heavenly bodies) are Gods, and that the divine encloses the whole of nature (περιέχει τὸ θεῖον τὴν ὅλην φύσιν). The rest of the tradition has been added later in mythical form, to persuade the multitude and for its utility with respect to the laws and expediency : they say the Gods are of human form, or like the other animals, and so on. But, if we separate the original point from these additions, and take it alone — that they thought the primary substances to be Gods, we might regard this as an utterance divinely inspired (θείως εἰρῆσθαι), and reflect that, while probably every art and science has often been developed as far as possible and perished again, these opinions have been preserved until the present, like relics of the ancient treasure.'

The importance of this attribute, ' divine,' as applied to the primary *physis* is overlooked by historians of philosophy ; yet it can hardly be over-emphasised. Philosophy is the immediate successor of theology, and the conceptions held by philosophers of the relation between the ultimate reality and the manifold sense-world are governed by older religious conceptions of the relation between God and the human group or Nature. The main purpose of the rest of this book will be to substantiate this statement. We shall try to show that there are two main currents in Greek philosophy which severally take their departure from those two types of religion—mystical and Olympian—which we distinguished at the end of the last

[1] *Phys.* γ 4, 203b 12.   [2] Frag. 5.   [3] *Met.* Λ 8, 1074b 1.

chapter. It was not for nothing that metaphysics was still called ' theology ' as late as the time of Aristotle.[1]

80. *The treatment of Physis by the philosophers*

We have argued above that when the earliest philosophers talked about *physis*, and declared that it was to be found in water, or air, or whatever it might be, the subject of these propositions—*physis* itself—was a soul-substance, a supersensible and yet material thing, which was embodied in this or that element, rather than identified with it (though on this point our information is, naturally, not always clear). We know that they regarded it as God and Soul ; and Gods and Souls have a material of their own, an extended but intangible substance, which is distinct from the tangible and visible ' body ' in which they may reside. This supersensible extended substance was, of course, from the first and always, not a natural object ; although it was called ' Nature,' it was really metaphysical—a representation whose mythical origin we have traced. Considered as matter, apart from its life, it differs from (say) the ether of modern physics chiefly in that it was not recognised to be a merely hypothetical substance, but believed to be actually existent.[2] Really, it was an entity of the same order as ether, and it was regarded in the same way as amenable to *a priori* mathematical treatment. You could take one or another of its recognised properties and deduce the consequences. Thus, the Eleatics emphasised its unity and perfect continuity to

---

[1] For the divinity of the elements see Eisler, *Weltenmantel*, ii. 664 ; O. Gilbert, ' Spekulation u. Volksglaube in der ionischen Philosophie,' *Arch. f. Relig.* xiii. 306 ff., and *Arch. f. Gesch d. Philos.* xxii. 279 : *die ganze ionische und eleatische, nicht minder auch die Pythagoreische Spekulation ist nicht als ein Suchen nach der Gottheit, d. h. nach der die Weltentwicklung bedingenden und tragenden Gottessubstanz.*

[2] It will be remembered that Dr. Frazer writes : ' Both branches of magic, the homœopathic and the contagious, may conveniently be comprehended under the general name of Sympathetic Magic, since both assume that things act on each other at a distance through a secret sympathy, the impulse being transmitted from the one to the other by means of what we may conceive as a sort of invisible ether, not unlike that which, I understand, is postulated by modern science for a precisely similar purpose— namely, to explain how things can physically affect each other through a space which appears to be empty' (*Lectures on the Early History of the Kingship*, 1905, p. 40).

such a point that they were driven to deny it any possibility of internal motion. This drove the Atomists to suppose that the substance consisted, not of one atom, but of an infinite number, and so they restored the possibility of motion. Now, in this procedure the Atomists were behaving exactly as a modern man of science would do, remodelling the hypothetical substance to 'save appearances'; only, the Atomists thought their atoms were real. The Eleatic Parmenides, on the other hand, starts, not from a scientific supposition, but from a religious belief—a passionate conviction that the real being, which is God, must be One. This conviction is the ultimate premiss of Eleaticism; it is a pure matter of religious faith, for which no reason was, or could be, given. Our present point is that the thing which Parmenides declared to be one, because it was God, was in origin the same thing as that which the Atomists declared to be innumerably many, because, having no prejudice in favour of monotheism, they did not object to plurality, and plurality had the scientific advantage of saving the obvious fact of motion from one part of space to another. The ' Being ' of both systems had the same properties : it was homogeneous soul-substance, diffused in space. The real question between them is whether the ' divinity,' which had all along been ascribed to this Being, implied ' unity,' in a sense that condemned all plurality and motion to be unreal, or merely implied immutability —a property which a polytheistic tradition could ascribe to material atoms without sacrificing plurality and motion. When we look at Atomism in this light, we see that although it goes the whole way to the extreme of ' materialism,' the properties of immutability and impenetrability ascribed to atoms are the last degenerate forms of divine attributes.

In fine, the various schools treat this substance in an *a priori* way, as if it were a mere scientific hypothesis ; but they all alike believe that they are speculating about an actually existing ultimate reality. The reason why they do not realise its hypothetical character is precisely that it was not invented by any of them, but taken over from pre-philosophic religious representation. Above all, the point on which we would insist is that the principal object of Greek speculation is not external nature as revealed through the senses, but a metaphysical representation of reality as a supersensible extended substance, which is at first both alive (Soul) and divine (Gôd), and also has a ' matter ' of its own, distinct, or distinguishable, from visible and tangible 'body' with its sensible properties. The problem, all along, was : given that reality is a substance of this sort, how can it be related to the sense-world ; how can it be adapted and remodelled so as to account for what we perceive ; how can we get out of it the world we see around us ?

81. *The causes of philosophic systems*

Our contention, then, is that, in accounting for the dogmatic systems of the first philosophers, who had nothing but theology behind them, the two main causes are to be found in two op-posed schemes of religious representation, and in the tempera-ments of the individual philosophers, which made one or other of those schemes the more congenial to them. As compared with these two causes, those questions of the ' influence ' of one system or another, so fully discussed by historians, are of secon-dary importance. One philosopher is influenced by another chiefly because his temperament predisposes him to a view which happens either to agree or to disagree with the other's. The form his reasonings take will, of course, be largely governed by the fact that he will develop his views mainly in antagonism to views which he detests. But this form is superficial, and often misleading. It will rarely represent any train of thought which really set him on the way to his conclusion. Almost all philosophic arguments are invented afterwards, to recommend, or defend from attack, conclusions which the philosopher was from the outset bent upon believing, before he could think of any arguments at all. That is why philosophical reasonings are so bad, so artificial, and so unconvincing. To mistake them for the causes which led to a belief in the conclusion, is generally to fall into a naive error. The charm of the early Greek philosophers lies in the fact that, to a large extent, they did not trouble to invent bad arguments at all, but simply stated their beliefs dogmatically. They produced a system as an artist produces a work of art. Their attitude was : ' That is how the world is to be ' ; and the system itself, as distinct from any arguments that may be constructed to buttress the fabric, is thrown out, like a statue or a poem, as the expression of some thought or emotion that lies within and will have utterance.

We shall, therefore, in what follows, say little of the influence of one system on another ; questions of that sort must, of course, be answered, but they have been excellently treated in the histories. It is, also, of little use to discuss the temperaments of individual thinkers, for the simple reason that in most cases we know nothing whatever of their temperaments, except that they must have been such as to lead them to this or that type of system. What remains, then, is the systems themselves, taken as coherent wholes, as typical schemes of representation, or possible ways of conceiving the world. We shall try to show that they can be better understood when we group them in two lines of tendency,[1] which originate in the two types of religious system above distinguished.

82. *The Scientific Tendency : explanations and causes*

It is now, perhaps, generally agreed that science has its principal root in magical art. Behind the systems of representation which science elaborates and remodels, lies the practical impulse which drives man to extend his power over Nature, an impulse which found its first collective expression in magic. In order to explain the characteristics of the scientific tendency in Greek speculation, we must, therefore, recur to certain features of magical practice which have already been described.

Sympathetic magic consists in the representation of the object of passionate desire. Primarily, this representation is mimetic —in other words, the realisation of the desired end in dramatic action. The emotion is satisfied by actually doing the thing which is willed. Besides this, there is also the verbal expression of the same emotion and desire—the element of myth, which at first is simply the statement of what is being done and willed.[2] At a later stage, the myth becomes ' aetiological,' that is to say,

---

[1] Cf. Diog. L. proem. 13, φιλοσοφίας δὲ δύο γεγόνασιν ἀρχαί, ἥ τε ἀπὸ Ἀναξιμάνδρου καὶ ἡ ἀπὸ Πυθαγόρου.

[2] For this view of Myth, see J. E. Harrison, *Themis*, p. 327.

a description of the action, alleged as an explanation of it ; but the content of the myth remains, as before, a transcript or representation of the action itself. The mimetic action and the verbal expression are thus, at first, only two modes in which the same desire finds vent and satisfaction.

In the earliest stage, we have supposed that the dramatic action and the desired effect are not distinguished. The rain-maker feels simply that he is making rain, not that he is imitating the fall of rain, in order to cause real rain to fall subsequently. When the faith in magic begins to weaken, some distinction must begin to arise between the mimetic action and the natural event ; some notion of *causality* makes its first appearance. This is a critical moment in the pre-history of science. It is of cardinal importance to grasp the form under which the relation of cause and effect was originally represented.

Now, the fundamental fact about the class of causes and effects which we are considering—a class which, from their social importance, will pre-eminently be the centre of attention —is that they are *alike*, since sympathetic magic produces its effects by imitation. In the second place, all likeness, as we have seen, is interpreted as kinship or membership of the same group. Finally, all kinship is represented by means of a material substrate or continuum, co-extensive with the group, and the medium of sympathetic interaction within it. On this basis, the emphasis is thrown entirely on the likeness, kinship, and material continuity of the two events, not on their temporal succession. The first notion of causality is, thus, not temporal but static, simultaneous, and spatial.[1] Magic, then, is not at all concerned with the order of time, but solely with classification. Its nascent science is occupied with more and more elaborate schemes, in which all objects are ranged in groups of kindred—clans of things which, being united by sympathetic continuity, can interact on one another. Its framework is not temporal, but spatial; it traces the boundaries of *moirai*.

---

[1] This is confirmed by the study of primitive languages. Lévy-Bruhl (*Fonct. ment.* p. 165) quotes Gatschet (*The Klamath Language*, p. 554): ' *Les catégories de position, de situation dans l'espace, et de distance sont, dans les représentations des peuples sauvages, d'une importance aussi capitale que celles de temps et de causalité le sont pour nous.*'

At the same time, to the magician knowledge is power; the impulse which drives him is still the desire to extend the influence of his *mana* (or the *mana* of the group, for the whole process is collective) to its utmost bounds. To form a representation of the structure of Nature is to have control over it.[1] To classify things is to name them, and the name of a thing, or of a group of things, is its soul; to know their names is to have power over their souls. Language, that stupendous product of the collective mind, is a duplicate, a shadow-soul, of the whole structure of reality; it is the most effective and comprehensive tool of human power, for nothing, whether human or superhuman, is beyond its reach. Speech is the *Logos*, which stands to the universe in the same relation as the myth to the ritual action: it is a descriptive chart of the whole surface of the real.

Early science seeks an intelligible representation or account (*logos*) of the world, rather than laws of the sequence of causes and effects in time—a *logos* to take the place of *mythoi*. We have spoken of the aetiological myth as the transcript in verbal expression of the ritual performed. Such a verbal equivalent was called an *aitia* or *aition*, in the sense rather of ' explanation ' than of ' cause.' It is true that the *aitia* is thrown into the past, by that curious psychological process which transformed the aorist tense (' this *is* done ') into the past (' this *was* done ');[2] but the *aitia* remains rather a *representation* of the significance of the rite than a mere historical account of its first enactment. Similarly, early science does not always clearly distinguish between explanatory representations and processes of genesis. It wavers between cosmogony and cosmology, easily reversing its own process of analysis, in taking the world to pieces, into a process by which it supposes that the world first arose. Thus, even when it appears to be describing how the universe came

---

[1] As late as Anaxagoras we shall find that Mind *masters* (κρατεῖ) the world because it *knows* it; 'for knowing defines and determines what is known' (Simpl. *de Caelo*, 608, ἡ γὰρ γνῶσις ὁρίζει καὶ περατοῖ τὸ γνωσθέν, *D.F.V.*[2], p. 329). For this conception of the work of the intellect, see Bergson's *Evolution Créatrice*.

[2] P. Beck, ' Erkenntnissth. d. prim. Denkens,' *Zeitschr. f. Phil. u. phil. Kritik*, Leipzig, 1904, bd. 124, p. 9 ff. has some valuable remarks on this phenomenon in connection with the concept of eternity.

into being, its interest really lies in the analysis of the world as it now is—its aetiological *logos*. It is bent on the static aspect of structure, arrangement, order, rather than on the temporal questions of cause and effect which become prominent in modern science.[1]

The view that will here be put forward is that the dominant aim of early philosophy, on what we have called the scientific side, is to perfect and simplify a new tool—a conceptual model of reality, starting from the notion of *physis* above defined. The first business of the intellect, driven by the impulse to power, is to find its way about the world, to trace out the shapes and contours of its parts, and to frame a perfectly clear plan of the cosmos. With this intent, it will take for its point of departure that aspect of *physis* which submits to this treatment—its aspect as material substance filling space. This aspect will be emphasised to the ultimate exclusion of Soul, or Life, and of God, in so far as these conceptions contain something that defies exact analysis and measurement, for you cannot make a map of vital energy. All that will be left of God is the attribute of immutability, which can be ascribed to matter; all that will be left of Soul is mechanical motion—change of position in space. Such philosophy is governed in its progress by the ideal which it finds in the science of space-measurement, geometry;[2] and it reaches its own perfect fulfilment in Atomism.

---

[1] Plato in the *Phaedo* shows the same desire to discover a fixed, immutable structure of the 'nature of things' (the Ideal World, which is his φύσις), and insists that this supersensible *ground* (αἰτία) of the sensible world is the only 'cause' worth looking for.

[2] Geometry is known to have had a strictly practical origin in an art of social importance—the land-measurement practised by the 'cord-fasteners' (*harpedonaptai*), who marked out the divisions of the soil in Egypt after the inundations of the Nile (see Burnet, *E.G.P.*[2], p. 24). Mr. Payne remarks that geometry is the only mathematic science, beyond arithmetic, the rudiments of which are found in aboriginal America. He adds that 'the primary stimulus to measurement appears to have been the division, sub-division, and redivision of land in densely peopled districts of limited extent, such as Egypt and Babylonia, and Peru. Only in the valleys of the latter district were these conditions produced in the New World; and it is significant that the Peruvian peoples, in general less advanced than the Mexicans, excelled the latter in the practice and the proximate applications of a rudimentary geometry' (*History of the New World called America*, ii. p. 281).

83. *Ionian Science and Olympianism*

The scientific tendency is Ionian in origin : it takes its rise among that race which had shaped Homeric theology, and it is the characteristic product of the same racial temperament. We may note, too, that its birthplace, Miletus, was one of the most important centres of commerce at that time. Science and commerce are, here as elsewhere, twin products of that daring spirit of exploration and adventure which voyages over strange seas with a strictly practical object in view. Baconian science insists upon ' fruit ' in exactly the same spirit as the buccaneering admirals of the same Elizabethan age went in pursuit of gold-dust, and accidentally discovered new lands. In the same way, Thales, bent upon measuring the distance from land of ships at sea, accidentally discovered trigonometry.

It will now be clear why we regard this tendency in philosophy as succeeding to the place left vacant by Olympian theology. They are two similar products of the same temperament. Both systems of thought are governed by the notion of *Moira*—the distribution of the world into spatial provinces. Both are pluralistic,[1] rationalistic, and fatalistic in tendency. Above all, both are realistic, in the sense that is opposed to other-worldliness. Science, no matter to what heights of disinterestedness its specific emotion of curiosity may sometimes rise, remains practical from first to last, and for it all value lies in the sense-world. True, it will mistake its own conceptual model of atoms and void for the real structure of the universe, and condemn the senses because we cannot see and touch the supersensible. But its affections are never set upon this metaphysical construction ; the spectral dance of imaginary dead particles has never smitten the human soul with homesickness. The intellect must find its satisfaction in the excitement of pursuit, not in the contemplative fruition of anything it can either discover or invent.[2]

---

[1] It is noteworthy that, whereas all the philosophers of the mystical tradition (Heracleitus, Pythagoras, Xenophanes, Parmenides, Empedocles, and Plato) assert that there is only *one* cosmos, the scientific tradition (Anaximander, Anaximenes, the Atomists) admit 'innumerable worlds' (ἄπειροι κόσμοι).

[2] The description of the mystic tendency, which we contrast with the scientific, is reserved to chap. vi.

V

THE SCIENTIFIC TRADITION

84. *The course of Science*

THE aim of science, described in the last chapter, was triumphantly achieved in Atomism. The course of what we have called the scientific tendency is marked by a line of thinkers which starts from the Milesian school, and leads, through Anaxagoras,[1] to Leucippus and Democritus. These Atomists succeeded in reducing *physis* to a perfectly clear, conceptual model, such as science desires, composed of little impenetrable pieces of homogeneous 'matter,' with none but spatial properties—tiny geometrical solids, out of which all bodies, of whatever shape or size, could be built up.

85. *The Milesian School :* ANAXIMANDER

As we saw at the outset, the really important member of the Milesian school is its second head, Anaximander. The closer study of his system, from the point of view we have now reached, will start us upon the track which leads science to its goal in Atomism. We may also hope to clear up some difficulties which have hitherto obscured the interpretation of his cosmology.

Anaximander's great achievement, which stamps him as a man of genius, is the partially successful effort of thought by which he attempted to distinguish the primary *physis* from the visible elements. He isolated in conception that soul-substance which we have called the primitive datum of philo-

---

[1] Cf. Burnet, *E.G.P.*[2], p. 292, who points out that the doxographers' statement that Anaxagoras was the 'pupil' or 'companion' of Anaximenes, though not literally true, correctly describes the relation between their systems.

sophy, from the water with which Thales had confused it, and kept it clear also of fire, air, and earth. This, as we can now see, was really an effort of abstraction, which drew a line of distinction between the supersensible soul-substance and its sensible embodiments. God once more gets clear of Nature, as he had done before in the age of religion ; only not this time in the personal form which anthropomorphising theology had reduced to absurdity, but in that older impersonal form from which theology had started on its long side-track of delusion. Anaximander, putting aside the humanised shapes of divinity, rediscovers the substance which had informed those shapes. He rechristens it *physis*, because its function now is to inform and animate, not Gods, but the world we see : it is the ' nature of things.'

But, although we can see that this was simply an effort of abstraction, it was not as such that it could present itself to Anaximander. He thought he had found, not a mythical representation, which was only entitled to be considered as hypothetical, but the actually existing primitive substance. Hence, instead of isolating it only in thought, he isolates it in time, and conceives it as the first state of the world, out of which the world we see must somehow have arisen. *Physis* is not to him an hypothesis, but a ' beginning' (ἀρχή). The problem is, how to get the world out of it.

Now, owing to causes we have already traced, the most important aspect of the visible world is the departmental distribution of the four elements in their appointed *moirai*. The breaking out of this division is, accordingly, the first act of cosmology, as it had been of cosmogony. The elements are parted by a process of *separation* (ἀπόκρισις) out of the primal continuous substance. Correspondingly, the important fact about that substance is the absence of these secondary departmental limits ; it is therefore described by the negative name, 'the Limitless' (ἄπειρον)—a word which specially suggested to the Greek mind the having no beginning, middle, or end. *Physis* is thus called ' the unlimited,' primarily in contradistinction to the elemental provinces which are limited, though, as we shall soon see, this sense of the word is not distinguished from others. Here, then, we have the first two stages of exist ence, which precede the birth of individual things—the third stage.

The next question is : how to account for the passage from the first stage to the second—how do the limits of the elemental provinces ever come to be imposed ?

To answer this question, Anaximander falls back upon the moral character which had clung to *physis* ever since it had come into existence as a representation of the social consciousness, felt precisely as a power which imposes limits on individual aggression. This character, as we have seen, had never passed altogether from *Moira* to be vested in the will of the supreme deity ; and, now that the Gods have vanished, it resides in the divine soul-substance, *physis* itself, which ' not only embraces but governs all other things.' [1] This governance is moral, showing itself in the dispensation of the elemental regions. In presence of this transparently mythical conception, it is probable that the ' eternal motion,' which is said to have caused the separation, should not be understood in a purely mechanical sense. It is ' eternal ' because native to the divine, the ' immortal and imperishable ' *physis*, whose motion, like itself, must be without beginning or end ; but, since *physis* is alive, its motion is probably not distinguished from growth—the characteristic movement of life. We may perhaps think of the opposed elements as developed, or unfolded, out of the one by a process of growth not clearly distinguished from a mechanical sifting, due to the rotation of the universe—a motion which, being circular, is without beginning or end, and so limitless or ' eternal.' There is here a tangle of confusion and obscurity, which it will be the business of Anaximander's successor to unravel so far as he can. [2]

Next, since the elements were separated out of the limitless thing, their specific qualities must at first have been somehow

---

[1] Arist. *Phys.* γ 4, 203*b* 6 : καὶ περιέχειν ἅπαντα καὶ κυβερνᾶν. O. Gilbert, 'Spekulation u. Volksglaube,' *Arch. f. Relig.* xiii. p. 312 : *Damit tritt aber dem tatsächlich bestehenden Kampf- und Raubzustande der Welt eine höhere sittliche Ordnung gegenüber und diese letztere kann nur auf τὸ θεῖον schlechthin, das absolut Göttliche des ἄπειρον, zuruckgeführt werden.*

[2] Eisler (*Weltenmantel*, ii. 666) identifies Anaximander's ἄπειρον with the ' Orphic ' supreme God *Chronos* or Αἰὼν ἄπειρος. If this is right, as I incline to think, ἄπειρος would mainly mean the *unending* revolution of Time.

fused in it. Later authorities, familiar with atomistic conceptions, call Anaximander's limitless *physis* a 'mixture' ($\mu\epsilon\hat{\iota}\gamma\mu a$). Once more, it seems right to interpret the name 'limitless' in a negative way. It is *not* fire or air or water or earth, and has not the distinct and li nited properties of any or all of them. These properties must have been latent in it, or they could not have come out of it; but we must not think of the primal mixture as containing portions of them all in a chaos. In that first stage, there was no such thing as fire or air, earth or water. They were mixed, rather, as wine is mixed with water, so that you cannot say that the mixture is either wine or water, or that any part of it is only water or only wine.

Finally, the moral character of the elemental disposition is strongly marked in the doctrine already dwelt upon, that individual things owe their existence to 'injustice,' consisting in the encroachment of one element upon another. The becoming of things ($\gamma\acute{\epsilon}\nu\epsilon\sigma\iota s$) is birth, and all birth results from the mixing of opposites. Anaximander emphasises the antagonism of opposites, rather than the necessity of their union to give birth to existence. In so doing, he unconsciously revives that primitive morality which emphasises the absolute supremacy of the group over the individual, and, as against the inflexible custom of the tribe, bans all individuality and personal freedom as arrogant aggression. The elements in his scheme correspond to individuals; the moral ordinance of *physis* enjoins them to keep within their regions, exactly as *Moira*, in Olympian theology, restricted the Gods to their departments.

We need not pursue, in further detail, the evolution of the visible world. Throughout our analysis of the various systems, we shall only be concerned with views about the fundamental 'nature of things,' our purpose being to show how they can be deduced from the primitive datum of philosophy.[1]

---

[1] If I have put Anaximander at the head of the scientific tradition, I do not overlook the mystical elements in his system, for which Eisler, *Weltenmantel*, vol. ii. p. 666 ff., should be consulted. He seems to me to hold both tendencies in solution, but his immediate successors went off in the scientific direction. Empedocles, as we shall see (p. 231), when he sought to reconcile mysticism and science, went back to Anaximander.

86. ANAXIMENES

Anaximander's successor, Anaximenes, was a lesser man than his master. So far from making any advance towards the truth that Anaximander's *physis* was a hypothetical entity, he could not even keep it distinct from one of the elements, dark and cold air, or mist (ἀήρ), which, by the way, had always been regarded as the appropriate clothing of divinities (ἠέρα ἐσσάμενοι). He thus reverted to the position of Thales, merely substituting air for water as the embodiment of *physis*, and no doubt thinking that he was effecting a simplification. In another direction, however, he really took a considerable step towards that clearness of conception at which science instinctively aims. He turned his attention to that point in Anaximander's scheme where obscurity and confusion most obviously reigned—the problem, how to get the qualitatively different elements out of the indeterminate *physis*.

To Anaximenes it seemed simple to identify the soul-substance with air; for air is breath, and breath is life, or soul. ' Just as our soul, being air, holds us together, so do a breath and air encompass the whole world.' [1] Thus, the soul-substance becomes again confused with an actually existing form of matter. The advantage of this theory is that the other elemental forms can be got out of it without resorting to the conception of *Moira*, which is accordingly eliminated. Air is of the same order of existence as the other elements, not a metaphysical substance on a higher plane. Consequently, its transformation into them can be interpreted in purely quantitative terms. For Anaximander qualitative differences were ultimate; his ' Limitless ' was a perfect fusion of all qualities, which were afterwards ' separated out.' Anaximenes reduced all change and transformation to ' thickening and thinning ': the real fact which underlies what we call qualitative differences is simply difference of quantity—more or less of the same stuff in a given space.[2] To get rid of quality in this way is to make an enormous advance in simplification. Instead of the infinitely subtle gradations, and innumerable varieties, of quality—colours, sounds, tastes, and so forth—we have now only to conceive one uniform material

---

[1] Frag. 2=Aet. i. 3. 4.   [2] Cf. Burnet, *E.G.P.*[2], p. 78.

with differences of density, which are comparatively distinct and, above all, commensurable.[1]

On the other hand, it may be remarked that you do not get rid of qualities by saying they are caused by thickening and thinning; you only get rid of the trouble and difficulty of thinking about them : nor can you be said to have explained them, until you can form some notion how qualitative differences could result from changes of density. The truth seems to be that Anaximenes' theory is motived by the desire to simplify and clarify the conceptual model of the world—to explain away, rather than to explain, the confused variety which our senses show us. From this point of view, the impulse of science, perpetually allured by the ideal clearness of geometrical conceptions, is to turn away from all sensible qualities, which it has not yet learnt how to measure, and to dismiss them as secondary, and derived from the spatial properties of body.

Finally, it is really only by confusion that the air which is *physis* and soul-substance can be identified with atmospheric air or mist. The latter is obviously not identical with fire or water or earth. It exists, side by side with them, in a region of its own, and has its own peculiar properties. The air which is soul-substance, on the other hand, exists, one and the same, in all the elements alike. Atmospheric air is considered to be the primary or fundamental form of matter only because it is confused with the mythical soul-substance. If it were taken simply as a natural substance, there would be no reason whatever for calling it *primary*, rather than fire or earth or water. It is selected for this position merely because it is the one of the four elements which seemed to Anaximenes to be most like soul-substance—the most appropriate vehicle of life. It is *qua* soul-substance, not *qua* natural element, that it is called divine, or God ; and it is really on the same metaphysical plane

[1] Cf. G. Milhaud, *Les philosophes géomètres de la Grèce* (1900), p. 18 ff. Aet. i. 24. 2, brings out the point that this abandonment of quality and transformation (ἀλλοίωσις) for quantity and 'coming together and separation' leads on to Atomism : Ἐμπεδοκλῆς, Ἀναξαγόρας, Δημόκριτος, Ἐπίκουρος, καὶ πάντες ὅσοι κατὰ συναθροισμὸν τῶν λεπτομερῶν σωμάτων κοσμοποιοῦσι, συγκρίσεις μὲν καὶ διακρίσεις εἰσάγουσι, γενέσεις δὲ καὶ φθορὰς οὐ κυρίως· οὐ γὰρ κατὰ τὸ ποιὸν ἐξ ἀλλοιώσεως, κατὰ δὲ τὸ ποσὸν ἐκ συναθροισμοῦ ταύτας γίνεσθαι.

as Anaximander's *physis*. From it, we are told, Anaximenes said, ' the things that are and have been and shall be, and the Gods and things divine, took their rise, while other things come from its offspring.' [1] Thus, it is clear that, in Anaximenes' system, *physis* does not really shake off its metaphysical character. It is not a natural substance, but only confused with one, and it retains properties which belong to God and Soul.

87. EMPEDOCLES *as man of science*

Empedocles, the wonder-worker, who went about among men as an immortal God, crowned with fillets and garlands, primarily belongs to the mystical tradition, whose home was in the western Greece of lower Italy and Sicily, where he was born. The detailed study of his system must, therefore, be postponed for the present ; but he has a place also in the scientific tradition, for his exuberant genius combined the temperament of a prophet with a really scientific turn of mind, which led him so far as to illustrate his theories by experimental demonstrations. As we shall see later, he makes a brilliant attempt to combine the mystic view of the world with Ionian science, and, in so doing, he takes a step beyond the Milesians in the direction of Atomism. It is in respect of this advance only that we are here concerned with his opinions.

The Milesians were hylozoists ; *physis*, for them, still retained its original meaning of something containing a vital principle within it and capable of growth. It was both a soul-substance, living and self-moving, and yet could be identified (or confused) with a bodily element. Now, in the spontaneous, procreant movement of life there is something which defies analysis in mechanical terms, something gratuitous and unaccountable, of supreme importance to the mystical temperament, and corre-

---

[1] Hippol. *Ref.* i. 7 : ἀέρα ἄπειρον ἔφη τὴν ἀρχὴν εἶναι, ἐξ οὗ τὰ γινόμενα καὶ τὰ γεγονότα καὶ τὰ ἐσόμενα καὶ θεοὺς καὶ θεῖα γίνεσθαι, τὰ δὲ λοιπὰ ἐκ τῶν τούτου ἀπογόνων. O. Gilbert, 'Spek. u. Volksglaube,' *Arch. f. Relig.* xiii. 313, holds that the three other elements are pre-eminently meant by θεοὶ καὶ θεῖα, and correspond to Anaximander's second stage ; while τὰ λοιπά = the ὄντα of Anaximander's third stage, particular things, which are born of those offspring (ἀπόγονοι) of God, the three inferior elements.

spondingly abhorrent to a science that is bent upon making physics conform to the perfect lucidity of geometry. The unconscious aim of such science must be to get the life out of matter, and finally to eliminate life altogether from its conceptual model of the real. Empedocles, mystic though he was, and little aware of what he was doing, forwarded this aim, and so has a place in the development of the scientific tradition.

It was even partly because he was a mystic, that he was led to this advance. Mystical religion, with its doctrine of immortality, emphasises the distinction between the soul and the body in which it is temporarily imprisoned. It is, therefore, specially easy for a man of science, bred up in mysticism, to get soul-substance clear of body-substance. Partly owing to this cause, and partly because a severe logic had led Parmenides, by another track, to assert the absolute rigidity and lifelessness of real being, Empedocles distinguished two kinds of material substance—the four elements, which are bodily, and two new soul-substances, Love and Strife, which move those bodily elements mechanically from without.[1]

The social origin of these two life-forces we have already traced, and explained how they came to be inherent in *physis*, so that Empedocles could get them out of it.[2] The detailed consideration of the part they play in forming worlds must be reserved for the present. The point which concerns us here is that these two constituents into which *physis* is analysed, as self-moving fluids, provide a vehicle for motion, outside, and between, the portions of the bodily elements, which accordingly lose their own inherent life. The coming into existence of individual bodies is, therefore, now no longer a birth. There is no such thing as ' coming into being,' no vital process of growth (φύσις); only a mixing of immutable elements, and a change

---

[1] Aristotle (*Met.* A 5) says that Empedocles was the first to introduce the cause of motion in a *double* form, assuming, not a single source of motion, but a pair which are opposed to one another ; and Aristotle implies that Empedocles was led to this because he saw the necessity of a cause of good things (Love) and a cause of evil things (Strife). See below, p. 230. Aristotle clearly regards these two principles of motion as different in kind from the four bodily elements.

[2] Above, § 31.

of what is mixed.[1] And this mixing and remixing is caused, from outside, by the two animate fluids.

In our view, then, these two fluids are not on a level with the four visible or bodily elements; when Empedocles declares them to be 'equal and coeval' with the rest, he merely means that all alike are eternal and immutable. Love and Strife are two life-forces, whose function is to perform mechanically those acts of separation and recombination which, in Anaximander's system, were left to the mythical figure of *Dike*. They thus fill a gap in the mechanical model of the world, and, at the same time, leave for Atomism only the final step of depriving these vital fluids both of life and matter, and reducing them to motion in a void.

Besides this advance, Empedocles contributed to science the notion, to which he had been helped by Parmenides, that each of the four forms of body is a 'thing,' eternally distinct from each of the others, an ultimate and irreducible 'element' (στοιχεῖον). Material substances are built up out of portions of these elements, which are conjoined in various proportions in a temporary combination, but remain distinct from one another, and simply come together and separate in space. We need not dwell upon the point that this conception of elements as discontinuous masses paves the way to a complete Atomism. It eliminates that element of continuity which still survived in Anaximenes' variations of density—his processes of 'thickening and thinning,' which were to lie behind changes of quality.

Empedocles, then, is an incomplete Atomist. He has reached the fundamental principle of the Atomistic conception, by building up bodies out of distinct parts, and treating motion as communicated from outside. Motion is still confused with life, and caused by vital fluids, running between the bodily elements; but it is a great step to have got it out of body, and deposited in a distinct soul-substance. The scientific tradition lays hold of these new conceptions, leaving aside the rest of Empedocles' extraordinary system.

[1] Emped. frag. 8 :

φύσις οὐδενός ἐστιν ἁπάντων
θνητῶν, οὐδέ τις οὐλομένου θανάτοιο τελευτή,
ἀλλὰ μόνον μίξις τε διάλλαξίς τε μιγέντων
ἐστί, φύσις δ' ἐπὶ τοῖς ὀνομάζεται ἀνθρώποισιν.

88. ANAXAGORAS

Anaxagoras of Klazomenae, who first transplanted Ionian science to Athens in the Periclean age, went a step beyond Empedocles in the direction of Atomism. He put a more rigorous construction upon the principle that *what is* cannot come out of *what is not*. He is not content to say, with Empedocles, that flesh, for instance, is made of earth and water etc., mixed in a certain proportion; for that would mean that what is flesh has come out of what is not flesh.[1] That implies a birth (φύσις), a sheer coming into existence, of something which did not exist before—the very thing Empedocles had denied to be possible, when he said that all becoming was nothing but mixing, and that ' birth ' (φύσις) was a mere name.

If you take a hair and cut it in half, the two pieces are still hair; suppose you continue cutting them up into smaller and smaller pieces, the same is true—they are still bits of hair. There is no moment at which you will suddenly find them dividing into a portion of earth and a portion of fire, or whatever it may be. Thus, every bodily substance is composed of parts which are like itself, and into these it is infinitely divisible.[2] But, in spite of this infinite divisibility, Anaxagoras speaks as if there were minimal parts, which could not actually be cut into smaller ones, but are, in fact, *atoms*; for he speaks of them as ' seeds ' (σπέρματα). The four elements of Empedocles are not ultimate and irreducible : each of these masses is a collection of heterogeneous seeds. The original indiscriminate mass, out of which the order of the world arose, is a ' mixture of all seeds.' [3] We have reached the notion of a primitive disorder or chaos, which has to be sorted out into a cosmos.

Like Empedocles, Anaxagoras needs a soul-substance or animate fluid, to run through the mixture of bodies and move

---

[1] Frag. 10: πῶς γὰρ ἂν ἐκ μὴ τριχὸς γένοιτο θρὶξ καὶ σὰρξ ἐκ μὴ σαρκός; Aet. i. 3. 5.

[2] Frag. 3 : ' Of the small there is no smallest, but always a smaller,' etc.

[3] Burnet (*E.G.P.*[2], p. 307) thinks Anaxagoras probably used the word πανσπερμία. It is not our purpose to follow out the details of Anaxagoras' interesting system.

them from without. It is characteristic of Anaxagoras that his soul-substance is not emotional, like love and hate, but intellectual: he calls it Mind (*Nous*). He dwells on the fact that it *knows* everything, in a way that suggests that its power or mastery over things was due to its understanding.[1] Its task is described as 'setting things in order' ($\delta\iota\alpha\kappa\sigma\mu\epsilon\hat{\iota}\nu$), 'distinguishing,' 'separating,' 'discriminating' ($\delta\iota\acute{\alpha}\kappa\rho\iota\sigma\iota\varsigma$, $\dot{\alpha}\pi\acute{o}\kappa\rho\iota\sigma\iota\varsigma$). It is nothing but the scientific intellect itself, which has taken the world to pieces, and now is projected to the further end, and charged with the task of sorting out the heap, and reducing it again to order. With an admirable scientific economy, its action is restricted within the narrowest limits. It is invoked to start mechanical motion: body, no longer being self-moving, must receive its first motion from something which can move itself, something which is alive, a soul-substance, a *physis*. But, once the motion is started, the more we can explain the structure of the world without falling back on this first cause, the better. From the scientific point of view, Anaxagoras' great merit lies in this economy, of which Socrates in the *Phaedo* (98 B) so bitterly complains. Socrates would have had Anaxagoras use his *Nous* at every turn, and explain every cosmic arrangement by showing how it was *best* that it should be so and not otherwise, making *Nous* a benevolent God, who designs everything for the best. Some modern writers appear to sympathise with Socrates, as if they were unaware that the progress of science demanded that, so far from endowing this mythical soul-substance with additional attributes, such as benevolence, it should be deprived even of intelligence and life and reduced simply to motion. A purely mechanical explanation of the world must be tried, before it is found wanting; and we ought rather to be thankful to Anaxagoras for refraining (if it ever occurred to him) from setting up a mythical teleology, and 'explaining' the known by the unknown.

---

[1] Frag. 12: $\kappa\alpha\grave{\iota}$ $\gamma\nu\acute{\omega}\mu\eta\nu$ $\gamma\epsilon$ $\pi\epsilon\rho\grave{\iota}$ $\pi\alpha\nu\tau\grave{o}\varsigma$ $\pi\hat{\alpha}\sigma\alpha\nu$ $\acute{\iota}\sigma\chi\epsilon\iota$ $\kappa\alpha\grave{\iota}$ $\acute{\iota}\sigma\chi\acute{\upsilon}\epsilon\iota$ $\mu\acute{\epsilon}\gamma\iota\sigma\tau\sigma\nu$. Cf. Simpl. *de Caelo*, 608 (*D. F. V.*[2], p. 316): $\pi\acute{\alpha}\nu\tau\alpha$ $\gamma\iota\gamma\nu\acute{\omega}\sigma\kappa\epsilon\iota\nu$ $\tau\grave{o}\nu$ $\nu\sigma\hat{\upsilon}\nu$ . . . $\mathring{\eta}$ $\gamma\grave{\alpha}\rho$ $\gamma\nu\hat{\omega}\sigma\iota\varsigma$ $\acute{o}\rho\acute{\iota}\zeta\epsilon\iota$ $\kappa\alpha\grave{\iota}$ $\pi\epsilon\rho\alpha\tau\sigma\hat{\iota}$ $\tau\grave{o}$ $\gamma\nu\omega\sigma\theta\acute{\epsilon}\nu$. Nous *constitutes* the world, as the scientific intellect constitutes its representation of it, by introducing distinctions and discriminations.

89. *The Atomism of* LEUKIPPUS

The author of the Atomic theory was a Milesian, who probably migrated to Elea, and certainly was influenced by the
arguments of the Eleatics, Parmenides and Zeno.[1] But, though
these arguments helped him to form his theory, he belongs,
in our view, to the scientific tradition which had originated
at his birthplace. The common opinion, reported by Theophrastus,[2] instinctively recognised that his standpoint is really
opposed to that of the mystics. ' Leukippus of Elea, or Miletus,
(for both accounts are given of him) had associated with Parmenides in philosophy, but he did not follow the same road
with Parmenides and Xenophanes in his explanation of things,
but, as is commonly believed, the opposite one. For, whereas
they held the All to be One, immovable, without beginning,
and limited, and did not allow us so much as to search for " what
is not," Leukippus posited unlimited and ever-moving elements,
namely the atoms. He made their shapes infinite in number,
because there was no reason why they should be of one sort
rather than another, and because he saw there was an unin-
terrupted becoming and change in things. Further, he held
that *what is* (*i.e.* atoms) is no more real than *what is not* (*i.e.*
empty space), and that both alike are needed to explain the
things that come into existence : for he postulated that the
substance of the atoms was " compact," or full, and called them
what is (ὄν), saying that they move in the void, which he called
what is not (μὴ ὄν), but declared to exist just as much as
what is.'

Leukippus accepted Parmenides' doctrine, that ' out of what
is in truth one, a plurality cannot come, nor yet a unity out of
what is really many '[3] ; but here the two ways part. The
mystic, ' transgressing against sense-perception and ignoring it,
holds that he ought to follow the argument '[4] ; and the premiss
of that argument, to which, as a mystic, he must hold, is :

---

[1] For the Pythagorean number-atomism, see below, § 114.

[2] Ap. Simpl. *Phys.* 28, 4 (*D.F. V.*², p. 344).

[3] Arist. *de Gen. et Corr.* 325 a 34: (Λεύκιππος ᾠήθη) ἐκ τοῦ κατ' ἀλήθειαν ἐνὸς
οὐκ ἂν γενέσθαι πλῆθος οὐδ' ἐκ τῶν ἀληθῶς πολλῶν ἕν.

[4] *Ibid.* l. 13 (of the Eleatics): ὑπερβάντες τὴν αἴσθησιν καὶ παριδόντες αὐτὴν
ὡς τῷ λόγῳ δέον ἀκολουθεῖν, alluding to *Parm.* frag. i. 33 ff.

The All is One, namely God. To save the unity of God, he will unhesitatingly condemn the world of seeming plurality as unreal. The scientific tradition, on the other hand, is not tied to this premiss, and Leukippus can follow the argument to an opposite conclusion. He feels, with Aristotle,[1] that ' so far as arguments go, the (Eleatic) conclusion seems to follow; but if we look at facts, such opinions border on madness; for no madman is so utterly out of his senses that fire and ice seem to him one.' That is the scientific temper, which starts with sensible facts, and will not fly in the face of them to save the unity of God. Accordingly, we are told[2] that ' Leukippus thought he had a theory which would agree with sense-perception, and not do away with becoming and perishing, or motion, or the plurality of things.' *What is* consists of an infinite number of indivisible bits of matter, impenetrable, and invisible because of their smallness. These atoms differ from one another, not qualitatively at all, but only in shape and position. The whole world and all it contains is resolvable into these tiny bodies. The coming into being and perishing of all things is nothing but the aggregation or dissipation of a set of atoms, moving mechanically in the void.

Besides atoms and void, there is motion, which had once been the spontaneous activity of life or soul. The incomplete Atomists, Empedocles and Anaxagoras, had, as we have seen, made this property reside in soul-substances, distinct from the elements, and penetrating between them. But now there is nothing between the elemental atoms save empty space, which gives them room to move, without any soul-substance running through. The soul-substance accordingly disappears; it has become a superfluous hypothesis. Leukippus took the strictly scientific course of not attempting to account for motion at all.[3] Aristotle, with his theistic prejudices, complains that to dismiss the question of the origin of motion was a piece of ' slackness.' The modern reader will prefer the Atomist's attitude to Aristotle's own grotesque doctrine of the *Primum Mobile*. Leukippus declared plainly that ' nothing happens at

---

[1] Arist. *de Gen. et Corr.* 325a 17.   [2] *Ibid.* 1. 23.

[3] Arist. *Met.* A iv. 985b : περὶ δὲ κινήσεως, ὅθεν ἢ πῶς ὑπάρχει τοῖς οὖσι καὶ οὗτοι (Leukippus and Democritus) . . . ῥᾳθύμως ἀφεῖσαν.

random ; but everything for some reason and of necessity.' [1]
What the necessity was, he did not, we are told, further define.
We may recognise in this *Ananke* the figure of *Moira*, still
pre-eminent in a world from which the Gods have utterly
vanished.

The soul, too, has become, like *physis*, a mere collection of
atoms. ' Democritus affirms the soul to be a sort of fire or heat.
For the " shapes " or atoms are infinite, and those which are
spherical he declares to be fire and soul : they may be compared
with the so-called motes in the air, which are seen in sunbeams
passing through windows. The aggregate of such seeds (*panspermia*), he tells us, forms the constituent elements of the whole
of nature (and herein he agrees with Leukippus), while those of
them which are spherical form the soul, because such figures
most easily find their way through everything, and, being themselves in motion, set other things in motion.' [2] If it is true, as
Aristotle says, that Leukippus gave no account of the origin
of motion, we must not conceive this motion of the soul-atoms
as an inherent principle of spontaneous activity, but as due, like
that of other atoms, to mechanical shock and collision.[3] The
soul-atoms merely differ in that their round shape makes them
more easily movable, and so they are the first to be set in motion,
and impart the shock to other atoms of more stable figures.
At death, the atoms are dispersed ; there can be no question of
immortality. ' The Atomists assume that it is the soul which
imparts motion to animals. Hence they take respiration as
the distinctive mark of life. For, when the surrounding air
compresses bodies and tends to extrude those atoms which,
because they are never at rest themselves, impart motion to
animals, then they are reinforced from outside by the entry
of other similar atoms in respiration, which, in fact, by helping
to check compression and solidification, prevents the escape

---

[1] Frag. 2 : οὐδὲν χρῆμα μάτην γίγνεται, ἀλλὰ πάντα ἐκ λόγου τε καὶ ὑπ' ἀνάγκης.
Hippol. *Ref.* l. 12 : τίς δ' ἂν εἴη ἡ ἀνάγκη, οὐ διώρισεν.   Dieterich, *Abraxas*, 75,
compares Plato. *Tim.* 48 A : μεμιγμένη γὰρ οὖν ἡ τοῦδε τοῦ κόσμου γένεσις ἐξ
ἀνάγκης τε καὶ νοῦ συστάσεως ἐγεννήθη.

[2] Arist. *de anim.* a ii. 403b 31.

[3] Alex. in Arist. *Met.* A iv. 985b : οὗτοι (Leukippus and Democritus) γὰρ
λέγουσιν ἀλληλοτυπούσας καὶ κρουομένας πρὸς ἀλλήλας κινεῖσθαι τὰς ἀτόμους.
Arist. *de anim.* a 2, §§ 3 and 4, contrasts the Atomists with those who
describe the soul as self-moving.

of the atoms already contained in the animals; and life, so they held, continues so long as there is strength to do this.'[1]

That other function of the soul—knowing—must be similarly explained. A soul which is nothing but a group of bodily atoms can only know or perceive other groups by colliding with them, or with filmy wraiths (*deikela, eidola*) thrown off by them.[2] Such, then, is the Atomists' doctrine of knowledge : they too 'follow the argument' to its most strange conclusions. The effect is that whatever is mysterious and unintelligible in the ideas of 'soul' and of 'life' is, as completely as may be, expurgated out of existence.

We are thus left with a conceptual model of the real, in which perfect clarity of conception triumphed, and which, accordingly, held the field in science till yesterday. The Gods and the immortal soul have vanished in the dance of material particles. *Physis*, though the name may be retained, has lost all its ancient associations of growth and life. There is no such thing as 'growth'; nothing but the coming together and separating of immutable atoms. All motion had once been the inherent property of the living thing, the proper expression of its inward life. Now the life is wrung out of matter ; motion, no longer a spontaneous activity, lies not within, but between, the impenetrable atoms. Instead of life, nothing is left but the change of space relations ; and the governance of the world returns to *Ananke-Moira*.

90. *Contrast with the Mystical Tradition*

In one very important respect, the scientific tradition differs from the mystic. Ionian science supersedes theology, and goes on its own way, without drawing any fresh supply of inspiration from religion. Science, with its practical impulse, is like magic in attempting direct control over the world, whereas religion interposes between desire and its end an uncontrollable and unknowable factor—the will of a personal God. The perpetual,

---

[1] Arist. *de anim.* a 2, 3.

[2] So all senses are reduced to one—Touching ; Arist. *de Sensu*, 442 a 29 : Δημόκριτος καὶ οἱ πλεῖστοι τῶν φυσιολόγων, ὅσοι λέγουσι περὶ αἰσθήσεως, ἀτοπώτατόν τι ποιοῦσι· πάντα γὰρ τὰ αἰσθητὰ ἁπτὰ ποιοῦσι.

if unconscious, aim of science is to avoid this circuit through the unknown, and to substitute for religious representation, involving this arbitrary factor, a closed system ruled throughout by necessity. The Gods may be exiled to the intermundane spaces, or pensioned off with the honorary position of First Cause; what science cannot allow is that their incalculable action should thrust itself in between the first cause and the last effect. Thus, science turns its back on theology, and works away from it with what speed it may; it reaches, in a few rapid strides, a very simple and clear model of the structure of reality, from which the supernatural has all but disappeared.

> *Ergo uiuida uis animi peruicit, et extra*
> *processit longe flammantia moenia mundi,*
> *atque omne immensum peragrauit mente animoque,*
> *unde refert nobis uictor quid possit oriri,*
> *quid nequeat, finita potestas denique cuique*
> *quanam sit ratione atque alte terminus haerens.*
> *quare-relligio pedibus subjecta uicissim*
> *opteritur, nos exaequat uictoria caelo.*[1]

In contrast with this steady advance away from religion and theology, the mystic tradition is continuously inspired by living religious faith. The mystical systems will be best understood if we consider them, not as following one upon another in a logical deduction, but as a series of efforts to translate a certain view of life, of God, and of the soul and its destiny, into terms of a physical system. Not, of course, that these efforts are independent of one another, or unaffected by science; each profits by the failures of its predecessor, and some at least borrow the results of the scientific tradition. But the inspiration and the impulse come fresh, each time, from a form of religious faith which was kept alive in the Pythagorean communities from the days of their founder, and survived their dispersion in the latter half of the fifth century. Thus, we regard the series of systems, now to be considered, as thrown off in succession by a mystical religion, whose view of life and of the world they, each and all, attempt to formulate.

[1] Lucr. i. 72.

VI

THE MYSTICAL TRADITION

91. *The representation of Time fundamental in Mysticism*

IN the foregoing chapter, we have seen how the scientific tradition
in philosophy is dominated throughout by the concept of
spatial externality, as Olympian theology had been dominated
by the figure of *Moira*, delimiting with rigid distinction the
provinces of all individual powers, divine and human. Guided
by that concept, science culminated in geometrical Atomism,
and the reign of *Moira*, under the name of Necessity. In the
mystical tradition, to which we now turn, the concepts of Time
and Number (the measure of Time [1]) hold the same predominant
position, and the notion of Righteousness (*Dike*) replaces that
of *Moira*. In the explanation of this central fact lies the key
to the interpretation of the mystical systems. It has already
been suggested that, as science is the legitimate successor of
Olympian theology, so the mystical philosophies derive their
inspiration and their conceptual scheme from the religion of
Dionysus. Before we come to details, we must point out why
the notion of Time is fundamental in this type of religion.

We may start from the structure of the group—the organisation of the cult-society itself; for there, as we have learnt,
the origin of its typical system of representation may be

---

[1] Cf. Plato, *Timaeus*, 39 B: ἵνα δ' εἴη μέτρον ἐναργές . . . ὁ θεὸς ἀνῆψεν
. . . ὃ δὴ νῦν κεκλήκαμεν ἥλιον, ἵνα ὅτι μάλιστα εἰς ἅπαντα φαίνοι τὸν οὐρανὸν
μετάσχοι τε ἀριθμοῦ τὰ ζῷα, ὅσοις ἦν προσῆκον, μαθόντα παρὰ τῆς ταὐτοῦ καὶ
ὁμοίου περιφορᾶς. Distance in space is measurable psychologically, by ex-
penditure of strength; but time-distance can be measured only by counting
the rhythmical repetition of the same occurrence. Hence the extent of
time-consciousness depends on the extent of the number-system. See
P. Beck, 'Erkenntnisstheorie des primitiven Denkens,' *Zeitschr. f. Philos.
u. philos. Kritik*, Leipzig (1904), bd. 123, p. 172 ff.

sought.[1] The Dionysiac cult-society, we have seen, is a single self-contained group, with a common life centred in its daemon. This life is continuous in several senses.

First, in the spatial or distributive sense, the group is continuously animated by one soul or daemon, which both resides in all its members at once, and also lies beyond any one of them. Since there is only one group—one church, no matter how far asunder its members may be scattered [2]—the organisation excludes any idea of its parts being confined within impenetrable provinces; the polytheistic notion of *Moira* is absent.

Next, in a temporal sense of continuity, the life of the group, being a common life which transcends every individual, is immortal, which, to the Greek, means ' divine.' This conception gives rise to several cardinal doctrines of mysticism.

The most primitive of these is Reincarnation (*palingenesia*). The essence of this belief is that the one life of the group, or tribe, extends continuously through its dead members as well as through the living; the dead are still part of the group, in the same sense as the living. This life, which is perpetually renewed, is reborn out of that opposite state, called ' death,' into which, at the other end of its arc, it passes again. In this idea of reincarnation, still widespread among savage races, we have the first conception of a cycle of existence, a Wheel of Life, divided into two hemicycles of light and darkness, through which the one life, or soul, continuously revolves.[3]

[1] Diodorus, v. 64, 4 (*D.F.V.*[2], p. 473), preserves the statement of Ephorus that Orpheus was the pupil of the Idaean Dactyls, who were magicians (γόητες) and practised spells, initiations, and mysteries, which Orpheus first introduced into Greece. Pythagoras also was initiated in Crete by the Idaean Dactyls and at Leibethra in Thrace. These traditions mark the continuity between the Orphic cult-societies and the magical fraternities, and also the fact that Orphism revived a primitive type of religion. See J. E. Harrison, *Themis*, p. 462.

[2] Cf. Porph. *de abst.* iv. 11 (of the Essenes) : μία δὲ οὐκ ἔστιν αὐτῶν πόλις, ἀλλ' ἐν ἑκάστῃ κατοικοῦσι πολλοί, κτλ.

[3] Lévy-Bruhl, *Fonct. ment.* p. 358, points out that the sharp distinction between living and dead does not exist at a low level of mentality : a ' dead' person still lives in a certain sense, and belongs both to the living society and to the dead. (We may note that 'immortality' so conceived precedes any clear conception of death. The belief in immortality is thus partly due to a failure to grasp the nature of death. There is no need to look further for a cause of the belief.) See also Dr. W. H. R. Rivers, *The Primitive Conception of Death*, Hibbert Journal, 1912, p. 393.

How did the doctrine of rebirth come to be moralised ? Among the Orphics and Pythagoreans, we find it associated with the notions of a fall of the soul from its original divine state, a purification of the soul's sins in this life and in an underworld purgatory, and a final restoration to the heavenly mansions whence it came. As we shall see later, this group of doctrines is of fundamental importance for the understanding of the mystic philosophy, and of the systems that emerged from the Pythagorean school. It concerns us, therefore, to give some account of the process by which the old savage doctrine of reincarnation came to have this moral significance.

92. *The Cycle of Reincarnation*

We need not discuss at length the origin of the belief in reincarnation, as it exists among savages. It is, probably, a very simple matter. When the totemist is engaged in multiplying his totem-species, his whole attention is bent upon the idea of new animals, or plants, that have to be brought into existence. The image of these animals or plants before his mind must be the memory-image of those that have already existed and been eaten. Thus, what he desires to bring into existence is to him *the same thing* as what has existed already. How could he help believing that the new animals and plants are the old ones, come back again from the other world ? [1] But, however that may be, it is certain that the notion of rebirth has none of those associations with sin and retribution which we find attached to it, when it recrudesces in Orphism. How did they come there ? We are not in a position to answer this question fully. It is complicated by the view, now being put forward, that the characteristic doctrines of Orphism were derived from Persian religion, and came into Greek thought in the sixth century, when Persia was in contact with the Ionian colonies of Asia Minor. [2] About this theory we must keep an open mind. Religious ideas, as we have remarked, are easily assimilated only when there already exists an indigenous system of thought

[1] For the supersensible reality attributed to memory-images, see P. Beck, *op. cit.*

[2] This theory is advanced by Eisler, *Weltenmantel u. Himmelszelt*, vol. ii., where a great mass of evidence is adduced.

into which they readily fit. Orphism is, indubitably, a revival and reformation of Dionysiac religion. Wherever the new ideas came from, it is probable that they were not totally foreign to the existing cults. Our object must be to throw into relief the chief elements of Dionysiac belief, and to distinguish from them the later factors which can be classed as specially Orphic. It will appear that, although Orphism was sufficiently like the older worship to emerge from it, or be grafted upon it, there is a latent contradiction between the two conceptions of immortality and of the soul, which severally belong to the two systems. This contradiction will give rise to two contrasted types of mystic philosophy.

The philosophy that lay implicit in the old doctrine of reincarnation is drawn out by Socrates, when, on the day of his death, he discusses with his Pythagorean friends the mystic view of life on earth and in the other world of the unseen. He recalls ' the ancient doctrine, that souls pass out of this world to the other, and there exist, and then come back hither from the dead, and are born again.' [1] One of the arguments by which this view is supported, is that there must be a constant process of repayment (ἀνταπόδοσις), according to which a set of souls that are born must be balanced by another set that die. If they did not thus ' go round in a circle,' but the process went forward in a straight line, instead of bending round again to its starting-point, a moment would come when all would reach the same state, and becoming (γένεσις) would be at a standstill. The living are constantly going over to the dead : unless the supply is renewed by a reverse process, life would be exhausted, and all would end in death.[2]

Although Socrates refers this argument to the more general principle, that all becoming is a passing from one to the other of two opposite states, the notions involved are very simple

---

[1] Plato, Phaedo, 70 c: παλαιὸς μὲν οὖν ἔστι τις λόγος, οὗ μεμνήμεθα, ὡς εἰσὶν ἐνθένδε ἀφικόμεναι ἐκεῖ, καὶ πάλιν γε δεῦρο ἀφικνοῦνται καὶ γίγνονται ἐκ τῶν τεθνεώτων.

[2] Plato, Phaedo, 72 B : εἰ γὰρ μὴ ἀεὶ ἀνταποδιδοίη τὰ ἕτερα τοῖς ἑτέροις γιγνόμενα, ὡσπερεὶ κύκλῳ περιιόντα, ἀλλ' εὐθεῖά τις εἴη ἡ γένεσις ἐκ τοῦ ἑτέρου μόνον εἰς τὸ καταντικρὺ καὶ μὴ ἀνακάμπτοι πάλιν ἐπὶ τὸ ἕτερον μηδὲ καμπὴν ποιοῖτο, οἶσθ' ὅτι πάντα τελευτῶντα τὸ αὐτὸ σχῆμα ἂν σχοίη καὶ τὸ αὐτὸ πάθος ἂν πάθοι καὶ παύσαιτο γιγνόμενα ; . . . εἰ γὰρ ἐκ μὲν τῶν ἄλλων τὰ ζῶντα γίγνοιτο, τὰ δὲ ζῶντα θνήσκοι, τίς μηχανὴ μὴ οὐχὶ πάντα καταναλωθῆναι εἰς τὸ τεθνάναι ;

and primitive. We are to conceive a limited quantity of soul-substance,[1] which passes out of the living body into the opposite state of separation from it, and, in perpetual revolution, re-appears again in new living bodies. Soul of this sort evidently has no organic connection with the series of bodies it temporarily informs,[2] and it must be conceived as impersonal, continuous, and homogeneous. The same soul-stuff passes through an endless succession of individual forms, and their individualities leave no abiding mark upon it. Such a description goes in no respect beyond the terms in which the savage doctrine of reincarnation could be described, in that there is, so far, no trace of a moral significance, but merely the notion of a stream of living stuff, flowing perpetually in a circle.[3]

93. *Grades of Initiation*

We advance one step further, when we add to this conception of continuous life the perhaps equally primitive idea of Initiation. Rites of initiation are the way-marks upon the road of life in savage communities. We must think of the complete circle of life and death as divided into a series of grades or phases, through each of which in succession that life must pass. The transition from each phase to the next is a rite of initiation— a *rite de passage*.[4] The infant is initiated into the living world

---

[1] The interpreters who speak of a 'constant quantity' of *absolutely immaterial* 'spirit' seem to me to be using words without meaning.

[2] Arist. *de anim.* 407 b 21 : ὥσπερ ἐνδεχόμενον κατὰ τοὺς Πυθαγορικοὺς μύθους τὴν τυχοῦσαν ψυχὴν εἰς τὸ τύχον ἐνδύεσθαι σῶμα.

[3] Cf. Plutarch, *Consol. ad Apoll.* 10 (after quoting Heracleitus, frag. 78, Byw.): ὡς γὰρ ἐκ τοῦ αὐτοῦ πηλοῦ δύναταί τις πλάττων ζῷα συγχεῖν καὶ πάλιν πλάττειν καὶ συγχεῖν καὶ τοῦθ' ἓν παρ' ἓν ποιεῖν ἀδιαλείπτως, οὕτω καὶ ἡ φύσις ἐκ τῆς αὐτῆς ὕλης πάλαι μὲν τοὺς προγόνους ἡμῶν ἀνέσχεν, εἶτα συνεχεῖς αὐτοῖς ἐγέννησε τοὺς πατέρας, εἶθ' ἡμᾶς, εἶτ' ἄλλους ἐπ' ἄλλους ἀνακυκλήσει. καὶ ὁ τῆς γενέσεως πόταμος οὕτως ἐνδελεχῶς ῥέων οὔποτε στήσεται, καὶ πάλιν ὁ ἐξ ἐναντίας αὐτῷ ὁ τῆς φθορᾶς. Zeller (*Phil. d. Griech.*[5], i. p. 640), following Bernays, thinks that Plutarch derived the general drift of this whole passage from Heracleitus, including the image of the potter. Cf. O. Gilbert, *Meteor. Theor.*, 335. Lévy-Bruhl, *Fonct. ment.* p. 398 : *Quand un enfant naît, une individualité définie reparaît, ou, plus exactement, se reforme. Toute naissance est une réincarnation. . . . La naissance est donc simplement le passage d'une forme de vie à une autre, tout comme la mort.*

[4] M. van Gennep, *Rites de Passage*, p. 107, has brought out this significance of initiatory rites.

soon after its birth ;[1] the youth is initiated into full membership of the tribe on attaining manhood, and so on. Each of these rites, moreover, is a new birth, and means the acquisition of a new soul, or rather, perhaps, the growth of the soul, its expansion to include new social rights and duties. The importance of these initiations overshadows the mere physical fact of birth ; the new-born child has little or no soul, until society confers it upon him.[2] Its growth culminates in the full privileges of manhood, and then passes into its decline. As his social effectiveness drops away from him, the man's soul dwindles, until, in old age, he has sunk again to a second, soulless, childhood and is dead already, the physical death being of little moment. This conception adds to the cycle of life the idea of promotion upwards through a series of grades, culmination, and degradation on the downward curve of the arc.[3]

94. *The Cycle of all Life in Nature*

At death, the soul passes into the underworld : the lower half of the circle moves through the nether darkness. The reason is that the earth is the source of all life.[4] The plants and trees spring up out of earth ; from her, too, must come the souls of animals and men ; and hence, when they are dead, they must be stored, like seeds, in the darkness of her womb. Spring festivals, such as the *Anthesteria*, are concerned alike with the seeds which man requires for his tillage, and with the revocation of souls ;[5] for, in the spring, all life needs to be

[1] Cf. the Omaha rites of infant initiation described by Miss Alice Fletcher. See above, p. 69.

[2] Cf. Dieterich, 'Mutter Erde,' *Arch. f. Relig.* viii. 1 ff.

[3] See Lévy-Bruhl, *Fonct. ment.* p. 360, and Hertz, 'Représent. collectives de la mort,' *Année sociol.* x.

[4] Eur. frag. 415, ap. Plut. *Consol. ad Apoll.* 104 B :
κύκλος γὰρ αὐτὸς καρπίμοις τε γῆς φυτοῖς
γένει βροτῶν τε, τοῖς μὲν αὔξεται βίος,
τῶν δὲ φθίνει τε κἀκθερίζεται πάλιν.

[5] See J. E. Harrison, *Prolegomena*, chap. ii., and *Themis*, p. 289. Cf. also Plato, *Politicus*, 272 E, where the souls, before each new birth, are described as falling into the earth as *seeds*, πάσας ἑκάστης τῆς ψυχῆς τὰς

magically revived after the death of winter. In such combinations we see the basis upon which a doctrine of trans-
migration (*metensomatosis*) can easily arise. If all life is one
and sympathetically continuous, the same soul-stuff may pass
at one time into a man, at another into an animal or plant.
All alike are creatures of earth.[1] Further, the life of Nature
in the cycle of the seasons follows the same curve as the life
of man. Nature, likewise, has her phases and grades. Her
life waxes in spring, culminates in summer, and in autumn
wanes again, till her fruits decay and leave only the seed, which
must be buried in death, and lie in hope of resurrection. The
year with its two seasons of light and dark, warmth and cold,
drought and wet, corresponds to the two halves of man's life-
circle. 'All mortal things, by necessity of Nature, revolve in
a wheel of changes. . . . When they are born they grow, and
when they are grown they reach their height, and after that
they grow old, and at last perish. At one time Nature causes
them to come to their goal in her region of darkness, and then
again out of the darkness they come back into mortal form,

γενέσεις ἀποδεδωκυίας, ὅσα ἦν ἑκάστῃ προσταχθέν, τοσαῦτα εἰς γῆν σπέρματα
πεσούσης. Cf. also *Timaeus*, 42 D, where God *sows* (ἔσπειρε) the souls into
earth, moon, and the other 'instruments of time.' *Phaedo*, 83 D : ὥστε
ταχὺ πάλιν πίπτειν εἰς ἄλλο σῶμα καὶ ὥσπερ σπειρομένη ἐμφύεσθαι. It is
significant that Anaxagoras calls his primary bodies, as yet unordered by
Nous, 'seeds' (σπέρματα), and (probably) described the primitive chaos, or
mixture of these, as a *panspermia* (see p. 153), the word used of the *pot of
all seeds* offered at the spring festival of Souls and Seeds (cf. J. E. Harrison,
Themis, p. 292). Democritus used the same term (Arist. *de anim.* 404 a 4)
to denote 'the elements of all *physis*,' the spherical seeds being soul-
atoms.

  [1] Musaeus, frag. 5 (*D.F.V.*[2], p. 485) :

ὡς δ' αὔτως καὶ φύλλα φύει ζείδωρος ἄρουρα·
ἄλλα μὲν ἐν μελίῃσιν ἀποφθίνει, ἄλλα δὲ φύει·
ὡς δὲ καὶ ἀνθρώπων γενεὴ καὶ φῦλον ἑλίσσει.

Aesch. *Choeph.* 128 :

καὶ Γαῖαν αὐτήν, ἣ τὰ πάντα τίκτεται
θρέψασά τ' αὖθις τῶνδε κῦμα λαμβάνει.

Eur. frag. 757 N. :

θάπτει τε τέκνα χἄτερ' αὖ κτᾶται νέα
αὐτός τε θνῄσκει· καὶ τάδ' ἄχθονται βροτοί
εἰς γῆν φέροντες γῆν· ἀναγκαίως δ' ἔχει
βίον θερίζειν ὥστε κάρπιμον στάχυν . . .

See Dieterich, 'Mutter Erde,' *Arch. f. Relig.* viii. 1 ff. for all this
subject.

by alternation of birth and repayment of death, in the cycle wherein Nature returns upon herself.' [1]

95. *The correspondence of Works and Days*

Nor is it Nature alone that urges life along its perennial round. Man, too, must do his share ; his Works must be fitted into the cycle of Days. The *Works and Days* of Hesiod is, significantly, both a treatise on agriculture and a hand-book of morality. The primitive art of agriculture is deeply tinged with magic : [2] mimetic ritual was, at first, even more important than digging and sowing. The mere practical operations will not be effective, unless there is a sympathetic correspondence between man's ways and Nature's course. He must keep straight upon the path of custom (*nomos*) or right (*dike*), or else the answering processes of natural life will likewise leave the track.[3] We seem to see in this the first interpretation of a moral maxim that fills a large place in the ethical consciousness of later days : Live according to Nature (ζῆν κατὰ φύσιν). We understand, also, why the *Works and Days* opens with a long discourse on Right (*Dike*). In the very first lines, too, we encounter the image of the wheel. The Muses are to sing of Zeus, through whom mortal men become illustrious or obscure ; ' easily he lifts them up to strength, and then, when they are strong, he casts them down ; easily he causes the light of one that shines to wane, and another to wax from obscurity.' [4]

---

[1] Hippodamus the Pythagorean, ap. Stob. *Flor.* 98, 71 : πάντα μὲν ὦν τὰ θνατὰ δι' ἀνάγκαν φύσιος ἐν μεταβολαῖς καλινδεῖται . . . τὰ μὲν ὑπὸ φύσιος εἰς τὸ ἄδηλον αὐτᾶς τερματιζόμενα καὶ πάλιν ἐκ τοῦ ἀδήλου ἐς τὸ θνατὸν ἐπισυνερχόμενα, ἀμοιβᾷ γενέσιος καὶ ἀνταποδόσει φθορᾶς, κύκλον αὐταύτας ἀναποδιζούσας. Compare the mystical passage in Plato, *Rep.* 546 A ff. : οὐ μόνον φυτοῖς ἐγγείοις ἀλλὰ καὶ ἐν ἐπιγείοις ζῴοις φορὰ καὶ ἀφορία ψυχῆς τε καὶ σώματος γίγνονται, ὅταν περιτροπαὶ ἑκάστοις κύκλων περιφορὰς συνάπτωσι, βραχυβίοις μὲν βραχυπόρους, ἐναντίοις δὲ ἐναντίας, κτλ.

[2] See J. E. Harrison, *Themis*, p. 423.

[3] Porph. *de abst.* iii. 27 : μιμησώμεθα τὸ χρυσοῦν γένος . . . μεθ' ὧν μὲν γὰρ Αἰδὼς καὶ Νέμεσις ἥ τε Δίκη ὡμίλει, ὅτι ἠρκοῦντο τῷ ἐκ γῆς καρπῷ· καρπὸν γάρ σφισιν ἔφερεν ζείδωρος ἄρουρα αὐτομάτη πολλόν τε καὶ ἄφθονον (Hes. *Erga*, 117).

[4] *Erga*, 3 : ὅν τε διὰ βροτοὶ ἄνδρες ὁμῶς ἄφατοί τε φατοί τε . . .
ῥέα μὲν γὰρ βριάει, ῥέα δὲ βριάοντα χαλέπτει,
ῥεῖα δ' ἀρίζηλον μινύθει καὶ ἄδηλον ἀέξει . . .
Ζεὺς ὑψιβρεμέτης.
Ar. *Lys.* 772 : τὰ δ' ὑπέρτερα νέρτερα θήσει Ζεὺς ὑψιβρεμέτης. Horat. *Carm.* i. 34, 12 : *ualet ima summis mutare et insignem attenuat deus obscura promens.*

Dike is the *Hora*, the Season, who brings wealth ; her sisters are *Eunomia* (Law-abidingness), and *Eirene* (Peace), who was represented in art, carrying the infant Wealth (*Ploutos*) in her arms. Their mother is *Themis*.[1] Wealth must not be snatched from another by robbery ; it is much better and more abiding when it is given of God, and comes in its duly appointed season (κατὰ καιρόν) in the circle of the year.[2]

This primitive correspondence between the ordered process of the year bringing fruits, and the appointed path of ' seasonable works ' (ὥρια ἔργα) which those fruits reward, helps to explain why the wheel of Time is also the wheel of Right. ' Time, in the length of his unnumbered years, gives birth to all things out of the darkness, and, when they have come into the light, hides them again.' [3] And so, too, there is a turn of the wheel

---

[1] Hesiod. *Theog.* 901 ; Pind. *Ol.* xiii. 6 : ἐν τῷ γὰρ Εὐνομία ναίει κασίγνηται τε. . . . Δίκα καὶ ὁμότροπος Εἰρήνα, ταμίαι ἀνδράσι πλούτου. Bgk.³ *Frag. Adesp.* 140, the *Moirai* are invoked to conduct *Eunomia, Dike*, and *Eirene* to the city. Cretan ' Hymn of the Kouretes' (*Brit. Sch. Annual*, xv. p. 357 ff.) :

Ὧραι δὲ βρ]ύον κατῆτος
καὶ βρότους Δίκα κατῆρχε
πάντα τ' ἄγρι' ἀμφεπ]ε ζῷ'
ἁ φίλολβος Εἰρήνα.

For this hymn, see J. E. Harrison, *Themis*, especially the concluding chapter on Themis.

[2] Hesiod, *Erga*, 320 :

χρήματα δ' οὐχ ἁρπακτά, θεόσδοτα πολλὸν ἀμείνω.
εἰ γάρ τις καὶ χερσὶ βίῃ μέγαν ὄλβον ἕληται . . .
ῥεῖα δέ μιν μαυροῦσι θεοί, μινύθουσι δὲ οἶκον
ἀνέρι τῷ, παῦρον δέ τ' ἐπὶ χρόνον ὄλβος ὀπηδεῖ.

Solon, frag. 13 (Bgk.⁴) 9 : πλοῦτον δ' ὃν μὲν δῶσι θεοὶ παραγίγνεται ἀνδρὶ ἔμπεδος . . . οὗ δ' ἄνδρες μετίωσιν ὑφ' ὕβριος, οὐ κατὰ κόσμον ἔρχεται. *Theognis*, 197 : χρῆμα . . . Διόθεν καὶ σὺν δίκῃ . . . παρμόνιμον, contrasted with ἀδίκως παρὰ καιρόν. *Bacch.* xiv. 50-64, *Dike, Eunomia*, and *Themis* give wealth ; *Hybris*, which snatches it from another, brings destruction. The use of καιρός, to mean ' due measure,' and κατὰ καιρόν as synonymous with μετρίως, goes back to this association of Right with Time. Iambl. *Vit. Pyth.* 182 (*D.F.V.*², p. 284) : συμπαρέπεσθαι τῇ τοῦ καιροῦ φύσει τήν τε ὀνομαζομένην ὥραν καὶ τὸ πρέπον καὶ τὸ ἁρμόττον. For Time and Justice see W. Headlam, *Journ. of Philol.* xxx. p. 290 ff. *Dike* is daughter of *Chronos* (Eur. frag. 223 N.).

[3] Soph. *Ajax*, 646 : ἅπανθ' ὁ μακρὸς κἀναρίθμητος Χρόνος
φύει τ' ἄδηλα καὶ φανέντα κρύπτεται.

Cf. ἐνιαυτός in Plato, *Cratylus*, 410 D : τὸ γὰρ τὰ φυόμενα καὶ τὰ γιγνόμενα προάγον εἰς φῶς καὶ αὐτὸ ἐν ἑαυτῷ ἐξετάζον . . . οἱ μὲν ἐνιαυτόν, ὅτι ἐν ἑαυτῷ,

that abases pride. Ajax, in the speech which opens with the above words, goes on to acknowledge this necessity of abasement. 'Even things dread and powerful yield to dignities (τιμαῖς): the snowy Winter gives place to fruitful Summer; Night's weary round makes room for Day, with her white steeds, to kindle light. . . . And shall not I also learn to curb my pride ? ' [1]

In the age of the Sophists, when controversial writings on the subject of politics began to appear, the disputants were eager to claim the authority of Nature for the particular form of government they were upholding. Several traces of one such treatise survive in Euripides.[2] The author bases the rule of justice, or equality, among men on the equality observed in Nature's course. Thus, Jocasta in the *Phoenissae* [3] argues with Eteocles :

' Equality is what is *naturally lawful* for mankind : the more

---

οἱ δὲ ἔτος, ὅτι ἐτάζει. See my note on 'Hermes, Pan, Logos,' *Classical Quarterly*, iii. p. 282. Nauck², frag. adesp. 483: ὁρῶ γὰρ χρόνῳ δίκαν πάντ' ἄγουσαν εἰς φῶς βροτοῖς. Dieterich, *Abraxas*, 96 : *das ist ein uralt mythischer Zusammenhang zwischen Schicksal, Recht, und Licht.*

[1] *Ajax*, 669 : καὶ γὰρ τὰ δεινὰ καὶ τὰ καρτερώτατα
τιμαῖς ὑπείκει· τοῦτο μὲν νιφοστιβεῖς
χειμῶνες ἐκχωροῦσιν εὐκάρπῳ θέρει·
ἐξίσταται δὲ νυκτὸς αἰανὴς κύκλος
τῇ λευκοπώλῳ φέγγος ἡμέρᾳ φλέγειν . . .
ἡμεῖς δὲ πῶς οὐ γνωσόμεσθα σωφρονεῖν ;

Note the references to Time in the preceding and following choruses, especially l. 711 : θέσμια (*Themis*) εὐνομίᾳ σέβων μεγίστᾳ ͵ πάνθ᾽ ὁ μέγας Χρόνος μαραίνει.

[2] See F. Dümmler, *Prolegomena zu Platons Staat*, Basel, 1891.

[3] 538 ff. : τὸ γὰρ ἴσον νόμιμον ἀνθρώποις ἔφυ,
τῷ πλέονι δ᾽ αἰεὶ πολέμιον καθίσταται
τοὔλασσον, ἐχθρᾶς θ᾽ ἡμέρας κατάρχεται.
καὶ γὰρ μέτρ᾽ ἀνθρώποισι καὶ μέρη σταθμῶν
ἰσότης ἔταξε κἀριθμὸν διώριο ε,
νυκτὸς δ᾽ ἀφεγγὲς βλέφαρον ἡλίου τε φῶς
ἴσον βαδίζει τὸν ἐνιαύσιον κύκλον
κοὐδέτερον αὐτῶν φθόνον ἔχει νικώμενον.
εἶθ᾽ ἥλιος μὲν νύξ τε δουλεύει βροτοῖς,
σὺ δ᾽ οὐκ ἀνέξει δωμάτων ἔχειν ἴσον
καὶ τῷδ᾽ ἀπονέμειν ;

So again in the *Suppliants*, 406, the principle of democracy is derived from the heavenly order (Dümmler, *op. cit.* p. 13) :

δῆμος δ᾽ ἀνάσσει διαδοχαῖσιν ἐν μέρει
ἐνιαυσίαισιν.

and the less are in eternal enmity, and herald the day of hatred. Equality it is, that ordained for man measure, and the divisions of weight, and the distinctions of number. Equal, on their yearly course, move the rayless eye of night and the light of the sun, and neither of them grudges the victory of the other. So the sunlight and the night are the servants of men; and can you not bear to hold an equal place with your brother, and allow him an equal share ? '

96. Heaven-worship

From the seasonal round of summer and winter, it is an easy step to the worship of the heavenly bodies, whose rhythmical revolution numbers the circuit of the years. Among many peoples, this shift has occurred when, first, the monthly waxing and waning of the moon, and, later, the annual periodicity of the sun, came to be regarded as sympathetically linked with the growth and decay of vegetation. Sunshine was, perhaps, at first regarded as a casual and capricious meteoric phenomenon, like the clouds and rain which interrupt it; the one, like the other, needing to be specially induced by magical ceremonies. But, with the first occurrence of a vague notion that the fruits of the earth, on which man's life depends, were not solely the offspring of earth herself, fertilised by the rains of heaven, but mysteriously connected with the periodic phases of the moon and with the waxing of the sun's power in summer and its waning in winter, moon and sun must become religious objects, and the old divisions of time, the seasons or Hours, will be worshipped with them as the givers of life and fertility.[1]

Sophocles compares the turning wheel of human destiny to the waxing and waning of the Moon, which can never stay in one form, but grows out of darkness to the full, and then melts away and returns to nothingness.[2] And again, the Women of

---

[1] The seasonal year being probably older than the solar or even the lunar calendar, the Horai would naturally be prominent before the moon and the sun were worshipped as the measurers of time and the givers of life. For the sequence of calendars—seasonal year, moon year, sun year, see Payne, *History of the New World called America*, i. 474 ff.

[2] Frag. 787 N[2] : ἀλλ᾽ οὑμὸς ἀεὶ πότμος ἐν πυκνῷ θεοῦ
τροχῷ κυκλεῖται καὶ μεταλλάσσει φύσιν·
ὥσπερ σελήνης ὄψις εὐφρόνας δύο

Trachis sing to Deianeira, how 'the son of Kronos has not appointed to mortal men a lot free from pain, but sorrow and joy come round to all, as the Bear moves in his circling paths. Nothing abides in one stay for men; not starry night, nor calamities; no, nor yet wealth; in a moment it is gone, and another has his turn of gladness or of loss.'[1] These images are not mere poetical comparisons, but look back to the old belief that the fate of man is sympathetically related to the circling lights of heaven. Any attentive reader of Pindar's most Orphic ode, the second *Olympian*, will see how the whole movement of its thought follows the turning wheel of Destiny (*Moira*) and Justice (*Dike*).[2] He will notice, too, the recurrence of Time, the Father of all things—Χρόνος ὁ πάντων πατήρ (l. 19). If he is also alive to Pindar's cryptic methods—one of those enlightened ones, to whom the poet's words are to have a voice[3]— he will observe that Zeus is addressed as the 'son of Kronos and Rhea,' and detect that these names signify *Time* and *Flow*.[4] The wheel of Time, in which all things flow and nothing abides, is the same as the wheel of Right (*Dike*).

στῆναι δύναιτ' ἂν οὔποτ' ἐν μορφῇ μιᾷ,
ἀλλ' ἐξ ἀδήλου πρῶτον ἔρχεται νέα
πρόσωπα καλλύνουσα καὶ πληρουμένη·
χὤταν περ αὐτῆς εὐπρεπεστάτη φανῇ,
πάλιν διαρρεῖ κἀπὶ μηδὲν ἔρχεται.

[Hippocr.] *de Victu*, i. 5 (after Heracleitus): χωρεῖ δὲ πάντα καὶ θεῖα καὶ ἀνθρώπινα ἄνω καὶ κάτω ἀμειβόμενα, ἡμέρη καὶ εὐφρόνη ἐπὶ τὸ μήκιστον καὶ ἐλάχιστον, ὡς σελήνη ἐπὶ τὸ μήκιστον καὶ ἐλάχιστον, <οὕτως> ἥλιος ἐπὶ τὸ μακρότατον καὶ βραχύτατον. πάντα ταὐτὰ καὶ οὐ ταὐτά, φάος Ζηνί, σκότος 'Αίδῃ, φάος 'Αίδῃ, σκότος Ζηνί. φοιτᾷ κεῖνα ὧδε καὶ τάδε κεῖσε, πᾶσαν ὥρην, πᾶσαν χώρην. . . . Selene is addressed as 'Ανάγκη, Μοῖρα, and Δίκη, *Orph. Hymn*, Abel, p. 292, l. 49.

[1] *Trach.* 125: ἀνάλγητα γὰρ οὐδ' ὁ πάντα κραίνων βασιλεὺς ἐπέβαλε θνατοῖς Κρονίδας· | ἀλλ' ἐπὶ πῆμα καὶ χαρὰ πᾶσι κυκλοῦσιν, οἶον ἄρκτου στροφάδες κέλευθοι. μένει γὰρ οὔτ' αἰόλα | νὺξ βροτοῖσιν οὔτε κῆρες | οὔτε πλοῦτος, ἀλλ' ἄφαρ | βέβακε, τῷ δ' ἐπέρχεται | χαίρειν τε καὶ στέρεσθαι. Herod. i. 207: μάθε, ὡς κύκλος τῶν ἀνθρωπηίων ἐστὶ πρηγμάτων, περιφερόμενος δὲ οὐκ ἐᾷ αἰεὶ τοὺς αὐτοὺς εὐτυχέειν (wheel of Τύχη).

[2] Note *e.g.* the recurrence of *Dike* in all the Epodes: l. 18, ἐν δίκᾳ καὶ παρὰ δίκαν; 41, wheel of Moira; 65, δικάζει; 83, Rhadamanthys; 106, δίκᾳ συναντόμενος.

[3] φωνάεντα συνετοῖσι (l. 93).

[4] l. 13, ὦ Κρόνιε παῖ 'Ρέας, an odd form of address, obviously used for the sake of introducing both names. That Kronos=Chronos is rendered practically certain by the tautometric responsion, l. 19, Χρόνος ὁ πάντων πατήρ= 85, πόσις ὁ πάντων 'Ρέας (=Kronos). The equation Chronos=Kronos is at

97. *Tao, Rta, and Asha*

Dike means ' Way.' [1] In a passage of the *Medea* of Euripides, the word means the ' course of Nature.' After Medea's threat of woman's vengeance upon man, the chorus opens : [2] ' The sacred river-founts flow upwards to their source, and *Dike* and all the world are turned backwards.' There is probably an allusion to the reversal of the revolution of the sky, which ancient legend connected with the strife of Atreus and Thyestes,[3] and which Plato curiously turns to account in the myth of his *Politicus*.[4] In the *Laws*, the solemn address to the citizens

least as old as Pherekydes (*D.F.V.*[2], ii. p. 507), whose principles were Zên, Chthonie, and Kronos : Ζῆνα μὲν τὸν αἰθέρα, Χθονίην δὲ τὴν γῆν, Κρόνον δὲ τὸν χρόνον . . . ἐν ᾧ τὰ γιγνόμενα. For the Orphic Time-God and his antiquity see below, p. 178, note 1, and Eisler, *Weltenmantel*, ii. chap. iv. especially p. 378. For Rhea=*Flow*, Plato, *Krat.* 402 A : τὸν Ἡράκλειτόν μοι δοκῶ καθορᾶν παλαί' ἄττα σοφὰ λέγοντα, ἀτεχνῶς τὰ ἐπὶ Κρόνου καὶ Ῥέας . . . ὅτι πάντα χωρεῖ καὶ οὐδὲν μένει (cf. Soph. *Trach.*, *loc. cit.* μένει γὰρ οὔτε . .) καὶ ποταμοῦ ῥοῇ ἀπεικάζων τὰ ὄντα λέγει ὡς δὶς ἐς τὸν αὐτὸν ποταμὸν οὐκ ἂν ἐμβαίης, followed by reference to the Orphic Okeanos and Tethys. In *Olympian* ii. the Emmenidai are εὐώνυμοι (l. 8), because their name means *abiding* (ἐμμένειν), though they dwell by a *river* (10), and mortals cannot reckon on unfailing happiness, but divers *streams* (ῥοαί) of joy and pain flow upon men at different times (ἀλλότε), and reverse of sorrow follows upon prosperity at another *time* (ἄλλῳ χρόνῳ). Cf. *Isth.* iii. 18 : αἰὼν δὲ κυλινδομέναις ἁμέραις ἄλλ' ἄλλοτ' ἐξάλλαξεν. *Ol.* vii. 94 : ἐν δὲ μιᾷ μοίρᾳ χρόνου ἄλλοτ' ἀλλοῖαι διαιθύσσοισιν αὖραι. [Eur.] frag. 594 N (Kritias, frag. 18, *D.F.V.*[2], p. 618) : ἀκάμας τε Χρόνος περὶ γ' ἀενάῳ ῥεύματι πλήρης φοιτᾷ τίκτων αὐτὸς ἑαυτόν, δίδυμοί τ' ἄρκτοι, κτλ. Time, as he moves forward, brings truth to light : ὁ τ' ἐξελέγχων μόνος ἀλάθειαν ἐτήτυμον Χρόνος. τὸ δὲ σαφανὲς ἰὼν πόρσω κατέφρασεν, *Ol.* x. (xi.) 53. There are other cryptic and etymological meanings in *Ol.* ii. ; for instance, the strange word ἀγροτέρα (μέριμνα), l. 60, is used because Θήρων is the 'hunter' after ἀρετή and fame ; cf. Arist. frag. 625 : 'Αρετὰ θήραμα κάλλιστον . . . σὰν ἀγρεύοντες δύναμιν.

[1] This sense is still common in Homer, *e.g. Od.* 11, 218, αὕτη δίκη ἐστὶ βροτῶν, 'this is the way of mortals.' Plato, *Laws*, 904 E, brings together this old use and the later, quoting αὕτη τοι δίκη ἐστὶ θεῶν οἳ Ὄλυμπον ἔχουσιν in connection with the Justice which assures that the soul shall be rewarded according to its deeds, δίκην . . . ἣν πασῶν δικῶν διαφερόντως ἔταξαν οἱ τάξαντες.

[2] 410 :   ἄνω ποταμῶν ἱερῶν χωροῦσι παγαί,

                          καὶ Δίκα καὶ πάντα πάλιν στρέφεται.

Verrall, *ad. loc.*, says, ' δίκα, the *custom* or *order* of nature,' and compares Parmenides, frag. 6, πάντων δὲ παλίντροπός ἐστι κέλευθος.

[3] Eur. *Electra*, 726. The chorus doubt whether the sun could be turned backwards, θνατᾶς ἕνεκ' ἀδικίας. Cf. also Electra's words in the following scene, 771: ὦ θεοί, Δίκη τε πάνθ' ὁρῶσ', ἠλθές ποτε. ποίῳ τρόπῳ δὲ καὶ τίνι ῥυθμῷ φόνου κτείνεις Θυέστου παῖδα, βούλομαι μαθεῖν, where the words Θυέστου παῖδα point the reference to the preceding chorus.

[4] 268 E ff.: τὸ γὰρ πᾶν τόδε τότε μὲν αὐτὸς ὁ θεὸς συμποδηγεῖ πορευόμενον

opens with the words : ' God, as the ancient doctrine also has it, containing the beginning and end and middle of all things that are, moves straight upon his revolving journey in the course of Nature. And always attendant upon him is *Dike*, the avenger of all negligence of the divine law, after whom follows closely, in orderly and humble fashion, whosoever desires that it shall be well with him.' [1] The next paragraph opens thus : ' What, then, is that conduct which is pleasing to God and follows after him ? ' And the answer is : the conduct which observes measure, and therefore is like God, who is to us the Measure of all things.

In these passages, the notion of Dike seems to come very

καὶ συγκυκλεῖ, τότε δὲ ἀνῆκεν, ὅταν αἱ περίοδοι τοῦ προσήκοντος αὐτῷ μέτρον εἰλήφωσιν ἤδη χρόνου, τὸ δὲ πάλιν αὐτόματον εἰς τἀναντία περιάγεται. In the former age of Kronos, men lived justly, without war or strife, or devouring one another (271 E, from Hesiod, *Erga*, 276 : Zeus gave men δίκη, that they should not eat each other like beasts), and ' the *seasons* were tempered to do them no hurt ' (τὸ τῶν ὡρῶν αὐτοῖς ἄλυπον ἐκέκρατο, 272 A). The period is the Great Year, which puts a term to the cycle of reincarnations of souls. Note also the mention of the Seasons' names in the parallel passage describing the rule of the daemons in the Golden Age of Justice, *Laws*, 713 E, ὁ θεὸς . . . γένος ἄμεινον ἡμῶν ἐφίστη τὸ τῶν δαιμόνων . . . εἰρήνην τε καὶ αἰδῶ καὶ εὐνομίαν καὶ ἀφθονίαν δίκης παρεχόμενον. For the reversal of the rotation of the universe see J. Adam, *Republic of Plato*, 1902, vol. ii. p. 295 ff.

[1] 715 E (included by Diels, *F. V.*[2], p. 474, among the older Orphic fragments) : ὁ μὲν δὴ θεός, ὥσπερ καὶ ὁ παλαιὸς λόγος, ἀρχήν τε καὶ τελευτὴν καὶ μέσα τῶν ὄντων ἁπάντων ἔχων, εὐθείᾳ περαίνει κατὰ φύσιν περιπορευόμενος· τῷ δ' ἀεὶ συνέπεται Δίκη τῶν ἀπολειπομένων τοῦ θείου νόμου τιμωρός, ἧς ὁ μὲν εὐδαιμονήσειν μέλλων ἑχόμενος συνέπεται ταπεινὸς καὶ κεκοσμημένος. . . . 716 C : Τίς οὖν δὴ πρᾶξις φίλη καὶ ἀκόλουθος θεῷ; Compare Euripides, *Troades*, 886 :

> Ζεύς, εἴτ' ἀνάγκη φύσεος εἴτε νοῦς βροτῶν,
> προσηυξάμην σε· πάντα γὰρ δι' ἀψόφου
> βαίνων κελεύθου κατὰ δίκην τὰ θνήτ' ἄγεις.

Cf. [Archytas] Mullach, *Frag. Phil. Gr.* i. 599 : the philosopher δυνατὸς ἐσσεῖται τὸν θεὸν κατοψεῖσθαι καὶ πάντα τὰ ἐν τᾷ συστοιχείᾳ καὶ τάξει τὰ ἐκείνω κατακεχωρισμένα, καὶ ταύταν τὰν ἁρματηλάταν ὁδὸν ἐκπορισάμενος τῷ νόῳ κατ' εὐθεῖαν ὁρμαθῆμεν καὶ τελεοδρομᾶσαι τὰς ἀρχὰς τοῖς πέρασι συνάψας τε καὶ ἐπιγνοὺς ὅτι ὁ θεὸς ἀρχά τε καὶ τέλος καὶ μέσον ἐστὶ πάντων τῶν κατὰ δίκαν τε καὶ τὸν ὀρθὸν λόγον περαινομένων. The language refers to the *Laws*, above quoted, and to *Phaedrus*, 246 E, where Ζεὺς, ἐλαύνων πτηνὸν ἅρμα, πορεύεται διακοσμῶν πάντα καὶ ἐπιμελούμενος, followed by the host of Gods and daemons. The immortals emerge on to the back of the οὐρανός, and are carried round by its περιφορά. Ps.-Archytas uses κατὰ δίκαν (περαίνεσθαι) as synonymous with Plato's κατὰ φύσιν (περαίνει). Soph. frag. 226 N[2] : ἀλλ' εἰς θεόν σ' ὁρῶντα, κἂν ἔξω δίκης | χωρεῖν κελεύῃ, κεῖσ' ὁδοιπορεῖν χρεών.

near to the Chinese *Tao*,[1] a term which, as we saw, also means
' Way '—the daily and yearly revolution of the heavens, and
of the two powers of light and darkness, day and night, summer
and winter, heat and cold. ' It is heaven's *Tao* or way to give
felicity to the good, and bring misfortune upon the bad.' [2] ' The
Tao, or order of the world, represents all that is correct, normal,
or right (*ching* or *twan*) in the universe; it does, indeed, never
deviate from its course. It consequently includes all correct
and righteous dealings of men and spirits, which alone promote
universal happiness and life. All other acts, as they oppose the
Tao, are incorrect, abnormal, unnatural.' [3] As in Hesiod's
Works and Days we traced a correspondence between the ordered
course of man's ways and the seasons called *Dike, Eunomia*, and
Eirene, so among the Chinese, ' *T'ai-sui* is the great year, the
planet Jupiter, whose path in the heavens governs the arrangements of the almanack which is annually published by imperial
authority, and gives the various days suitable for the transactions
of the various business of life. This god thus rules the *Tao*, or
revolution of the universe, and, as a consequence, the *Tao* of
human life, which, in order to bestow happiness and prosperity,
must fit in with the universal *Tao*.' [4]

When Buddhism was transplanted to China, the Chinese
unhesitatingly identified with their own *Tao* the *Dharma* of
Mahayanism. ' Dharma, the universal law, embraces the world
in its entirety. It exists for the benefit of all beings, for does not
its chief manifestation, the light of the world, shine for blessing on
all men and all things ? Salvation, which means conformity of life
to the dharma, consequently means in the first place manifestation
of universal love, both for men and animals. Indeed, as men and
animals equally are formed of the elements which constitute the

---

[1] See above, § 57.   [2] De Groot, *Religion of the Chinese*, 1910, p. 18.
[3] De Groot, *Religion of the Chinese*, 1910, p. 45. The Greek would be
παρὰ δίκην. Pind. *Ol.* ii. 17 : τῶν πεπραγμένων ἐν δίκᾳ τε καὶ παρὰ δίκαν
ἀποίητον οὐδ᾽ ἂν Χρόνος ὁ πάντων πατὴρ δύναιτο θέμεν ἔργων τέλος. The original
sense of δίκη remains clear in the compound ἔνδικος. Cf. Solon, frag. 36
(Bgk.⁴) ap. Ar. *Ath. Pol.* 12 : συμμαρτυροίη ταῦτ᾽ ἂν ἐν δίκῃ χρόνου μήτηρ
μεγίστη . . . Γῆ κτλ.
[4] *Ibid.* p. 114. Cf. Iambl. *Vit. Pyth.* 137 (ὁ Πυθαγόρειος) βίος ἅπας συντέτακται
πρὸς τῷ ἀκολουθεῖν τῷ θεῷ, καὶ ὁ λόγος οὗτος ταύτης ἐστὶ τῆς φιλοσοφίας, ὅτι
γελοῖον ποιοῦσιν ἄνθρωποι ἀλλοθέν ποθεν ζητοῦντες τὸ εὖ ἢ παρὰ τῶν θεῶν
(*D.F.V.*², p. 283).

universe itself, animals may become men, and through the human state be converted into arhats, boddhisattwas and buddhas.' [1]

Buddhism takes us to India, where a similar conception was dominant in religion long before the time of Buddha. It goes back, indeed, in all probability to a time before the separation of the Indian and Iranian stocks, for it is found both in the Veda and in the Persian Avesta.[2] The Vedic name for it is Ṛta; the Persian equivalent is Asha. ' The processes, whose perpetual sameness or regular recurrence give rise to the representation of Order, obey Ṛta, or their occurrence is Ṛta. " The rivers flow Ṛta." " According to Ṛta the light of the heaven-born morning has come." . . . The year is the path of Ṛta.' [3] The Gods themselves are born of the Ṛta or in the Ṛta; they show by their acts that they know, observe and love the Ṛta. In man's activity, the Ṛta manifests itself as the moral law.

The sun is called the wheel of Ṛta; the ritual and symbolism of the wheel are closely associated with this conception. The so-called praying-wheel of Buddhist religion is really an instrument of sympathetic magic, a wheel turned, the way of the sun, for the purpose of keeping the rotation of the heaven or of the sun going upon the path of the cosmic order.[4] The wheel of Fortune, familiar to us, does not symbolise chance or accident, but the very reverse. The wheel is essentially a symbol of regular recurrence. It is the wheel of Order and Right, on the observance of which all prosperity or fortune depends.

When we have traced this conception across Asia from the furthest east to Persia, we have reached a point at which the possibility of contact with Greek thought cannot be ruled out as impossible. Herodotus [5] remarks that the Persians above

---

[1] De Groot, *Religion of the Chinese*, 1910, p. 166. Cf. below, p. 182.

[2] Maurice Bloomfield, *The Religion of the Veda*, 1908, p. 125 ff. It is held that the Tel-el-Amarna tablets guarantee for this notion an antiquity of at least 1600 years B.C.

[3] Oldenberg, *Veda*, p. 196.

[4] W. Simpson, *The Buddhist Praying Wheel*, 1910. Theopompus, ap. Diog. L. proem. 13, reports that the Magians said that they 'maintained the order of the world by their invocations,' τὰ ὄντα ταῖς αὐτῶν ἐπικλήσεσι διαμένειν.

[5] i. 139. Herodotus says (*ibid.*) that the Persian names correspond (in their meaning) to the nobleness of the individuals who bear them, and tells us (vi. 98) that Arta-xerxes means μέγα(s) ἀρήιος. Did he know that *Arta-*

all things hate lies, and in the next place debts, because they
bring with them lying and fraud, which are punished by the
God of Light with leprosy. The *Avesta* confirms the truth of
this statement. Lying and Ahriman are so closely allied that
not only are the demons always treated as liars, because they
try to deceive the world with false doctrine, but falsity itself
is a work of the devil. Further, ' the practical side of veracity
is Justice, whose celestial representative is the *Asha*. Justice
is the rule of the world's life, as *Asha* is the principle of all well-
ordered existence, and the establishment or accomplishment
of justice is the end of the evolution of the universe.' [1]

Whether or not we accept the hypothesis of direct influence
from Persia on the Ionian Greeks in the sixth century, any
student of Orphic and Pythagorean thought cannot fail to see
that the similarities between it and Persian religion are so close
as to warrant our regarding them as expressions of the same
view of life, and using the one system to interpret the other.
The characteristic preoccupation of Pythagoreanism with
astronomy and the contemplation ($\theta\epsilon\omega\rho\iota\alpha$) of the heavens,
becomes transparently clear, when we see it in the light of
notions like *Tao*, *Rta*, and *Asha*.

We cannot here follow further the various developments of
the wheel of Time, Fate, and Justice in Greek religious representation ; [2] but we may note that in philosophy this notion of
periodicity has an important consequence. It excludes the
possibility of conceiving the process of change and evolution
as a progress in a straight line, a history which never repeats
itself. Onwards from Anaximander, who declares that all that
comes into being must pay the penalty of injustice by perishing
again, *according to the order of time* ($\kappa\alpha\tau\grave{\alpha}$ $\tau\grave{\eta}\nu$ $\tauο\hat{\upsilon}$ $\chi\rhoό\nuο\upsilon$ $\tauά\xi\iota\nu$)
and the ordinance of destiny, Greek philosophers are haunted

is the same as *Asha*=*ṛta*? It seems possible that, if he could discuss the
derivation of names, his informants might have explained the idea.

[1] Chantepie de la Saussaye, *Manuel d'histoire des religions*, Paris, 1904,
p. 467. Porph. *Vit. Pyth.* 41: τοιαῦτα παρῄνει (Πυθαγόρας) μάλιστα δὲ
ἀληθεύειν· τοῦτο γὰρ μόνον δύνασθαι τοὺς ἀνθρώπους ποιεῖν θεῷ παραπλησίους,
ἐπεὶ καὶ τοῦ θεοῦ, ὡς παρὰ τῶν Μάγων ἐπυνθάνετο, ὃν Ὡρομάζην καλοῦσιν ἐκεῖνοι,
ἐοικέναι τὸ μὲν σῶμα φωτί, τὴν δὲ ψυχὴν ἀληθείᾳ. Plut. *Is. et Os.* 370, renders
Asha-Arta by ἀλήθεια.

[2] See Lobeck: *Aglaoph.* 798 ff. ; Dieterich, *Nekyia*, 88.

by the idea of the periodic growth, culmination, and destruction of the world and all that it contains. They thought of the life of the universe as following the same curve as the life of an animal—birth, growth, maturity, decay, and death, to be followed by rebirth, and the same repeated round.

98. Orphic revival of Heaven-worship

The Orphic reformation of Dionysiac religion seems to have meant, among other things, the revival of the primitive worship of the heavenly bodies, and especially of the Sun. Orpheus is said to have honoured Helios instead of Dionysus, ' and rising early in the morning he climbed the mountain called Pangaion, and waited for the rising of the Sun.' [1] That the worship of the heavenly measurers of time had belonged to an early phase of religion in Greece is probable, and Plato seems to preserve the tradition of it. Socrates in the *Kratylus* (397 c) suspects that ' the first men in Hellas recognised only those Gods who are now recognised by many other nations—sun, moon, earth, stars, and sky.' [2] ' The Persians,' says Herodotus (i. 131), ' do not erect images, temples, or altars ; indeed, they charge those who do so with folly, because, I suppose, they do not, like the Greeks, think that the Gods are of human shape. Their custom is to go up on to the mountain-tops and sacrifice, and they give the name of Zeus to the whole circle of the sky.' When Xenophanes, the satirist, took that step, which we have described in a previous chapter, of deliberately wiping out the figures of the anthropomorphic Gods, he too went back to an earlier phase of religion which had preceded those too clear-cut human figures. We are told of him that ' he looked at the whole sky, and declared that the One is, namely God.' [3] He disinterred, as it were, that older nature-worship, in which the circle of the sky

---

[1] Eratosth. *Catast.* xxiv. Cf. J. E. Harrison, *Prolegomena*, p. 461 ; *Themis*, p. 465 ; Roscher, Lex. s.v. 'Orpheus.'

[2] Cf. also *Laws*, 885 E, where the first Gods whose existence is asserted are γῆ καὶ ἥλιος ἄστρα τε τὰ σύμπαντα καὶ τὰ τῶν ὡρῶν διακεκοσμημένα καλῶς οὕτως, ἐνιαυτοῖς τε καὶ μησὶ διειλημμένα ; and it is implied that all nations recognise these as divine.

[3] Arist. *Met.* A v. 986 : εἰς τὸν ὅλον οὐρανὸν ἀποβλέψας τὸ ἓν εἶναί φησι τὸν θεόν.

and the heavenly bodies had ruled the destinies of man.   The
Orphics seem to have stood for a similar revival of heaven-
worship.   The ' Rhapsodic Theogony,' which our best authorities
now agree to date from before the Persian wars,[1] starts, like
Pherekydes, from the divinity of Endless Time.

99. *The heavenly origin and fall of the Soul*

Whether or not this revival was occasioned by Oriental
influence, it is easy to see how well it agrees with the doctrines
characteristic of Orphism.[2]   The wheel of birth or becoming
is now governed by the circling of the starry heaven.   From
the stars the soul of man is believed to have fallen into the prison
of this earthy body, sinking from the upper region of fire and
light into the misty darkness of this ' roofed-in cave.'[3]   The
fall is ascribed to some original sin, which entailed expulsion
from the purity and perfection of divine existence, and has to
be expiated by life on earth and by purgation in the underworld.
Caught in the wheel of birth, the soul passes through the forms
of man and beast and plant.   But the cycle, instead of going
on for ever, is terminated by the limit of the Great Year of
ten thousand solar years ; at the end of this period, the soul
may escape and fly aloft to the fiery heaven whence it came,
regaining perfection and divinity.   Then a new Great Year
begins (for the cycle of Time is endless), and a new world is
born, to pass away in its season, and give place to another.[4]

When we analyse this conception, it becomes clear that the
cycle of the Great Year, which must have an astral origin,[5] has

---

[1] This date for this Orphic Theogony (Abel, frag. 48 ff. *D.F.V.*[2], p. 476)
was held by Lobeck, and is now accepted by Diels, Gomperz, Kern, Gruppe,
and Eisler ; see Eisler, *Orpheus, the Fisher* (Third Internat. Congress for
the History of Religions, Oxford), who discusses its affinities to Iranian
Zrvanism, especially the similarity of χρόνος ἀγήρατος to *Zrvān akarana*
(endless time).   For the detailed statement of the theory of Persian
influence, see his *Weltenmantel*, vol. ii.

[2] For references see Gruppe, *Griech. Myth. u. Relig.* pp. 1028 ff.

[3] Emped. frag. 120 ; Eisler, *Weltenmantel*, ii. p. 618.

[4] Eudem. *Phys.* 51 (Simpl. *Phys.* 732, 26) : ὁ δὲ αὐτὸς χρόνος πότερον γίγνεται . . . ἢ οὔ, ἀπορήσειεν ἄν τις . . . εἰ δέ τις πιστεύσειε τοῖς Πυθαγορείοις,
ὥστε πάλιν τὰ αὐτὰ ἀριθμῷ, κἀγὼ μυθολογήσω τὸ ῥαβδίον ἔχων ὑμῖν καθημένοις
οὕτω, καὶ τὰ ἄλλα πάντα ὁμοίως ἕξει, καὶ τὸν χρόνον εὔλογόν ἐστι τὸν αὐτὸν εἶναι.

[5] Eisler, *Weltenmantel*, ii. 502.

been superimposed upon the old cycle of reincarnation. That primitive belief belonged to earth, not to heaven : it taught the revolution of all life or soul in man and nature, passing in an endless round from the underworld into the light of day, and back again. There was no hope or possibility of any release ; indeed, such an idea would have no meaning, since the individual soul did not persist after death, but was reabsorbed in the one life of all things. No part or fragment of this life had any separate persistence. It had not come from the aether, and could not fly off thither ; it came from earth, and returned to earth again. In the later doctrine, a series of such periods is fitted into a larger period or Great Year, based upon astronomical theories, probably of Babylonian origin, of the length of time required for all the heavenly bodies, in their various revolutions, to come back to the same relative positions.[1] The focus is thus shifted from the annual recurrence of earthly life to the periodicity of the stars ; and with this change goes the doctrine that, while the body is of earth, the soul comes from the starry sky and claims to be of heavenly descent.[2]

This contrast brings out what seems to be the essential difference between the ' Dionysiac ' view of immortality (as we may call it) and the Orphic. Orphism is focused on the individual soul, its heavenly origin and immutable nature, and its persistence, as an individual, throughout the round of incarnations. It is ' an exile from God and a wanderer ' ;[3] and it is reunited with God, and with other souls, only after its final escape at the end of the Great Year. Hence, the Orphic is preoccupied with the salvation, by purifying rites, of his individual soul.

This insistence on the individual soul, perhaps, gives us the

---

[1] See W. Schultz, *Pythagoras u. Heraklit*, 1905, p. 68. Plato, *Timaeus*, 39 D : ὅ γε τέλεος ἀριθμὸς χρόνου τὸν τέλεον ἐνιαυτὸν πληροῖ τότε, ὅταν ἀπασῶν τῶν ὀκτὼ περιόδων τὰ πρὸς ἄλληλα ξυμπερανθέντα τάχη σχῇ κεφαλὴν τῷ τοῦ ταύτοῦ καὶ ὁμοίως ἀναμετρηθέντα κύκλῳ.

[2] Orphic tablet from Petelia, *D.F.V.*[2], ii. p. 480, J. E. Harrison, *Prolegomena*, 661 ff. :

γῆς παῖς εἰμι καὶ οὐρανοῦ ἀστερόεντος·
αὐτὰρ ἐμὸν γένος οὐράνιον.

[3] Emped. frag. 115 : φυγὰς θεόθεν καὶ ἀλήτης. Plotinus, *Enn.* iv. 8. 1 : Ἐμπεδοκλῆς τε εἰπὼν ἁμαρτανούσαις νόμον εἶναι ταῖς ψυχαῖς πεσεῖν ἐνταῦθα καὶ αὐτὸς φυγὰς θεόθεν γενόμενος . . . τοσοῦτον παρεγύμνου ὅσον καὶ Πυθαγόρας, οἶμαι, καὶ οἱ ἀπ' ἐκείνου ἠνίττοντο.

psychological key to the phenomena of Orphism. The cosmic dualism, with its contrast of the principles of light and darkness, identified with good and evil, reflects outwards upon the universe that inner sense of the double nature of man and the war in our members, which is called the ' sense of sin.' It is also the sense of separation from ' God,' which goes with the intense desire for reunion. We may, perhaps, see the psychological cause of all this in the development of self-conscious individuality, which necessarily entails a feeling of isolation from the common life, and at the same time an increasing conflict between self-assertive instincts and that part of the common consciousness which resides in each of us, and is called ' conscience.' If this is so, it is significant that the conflict is represented as between ' body ' and ' soul.' To ' body ' are assigned those senses and lusts whose insurrection destroys the inward harmony. ' Soul ' still covers the field of the common consciousness, or ' conscience '; but it has shrunk from being the pervasive soul of the whole group to being one among an aggregate of individual selves, weakened by their novel isolation, and always longing for the old undivided communion.

In the terms of religious representation, this is expressed as ' separation from God,' the loneliness of exile. As the barriers of individuality close in upon the soul, the old Dionysiac faith, with its sense of a communion easily and perpetually renewed, grows fainter, and calls for ever greater efforts, if it is to be recovered. The Orphic could no longer find a complete satis-faction in the immediate union with his God in orgiastic ecstasy ; his Way of Righteousness was a long and painful round of ritual forms, which easily degenerated into external observances, the preservation of ceremonial purity, and all the vacant futilities of ecclesiasticism. We know, too, that the baser sort of Orphics, in the decline of the movement, believed that the mere fact of initiation would secure to the believer the some-what gross enjoyments of Elysium. Such debasements are common in this type of religion ; but, on the other hand, the conception of life which lies behind it is full of inspiration to the mystical temperament, and the old forms may at any time be reanimated, when a new prophet arises to rekindle faith, by means of what seems a profounder and more spiritual interpretation. Such a prophet was Pythagoras; the 'Pythagorean Life' was a new Way of Righteousness, which followed the old tracks, but made it possible for the intellectually enlightened to travel along them, by substituting a purification by 'music' (philosophy) for the mere ritual washing away of sin.[1]

100. *Mystical morality*

Long and painful as this Way of Righteousness may be, at least it is a way, and it leads, at the end, to God. It is here that the morality of the mystic is in sharp contrast with Olympianism. Olympian morality, as we have seen, rested on the idea of *Moira*. The type of all offences was going beyond your allotted province, overstepping its limits ($\hat{v}\pi\epsilon\rho\beta\alpha\sigma\acute{\iota}\alpha$), trying to have more than your due share ($\pi\lambda\epsilon o\nu\epsilon\xi\acute{\iota}\alpha$). *Eros* and *Elpis* are the two fatal passions; *Hybris*, the cardinal sin. The whole conception is static and geometrical; everything has its limited field, with bounds that must not be passed. Mystical morality is totally different; its fundamental idea is the Way of Righteousness. The cycle of life is, indeed, divided into grades or phases, but these are not impermeable compartments; on the contrary, all life must pass through every phase; there is a rightful way that leads through the whole round of existence, and, along it, life moves from the lowest forms to the highest.

It is easy to see how a philosophy, starting from this standpoint, must take a different course from a philosophy dominated by *Moira*. The properties of the original datum to which it must cling, will be precisely those which Science progressively and triumphantly eliminated—unity and continuity, Life (soul), and God.

The mystic conception of *Nomos* shows a corresponding contrast with that notion of a dispensation of rigidly exclusive provinces which we analysed in the first chapter. Aristotle, when he draws the distinction between the law peculiar to any given state and that 'common law' ($\kappa o\iota\nu\grave{o}\varsigma$ $\nu\acute{o}\mu o\varsigma$) which is 'according to nature' and embodies what is *naturally* right and wrong, cites Empedocles' declaration that the killing and eating

---

[1] Aristoxenus (*D.F.V.*[2], p. 282): οἱ Πυθαγορικοὶ καθάρσει ἐχρῶντο τοῦ μὲν σώματος διὰ τῆς ἰατρικῆς, τῆς δὲ ψυχῆς διὰ τῆς μουσικῆς.

of things that have souls, is not right for some and wrong for others, but is forbidden by that universal law which pervades the whole universe.[1] This passage significantly connects the idea of a Law of Nature with the unity of all Life. Sextus,[2] again, observes that ' the schools of Pythagoras and Empedocles and the Italian philosophy in general teach that we have community and fellowship (κοινωνία) not only with one another and with the Gods, but also with irrational animals; for there is one spirit, which, like a soul, pervades the whole cosmos and unites us to them. To kill them is therefore an act of impiety.' To the mystic, the whole of Nature is bound together in one society (κοινωνία), of which human communities are microcosmic parts.[3] All living things are under the universal sway of *Dike*.

In contrast with this view, the Olympian tradition draws its fast line, not only between men and Gods, but between human society and the rest of Nature. As a consequence of this separation, the rule of *Dike* is confined to the ordered structure of the human state. Hesiod tells us that fishes, beasts, and birds prey upon one another because they have no *Dike*; but the son of Kronos gave *Dike* to man, that he might not follow their example.[4] The same notion is repeated in the myth which Plato puts into the mouth of Protagoras.[5] There, *Aidôs* and *Dike* are the final gift of God to mankind, who up to that time had lived, scattered and without cities, at the mercy of the beasts of prey. Two characteristic

---

[1] Arist. *Rhet.* a 13, 2 : ἔστι γάρ, ὃ μαντεύονταί τι πάντες, φύσει κοινὸν δίκαιον καὶ ἄδικον, κἂν μηδεμία κοινωνία πρὸς ἀλλήλους ᾖ μηδὲ συνθήκη . . . ὡς Ἐμπεδοκλῆς λέγει περὶ τοῦ μὴ κτείνειν τὸ ἔμψυχον· τοῦτο γὰρ οὐ τισὶ μὲν δίκαιον τισὶ δ' οὐ δίκαιον,

ἀλλὰ τὸ μὲν πάντων νόμιμον διά τ' εὐρυμέδοντος
αἰθέρος ἠνεκέως τέταται διά τ' ἀπλέτου αὖ γῆς (Frag. 135).

[2] The text is quoted below, p. 202, note 1. Compare also Pythagoras' doctrine of *Themis*, *Dike*, and *Nomos*, and the rule of Law in every part of the universe, above, p. 54, note 1; and Heracleitus' universal Law identified with the *Logos*, which is the Life of the world, below, p. 191.

[3] Cf. Heracleitus, frag. 91 b : τρέφονται γὰρ πάντες οἱ ἀνθρώπειοι νόμοι ὑπὸ ἑνὸς τοῦ θείου· κρατεῖ γὰρ τοσοῦτον ὁκόσον ἐθέλει καὶ ἐξαρκεῖ πᾶσι καὶ περιγίνεται. Hippocrates, *de Victu*, 11 (*D.F.V.*², p. 83).

[4] *Erga* 276 : τόνδε γὰρ ἀνθρώποισι νόμον διέταξε Κρονίων, ἰχθύσι μὲν καὶ θηρσὶ καὶ οἰωνοῖς πετεηνοῖς ἐσθέμεν ἀλλήλους, ἐπεὶ οὐ δίκη ἐστὶν ἐν αὐτοῖς· ἀνθρώποισι δ' ἔδωκε δίκην . . .

[5] Plato, *Protag.* 320 D ff.

opinions are contained in this representation. In the first place, Law and Right are held to be peculiar to man, who lives within his ring-fence of custom and convention, while the rest of Nature is given over to a lawless struggle for existence. Second, Right, or Justice, dates only from the formation of civil communities. In the hands of other sophists, this theory became a weapon in a general attack upon the validity of all human morality. 'Justice' was assailed as a mere arbitrary convention, under which men, originally independent and free from any restraint, surrendered their *natural* right of getting the better of one another ($\pi\lambda\epsilon o\nu\epsilon\xi i a$).[1] The Social Contract theory marks an age of individualism. This view, moreover, that Society is an aggregate, arbitrarily formed by the coming together of independent individuals, is nothing but the equivalent, in political theory, of the physical doctrine of Atomism, according to which all things are casual aggregates of distinct atoms, temporarily cohering. The two theories make their appearance at the same time, and both belong to the scientific tradition. Plato, who condemned both alike as atheistical and immoral, devoted the argument of the *Republic* to the refutation of political Atomism and the proof that the State is natural, and, if reconstructed on ideal lines, might embody the same principle of Justice that rules through every part of the cosmos.

Before we consider Pythagoreanism, we have first to deal with Heracleitus. His system of thought is dominated by the twin conceptions of Time and Flow, *Chronos* and *Rhea*. But the type of his philosophy is distinct from the Pythagorean. It is not Orphic, but Dionysiac. It is not inspired by any doctrine of individual immortality, or of the persistence, through all transformations, of a plurality of soul-atoms, fallen from the heavenly fires. Rather, he goes back to the older notion of the one continuous and homogeneous Soul, or Life, in all things— a perennial stream, on whose surface individual forms are mere

---

[1] Callicles in Plato's *Gorgias*, 483; Thrasymachus in the *Republic*, Book i.; and the restatement of his argument by Glaucon, *Rep.* ii. 358 E ff., especially 359 C : διὰ τὴν πλεονεξίαν, ὃ πᾶσα φύσις διώκειν πέφυκεν ὡς ἀγαθόν, νόμῳ δὲ βίᾳ παράγεται ἐπὶ τὴν τοῦ ἴσου τιμήν.

momentary bubbles, bursting and leaving no trace of their transient existence.[1]

101. HERACLEITUS

In Heracleitus we see the mystic temperament in violent reaction against Ionian rationalism and the mechanical tendencies of Science. His exalted contempt for 'polymathy' includes all the characteristic manifestations of the Ionian spirit—the popular polytheism of Homer, and, equally, the rationalising critic of that polytheism, Xenophanes; the 're-search' (ἱστορίη) of travellers like Hekataeus; and physical science. It has been pointed out that in cosmology and astronomy Heracleitus was, from the scientific standpoint, actually behind the Milesians; manifestly, the science of nature, as they understood it, was a thing he rejected and despised as radically on false lines.[2] Any attempt to represent Heracleitus as continuing the work of the Milesian School is utterly mistaken. He is pre-eminently an exponent of the opposed, mystical tendency, which we have just described; the older doctrines characteristic of it are affirmed by him, in undisguised revolt against rationalising science.

The frame of his cosmological scheme is temporal—the cycle of existence, that circle ' whose beginning and end are the same ' (frag. 70); [3] indeed, he appears to have actually identified Time with his one primary substance.[4] The movement round this circle is not the mechanical motion of body, but the movement of Life itself—of the one, living and divine, soul-substance, embodied in Fire, which perpetually dies into all other transformations and is reborn again. It will soon appear how this fundamental conception leads him to contradict all those

---

[1] None of Heracleitus' obscure utterances about the fate of the soul seem to me to point to a belief in personal immortality. Frag. 68 (Byw.) ψυχῆσι θάνατος ὕδωρ γενέσθαι seems expressly to deny it. See Rohde, Psyche [3], ii. 150.

[2] Pfleiderer, Heraklit von Ephesus (1886), p. 19 ff. ; Diels, Heraklit von Ephesos (1901), p. vi.

[3] For the fragments of Heracleitus I give Bywater's numbering, which Professor Burnet also follows in his Early Greek Philosophy.

[4] Sext. adv. Math. x. 216: σῶμα μὲν οὖν ἔλεξεν εἶναι τὸν χρόνον Αἰνησίδημος κατὰ τὸν Ἡράκλειτον· μὴ διαφέρειν γὰρ αὐτὸν τοῦ ὄντος καὶ τοῦ πρώτου σώματος. Cf. O. Gilbert, Griech. Religionsphilosophie, Leipzig (1911), p. 60.

principles of mechanical and materialistic explanation which were already implicit in Anaximander.

We have seen how, in Anaximander's Olympian cosmology, the important fact about the order of the world was the separation of the elements in rigidly defined, spatial provinces; so that the mutual invasion of one another's spheres was an act of unjust aggression. Heracleitus, on the contrary, insists that they form a permeable cycle of transformations, which, so far from being rigidly distinct, are perpetually passing one into another. ' Fire lives the death of air, and air lives the death of fire; water lives the death of earth, earth that of water ' (frag. 25).[1]

As this fragment, and others like it, show, the movement of becoming or change is the movement of Life. The Dionysiac mystic holds to the truth that life is not stationary, and that there is no such thing as that fixed and changeless immortality which Olympian theology ascribed to its Gods. Life and Death, Dionysus and Hades, are the same (frag. 127). Whereas Milesian science interprets the becoming of the elements as a mere process of mechanical separation (ἀπόκρισις), Heracleitus will have it that all becoming is the becoming of life, namely birth; and, as in the wheel of reincarnation, every birth is, also and equally, a death. ' Mortals are immortals, and immortals are mortals, the one living the other's death, and dying the other's life ' (frag. 67).[2] Fire is not ' deathless ' (ἀθάνατον), but ' ever-living ' (ἀείζωον); and it lives by death and rebirth into all other forms.

Thus, ' it is wisdom to confess that all things are one ' (frag. 1); ' all things come out of one, and one out of all things ' (frag. 59). We encounter here, as we should expect, the mystical belief that the One can pass out of itself into the manifold, and yet retain its oneness. The secret seemed to Heracleitus to lie in the notion that the continuity of life is not broken by death, but rather renewed. Death, in fact, is not ' perishing '; it is neither an end nor a dissolution; the One Life revolves in

---

[1] Cf. Arist. de Gen. et Corr. 337 a 1: διὸ καὶ τἆλλα ὅσα μεταβάλλει εἰς ἄλληλα . . . οἷον τὰ ἁπλᾶ σώματα, μιμεῖται τὴν κύκλῳ φοράν· ὅταν γὰρ ἐξ ὕδατος ἀὴρ γένηται καὶ ἐξ ἀέρος πῦρ καὶ πάλιν ἐκ πυρὸς ὕδωρ κύκλῳ φάμεν περιεληλυθέναι τὴν γένεσιν διὰ τὸ πάλιν ἀνακάμπτειν.

[2] This is the only occurrence of the word ἀθάνατος in the fragments.

an endless circle, and its unity is such that it cannot be dissolved, or broken up into parts, like Anaximander's ' Limitless.' Its unity is not that of a mixture, out of which the elemental forms could come by separation ; it is continuous in substance, as in time. Heracleitus insists on the unity and continuity of the one real Being, just as emphatically as Parmenides ; and, from this point of view, the histories of philosophy are misleading, when they set the two systems in polar antagonism.

From the unity of the real follows the inevitable condemnation of the many to comparative unreality or ' seeming.' This is the true ground of Heracleitus' contempt for Ionian science and rationalism. He calls it ' polymathy,' a ' learning of *many* things,' which ' does not teach insight ' (frag. 16). Of what use, he seems to argue, are their various explanations of natural phenomena ? By what do they explain them ? By other phenomena of the same order of unreality. Why run about the world, like Hekataeus, picking up scraps of information, and call that ' research ' (or ' science,' ἱστορίη) ? You will come back no wiser than you started. There is only one truth, and that truth is within you, and in all things around you. There is one *logos*, one reason for everything, throughout ' the one cosmos, which is the same for all ' (frag. 20). Of this one meaning all particular things are merely symbols ; no one of them is a complete and independent expression of it ; taken as such, they are as false as the idols which polytheism mistakes for individual Gods, ' for they know not what Gods and Heroes are ' (frag. 126). ' Wisdom is one only ; it is willing and unwilling to be called by the name of Zên ' [1] (Life, which is God, Zeus, frag. 65). ' I searched myself ' (frag. 80) [2] ; for ' it is open to all men to know themselves and to be wise ' (frag. 106). But they will not find wisdom by running to the ends of the earth, and trusting to their ' eyes and ears, which are bad witnesses to men, if they have not souls that understand their language ' (frag. 4).[3] ' Nature loves to hide herself ' (frag. 10) ; she hints her

---

[1] Ζηνός. The nominative Ζήν was used by Pherekydes (frag. 1), and probably by Empedocles (=ξέσις, D.F.V.², p. 159, l. 17). See Eisler, *Weltenmantel*, ii. p. 357.

[2] Plot. *Enn.* iv. 8. 1 : ὁ Ἡράκλειτος . . . ἀμελήσας σαφῆ ἡμῖν ποιῆσαι τὸν λόγον, ὡς δέον ἴσως παρ' αὐτοῖς ζητεῖν, ὥσπερ καὶ αὐτὸς ζητήσας εὖρεν.

[3] I understand frag. 49, χρὴ γὰρ εὖ μάλα πολλῶν ἵστορας φιλοσόφους ἄνδρας

one meaning under many forms, which delude the senses of the fool; she is like 'the lord at Delphi, who neither declares plainly, nor yet conceals, his meaning, but shows it by a sign.'[1] To the mysticism of all ages, the visible world is a myth, a tale half true and half false, embodying a *logos*, the truth which is one.[2]

102. *Soul and Logos*

What, then, is the one truth, the one reality which runs through all these manifold transformations ? It is, as before, the divine soul-substance, *physis*, only with all the emphasis thrown, not upon its nature as material filling space, but upon its life, one and continuous in the round of death and rebirth, which is like the cycle of 'the seasons that bear all things.'[3] It is God, who is 'day and night, winter and summer, war and peace, surfeit and hunger; only, he takes various shapes, just as fire, when it is mingled with spices, is named according to the savour of each' (frag. 36). It is also Soul ($\psi\nu\chi\dot{\eta}$), the principle of life. 'Heracleitus takes soul for his first principle, as he identifies it with the vapour from which he derives all other things, and further says that it is the least corporeal of things and in cease-

εἶναι, 'Lovers of Wisdom must know a great many things indeed,' as an ironical sneer at 'polymaths,' perhaps especially directed at Pythagoras, whose humility led him to call himself not 'wise,' but a 'lover of wisdom.' To Heracleitus, convinced that 'wisdom is one' (frag. 19), and that he possessed it, such humility seemed mawkish and hypocritical. πολλῶν ἴστορες in his language is a term of contempt; cf. frag. 35: διδάσκαλος δὲ πλείστων Ἡσίοδος· τοῦτον ἐπίστανται πλεῖστα εἰδέναι, ὅστις ἡμέρην καὶ εὐφρόνην οὐκ ἐγίνωσκεν· ἔστι γὰρ ἕν.

[1] Frag. 11: ὁ ἄναξ, οὗ τὸ μαντεῖόν ἐστι τὸ ἐν Δελφοῖς, οὔτε λέγει οὔτε κρύπτει ἀλλὰ σημαίνει. Cf. p. 218, note 1, for meaning of σῆμα (σημαίνειν).

[2] Sallustius, *de Diis et Mundo*, 3: ἔξεστι γὰρ καὶ τὸν κόσμον μῦθον εἰπεῖν, σωμάτων μὲν καὶ χρημάτων ἐν αὐτῷ φαινομένων, ψυχῶν δὲ καὶ νόων κρυπτομένων. See Plato, *Krat.* 408 A, on derivations of Hermes, Pan, Logos, especially ὁ λόγος πᾶν σημαίνει καὶ κυκλεῖ καὶ πολεῖ ἀεί, καὶ ἐστι διπλοῦς, ἀληθής τε καὶ ψευδής . . . τὸ μὲν ἀληθὲς αὐτοῦ . . . θεῖον καὶ ἄνω οἰκοῦν ἐν τοῖς θεοῖς, τὸ δὲ ψεῦδος κάτω ἐν τοῖς πολλοῖς τῶν ἀνθρώπων. For the antiquity of this Hermes-Logos doctrine, see Zielinski, 'Hermes und die Hermetik,' *Arch. f. Relig.* ix. The equation Hermes=Logos goes back to Theagenes of Rhegium in the sixth century; see *D.F.V.*², ii. p. 511.

[3] Frag. 34: ὧραι αἳ πάντα φέρουσι. φέρειν, like 'bear,' has a double sense: (1) 'keep all things moving' in the yearly round, (2) 'bring all things to birth.'

less flow ; and that it is by something in motion that what is
in motion is known ; for he, like the majority, conceived all
that exists to be in motion.' [1]

Heracleitus, like the rest, could not conceive the divine Soul
as immaterial ; it is only ' the least corporeal of things ' ; and
its appropriate vehicle is Fire, the element which is ' ever-living '
and ever-moving.   Here again, the argument we put forward
about the ' Air ' of Anaximenes (p. 149) holds of the Fire of
Heracleitus.   Visible flame—fire as a natural object—is only one
of many forms in the sense world, and, as such, is on a level
with water, air, and earth ; fire dies into air, just as air dies into
water, or water into earth.   It is only one embodiment of a
substance which must, in some way, be other than it, since that
substance persists the same through all embodiments and
transformations.   Fire is considered primary, only because its
mobile nature seems nearest to the moving force of life, and to
be its most transparent medium.   The soul-substance itself is
a sort of metaphysical Fire, composed of the supernatural,
daemonic *mana* of fire, the least corporeal or most ' spiritual '
form of matter, which can be identified with the force of life.

What is really constant, throughout all the transformations, is
Logos, which, in one of its senses, means the proportion of equiva-
lence.   Every transformation is an exchange : ' all things are
an exchange for Fire, and Fire for all things, even as wares for
gold, and gold for wares ' (frag. 22).   That is to say, the ' measure '
or value remains constant, though the form assumed is different.
When earth becomes liquid sea, ' it is measured by the same
tale as before it became earth ' (frag. 23).   The ever-living Fire
is described as ' with measures kindling and with measures
going out ' (frag. 20).

103. *The Way of Justice*

This maintenance of measure, or constancy of proportion,
is the principle of Justice, and it is important as bringing out
another contrast between Heracleitus and Anaximander.   To
Anaximander, as we have seen, Justice meant the keeping of
bounds : *Dike*, for him, is not the ' Way,' but the barrier, or the

[1] Arist. *de anim.* a 2, 405 a 25.

avenging power who guards the frontiers of *Moira*. Heracleitus takes the opposite view : he identifies Justice precisely
with the living power which owns no barriers between the
elemental regions, but passes, on its ordered course, through
every phase and form. The doctrine is preserved for us in the
Kratylus of Plato (412 c). Discussing the derivation of δίκαιον
(*just*), Socrates says that the school of thinkers who hold that
all things are in motion, say that there is something which
passes through the whole universe, and causes all things to come
into existence. It is the swiftest and subtlest of things :
nothing can keep it out, and it treats other things as if they
were stationary. Since, then, it governs all things, *passing
through* (διαϊόν) them, it is rightly called ' just ' (δί(κ)αιον).

Socrates complains that, to further questioning as to the nature
of Justice, he could only get conflicting answers. One would
reply that Justice is the Sun ; for he alone ' passing through and
burning ' (διαϊόντα καὶ κάοντα, i.e. δια-κα-ιον) governs all
things. Another says, it is Fire ; another, the Heat that is in
Fire.[1] Another laughs at this, and says, with Anaxagoras, that
Justice is Mind ; for Mind has absolute mastery, and mixes with
nothing, and orders all things, and passes through all things.

It is evident that the successors of Heracleitus were puzzled
by their master's famous obscurity, and caught at various explanations. In so doing, they introduced new distinctions
which were becoming obvious to them, but were foreign to the
mystical thought of Heracleitus. To him, the living Fire, which,
through all the cycle of its transformations, preserved its
measures, actually *was* Reason (another meaning of *Logos*) and
the principle of Justice. Its chief embodiment was the Sun,
who ' will not overstep his measures, or the Spirits of Vengeance,
the ministers of Justice, would find him out ' (frag. 29). Later
writers, as we should expect, identify this Justice with Destiny.
' The all is finite, and the world is one. It arises from fire, and is
consumed again by fire, alternately, through all eternity, in certain
cycles. This happens according to Fate (καθ᾽ εἱμαρμένην).'[2]

---

[1] A material way of expressing what I have called the *mana* or daemon
of the fire. It shows that this fieriness, or spirit of the fire, was half
distinguished from visible flame.

[2] L. Diog. ix. 8.

Theophrastus adds, ' He lays down a certain order (τάξις) and a determined time for the changing of the world, according to a certain fated necessity.' [1] But, in Heracleitus' own time, the principle of *Dike*, as he understood it, was in opposition to the principle of *Moira* or Destiny, as understood by Ionian science. His divine Fire is the Way, as well as the Truth and the Life.

104. *The Harmony of Opposites*

When once we understand that Justice is the Way of Life, and also the force that moves along that way and owns no barriers, the doctrine of the harmony of opposites falls into line, as another contradiction of Anaximander's view. Anaximander held that all individual existence is unjust, because it results from the mixing of the elements which ought to be distinct, and can only combine by invading each other's provinces. The penalty is paid, and the reign of *Moira* restored, by death or dissolution. Heracleitus convicts him out of his own mouth. You admit, he seems to say, that ' War (Πόλεμος) is the father of all things ' (frag. 44), and yet you condemn the parent of all life as unjust. The end of warfare would be the end of life itself. ' Homer was wrong when he said : " Would that Strife might perish from among Gods and men ! " He did not see that he was praying for the destruction of everything ; for, if his prayer were heard, all things would pass away ' (frag. 43). Death is not dissolution, but rebirth ; so, war is not destruction, but regeneration. ' War is common to all, and Strife is Justice, and all things come into being through Strife.' [2] Strife is Justice ; if it were not for these acts of ' injustice,' as you call them, men would not have known the name of Justice.[3] Justice is not the separation of opposites, but their meeting in attunement or ' harmony.' Without opposition there were no agreement. ' What is at variance agrees with itself. It is the attunement

---

[1] Theophr. ap. Simpl. *Phys.* 6ʳ 24, 4 D : ποιεῖ δὲ καὶ τάξιν τινὰ καὶ χρόνον ὡρισμένον τῆς τοῦ κόσμου μεταβολῆς κατά τινα εἱμαρμένην ἀνάγκην.

[2] Frag. 62 : εἰδέναι δὲ χρὴ τὸν πόλεμον ἐόντα ξυνόν, καὶ Δίκην Ἔριν, καὶ γιγνόμενα πάντα κατ᾽ ἔριν. . . .

[3] Frag. 60 : Δίκης ὄνομα οὐκ ἂν ᾔδεσαν, εἰ ταῦτα μὴ ἦν. I agree with Burnet (*E.G.P.*², p. 151, note 5) that ταῦτα means ' all kinds of injustice '; but I think he especially meant what Anaximander called ' injustice,' as Burnet seems to recognise (pp. 158, 160).

of opposite tensions, like that of the bow and the lyre' (frag. 45). The give and take between the elements, then, without which nothing can come into being, is an 'injustice' that is also the very essence of justice, a war that is peace—not the peace of changeless, 'immortal' stagnation, but the peace of 'harmony,' that hidden attunement of opposite tensions, which is better than any that appears to the senses (frag. 47).

105. *The Common Reason*

This Justice or Harmony, again, is the *Logos*, the Spirit of Life, observing measure, but passing all barriers. It is the divine soul-substance, whose life consists in movement and change. It is also the one divine Law, the law of Nature (*physis*), which is the Will of God. 'It is Law (*nomos*) to obey the will of One' (frag. 110). This is true for the universe, no less than for human society; it is *common* (ξυνός) to all things. 'Those who speak with understanding must hold fast to what is common to all, as a city holds fast to its law, and even more strongly. For all human laws are fed by the one divine law. It prevails as much as it will, and suffices for all things with something to spare' (frag. 91 *b*). 'So we must follow what is common; yet the many live as if they had a wisdom of their own' (frag. 92). 'It is not meet to act and speak like men asleep. The waking have one common world, but the sleeping turn aside each into a world of his own' (frag. 94, 95).

When we take these sayings in conjunction, we are tempted to say that (strange as it may seem) Heracleitus had all but divined what this book is intended to prove—that *physis* is, ultimately and in origin, a representation of the social consciousness. At any rate, our theory could hardly have a stronger confirmation than a system which identifies the one continuous soul-substance, or nature of things, not only with Justice and Law, but with that 'common world' or 'common reason' which is accessible to all and present in all, if only their eyes are open to perceive it, and they do not turn aside, as the many do, to slumber each in his individual world of private opinion or 'seeming.' Heracleitus comes as near to describing the social consciousness, as was possible for a man whose intellectual apparatus was not yet refined enough to enable him to distinguish it from a material continuum, and who still thought, as theologians have thought before and since, that the social consciousness, as the source of morality, was the will of God.

Further, it was Heracleitus' respect for the common consciousness that led him to seek true wisdom in the most marvellous product of its collective activity, language. He and his followers, as we may see from Plato's *Kratylus*, constantly appealed to words as embodying the nature of things, because he saw in language an expression of that common wisdom which is in all men, and thought that, as a collective product, it might be free from, or at least only partly obscured by, the false private opinions of individuals. The *Logos* is revealed in speech.[1] The structure of man's speech reflects the structure of the world; more, it is an embodiment or representation of it. The *Logos* is contained and immanent in it, as one meaning may be contained in many outwardly different symbols. When Heracleitus says that the Wise, which is One only, ' is willing and unwilling to be called by the name of *Zên*' (Zeus, Life), we are to understand that it is willing to be so called, because that name reveals some of the truth about it; unwilling, because it is only some of the truth that is revealed, and more is concealed. Language, like the visible world, is a manifold, and so half unreal and false;[2] yet, for those who have ears, the one truth lives through all its varied forms.

We have dealt with Heracleitus at some length, because he has been so frequently misunderstood by interpreters who did

[1] The modern interpreters of the *Kratylus* who imagine that these mystical interpretations of names are simply bad attempts at philological derivation of one word from another, are utterly at fault. Taken as such, they are too obviously false and ridiculous for any sane person, however innocent of philology, to mistake them for derivations. The point that matters in mystical philology is what significant elements the name contains; the historical question, how they came to be there, is irrelevant and never considered. To the mystic the 'derivation' of the name Nero is not of the smallest account, nor does he inquire into it; what matters is that the number value of the letters (no matter how they came there) adds up to the number of the Beast. For the number-mysticism of Heracleitus' *logos*-doctrine see Eisler, *Weltenmantel*, ii. 694 ff.

[2] Plato, *Krat.* 408 c: οἶσθ' ὅτι ὁ Λόγος τὸ Πᾶν σημαίνει καὶ κυκλεῖ καὶ πολεῖ ἀεί, καί ἐστι διπλοῦς, ἀληθής τε καὶ ψευδής.

not know that the mystical representation of *physis* is the key to his famous obscurities, and supposed that he was working on the same lines as the Milesians. One further point remains. His insistence, in the truly mystical spirit, on the unity and continuity of all Life seems, at first sight, inconsistent with his personal attitude of solitary disdain towards his fellow-men. Are we justified in classing him with Pythagoras, the founder of a community and preacher of the common life ?

After what has been said of Heracleitus' respect for the common consciousness, we need not be misled by his contempt for the mass of mankind, whom he condemned precisely because they slumbered, and could not wake to the wisdom that was in them. All mystics have fled from the world to find their own souls, as Jesus went into the wilderness, and Buddha into the jungle.[1] Some, when they have found themselves, can stand alone, in fiery freedom of spirit, and despise their followers far more than their opponents. Such were Heracleitus and Friedrich Nietzsche ; for the author of *Beyond Good and Evil*, more than any other modern man, could understand the philosopher who said that ' Good and Ill are one,' and know the temper in which, instead of founding a church or publishing his book, Heracleitus dedicated the single copy of his *Logos* in the temple of Ephesian Artemis, careless whether the ' asses who prefer straw to gold,' went there to drink its wisdom, or quenched their thirst elsewhere.[2] Pythagoras, to whom we turn next, was a preacher as well as a prophet, and, like Jesus and Buddha, must needs have disciples, and cannot leave the world to go its own way unenlightened. These, when they have discovered the truth by searching themselves, will not find peace in a hermitage, but are driven to externalise the common life in a monastic church.

---

[1] Porph. *de abst.* i. 36: οὕτως γὰρ καὶ τῶν πρόσθεν ἀκούομεν κλέα ἀνδρῶν, Πυθαγορείων τε καὶ σοφῶν, ὧν οἱ μὲν τὰ ἐρημότατα χωρία κατῴκουν, οἱ δὲ (*e.g.* Apollonius of Tyana) καὶ τῶν πόλεων τὰ ἱερὰ καὶ τὰ ἄλση.

[2] The successors of Heracleitus, satirised by Plato (*Theaet.* 179 E ff.), refused to be taught by one another, but ' sprang up like mushrooms,' each claiming a private inspiration, and denying that any of the others knew anything at all.

106. PYTHAGORAS

The School of Pythagoras, in our opinion, represents the main current of that mystical tradition which we have set in contrast with the scientific tendency. The terms 'mystical' and 'scientific,' which have been chosen in default of better, are, of course, not to be understood as if we supposed that all the philosophers we class as mystic were unscientific. The fact that we regard Parmenides, the discoverer of Logic, as an off-shoot of Pythagoreanism, and Plato himself as finding in the Italian philosophy the chief source of his inspiration, will be enough to refute such a misunderstanding. Moreover, the Pythagorean School itself developed a scientific doctrine closely resembling the Milesian Atomism; and Empedocles, again, attempted to combine the two types of philosophy.

What we do hope to establish is that the philosophy of the western Greek colonies, however much its individual thinkers may be influenced by the Milesians and their followers in the East, however far they may severally go to join hands with 'science,' has at its root a different and opposed view of life, a different type of religion, and, consequently, a different conceptual scheme of the nature of things, which lies behind all its manifestations, and is the point of departure which they all have in common. What this was, we have already tried at some length to describe. It was that type of religion, centred in Greece round the figure of Dionysus, which has some claim to be called the only form of religion that possesses the secret of vitality, just because it is, at bottom, the religion of the Life of earth and man, the life which, though it dies, is perpetually reborn. As if because its faith has been rooted in this life, mystical religion has itself been reborn a thousand times. Its history is a series of revivals; and every such revival is heralded by the doctrine of regeneration: 'Ye must be born again.' But he that would save his life must lose it; this religion is also the religion of death and renunciation: Hades and Dionysus are the same. Herein lies its almost irresistible attraction for a certain type of emotional ascetic—the man whose nature demands intensity of passion, and who yet rejects 'bodily' passions as impure.

107. *The Orphic Revival*

Behind the School of Pythagoras, we can discern, in the so-called Orphic revival, one of these reformations of Dionysiac religion. It is important for us to grasp its nature, because the reforming principle, represented in the figure of Orpheus, is Apolline in character, and therefore drawn partly within the circle of Olympian theology. Orpheus, the ideal of the Orphic, is a Dionysus tamed, and clothed, and in his right mind—in a word, Apollinised.[1] When we come to the Pythagorean School, which carries on this representation into philosophy, the same combination of Dionysiac with Apolline elements will reappear ; and we shall see, moreover, that (as we should expect) there is, between the two ideals, a deep-lying contradiction, which defies reconciliation. Dionysus may become Orpheus, without losing all his life and mystery ; but, if he takes the further step (which perhaps, in a sense, he actually did take at Delphi [2]) and becomes Apollo, then he ceases to be Dionysus. He has left the earth and her cycle of life, which dies and is born again, and ascended to his seat among the ' deathless ' ones, above the reach of mortality. He is no longer a daemon in communion with his church, but a God beyond the great fixed gulf of *Moira*. This fatal sequence, from the group-daemon to the personal God, is reflected in a curious way in the Pythagorean philosophy, which is always passing from mysticism to science, as its religion had passed from Dionysus to Apollo. Yet, philosophy and religion alike do not cease to be mystical at the root ; and the attempt to hold the two ends together involves religion in certain contradictions, and leads philosophy to corresponding dilemmas, which it will be our business to bring to light.

It is important to observe that the Orphic movement was a revival, as well as a reformation ; that is to say, it was a return to a type of religion more primitive than the prevailing Olympianism. It must have been caused by one of those outbursts of mystic fervour which, from time to time, upheave and shatter the crystallised forms of theology and ecclesiasticism, when the

---

[1] For Orpheus as son, or ἐρώμενος, or ἕταιρος of Apollo, see Roscher Lex. s.v. 'Orpheus'; Eisler, *Weltenmantel*, ii. p. 681.

[2] See J. E. Harrison, *Themis*, p. 443.

life that created them has died out of them, and they have drifted away from all touch with genuine emotion. The rule in such cases is that, with much clearing away of lumber, there is a return to the simple, primitive type of organisation shaped by the first impulse of the same spirit, which now resurges and seeks once more to clothe itself in the bare essential form. The Orphic movement was thus, in some degree, a return to Dionysus and his *thiasos*—the daemon and his church, held in one by the unique, mystical relation. It is the organisation of the magical secret society, adapted once more to a reviving human need.

But history never repeats itself. The Dionysus to whom the Orphics return, is not the old Dionysus of a group of satyrs, but the Orpheus who was more at home with the Muses than with the Maenads. It was the Maenads, indeed, that tore him, the Muse's enchanting son, to pieces. Thus, Dionysus, though revived, is also reformed ; the more savage parts of his ritual are expurgated, or toned down to a decent symbolism.

Above all, what had formerly been the religion of earth and of the life and death of her trees and plants in the circling seasons, becomes now a religion of the heavenly bodies, and especially of the Sun. The Sun also moves through the circle of the year, waxing in summer and waning in winter ; but he too easily comes to be conceived as an immutable and deathless God.[1] The Olympian notion of immortality (*athanasia*), as a life that negates change and death, intrudes itself. With the doctrine of the fall of the soul from the stars, went, as we have seen, the belief in an indestructible individual soul, persisting throughout its round of reincarnation.

After what has been said above of Heracleitus, it will be clear that this Orphic notion of individual immortality is in contradiction with the other mystic representation, to which Heracleitus remains true, that there is no life without death, and that there is only one life, which dies and is reborn in every shape of existence. This representation is the older, for it goes back to days when only the group had a soul, and the atomic individual soul was not yet invented. The soul of Heracleitus' world is like the soul of the tribe which passes from the

---

[1] Heracleitus characteristically protested against this, declaring that the Sun, like everything else, changes, and is 'new every day' (frag. 32).

living state to the dead, and round again. This was no ' sorrowful weary wheel,' from which any escape was either possible or to be desired. The cyclic movement simply was the movement of life, and life could take no other course, no upward flight to a mansion in the stars. Thus, the Orphic religion already contains two contradictory notions of the nature and destiny of the soul, one Dionysiac, the other Ouranian. Modern writers have failed to see this contradiction, because they have been blinded by the compromise in which Orphism attempts to ' reconcile ' the incompatible.

Further, throughout the mystical systems inspired by Orphism, we shall find the fundamental contrast between the two principles of Light and Darkness, identified with Good and Evil. This cosmic dualism is the counterpart of the dualism in the nature of the soul; for, as always, *physis* and soul correspond, and are, indeed, identical in substance. The soul in its pure state consists of fire, like the divine stars from which it falls; in its impure state, throughout the period of reincarnation, its substance is infected with the baser elements, and weighed down by the gross admixture of the flesh.[1] In the cosmologies inspired by this conception, we may expect to find, first, that the element of fire will be set in contrast with the other three,[2] and second, that the manifold world of sense will be viewed as a degradation from the purity of real being. Such systems will tend to be other-worldly, putting all value in the unseen unity of God, and condemning the visible world as false and illusive, a turbid medium in which the rays of heavenly light are broken and obscured in mist and darkness. These characteristics are common to all the systems which came out of the Pythagorean movement—Pythagoreanism proper, and the philosophies of Parmenides, Empedocles, and Plato.

[1] All this is very clearly brought out by Socrates in Plato's *Phaedo* ; see below, p. 246.

[2] It must be remembered, too, that Fire is the element of which the Measurers of *Time* (the heavenly bodies) consist. Diog. Laert. viii. 1, 27 (Pythagoras): ἥλιόν τε καὶ σελήνην καὶ τοὺς ἄλλους ἀστέρας εἶναι θεούς· ἐπικρατεῖν γὰο τὸ θερμὸν ἐν αὐτοῖς, ὅπερ ἐστὶ ζωῆς αἴτιον . . . καὶ ἀνθρώποις εἶναι πρὸς θεοὺς συγγένειαν, κατὰ τὸ μετέχειν ἄνθρωπον θερμοῦ· διὸ καὶ προνοεῖσθαι τὸν θεὸν ἡμῶν. So, in aboriginal America, ' the Fire-God was especially associated with the lapse of time,' and his vital force, enfeebled by use, was periodically renewed by the kindling of new fire. Payne, *History of the New World*, ii. 330.

108. *The Pythagorean reformation of Orphism*

As Orphism was a reformation of Dionysiac religion, so Pythagoreanism may be regarded as a further reformation of Orphism,[1]
which takes yet another step, away from Dionysus, away even
from Orpheus, towards Apollo. It is a further movement from
emotion towards intellect and reason, from religion towards
philosophy. Orphism was still a cult, in which the initiate, as
Aristotle[2] says, ' was not expected to learn or understand anything, but to feel a certain emotion and get into a certain state
of mind, after first becoming fit to experience it.' The means
to that emotional state of mind had formerly been ' orgiastic '
ritual, and especially those dramatic representations of the
passion and resurrection of the life-daemon, which point back
to the old mimetic dances of magic, and forward to the tragic
drama. The state of mind is that of passionate sympathetic
contemplation ($\theta\epsilon\omega\rho\iota a$), in which the spectator is identified
with the suffering God, dies in his death, and rises again in his
new birth. By these and other ritual means—the eating of
flesh or the drinking of wine—the old sense of mystical oneness and participation can be renewed, and the daemon-soul of
the group re-created in collective emotion. The only doctrine
is the myth, the verbal counterpart of the action of the rite,
the life-history of the God, which is also the life-history of
the soul.

The doctrines of mysticism are secret, because they are not
cold, abstract beliefs, or articles in a creed, which can be taught
and explained by intellectual processes ; such beliefs no one has
ever desired to conceal, except from fear of persecution. The
' truth ' which mysticism guards is a thing which can only be
learnt by being experienced ($\pi a\theta\epsilon\hat{\iota}\nu \mu a\theta\epsilon\hat{\iota}\nu$); it is, fundamentally,
not an intellectual, but an emotional experience—that invasive,
flooding sense of oneness, of reunion and communion with the

---

[1] For Pythagoras' relation to the Orphic communities in Western Greece
see Eisler, *Weltenmantel*, ii. p. 679.

[2] Arist. frag. 45, 1483 *a* 19 : καθάπερ Ἀριστοτέλης ἀξιοῖ τοὺς τελουμένους οὐ
μαθεῖν τι δεῖν, ἀλλὰ παθεῖν καὶ διατεθῆναι δηλονότι γενομένους ἐπιτηδείους. Cf.
Burnet, *E.G.P.*[2], p. 91, who, however, ignores the importance of the emotional state of mind. This, surely, not the ritual action, is the essential
thing.

life of the world, which the mystical temperaments of all ages seem to have in common, no matter in what theological terms they may happen to construe it afterwards. Being an emotional, non-rational state, it is indescribable, and incommunicable save by suggestion. To induce that state, by the stimulus of collective excitement and all the pageantry of dramatic ceremonial, is the aim of mystic ritual. The ' truth ' can only come to those who submit themselves to these influences, because it is a thing to be immediately felt, not conveyed by dogmatic instruction. For that reason only—a very sufficient one—' mysteries ' are reserved to the initiate, who have undergone ' purification,' and so put themselves into a state of mind which fits them for the consummate experience.

Pythagoreanism presents itself as an attempt to intellectualise the content of Orphism, while preserving its social form, and as much as possible of the spirit which that form had originally clothed. Like Orphism itself, it is both a reformation and a revival. Like all reformations, it means that much of the ceremonial overgrowth is shaken off : Orphism ceases to be a cult, and becomes a Way of life. As a revival, Pythagoreanism means a return to an earlier simplicity, a disinterring of the essential form, whose outline is simple enough to adapt itself to a new movement of the spirit. Pythagoreanism is thus, from the very first, a complex phenomenon, containing the germs of several tendencies, which, when we come to the philosophies that emerged from the school, we shall find separating towards divergent issues, or intertwined in ingenious reconciliations. Our analysis must take account of three strata, superimposed in the order we have described—Dionysus, Orpheus, Pythagoras. From Dionysus come the unity of all life, in the cycle of death and rebirth, and the conception of the daemon or collective soul, immanent in the group as a whole, and yet something more than any or all of the members that partake of it. To Orpheus is due the shift of focus from earth to heaven, the substitution for the vivid, emotional experience of the renewal of life in nature, of the worship of a distant and passionless perfection in the region of light, from which the soul, now immortal, is fallen into the body of this death, and which it aspires to regain by the formal observances of asceticism. But the Orphic still clung to the emotional experience of reunion and the ritual that induced it, and, in particular, to the passionate spectacle (*theoria*) of the suffering God. Pythagoras gave a new meaning to *theoria* ; he reinterpreted it as the passionless contemplation of rational, unchanging truth, and converted the way of life into a ' pursuit of wisdom ' (*philosophia*). The way of life is still also a way of death ; [1] but now it means death to the emotions and lusts of this vile body, and a release of the intellect to soar into the untroubled empyrean of *theory*.[2] This is now the only avenue by which the soul can ' follow God ' (ἕπεσθαι θεῷ), who has ascended beyond the stars.[3] Orgiastic ritual, which plays upon the emotions, only drives a new nail into the coffin of the soul, and binds it by a new chain to its earthly prison-house. All that must go ; only certain ascetic prescriptions of the Orphic *askesis* are retained, to symbolise a turning away from lower desires, that might enthral the reason.[4]

Such, in our opinion, is the trend of this new movement, called Pythagoreanism. But, though it moves further from Dionysus towards Apollo, it remains Dionysiac at the root, and keeps alive something of the faith first delivered to the saints of mysticism. Hence, in the analysis to which we now turn, we shall try to distinguish what Pythagoreanism preserves from each

---

[1] Plato, *Phaedo*, 64 A : κινδυνεύουσι γὰρ ὅσοι τυγχάνουσιν ὀρθῶς ἁπτόμενοι φιλοσοφίας λεληθέναι τοὺς ἄλλους, ὅτι οὐδὲν ἄλλο αὐτοὶ ἐπιτηδεύουσιν ἢ ἀποθνήσκειν τε καὶ τεθνάναι.

[2] Not to be confounded with the θεωρία of Ionian science, which characteristically means *curiosity*, such as led Hekataeus or Solon to travel about the world as *spectators* of its marvels. The θεωρία of Pythagoras meant especially contemplation of the heavens. Cf. his sermon on the Three Lives, Heracl. Pont. ap. Cic. *Tusc.* v. 3 ; Iambl. *Vit. Pyth.* 58 : εἰλικρινέστατον δὲ εἶναι τοῦτον ἀνθρώπου τρόπον, τὸν ἀποδεξάμενον τὴν τῶν καλλίστων θεωρίαν, ὃν καὶ προσονομάζειν φιλόσοφον. καλὴν μὲν οὖν εἶναι τὴν τοῦ σύμπαντος οὐρανοῦ θέαν καὶ τῶν ἐν αὐτῷ φορουμένων ἀστέρων, εἴ τις καθορῴη τὴν τάξιν . . . Plato, though impatient of this star-gazing (*Rep.* 529 A), and of those who study the ' proportion (συμμετρία) of day to night, and of day and night to month, and of month to year, and of the other stars to sun and moon' (530 A), still speaks of the philosopher as the ' spectator of all *time*.'

[3] For the escape of the soul from the wheel of birth, as Pythagorean doctrine, see Rohde, *Psyche*,[3] ii. 165. Plato, *Theaet.* 176 A : διὸ καὶ πειρᾶσθαι χρὴ ἐνθένδε ἐκεῖσε φεύγειν ὅτι τάχιστα. φυγὴ δὲ ὁμοίωσις θεῷ κατὰ τὸ δύνατον.

[4] Plato's rejection of the drama and of the orgiastic kinds of music is partly motived by a similar condemnation of violent states of non-rational emotion.

of the two strata—Dionysiac and Orphic—that lie below it. In the actual history of the school, all the elements are, of course, present from the outset and blended together ; but, in analysis, it is worth while to isolate them, with a view to following out their shifting combinations in the systems which derive from the Pythagorean tradition.

109. *Pythagoras as Daemon of his School*

Dikaiarchos,[1] after describing the founding of the community at Kroton, says that it is hard to get any certain knowledge of what Pythagoras taught his disciples ; but his best known doctrines were, ' first, that soul is an immortal thing, and that it is transformed into other kinds of living things; further, that whatever comes into existence is born again in the revolutions of a certain cycle, nothing being absolutely new; and that all things that are born with life in them ought to be treated as kindred ' (ὁμογενῆ).

We have already dwelt at length on the significance of these doctrines, of the unity and kinship of all life or soul, and its continuous rebirth in periodic revolutions. Later legend told how Pythagoras, like Francis of Assisi and the Spanish Carmelites, preached to animals ; [2] and, when we remember that Orpheus before him had made the wild things gather to his music, there is no reason to doubt the substantial truth of the tradition. What specially concerns us is to note that, for anything Dikaiarchos says, the Master himself, like Heracleitus,

---

[1] Ap. Porph. *Vit. Pyth.* 18, 19 : πρῶτον μὲν ὡς ἀθάνατον εἶναί φησι τὴν ψυχήν, εἶτα μεταβάλλουσαν εἰς ἄλλα γένη ζῴων, πρὸς δὲ τούτοις ὅτι κατὰ περιόδους τινὰς τὰ γενόμενά ποτε πάλιν γίγνεται, νέον δὲ οὐδὲν ἁπλῶς ἐστι, καὶ ὅτι πάντα τὰ γινόμενα ἔμψυχα ὁμογενῆ δεῖ νομίζειν.

[2] Iambl. *Vit. Pyth.* xiii. ; Porph. *Vit. Pyth.* 24 ; G. Cunninghame Graham, *Santa Teresa* (1907), p. 51. Compare also the Golden race of the Age of Kronos in the *Politicus* of Plato (272 B), who ' have the power to converse not only with men but with beasts,' and use their opportunity εἰς φιλοσοφίαν, ' inquiring from all nature ' (παρὰ πάσης φύσεως), in case any part of nature may have some peculiar faculty, so as to perceive, better than any other, what might contribute to the ingathering of wisdom. In the *Meno*, 81 c, where the Orphic doctrine of *palingenesia* is stated, it is the ' kinship of all nature ' (ἅτε τῆς φύσεως ἁπάσης συγγενοῦς οὔσης) that makes it possible for the soul, which has learnt all things in the other world, to recover its knowledge here by reminiscence (*anamnesis*).

may have held, more closely than his later followers, to the primitive Dionysiac belief in one all-pervading Soul, the substratum of kinship which unites all forms of life into ' one clan ' (ὁμογενή).[1] It seems probable that he dwelt upon this unity, rather than upon the inconsistent idea of a plurality of indestructible, atomic souls, which always asserts itself in the popular mind as soon as the sense of individuality has grown strong enough to insist upon a personal immortality. Not that we are convinced that Pythagoras himself saw the inconsistency or tried to avoid it ; only, the very form which he gave to his community embodied the value he set on unity and his attempt to keep in check the self-assertion of individualism.

To this society men and women were admitted without distinction ; they had all possessions in common, and a ' common fellowship and mode of life.'[2] In particular, no individual member of the school was allowed to claim the credit of any discovery he might make. The significance of this rule has not been fully understood. It was vulgarly supposed that the school must have wished to keep its knowledge to itself as a ' mysterious ' doctrine, as if there were any conceivable reason

---

[1] Sextus Emp. *Math.* ix. 127: οἱ μὲν οὖν περὶ τὸν Πυθαγόραν καὶ τὸν Ἐμπεδοκλέα καὶ τῶν Ἰταλῶν πλῆθος φασὶ μὴ μόνον ἡμῖν πρὸς ἀλλήλους καὶ πρὸς τοὺς θεοὺς εἶναί τινα κοινωνίαν, ἀλλὰ καὶ πρὸς τὰ ἄλογα τῶν ζώων. ἐν γὰρ ὑπάρχειν πνεῦμα τὸ διὰ παντὸς τοῦ κόσμου διῆκον ψυχῆς τρόπον, τὸ καὶ ἑνοῦν ἡμᾶς πρὸς ἐκεῖνα. Iamblichus (*Vit. Pyth.* 108) well expresses the doctrine in the following words : Pythagoras ' taught them to abstain from things that had life (soul) in them (ἐμψύχων) ; for, if they wished to reach the height of just behaviour, they must of course do no wrong to any of the living things that were their kindred (συγγενῶν ζώιων). How could they induce others to behave justly if they themselves were convicted of aggression (πλεονεξία), although bound in the participation of kinship (συγγενικῆι μετοχῆι) with living things, which are linked to us, as it were, in brotherhood by fellowship (κοινωνίαν) in the same life and elements and the same mixture composed of them.' If Aristoxenus (see Burnet, *E. G. P.*[2], p. 102) is right in stating that Pythagoras only prohibited, among animals, the ploughing ox and the ram, he probably did so because the ram stood for the male fertilising principle of animal life, and the ox which ploughs the earth for the same principle in vegetation, which springs from the ploughed earth. The two animals would be symbols of *all* life. Compare the doubtful fragment of Empedocles 154 *b* (*D. F. V.*[2]) which says that the first miserable men who ate flesh βοῶν ἐπάσαντ' ἀροτήρων.

[2] κοινὴ συνουσία καὶ δίαιτα, Iambl. *Vit. Pyth.* 246. The admission of women was ' Dionysiac ' (the Maenads) rather than Orphic. Orphism was anti-feminine.

for hiding a theorem in geometry or harmonics. The truth comes out in the story of Hippasos of Metapontion, who ' was of the Pythagoreans, but, because he published a treatise on the sphere of the twelve pentagons, was cast away at sea, as having committed an impiety and taken glory to himself for his discovery, whereas all discoveries belonged to " Him " (ἐκείνου τοῦ ἀνδρός), for so they call Pythagoras. They say that a supernatural vengeance overtook (τὸ δαιμόνιον νεμεσῆσαι) those who published what belonged to Pythagoras.' [1] This supernatural or daemonic anger was the wrath of Pythagoras himself, who after his death remained what he had been in life—the daemon in whom all the life of his church was centred and incarnated. That Pythagoras worked miracles and was conscious of supernatural power, there is no reason whatever to doubt ; he was probably the author of the doctrine : ' There are Gods, and men, and beings like Pythagoras '—beings who are half-divine, daemons in human shape. [2] What is to be gathered from the story of Hippasos is that the pious Pythagoreans believed that the Master's spirit dwelt continually within his church, and was the source of all its inspiration. [3] The impiety lay, not in divulging a discovery in mathematics, but in claiming to have invented what could only have come from ' Him.'

Thus Pythagoras seems to have held to the conception of a group-soul, incarnate in himself, but living on after his death as the *Logos* of his disciples. Heracleides, who preserves the famous story of his previous incarnations, reports him as saying that Hermes had offered him anything he wished for, except deathlessness (*athanasia*) ; and that he chose to preserve, through life and death, the memory of what happened to him. [4] The legend may enshrine the truth that the ' immortality ' Pythagoras desired and claimed was not the deathless continuation

---

[1] Iambl. *Vit. Pyth.* 88 = *D.F.V.*[2] s. tit. 'Hippasos,' 4.

[2] *D.F.V.*[2], p. 24. Cf. the Introd. to the Hindu Tales of Somadeva : 'The Gods have perpetual happiness, men are in constant unhappiness ; the actions of those who are *between men and Gods* are, by the diversity of their lot, agreeable. Therefore I will recount to you the life of the Vidyâdhâras,' *i.e.* demons and magicians (*Kâtha-Sâra-Sârit-Sagara*, 1. i. 47).

[3] Cf. Procl. *in Eud.* i. p. 419 : ἔστι μὲν ἀρχαῖα, φασὶν οἱ περὶ τὸν Εὔδημον, καὶ τῆς τῶν Πυθαγορείων Μούσης εὑρήματα.

[4] Heracl. Pont. ap. Diog. viii. 4 (*D.F.V.*[2], p. 24).

of individual personality, but the older Dionysiac continuity of the one life that is born again in every generation of the group.[1] But, as usual, his followers could not be content to live in communion with a spirit of like passions with themselves, but must needs exalt their daemon to the highest grade of divinity. Pythagoras soon becomes the son of Apollo by a virgin birth,[2] and even an incarnate God, Apollo Hyberoreios himself.[3] But, through all the overgrowth of decadent superstition in the later legend, enough remains of the older faith to warrant us in refusing to attribute these frigid inventions to the Master himself. *Apotheosis* and *athanasia* are precisely the fatal steps in the career of a ' being like Pythagoras,' because they put an end to the reality of that communion in which the originators of such churches find the very meaning of the common life.

If our view, then, be correct, the society of Pythagoras, so long as the influence of his own ideal survived, realised once more the primitive type of religious group, and that peculiar relation, best called ' participation ' (*methexis*), in which such a group stands to its immanent collective soul. The passage from the divine plane to the human, and from the human to the divine, remains permeable, and is perpetually traversed. The One can go out into the many ; the many can lose themselves in reunion with the One. This essential conception is the key to the understanding of the number doctrine, on which rests Pythagoras' claim to be a philosopher, as well as a founder of mathematics.

110. *The Tetractys* [4]

The misguided followers who reckoned Pythagoras among the Gods, were accustomed, Porphyry tells us,[5] to swear by

---

[1] It will be remembered how Diotima in Plato's *Symposium* (207 D) explains this immortality of perpetual renewal. Plato, too, thought of his *logoi* as living on in the souls of his school and perpetually giving birth to new thoughts in each generation that arose and passed away.

[2] His mother is called Parthenis, in legend. See Eisler, *Weltenmantel*, ii. p. 679 ff.; W. Schultz, *Altionische Mystik*, p. 97.

[3] Arist. frag. 186 ; Porph. *Vit. Pyth.* 20: μετὰ τῶν θεῶν τὸν Πυθαγόραν κατηρίθμουν.

[4] For the *tetractys* see W. Schultz, ΑΤΤΟΣ, *Memnon*, 1910 ; Eisler, *Weltenmantel*, ii. p. 684.   [5] *Vit. Pyth.* 20.

him, as the God who had left with them a symbol applicable to the solution of many problems in nature—the *tetractys*.

' The so-called Pythagoreans,' says Aristotle,[1] ' attached themselves to the mathematics, and were the first to advance that science by their education, in which they were led to suppose that the principles of mathematics are the principles of all things. So, as numbers are logically first among these principles, and they fancied they could perceive in numbers many analogies of what is and what comes into being, much more readily than in fire and earth and water . . . and since they further observed that the properties and determining ratios of harmonies depend on numbers—since, in fact, everything else manifestly appeared to be modelled in its entire character ($\phi\acute{v}\sigma\iota\nu$) on numbers, and numbers to be the ultimate things in the whole universe, they became convinced that the elements of numbers are the elements of everything, and that the whole " Heaven " is harmony and number.' Aristotle adds that the decad was held to be perfect, and to embrace the whole ' nature ' of number.[2] We may therefore look for the ' nature ' of all things in the decad, as expressed in the symbol called the *tetractys*, which, we have every reason to believe, goes back to Pythagoras himself.

The original *tetractys* appears to have been the ' *tetractys* of the decad,' obtained by the addition, $1+2+3+4=10$:

' This *tetractys*,' says Theon of Smyrna,[3] ' is of great importance in music, because all the consonances are to be found

---

[1] *Met.* A 5, trans. A. E. Taylor.

[2] *Met.* A 5, 986 a : ἐπειδὴ τέλειον ἡ δεκὰς εἶναι δοκεῖ καὶ πᾶσαν περιειληφέναι τὴν τῶν ἀριθμῶν φύσιν. Cf. Philolaus, frag. 11 : θεωρεῖν δεῖ τὰ ἔργα καὶ τὴν οὐσίαν τῶ ἀριθμῶ καττὰν δύναμιν ἅτις ἐστὶν ἐν τᾷ δεκάδι· μεγάλα γὰρ καὶ παντελὴς καὶ παντόεργος καὶ θείω καὶ οὐρανίω βίω καὶ ἀνθρωπίνω ἀρχὰ καὶ ἁγεμὼν κοινωνοῦσα. Lévy-Bruhl (*Fonct. ment.* p. 237) has an interesting discussion of the mystic properties of numbers. He remarks that the numbers so enveloped with a mystical atmosphere rarely go above 10. The higher numbers have not, together with their names, passed into collective representations, but have generally been mere arithmetical numbers from the first.

[3] περὶ τετρακτύος, p. 154, Dupuis (1892).

contained in it. But it is not only on this account that it has been held in the highest honour by all Pythagoreans ; but also because it is held to contain the nature of the universe. Hence it was an oath by which they swore :

' By him who gave to our soul the *tetractys*, which hath the fountain and root of ever-springing " nature " (*physis*).' [1]

Theon proceeds to enumerate other forms of the *tetractys*. The second is that used by Plato in the *Timaeus* to symbolise the harmonic constitution of the world-soul :

These two *tetractyes* ' contain the musical, geometrical, and arithmetical ratios, of which the harmony of the whole universe is composed.'

The later Pythagoreans delighted in using this symbol as the master-key to the interpretation of the world. The third *tetractys* is point, line, surface, solid ; the fourth is fire, air, water, earth ; the fifth is pyramid, octahedron, eikosahedron, cube ; the sixth is ' of things that grow ' (τῶν φυομένων) : the seed, growth into length, into width, into height ; [2] the seventh is that of societies : the individual, the family, the village, the

---

1   οὐ μὰ τὸν ἀμετέρᾳ ψυχᾷ (γενέᾳ, al.) παραδόντα τετρακτύν,
παγὰν ἀενάου φύσιος ῥίζωμά τ' ἔχουσαν.

Diels, *Arch. f. Gesch. d. Phil.* iii. 457, conjectures that these lines were the opening of the poem often cited as the Ἱερὸς Λόγος or Περὶ θεῶν, in which, according to *Theol. Arith.* p. 17, the might of the number 4 was celebrated, and Metaphysics connected with it.

Cf. Payne, *History of the New World*, ii. 283, 410 : ' Nauh-, the Mexican particle for this number (4), in the abstract form " Nahui " probably embodies some conception analogous to " Nahua," the Command or Rule of Life, and suggesting wholeness, perfection, or indefeasibility ; these austere and orderly barbarians recall the Pythagorean philosophers, who held the number 4 to be the root or source of all things.' Nahuatlacâ is a general name used by the Mexicans to denote ' tribes living mainly by agriculture in accordance with a settled Nahua or Rule of Life, dictated by a custom administered by hereditary chiefs.'

2 Note this as the primitive form of the three 'dimensions' (αὔξαι, ' growths ').

state ; the eighth is the four cognitive faculties : reason, knowledge, opinion, sense ; [1] the ninth is the rational, spirited, and appetitive parts of soul, and the body ; the tenth is spring, summer, autumn, winter—the seasons by which all things come into being ; the eleventh is the four ages of man : infancy, youth, manhood, old age.

' The cosmos composed of these *tetractyes* is geometrically, harmonically, and arithmetically adjusted, potentially containing every nature of number, and every magnitude and every body, whether simple or composite. It is perfect because all things are parts of it, and itself is not a part of anything. That is the reason why the Pythagoreans swore by it, and said " all things are like number." '

The details of some of these interpretations of the *tetractys* are, of course, late ; they are expressed partly in Platonic terms.[2] But they are in a line with the earliest traditions of Pythagoreanism, and are typical of the whole tendency of the school. They satisfy the mystic's passion for unity, his desire to find the meaning and nature of the whole in every part.

111. *The Procession of Numbers*

The real significance of the *tetractys* comes out in the second line of the Oath, which describes it as ' containing the fountain and root of ever-springing nature (*physis*).' No words could better express what we take to be the genuine Pythagorean conception of the process by which the One goes out into the manifold world. The *tetractys* is not only a symbol of static relations linking the various parts of the cosmos ; it contains also the cosmogonical movement of life, evolving out of primal unity the harmonised structure of the whole. It is a fountain of ever-flowing life.

The *tetractys* of the decad is a numerical series, the sum of which is the perfect number, ten, which we are told that Pythagoras regarded as ' the nature of number, because all men,

---

[1] Arist. *de Anim.* a 2, 404 *b* 21.

[2] Cf. Arist. *de Anim.* a 2, 404 *b* 18. ' It was explained in (Plato's) lectures on philosophy that the self-animal (universe) is composed of the form of One, and the first length (Two), breadth (Three), and depth (Four),' etc.

whether Hellenes or not, count up to ten, and, when they reach it, revert again to unity.'[1]   The word ' revert ' ($\dot{a}\nu a\pi o\delta\delta\omega$) recalls the fragment, already quoted, of the Pythagorean Hippodamus, which tells us that this reversion is to be conceived as the revolution of a wheel. ' All mortal things under constraint of Nature revolve in a wheel of changes. . . . When they are born they grow, and when grown they reach their height, and after that they grow old, and at last perish. At one time, Nature causes them to come to their goal in her region of darkness, and then back again out of the darkness they come round into mortal form, by alternation of birth and repayment of death, in the cycle wherein Nature *reverts* upon herself ' ($\dot{a}\nu a\pi o\delta\iota\zeta o\acute{\nu}\sigma a\varsigma$).[2]

We have seen that the whole nature of things, all the essential properties of *physis*, were believed by the Pythagoreans to be contained in the *tetractys* of the decad ; and it now appears that, just as we should expect, this ' fountain of ever-flowing nature ' contains the periodic movement of life, evolving out of unity and reverting to unity again, in the recurrent revolution of a wheel of birth. It embodies the fundamental Dionysiac representation of *palingenesia*.

But there is something more in it than this. Pythagoras inherited the music of Orpheus, as well as the reincarnation doctrine of Dionysus. From the Orphics he inherited also the doctrine of the fall of the soul from its first perfect state of union with the divine, its degradation into the darkness of this life and of the underworld, and its final restoration to peace and unity. Now, on the model of this doctrine of the fall of the soul, the Pythagorean philosophy must hold that all existence proceeds out of the One and returns to it again ; and that the One alone is perfect, while the manifold world of visible body is a turbid medium of appearance, in which the one truth is half-revealed and half-concealed, as the divine soul is manifest in the flesh and yet obscured by it and degraded.

There is thus, inherent in the representation handed down

---

[1] Aetius, i. 3. 8 : $\epsilon l\nu a\iota$ $\delta\grave{\epsilon}$ $\tau\grave{\eta}\nu$ $\phi\acute{\nu}\sigma\iota\nu$ $\tauο\hat{\nu}$ $\dot{a}\rho\iota\theta\muο\hat{\nu}$ $\delta\acute{\epsilon}\kappa a\cdot$ $\mu\acute{\epsilon}\chi\rho\iota$ $\gamma\grave{a}\rho$ $\tau\hat{\omega}\nu$ $\delta\acute{\epsilon}\kappa a$ $\pi\acute{a}\nu\tau\epsilon\varsigma$"$E\lambda\lambda\eta\nu\epsilon\varsigma$, $\pi\acute{a}\nu\tau\epsilon\varsigma$ $\beta\acute{a}\rho\beta a\rho o\iota$ $\dot{a}\rho\iota\theta\muο\hat{\nu}\sigma\iota\nu$, $\dot{\epsilon}\phi'$ $\mathring{a}$ $\dot{\epsilon}\lambda\theta\acute{o}\nu\tau\epsilon\varsigma$ $\pi\acute{a}\lambda\iota\nu$ $\dot{a}\nu a\pi o\delta o\hat{\nu}\sigma\iota\nu$ $\dot{\epsilon}\pi\grave{\iota}$ $\tau\grave{\eta}\nu$ $\muο\nu\acute{a}\delta a$.   Professor Burnet (*E.G.P.*[2], p. 114) thinks we are probably justified in referring this to Pythagoras himself.   For $\pi\rho o\pi o\delta\iota\sigma\mu\acute{o}\varsigma$ (' procession '), the opposite of $\dot{a}\nu a\pi o\delta\iota\sigma\mu\acute{o}\varsigma$, see below, p. 209, note 1.

[2] Hippodamus, ap. Stob. *Flor.* 98, 71, see above, p. 167, note 1.

from Orphism to Pythagoras, not only the primitive wheel of
birth, but another aspect of the movement of life, which is best
described as a *processional* movement (προποδισμός) out of unity
into plurality, out of light into darkness.[1] This movement, also,
must be revealed in the nature of numbers, and contained in the
tetractys. Pythagoras found it in the procession of numerical
series, the study of which he originated, thereby founding the
science of number. It is practically certain, also, that in music
he discovered the ratios of the octave, the fifth, and the fourth,
contained in the harmonic proportion 12 : 8 : 6.[2] Now a pro-
gression like those contained in the *tetractys* of Plato's world-
soul (p. 206)—the series, 1 : 2 : 4 : 8, 1 : 3 : 9 : 27—is what the
Pythagoreans called an *harmonia* ; it is a continuous entity knit
together by a principle of unity running through it, namely the
logos or ratio ($\frac{1}{2}$ or $\frac{1}{3}$) which links every term to its predecessor
by the same bond.[3] Both series, moreover, radiate from the One,
which in Pythagorean arithmetic was not itself a number, but
the source in which the whole nature of all numbers was gathered
up and implicit. When we note, further, that every number is
not only a many, but also *one* number, we can see how Pythagoras would find the whole movement of cosmic evolution contained in the procession of series, in which the One passes out of
itself into a manifold, yet without losing all its unity, and a
return from the many to the One is secured by that bond of
proportion which runs, backwards and forwards, through the
whole series and links it into a ' harmony.' It is thus that we
must understand the doctrine that ' the whole Heaven is harmony and number.' The processional movement of *physis* is
modelled upon that of soul, which falls from its first state of
union with the divine, but yet remains linked to the One life

---

[1] *Theon Smyrn.* p. 29 (Dupuis) : ἀριθμός ἐστι σύστημα μονάδων (the atomic
view discussed below, p. 212) ἤ προποδισμὸς πλήθους ἀπὸ μονάδος ἀρχόμενος καὶ
ἀναποδισμὸς εἰς μονάδα καταλήγων.

[2] See Burnet, *E.G.P.*[2], p. 118.

[3] Aetius, i. 3. 8 : Πυθαγόρας . . . ἀρχὰς τοὺς ἀριθμοὺς καὶ τὰς συμμετρίας τὰς
ἐν τούτοις, ἃς καὶ ἁρμονίας καλεῖ. Compare the *logos* of Heracleitus, as constancy of ' measures ' preserved throughout transformation, above, p. 188.
Plato, *Tim.* 31 c, on the ' bond ' of proportion : δεσμῶν δὲ κάλλιστος ὃς ἂν αὐτόν
τε καὶ τὰ συνδούμενα ὅτι μάλιστα ἒν ποιῇ· τοῦτο δὲ πέφυκεν ἀναλογία κάλλιστα
ἀποτελεῖν.

by mysterious bonds of harmony, and can return to it again, purified by music.[1]

In discussing the segregation of opposites and its possible origin, as reflecting the exogamous segmentation of the undifferentiated human herd, we have already pointed out that the Pythagorean One, or Monad, splits into two principles, male and female, the Even and the Odd, which are the elements of all numbers and so of the universe.[2]   The analogy reminds us that the One is not simply a numerical unit, which gives rise to other numbers by a process of addition. That conception belongs to the later atomistic number-doctrine, presently to be considered.[3]   In the earlier Pythagoreanism, we must think of the One (which is not itself a number at all) as analogous to Anaximander's ἄπειρον. It is the primary, undifferentiated group-soul, or *physis*, of the universe, and numbers must arise from it by a process of differentiation or ' separating out ' (ἀπόκρισις). Similarly, each of these numbers is not a collection of units, built up by addition, but itself a sort of minor group-soul—a distinct ' nature,' with various mystical properties. In the same way, it is by dividing up the whole interval of the octave that the harmonic proportions are determined.[4]

---

[1] See *Theon Smyrn.* p. 18 ff. (Dupuis) for philosophy as purification and initiation; Procl. Μέλισσα, *Anec. Gr. et Lat.* ii. p. 25 : ἡ μέν γε μυριάς, ἥτις ἐστὶν ἁρμονία κρείττων, ἐκ τῆς τριωδουμένης γενομένη μονάδος ἐπιστραφείσης εἰς ἑαυτήν (*i.e.* 100 × 100), ἀποκαταστατικὴ τίς ἐστι καὶ τελεσιουργὸς τῆς ψυχῆς, ἐπανάγουσα πεσοῦσαν εἰς τὴν οἴκησιν πάλιν ὅθεν ἥκει δεῦρο, καθάπερ φησὶν ὁ ἐν Φαίδρῳ Σωκράτης.   The reference is to *Phaedrus*, 248 E, εἰς μὲν γὰρ τὸ αὐτὸ ὅθεν ἥκει ἡ ψυχὴ ἑκάστη οὐκ ἀφικνεῖται ἐτῶν μυρίων, and, since this agrees with Empedocles' doctrine that the fallen soul is exiled for 30,000 ὧραι = 10,000 years (see below, p. 228), it is probable that Proclus' connection of the return of the soul with the return to the monad is of old Pythagorean origin, as indeed the character of the doctrine would lead us to expect.

[2] Above, p. 70.   Also *Theon Smyrn.* p. 34 (Dupuis) : Ἀριστοτέλης ἐν τῷ Πυθαγορικῷ τὸ ἕν φησιν ἀμφοτέρων (ἀρτίου καὶ περίττου) μετέχειν τῆς φύσεως.

[3] The methods of Eurytos described by Burnet (*E. G. P.*[2], p. 110) belong, as he points out, to the fourth century. By that time the atomistic doctrine was developed.

[4] Cf. the division of the soul in Plato's *Timaeus*, 35 B, and the distribution of the whole mass of soul-substance, first into a number of portions, one for each star, and secondly into individual souls (*ibid.* 41 D).

112. *Pythagorean Ethics*

The Pythagorean conception of goodness (ἀρετή), including both moral virtue and the physical excellences of health and strength, is based entirely on the notion of ' arrangement ' (τάξις) and ' order ' (*cosmos*). The best expression of it is to be found in Plato's *Gorgias*. Socrates there argues that the good artist will not work at random, but always with reference to an ideal or pattern. Guided by this model, he will put his material into a certain arrangement, making one part suitable and fitting to another, until he has marshalled the whole into ' an arranged and ordered thing.' [1] Trainers of the body and physicians order and systematise the body (κοσμοῦσι τὸ σῶμα καὶ συντάττουσι), and this *cosmos* is health and strength. The similar *cosmos* that is introduced into the soul, is Law, which makes men law-abiding and orderly ; and this is Justice and Temperance.[2] The source from which this conception is derived is acknowledged later, where Socrates says that ' the wise say that heaven and earth and Gods and men are held together by fellowship, and friendship, and orderliness, and Temperance, and Justice, and, for that reason, call this universe *Cosmos*.' Their knowledge of geometry has taught them the great power, among Gods and men, of Proportion ; whereas the ignorant believe in grasping more than one's due share.[3]

---

[1] *Gorg.* 503 E : εἰς τάξιν τινὰ ἕκαστος τίθησιν ὃ ἂν τιθῇ, καὶ προσαναγκάζει τὸ ἕτερον τῷ ἑτέρῳ πρέπον τε εἶναι καὶ ἁρμόττειν, ἕως ἂν τὸ ἅπαν συστήσηται τεταγμένον τε καὶ κεκοσμημένον πρᾶγμα. Iambl. *V.P.* 182, after Aristoxenus (*D.F.V.*[2], p. 284) : συμπαρέπεσθαι τῇ τοῦ καιροῦ φύσει τήν τε ὀνομαζομένην ὥραν καὶ τὸ πρέπον καὶ τὸ ἁρμοττον.

[2] 504 D : ταῖς δὲ τῆς ψυχῆς τάξεσι καὶ κοσμήσεσι νόμιμον καὶ νόμος, ὅθεν καὶ νόμιμοι γίγνονται καὶ κόσμιοι· ταῦτα δ' ἐστι δικαιοσύνη τε καὶ σωφροσύνη. Cf. *Rep.* 432 A, where Temperance is the concord (ἁρμονία), compared to the harmony of the octave (δι' ὅλης ἀτεχνῶς τέταται, διὰ πασῶν παρεχομένη συνᾴδοντας), an ὁμόνοια, συμφωνία. See also *Phaedo*, 93 c, for virtue as *harmonia*.

[3] 507 E : φασὶ δ' οἱ σοφοὶ (Pythagoreans and Empedocles, Olympiod.) καὶ οὐρανὸν καὶ γῆν καὶ θεοὺς καὶ ἀνθρώπους τὴν κοινωνίαν συνέχειν καὶ φιλίαν καὶ κοσμιότητα καὶ σωφροσύνην καὶ δικαιότητα, καὶ τὸ ὅλον τοῦτο διὰ ταῦτα κόσμον καλοῦσιν . . . λέληθέ σε ὅτι ἡ ἰσότης ἡ γεωμετρικὴ καὶ ἐν θεοῖς καὶ ἐν ἀνθρώποις μέγα δύναται· σὺ δὲ πλεονεξίαν οἴει δεῖν ἀσκεῖν· γεωμετρίας γὰρ ἀμελεῖς. Plutarch, *Symp. Q.* viii. 2. 2, says that this principle of proportion is called Δίκη and Νέμεσις (Aristotle's ' distributive justice,' *E.N.* v. 3. 13). Alex. in Arist. *Met.* A 5, 985b 26 : τῆς μὲν γὰρ δικαιοσύνης ἴδιον ὑπολαμβάνοντες εἶναι τὸ ἀντιπεπονθός τε καὶ ἴσον (οἱ Πυθαγόρειοι), ἐν τοῖς ἀριθμοῖς τοῦτο εὑρίσκοντες ὄν,

113. *Pythagorean Science*

The earliest 'science' of the Pythagoreans is simply a transcript of the procession of numbers into terms of space and space-filling matter ; or, rather, we should say that they were at first unable to conceive number and its behaviour except under the forms of space and motion, and hence did not distinguish at all between the procession of numbers out of the Monad and the process which generates the visible world in space. This process presented itself in the only possible way—as the progressive conquest of a formless and unlimited field ($\chi\acute{\omega}\rho\alpha$) of darkness (the dark and cold air) by the light and warmth radiating from a central nuclear unit.[1] We may note, by the way, that this led to the displacement of earth from the central position in the universe, which must be occupied by the nuclear Fire, *Hestia*. The first great step away from geocentric astronomy was thus due to the bold acceptance of the consequences of an *a priori* theory, which simply restated a purely mythical representation. Its importance for us is the way it illustrates once more the truth of our hypothesis, that the nature and behaviour of *physis* reproduce mythical and religious beliefs about the nature and behaviour of Soul.

114. *Number Atomism*

Guided by the same hypothesis, we can predict the final stage of Pythagorean science. It will inevitably reproduce the later and inconsistent conception of the atomic, indestructible, individual soul. This, as we saw, was already present in Orphic religion, fallen from its first Dionysiac faith in the one continuous life in all things, towards the Olympian conception of *athanasia*. The later Pythagoreans of the fifth century ' construct the whole world out of numbers, but they suppose the units to have magnitude. As to how the first unit with magnitude arose, they

---

διὰ τοῦτο καὶ τὸν ἰσάκις ἴσον ἀριθμόν (either 4 or 9) πρῶτον ἔλεγον εἶναι δικαιοσύνην. The mathematical education in *Rep.* vii. (530 A) culminates in the conceptions of συμφωνία in harmonics and συμμετρία in astronomy, and these provide a bridge to dialectics and the study of beauty and goodness (531 c).

[1] See Burnet, *E.G.P.*[2], p. 120.

appear to be at a loss.' [1]   They might well be at a loss, because
they could not realise that this physical doctrine was nothing
but a reflection of the belief in a plurality of immortal souls,
which contradicted their older faith that Soul was a Harmony
—a bond linking all things in one.[2]   This Soul had formerly been
the One God manifest in the *logos* ;   now it is broken up into a
multitude of individual atoms, each claiming an immortal and
separate persistence.   And the material world suffers a corresponding change.   In place of the doctrine of procession from the
Monad, bodies are built up out of numbers, now conceived as
collections of ultimate units, having position and magnitude.
Thus, Pythagoreanism is led on from a temporal monism to a
spatial pluralism—a doctrine of number-atoms hardly distinguishable from the atoms of Leukippus and Democritus, who,
as Aristotle says,[3] like these Pythagoreans, 'in a sense make
all things to be numbers and to consist of numbers.'   But the
development of this number-atomism was predestined by
religious representations of the nature of soul older than Pythagoreanism itself, and already contained in the blend of Dionysiac
and Olympian conceptions inherited by Pythagoras from
Orphism.

The tendency which impelled Pythagorean science towards a
materialistic atomism is only the recoil of that same tendency
which exalted Pythagoras, from his position as the indwelling
daemon of his church, to the distant heaven of the immortals.
It is the tendency to dualism.   When God ceases to be the
immanent Soul of the world, living and dying in its ceaseless
round of change, and ascends to the region of immutable per-

---

[1] Arist. *Met.* μ 6, 1080*b* 18 ff.   See Burnet, *E.G.P.*[2], p. 336 ff.

[2] Burnet (*E.G.P.*[2], p. 343) says that the view that the soul is a harmony
cannot have belonged to the earliest form of Pythagoreanism, 'for, as shown
in Plato's *Phaedo*, it is quite inconsistent with the idea that the soul can
exist independently of the body.'   The inference would hold, if it were
impossible for religious, or even philosophic, representation to be inconsistent.   I doubt, however, if it is even inconsistent ; see below on Empedocles'
logos-soul, p. 235.   The doctrine that the soul is a harmony is attributed
to Pythagoras by Macrobius, *Somn. Scip.* i. 14, 19.   Cf. Rohde, *Psyche*[3], ii.
169.

[3] *De Caelo*, γ 4, 303*a* 8.   Cf. *de Anim.* a 5, 409*b* 7, on the monads of
Xenocrates and their likeness to atoms.

fection, it is because man has acquired a soul of his own, a little indestructible atom of immortality, a self-subsistent individual. ' Nature ' likewise loses her unity, continuity, and indwelling life, and is remodelled as an aggregate of little indestructible atoms of matter. But note the consequence : she, too, is now self-subsistent. The world of matter becomes the undisputed dominion of Destiny, or Chance, or Necessity—of *Moira, Lachesis, Ananke*. There is no place in it for the God who has vanished beyond the stars. We shall watch, in the sequel, the mystic philosophers, who cannot dispense with God, exhausting their ingenuity in devices to get him back into touch with Nature, to restore to him the *raison d'être* which he lost from the moment that he ceased to animate the world from within, to *be* the ' nature of things ' itself. All such attempts seem now to us like efforts to draw down Apollo from the skies, and change him back into Dionysus ; or, if that is impossible, to find a mediator between God and Nature, some daemonic power, half-natural, half-divine, an Eros who will fill up the chasm, and bind all things again into one. But the time for these efforts is not yet. We have first to consider two systems that emerged from the Pythagorean tradition, before that tradition went all the way to join hands with scientific Atomism, and so became fatally Olympianised. These are the systems of Parmenides and Empedocles.

115. PARMENIDES

Parmenides wrote what he had to say ' about the Nature of Things ' (περὶ φύσεως) in hexameter verse, which combines a certain oracular dignity and earnestness with the closely knit sequence of logical argument. He is the first philosopher, so far as we know, who cast his theory of Nature into the form of a deduction, in this respect justifying the historians who throw him into the sharpest contrast with the cryptic and interjectional Heracleitus. But it is characteristic of him, too, that his theory is stated as a revelation, accorded to him by the Goddess who governs all things in person. Certain features of the proem call for our attention.

Like Orpheus, Parmenides seeks wisdom by a descent, through the western gate of the sunset, into the darkness of the underworld.[1] He travels thither on the chariot of the Sun, attended by the sun-maidens. In the nether darkness he remains with the Goddess *Dike*, after she has opened the gates of sunrise for the chariot to pass up again to the region of light. She tells him, in words which now have for us a new significance, that he has been ' conducted on his journey, not by an evil *Moira* (for the way lies far apart from the path which mankind tread), but by *Themis* and *Dike*.' The Goddess tells him that he must learn ' both the unshaken heart of rounded Truth, and the opinions of mortals, in which there is no true belief.'[2] Accordingly, the poem is divided into two parts—the Way of Truth and the Way of Opinion. These are ' the only two ways of search that can be thought of' (frag. 4). The one is a ' much disputed proof,' which Parmenides is told to judge by reasoning (λόγῳ); the other is at the mercy of the senses, ' the objectless eye, the droning ear, and the tongue ' (which fashions ' names ' without meaning). From this second path he is warned to turn away his thought, and not to let ' custom force him ' along its misleading track.[3]

The Way of Truth is excellently described as a proof which must be judged by reasoning, in abstraction from, and in defiance of, the witness of the senses.[4] The nature of things is a

---

[1] Parmenides' journey is generally regarded as a Heaven Journey ; see Diels, *Parmenides Lehrgedicht*; but O. Gilbert, *Arch. f. Gesch. d. Philos.* xx. p. 25 ff., has argued that it is a journey to the Underworld. See, however, below, note 3 on p. 222. Epimenides, during his initiatory sleep in the Dictaean Cave, communed with *Aletheia* and *Dike*, Max. Tyr. p. 286 (*D.F.V.*[2], ii. 494). In the Ps.-Platonic *Axiochus* (371B) the πέδιον Ἀληθείας is in the Underworld.

[2] Frag. 1. 28 :　　　χρεὼ δέ σε πάντα πύθεσθαι

　　　　ἠμὲν Ἀληθείης εὐκυκλέος ἀτρεμὲς ἦτορ

　　　　ἠδὲ βροτῶν δόξας, ταῖς οὐκ ἔνι πίστις ἀληθής.

[3] Frag. 1. 33 : ἀλλὰ σὺ τῆσδ' ἀφ' ὁδοῦ διζήσιος εἶργε νόημα

　　　μηδέ σ' ἔθος πολύπειρον ὁδὸν κατὰ τήνδε βιάσθω,

　　　νωμᾶν ἄσκοπον ὄμμα καὶ ἠχήεσσαν ἀκουήν

　　　καὶ γλῶσσαν, κρῖναι δὲ λόγῳ πολύδηριν ἔλεγχον

　　　ἐξ ἐμέθεν ῥηθέντα.

I interpret ἄσκοπον as meaning 'having no (real) object,' guided by Parmenides' identification of the object of thought with ' that *for the sake of which* the thought exists' (frag. 8. 34). He does not distinguish 'object' from 'aim' or 'mark.'

[4] Cf. Arist. *de Gen. et Corr.* 325 a 13 (of the Eleatics) : ὑπερβάντες τὴν αἴσθησιν καὶ παριδόντες αὐτὴν, ὡς τῷ λόγῳ δέον ἀκολουθεῖν.

rounded sphere of logical consistency, which threatens to leave the world as known to the senses an inexplicable tissue of delusion.

116. *The Way of Truth*

In the *Thing which is* (τὸ ἐόν), as Parmenides called it, we recognise, transparently enough, the primitive datum of philosophy—*physis* conceived as a material continuum, and, above all, as divine. The ancients recognised the parent of Eleaticism in Xenophanes,[1] who ' looked at the whole sky and declared that the One is, namely God '; and this view expresses the truth that Parmenides' ultimate premisses are : that God alone is, and that he is One. It is from the divinity of *physis* that his system is deduced. What he does is to argue, with his unrelenting logic, that the attributes of unity, perfect continuity, and divinity (now construed in the Olympian sense of deathless immutability) exclude and negate plurality, discontinuity, and the changing movement of life. The system of Heracleitus, Ionian science, and the earlier forms of Pythagoreanism, all in their various ways attempted to combine the two sets of predicates, and to get the One to evolve somehow into the many. Parmenides declares that no such evolution is possible. His cosmology faces, and accepts as unanswerable, an objection that besets pantheism, and some other theisms, in all ages. If God is one and perfect in himself, why should he ever leave that state and go forth into unreality and imperfection ? Yet, if he does not do so, he ceases to be the pervasive life and moving soul of the world ; he crystallises into a being that cannot become, or move, or change ; and, since life is change, he is lifeless —a complete, immovable, continuous, homogeneous substance, unbegotten and imperishable. Necessity in all her forms, moral, physical, fatal (and, we must now add, logical), deprives him of the creative force of life. ' *Dike* does not loose her fetters and let anything come into being or pass away, but holds it fast.'[2] ' Mastering *Ananke* holds it in the bonds of the

---

[1] See above, p. 177.
[2] Parm. frag. 8. 13 : οὔτε γενέσθαι
οὔτ' ὄλλυσθαι ἀνῆκε Δίκη χαλάσασα πέδῃσιν
ἀλλ' ἔχει.

limit that fences it on every side.'[1] 'Moira has fettered it so as to be whole and immovable.'[2] Thus all the original life of the ultimate *physis* is frozen out of it; the World Egg is hardened to adamant, and cannot hatch. That it should become and perish, both be and not be, change its place, or vary its colour—all these are mere 'names,' which mortals have agreed to use, believing them to be true.[3] Thus, Parmenides absolutely rejects the Heracleitean harmony of opposites.

The One Being of Parmenides' vision is the Monad of the Pythagoreans, but it is no longer a 'fountain of ever-flowing nature.' The whole doctrine of the procession of numbers out of the One is shorn away, because that One can no longer contain within itself the principle of the manifold; since it is absolutely and strictly One, the opposites and the many are not implicit within its nature, and therefore cannot come out of it. It is also the 'Limitless' of Anaximander; but *Moira*, instead of portioning it out into provinces, has now 'fettered it so as to be whole.' There can be no division or 'separating out' ($\dot{a}\pi\acute{o}\kappa\rho\iota\sigma\iota\varsigma$) of opposites or elements. 'Thou canst not cut off *what is* from holding fast to *what is*, neither scattering itself abroad in an order (*cosmos*) nor coming together.'[4] Aristotle[5] called Parmenides an 'unphysicist' ($\dot{a}\phi\upsilon\sigma\iota\kappa\acute{o}\varsigma$), because he did away with the principle of motion, which is *physis*.

The disappearance of the doctrine of the procession of numbers out of the One, which is cut off at one blow of Parmenides' logic, has disguised from critics, ancient and modern, the fact that the Way of Truth starts from Pythagoreanism; but the Pythagorean character of the Way of Opinion is recognised. In considering this second way of search, we will put aside for the

---

[1] Frag. 8. 30 :
κρατερὴ γὰρ Ἀνάγκη
πείρατος ἐν δεσμοῖσιν ἔχει, τό μιν ἀμφὶς ἐέργει.

[2] Frag. 8. 37 :
ἐπεὶ τό γε Μοῖρ' ἐπέδησεν
οὖλον ἀκίνητόν τ' ἔμεναι.

[3] Frag. 8. 38 :
τῷ πάντ' ὄνομ' ἔσται
ὅσσα βροτοὶ κατέθεντο πεποιθότες εἶναι ἀληθῆ,
γίγνεσθαι τε καὶ ὄλλυσθαι, εἶναί τε καὶ οὐχί,
καὶ τόπον ἀλλάσσειν διά τε χρόα φανὸν ἀμείβειν.

[4] Frag. 2 :
οὐ γὰρ ἀποτμήξει τὸ ἐὸν τοῦ ἐόντος ἔχεσθαι
οὔτε σκιδνάμενον πάντῃ πάντως κατὰ κόσμον
οὔτε συνιστάμενον.

[5] Ap. Sext. *Adv. Math.* x, 46.

moment the disputed question, what a philosopher can mean by propounding a cosmology (the details of which, so far as we know, were his own, and have been taken as such by most, if not all, of his readers), and yet declaring that ' there is no true belief ' in them. Our first business must be to establish the type of this physical system, and determine from what part of the Pythagorean scheme of thought it is derived.

117. *The Way of Opinion*

This second part of the poem begins as follows (frag. 8. 50) : ' Here do I close my trustworthy speech and thought about the truth. Opinions (δόξας), mortal opinions, thou must henceforward learn, hearkening to the deceptive ordering of my words.

' Two forms (μορφάς) there are, which mortals have made up their minds to name (ὀνομάζειν), one of which they ought not to name, and that is where they have gone astray. They have distinguished them as opposite in body (δέμας), and assigned them visible tokens [1] distinct from one another—to the one the Fire of heaven, a gentle thing, very light, in every direction the same as itself, but not the same as the other. The other is just the opposite to it, indiscernible Night, a dense and heavy body (δέμας). Of these I declare to thee the whole disposition, as it seems likely ; for so no mortal judgment shall outstrip thee.'

Two other fragments give us little more light : ' Now that all things have been named (ὀνόμασται) Light and Night, and the names which belong to their several powers have been assigned to these things and to those, everything is full at once

---

[1] σήματα. The word seems to mean 'visible signs,' 'tokens,' almost ' symbols.' Fire, for instance, may be regarded as a visible embodiment (δέμας) of one 'form,' rather than completely identical with it. It stands for it, represents it visibly. That body is a *mark* or *visible sign*, is one of the meanings of the Orphic dictum, σῶμα σῆμα, for σῆμα means 'tomb' only because it meant a mark or sign of a place which is taboo, or 'impure,' and so a gravestone or pillar. Plato (*Phaedr.* 250c) avails himself of both senses : καθαροὶ ὄντες καὶ ἀσήμαντοι τούτου ὃ νῦν σῶμα περιφέροντες ὀνομάζομεν, where ἀσήμαντοι means that we are not *marked by this gravestone* called a body. Cf. Heracleitus' use of σημαίνειν above, p. 187. See also J. Adam, *Religious Teachers of Greece* (1908), p. 96.

of Light and unapparent Night, both equal, since neither has any part in the other.' [1]

At the end of the poem (frag. 19): ' Thus, according to Opinion, did these things come into being (ἔφυ), and thus they are now, and after this shall grow and come to their end. Men have stamped them each with a name to know them by.' [2]

The two fundamental ' forms ' in this scheme are Light and Dark, and the other pairs of contrary attributes may be regarded as attaching to these two substances (if substances they be):

> That which Is and That which Is Not
> Light and Dark
> Warm and Cold (Aristotle)
> Light and Heavy
> (Rare) and Dense
> Fire (Heaven) and Earth
> Male and Female.[3]

Now, we know that the Orphic said of himself: ' I am the child of Earth and of the starry Heaven,' [4] believing that the divine and immortal soul came down from the heavenly fires, and was imprisoned in the darkness of the earthy body. The same truth is symbolised in the descent of Orpheus and Parmenides into the dark underworld and their resurrection into the light of day. Aristotle speaks of the ' theologians ' (Orphic) who made all things come into being out of Night, and contrasts with the ancient poets who said that Zeus was king of all, others who held that the eldest Gods were Night and Heaven.[5] In the Way of Opinion we are on Orphic ground, and the fundamental scheme is the fall and descent from the region of heavenly light, reality, and truth, to the darkness, unreality, and falseness of bodily existence.

---

[1] Frag. 9: αὐτὰρ ἐπειδὴ πάντα φάος καὶ νὺξ ὀνόμασται
καὶ τὰ κατὰ σφετέρας δυνάμεις ἐπὶ τοῖσί τε καὶ τοῖς,
πᾶν πλέον ἐστὶν ὁμοῦ φάεος καὶ νυκτὸς ἀφάντου,
ἴσων ἀμφοτέρων, ἐπεὶ οὐδετέρῳ μέτα μηδέν.

[2] τοῖς δ' ὄνομ' ἄνθρωποι κατέθεντ' ἐπίσημον ἑκάστῳ. A 'name' also is a σῆμα, embodying or entombing a thing or meaning, which it σημαίνει.

[3] See O. Kern, Arch. f. Gesch. d. Phil. iii. p. 174, for the male and female character of the two principles and the bisexed Eros in Parmenides.

[4] Orphic tablets, D.F.V.², ii. 480; above, p. 179.

[5] Met. λ 6, 1071 b 26; ν 4, 1091 b 4. D.F.V.², ii. 475.

What Parmenides does in the Way of Opinion is to take this purely Orphic conception of a descent from light to darkness, and expurgate that other, Dionysiac, view of life and death as a perpetual process of change revolving in a cycle, which Heracleitus had championed against the Orphic and Olympian notions of the destiny of the soul. Both views, we have seen, were inherent in the religious tradition of mysticism, before philosophy appeared; they are now separated out, as their inconsistency becomes apparent, by Heracleitus and Parmenides. If we start from this point, we can deduce the other characteristics of the Way of Opinion, and perhaps gain new light upon them.

Let us note, in the first place, that Parmenides says that mortals have decided to *name* two 'forms'; and that where they have gone wrong is in naming the second. He does not say they were wrong to name the first. Aristotle, moreover, says that 'he ranks the Warm under the head of That which Is, its opposite under the head of That which Is Not.' [1] The natural conclusion is that Parmenides meant that Fire, the principle of light and warmth, is the embodiment (δέμας), or visible token (σῆμα), of the real, as it were an effluence from that inward omnipresent God who alone Is, into the world of 'seeming' (δόξα). Parmenides must have had in his mind some distinction between 'reality' and 'appearance.' Probably he did not distinguish 'appearance' from 'opinion': both are what 'seem' to mortals, and δόξα probably covers both meanings. The confusion makes Parmenides speak as if mortals were responsible for the appearance of the world. He cannot have really thought this, in any sense that we should put upon it; his difficulties arise largely because he cannot get his thought clear about the meaning of δόξα.

If mortals were not wrong when they named the first 'form' fire, they did go astray when they named the second, and they ought not to have named it at all. Why not? Because there is no *thing* (ὄν) to correspond to these names in the second column of contraries. As Aristotle says, they come 'under the head of That which Is Not.' These opposites, or antagonists, of the principle of Light simply *are not*; they are names which

---

[1] *Met.* A5, 986b 35: τούτων δὲ κατὰ μὲν τὸ ὂν τὸ θερμὸν τάττει, θάτερον δὲ κατὰ τὸ μὴ ὄν.

denote nothing, or a ' *not-thing* ' (μὴ ἐόν), words that stand for no positive existing things whatever.[1]

It is here that Parmenides joins issue with Ionian science and with Heracleitus. Both these types of system had explained ' becoming ' by the separation and conflict, or harmony and reconciliation, of opposites, regarded as equal and balancing powers, each with a domain, or a force, of its own. Parmenides sweeps this whole conception away. In these pairs of antagonists which ' men have agreed to name,' one member is a *not-thing*, a mere word ; only the other stands for anything real. The War of Opposites, and all those views of life and death which hang with it, are banished, by the same uncompromising logic that banished life from the real being of God.

If this is so, we can explain frag. 9, quoted above (p. 218), as follows : When these *names*, Light and Night, have once been given, and all the other pairs of contrary names that go with them, then we have all things ' full at once of Light and Night,' and these are equal, and independent of one another. The two antagonists are set up, and they can go about their wars and reconciliations. But the whole process is illegitimate : one set of names denotes no positive things.

What, then, can Parmenides mean by declaring that cold, heavy, dark, etc., are mere names, without things to correspond ? Only one explanation seems possible ; it is simple, and surely it would easily occur to the father of Logic. It is that cold only means not-hot, dark means not-light, and so on.[2] Heat and light exist (or represent something that exists) ; cold and darkness are absences of them. This explanation has the authority of Aristotle ;[3] and we cannot see what other conclusion

---

[1] I do not think Parmenides meant by τὸ μὴ ὄν the *absolutely non-existent* as we conceive it ; rather it was, as it were, a subject with no predicates, only to be described negatively, like Anaximander's ἄπειρον, or Aristotle's formless matter. The distinction between negative existential propositions (x does not exist) and negative Subject-Predicate propositions (x is not A) was not yet drawn. Parmenides' μὴ ὄν is an x which is not A, not B, etc., for all positive predicates.

[2] Cf. the 'not-things' (μὴ ὄντα) which the Eleatic Stranger in Plato's *Sophist* allows himself, with due respect to Parmenides, to reinstate from being *nothing* to being *other things*.

[3] *De Gen. et Corr.* 318 b, 3 ff.: οἷον τὸ μὲν θερμὸν κατηγορία τις καὶ εἶδος, ἡ δὲ ψυχρότης στέρησις. O. Gilbert, *Griech. Religionsphilosophie*, p. 49, note 1.

Parmenides could have reached from his rigidly monistic premisses, or what difficulty there was, that could arrest a mind so powerful as his before he reached it.

We hold, then, that to Parmenides the process of becoming which brought the visible world into existence was like the fall of the Orphic soul—a declension or degradation of light, till it fails and dies out in darkness and nonentity. The fact that the earth itself, which to the ordinary materialist seems so solid and real, is at the lower end of this scale, did not stagger Parmenides : in the language of any mystic, ' earthy ' means dark, unreal, false. When he calls dark Night ' a compact and heavy body,' he evidently means the earth ; [1] the more compact and heavy it is, the further is it from being a true embodiment of the substance of God. But even the earth, though low in the scale, has still some fire and heat and light in it.

If we sink still further, what do we reach at the nadir ? The power of darkness, *Moira, Lachesis, Ananke.* Modern critics apparently think of this figure, as of a lady whom it is not quite decorous to accommodate with a seat in the centre of the earth, presumably because they do not realise that the earth is verging on non-existence.[2] She is Necessity, on whose knees is the spindle with its turning whorls, in the vision of Er. But she is also Aphrodite, who contrived Eros, first of the Gods, and the axis of her spindle passes through the midst of the ' crowns ' up to the limits of the world. It is the path of souls, who ascend upwards and fall downwards.[3] Light is also Soul ;

---

[1] Cf. O. Gilbert, *Arch. Gesch. Phil.* **xx.** p. 42.

[2] Professor Burnet, who feels this impropriety (*E.G.P.*[2], p. 219), now politely hands her to a place in the Milky Way, good-humouredly abandoning his former effort to make a hole through the earth for her and turn it from a sphere into a ring.

[3] Simpl. *Phys.* 39, 18 : ταύτην ('Αφροδίτην) καὶ θεῶν αἰτίαν εἶναί φησι λέγων (frag. 13), "πρώτιστον μὲν "Ερωτα θεῶν μητίσατο πάντων," καὶ τὰς ψυχὰς πέμπειν ποτὲ μὲν ἐκ τοῦ ἐκφανοῦς εἰς τὸ ἀειδές, ποτὲ δὲ ἀνάπαλιν φησιν. Plato, *Rep.* 616 B ff., describes a ' straight pillar of light, stretched all through the heaven and the earth,' which is apparently the axis of the cosmos and the shaft of the spindle of Necessity (see J. Adam, *ad loc.*). The souls journey to the centre of this light, *i.e.* the centre of the earth and of the universe. I believe that Parmenides' path of souls is similar, and that his *Dike* is at the centre. The difficulties of interpretation which beset both Parmenides' and Plato's descriptions are ultimately due to the attempt to combine the ' Dionysiac ' and ' Orphic ' conceptions, whose in-

hence we are told that men were first born from the sun,[1] and that the dead body cannot perceive light and warmth and sound, because the fire has failed out of it.[2] Fire, or Light, is thus the soul-substance, and nearest akin to the substance of God.

But, finally, let us observe that the life which has gone out of God, has come back into Nature. The Goddess, throned in the centre, is the Queen of Life, Aphrodite ; and of her, Eros, banished by Olympianism, is born again. The downward fall of life from the heavenly fires is countered by an upward impulse which ' sends the souls back from the seen to the unseen.' We have here a hint of the movement of life interpreted as desire for perfection, which leads to important developments in later conceptions of *physis*. The last resource of Nature, deserted by God, is to aspire towards that perfection which lies above and beyond her reach, and in that aspiration she regains the life which God has lost.

We would not leave the impression that Parmenides was satisfied with this physical system, obtained by developing the Orphic view to its logical conclusion and expurgating the Dionysiac. He was too much in earnest with his monism to be content, and too penetrating and sincere to hide from himself or others that he had not really reduced the power of darkness to an empty name. So he calls the Way of Opinion misleading.

consistency we have pointed out. The ' Dionysiac' path of souls is a circle, from the upper region of light above the earth to the dark region below and back again. Parmenides adopts this for his own journey to the underworld. But according to that view *Dike* ought to be in Tartarus, *under* the earth, not in the centre. The Orphic path of souls is from heaven down to earth, and the lowest point is the centre of earth, where the Pythagorean central fire and *Dike* ought to be. Cf. *Theol. Arith.* p. 6 ff. ed. Ast, which states that the Pythagoreans place a ἐναδικὸς διάπυρος κύβος περὶ τὸ μέσον τῶν τεσσάρων στοιχείων, and οἱ περὶ Ἐμπεδοκλέα καὶ Παρμενίδην follow them in so far as they maintain τὴν μοναδικὴν φύσιν Ἑστίας τρόπον ἐν μέσῳ ἱδρῦσθαι καὶ διὰ τὸ ἰσόρροπον φυλάσσειν τὴν αὐτὴν ἕδραν (see O. Gilbert, *loc. cit.* p. 42 ; and *Griech. Religionsphilosophie* (1911), pp. 185, 189 ff.). Plato (*Rep.* 616) attempts to combine both by making the pillar of light at its two poles spread out into a belt which runs all round the heavenly sphere (if Adam, *ad loc.*, is right). The very fact that scholars are divided on the question whether Parmenides' journey is to heaven or the underworld points to Parmenides not being clear in his own mind.

[1] Diog. ix. 22.   [2] Theophr. *de Sensu*, 3.

We take his position to be this. If God is really and absolutely
One and perfect, then there is nothing to be made of the world
we see, with its plurality and changing life. The Way of Opinion
is the best that can be made of it ; but still it will not do. God,
with his unity and immutable perfection, has gone out of the
world, and animates it no longer. One or the other must be
given up : either such a God is not, or the world infected with
darkness and evil cannot come from him. It is Parmenides'
glory to have formulated this dilemma with unfaltering courage,
and made his choice—the choice of the ' unphysicist,' the Mystic.

118. Empedocles

We have considerable fragments of two long poems by Empedocles, called *Purifications* and *About Nature*. The current
opinion is that the religious views contained in the *Purifications*
are inconsistent with the physical theory of the other poem ;
and Professor Burnet adds that ' this is just what we should
expect to find. All through this period, there seems to have
been a gulf between men's religious beliefs, if they had any, and
their cosmological views. The few points of contact (between
the two poems) which we have mentioned may have been
sufficient to hide this from Empedocles himself.' [1]

This is a hard saying ; and the following account of Empedocles will, we hope, make it clear that it is not a true one.
In our view, there is no more inconsistency in Empedocles'
system of things—religious and scientific—than that which we
have pointed out as already inherent in the Orphic and Pythagorean doctrines of immortality. Empedocles seems to us to
make a heroic and amazingly ingenious effort to reconcile these
views of the nature and destiny of the soul with Ionian physical

[1] *E.G.P.*[2], p. 289. Cf. Zeller, *Phil. d. Griech.*[5], i. p. 806 : Anders verhält
es sich mit gewissen religiösen Lehren und Vorschriften, welche . . . mit
den wissenschaftlichen Grundsätzen unseres Physikers in keiner sichtbaren
Verbindung stehen. In diesen Sätzen können wir nur Glaubensartikel
sehen. . . . Rohde, *Psyche*[3], ii. 175 : Zumeist aber stehen in seiner Vor-
stellungswelt Theologie und Naturwissenschaft unverbunden neben ein-
ander. In spite of these authorities, the entertaining of religious beliefs
which will not square with the same person's philosophical opinions, seems
to me characteristic rather of modern orthodoxy than of the Greek
philosophers.

science, and he comes within an ace of succeeding. We regard his physical system as modelled on his religious beliefs and dictated by them. We shall, therefore, reverse the usual practice of discussing first the poem *About Nature* and explaining its conclusions as reached by purely rational processes of reasoning, mainly in reaction against Parmenides. There is, of course, truth in that point of view ; but what we are concerned to discover is the innermost convictions of Empedocles, the view of life and of the world, which made him dissent from Parmenides in some points and agree with him in others. The driving power, the *cause* of Empedocles' system, is not only, or chiefly, intellectual dissatisfaction with Parmenides' theories, but a profound belief that a somewhat different interpretation of the mystic view of the soul and God provides a scheme which, when we use it to interpret nature, leads to conclusions not so paradoxically at variance with sense-data and with Ionian science as those of Parmenides. We shall, accordingly, begin with the religious poem, in which that interpretation is plainly set forth. It states in mythical form the very doctrine which the poem *About Nature* attempts to throw into more scientific language.

We learn from Aristotle [1] that Empedocles' poems were ' esoteric,' in the sense explained by Professor Margoliouth in his recent edition of the *Poetics*.[2] They were, that is to say, first learnt by heart, without being understood, because it ' took time for them to be assimilated.' When the whole text had thus got into the mind, one part of it would throw light upon another, and so the hidden meaning would gradually come out. If Empedocles' writings were of this character, we should beware of charging him with inconsistency, and rather look out for cross-references, characteristic of this method of writing, of which, in fact, we shall encounter some instances.[3] Probably it will be found that Parmenides' poems are similarly esoteric. This would explain the metrical form used by both philosophers ;

---

[1] *Eth. Nic.* η 5, 1147 a 18: καὶ γὰρ οἱ ἐν πάθεσι τούτοις (states of drunkenness, etc.) ὄντες ἀποδείξεις καὶ ἔπη λέγουσιν Ἐμπεδοκλέους, καὶ οἱ πρῶτον μαθόντες συνείρουσι μὲν τοὺς λόγους, ἴσασι δὲ οὔπω· δεῖ γὰρ συμφυῆναι, τοῦτο δὲ χρόνου δεῖται. Schol. *ad loc.* : συμφυῆναι· οἱονεὶ φύσιν γενέσθαι τὴν ἕξιν ἐν αὐτοῖς.

[2] D. S. Margoliouth, *The Poetics of Aristotle*, p. 22. London, 1911.

[3] I had already observed these cross-references before I learned from Professor Margoliouth the nature of esoteric composition.

for it is convenient that such writings should be both compact and easily committed to memory.[1]

119. *The* PURIFICATIONS

Parts of the introductions to both poems are fortunately preserved ; and the impression we get by comparing them is that Empedocles regarded the *Purifications* as containing a fuller revelation of truth than the other. Addressing Pausanias at the beginning of the physical poem, he dwells on the difficulty and darkness that beset men in this mortal life ; how hard it is for their mind to grasp truth through their eyes and ears. Pausanias is not to distrust his senses altogether ; they leave some 'opening for understanding' (frag. 4). But it is only an imperfect comprehension that can come that way. 'Thou, then, since thou hast found thy way hither, shalt learn no more than mortal mind hath power.' [2]

He calls upon the Muse to allow him to hear what is lawful for the children of a day, and tells her that no garlands of honour offered by mortals shall force her to lift them from the ground, at the cost of her speaking more than is religiously permissible (ὁσίης πλέον), or taking a seat upon the heights of wisdom (frag. 4).

Contrast with this the opening of the *Purifications*. Empedocles there says that he goes about among men ' an im-

---

[1] Our view of Empedocles agrees with that taken by Aristotle (*Met.* β 4, 1001 a 5 ff.), who discusses him under the head of 'the school of Hesiod and all theologians' (θεολόγοι), who only think of what convinces themselves and take no trouble about persuading us. He singles out Empedocles as 'the one whose statements *might be expected to be most consistent*' (ὅνπερ οἰηθείη λέγειν ἄν τις μάλιστα ὁμολογουμένως αὐτῷ), and says that 'even he' makes the principle of destruction (*Neikos*) also that which produces everything, except the One, that is God. This is not the inconsistency which modern writers discover between the two poems, but belongs to both equally, and in itself it is no more an inconsistency than Heracleitus' corresponding doctrine that 'Strife is Justice,' explained above, p. 190.

[2] Frag. 2 :   σὺ δ' οὖν, ἐπεὶ ὧδ' ἐλιάσθης,
πεύσεαι οὐ πλεὸν ἠὲ βροτείη μῆτις ὄρωρεν.
I take this as meaning that Pausanias' soul, having 'found its way' into this mortal body, must be content to look out through the senses and so gain what imperfect knowledge can come to it through them.

mortal God, no mortal now, honoured among all as is meet, wreathed with fillets and flowery crowns.' He seems to have no fear that ' garlands of honour ' will uplift him too high ; [1] he has attained the heights of wisdom, and now does not scruple to declare it. ' Why should I harp on these things, as if it were any great matter that I should surpass mortal, perishable men?' (frag. 113). ' Friends, I know indeed that truth is in the words I shall utter ; but it is hard for men, and jealous are they of the assault of belief in their souls ' (frag. 114). Empedocles does not now invoke the Muse, or pray that his lips may be pure and not go beyond what is lawful. He speaks as an immortal God, uttering truth from the heights of wisdom. It is strange that his modern interpreters should not seek in this poem the real convictions of Empedocles, but should treat it as so much mere ' religious belief,' which we may expect to be inconsistent with his theory of nature. On the contrary, his violent disapproval of Parmenides—to whom the words, ' O ye Gods, turn aside my tongue from the madness of those men ! ' [2] are supposed to refer —may well have been due to the very fact, so creditable to Parmenides' logic and candour, that he had not been able to construct a physical theory that would harmonise with the Way of Truth. Empedocles' principal motive is to find a new Way of Opinion, which will not contradict the religion he passionately proclaims. He almost says as much when, in open contrast with Parmenides, he bids Pausanias ' listen to the course of his argument which is *not deceptive.*' [3] True, no theory of the sense world can be free from that element of falsity and darkness which

---

[1] Compare Περὶ Φύσεως, frag. 4. 6 (above paraphrased) :

μηδέ σέ γ' εὐδόξοιο βιήσεται ἄνθεα τιμῆς
πρὸς θνητῶν ἀνελέσθαι, ἐφ' ὧι θ' ὁσίης πλέον εἰπεῖν
θάρσεϊ καὶ τότε δὴ σοφίης ἐπ' ἄκροισι θοάζειν

and Καθαρμοί, frag. 112 :

ἐγὼ δ' ὑμῖν θεὸς ἄμβροτος, οὐκέτι θνητός,
πωλεῦμαι μετὰ πᾶσι τετιμένος, ὥσπερ ἔοικα,
ταινίαις τε περίστεπτος στέφεσιν τε θαλείοις.

I take this for an esoteric cross-reference.

[2] Frag. 4.

[3] Frag. 17. 26 : σὺ δ' ἄκουε λόγου στόλον οὐκ ἀπάτηλον, contrasted with Parm. 8, 52 : μάνθανε κόσμον ἐμῶν ἐπέων ἀπατηλὸν ἀκούων. Note that Empedocles uses λόγος where Parmenides has ἐπέων. Parmenides' physical system is (partly) a cosmos of *words, names* ; Empedocles' system is a λόγος, with a rational and consistent meaning.

infects its object; but Empedocles is determined that it shall not be in open conflict with the Truth.

120. *The Exile of the Soul*

The basis of Empedocles' position is disclosed in the famous fragment describing the exile of the soul and its wanderings round the wheel of rebirth : [1]

'There is an oracle of Necessity, a decree of the Gods from of old, everlasting, with broad oaths fast sealed, that, whensoever one of the daemons, whose portion is length of days, has sinfully stained his hands with blood, or followed Strife [2] and sworn a false oath, he must wander thrice ten thousand seasons [3] away from the Blessed, being born throughout the time in all manner of mortal forms, passing from one to another of the painful paths of life.

'For the power of the Air drives him seaward ; and the Sea spews him out on the dry land ; Earth hurls him into the rays of the blazing Sun, and Sun into the eddies of Air. One from another receives him, and he is loathed of all.

'Of these now am I also one, an exile from God and a wanderer, having put my trust in raging Strife.'

That the doctrine contained in these lines was not invented by Empedocles is certain from the fact that the essential features of it are to be found in Pindar's second *Olympian*,[4] written for

---

[1] Frag. 115 : ἔστιν Ἀνάγκης χρῆμα, θεῶν ψήφισμα παλαιόν,
ἀΐδιον, πλατέεσσι κατεσφρηγισμένον ὅρκοις·
εὖτέ τις ἀμπλακίῃσι φόνῳ φίλα γυῖα μιήνῃ,
<Νείκεΐ θ'> ὅς κ' ἐπίορκον ἁμαρτήσας ἐπομόσσῃ,
δαίμονες οἵτε μακραίωνος λελάχασι βίοιο,
τρίς μιν μυρίας ὥρας ἀπὸ μακάρων ἀλάλησθαι,
φυομένους παντοῖα διὰ χρόνου εἴδεα θνητῶν
ἀργαλέας βιότοιο μεταλλάσσοντα κελεύθους.

αἰθέριον μὲν γάρ σφε μένος πόντονδε διώκει,
πόντος δ' ἐς χθονὸς οὖδας ἀπέπτυσε, γαῖα δ' ἐς αὐγὰς
ἠελίου φαέθοντος, ὁ δ' αἰθέρος ἔμβαλε δίναις·
ἄλλος δ' ἐξ ἄλλου δέχεται, στυγέουσι δὲ πάντες.
τῶν καὶ ἐγὼ νῦν εἰμι, φυγὰς θεόθεν καὶ ἀλήτης,
Νείκεΐ μαινομένῳ πίσυνος.

[2] I accept Diels' Νείκεΐ as a certain restoration of the word lost at the beginning of this line. Its appropriateness will appear later.

[3] *i.e.* 10,000 years. Cf. Dieterich, *Nekyia*, 119.

[4] The fragments of Pindar's *Threnoi* supply further details. Rohde, *Psyche*³, ii. 216.

Theron of Acragas, where Empedocles was born, at a date when Empedocles was a boy. Throughout the course of that majestic Ode revolves, as we have seen, the wheel of Time, Destiny, and Judgment.[1] The doctrine can be classed unhesitatingly as 'Orphic.' The soul is conceived as falling from the region of light down into the 'roofed-in Cave,' the 'dark meadow of Ate' (frag. 119, 120, 121). This fall is a penalty for sin—flesh-eating or oath-breaking.[2] Caught in the wheel of Time, the soul, preserving its individual identity, passes through all shapes of life. This implies that man's soul is not 'human': human life (ὁ ἀνθρώπινος βίος) is only one of the shapes it passes through.[3] Its substance is divine and immutable, and it is the same substance as all other soul in the world. In this sense, the unity of all life is maintained; but, on the other hand, each soul is an atomic individual, which persists throughout its ten thousand years' cycle of reincarnations. The soul travels the round of the four elements : ' For I have been, ere now, a boy and a girl, a bush (earth), a bird (air), and a dumb fish in the sea ' (frag. 117). These four elements compose the bodies which it successively inhabits.

The soul is further called ' an exile from God (θεόθεν) and a wanderer,' and its offence, which entailed this exile, is described as ' following Strife,' ' putting trust in Strife.' At the end of the cycle of births, men may hope to ' appear among mortals as prophets, song-writers, physicians, and princes ; [4] and thence they rise up, as Gods exalted in honour, sharing the hearth of the other immortals and the same table, free from human woes, delivered from destiny (ἀπόκληροι ?) and harm ' (frag. 146, 147). Thus the course of the soul begins with separation from God, and ends in reunion with him, after passing through all the *moirai* of the elements.

---

[1] Χρόνος, Μοῖρα, Δίκη are the keywords throughout. See above, p. 171.

[2] That ' defiling the hands (or limbs, γυῖα) with blood' means flesh-eating and animal sacrifice is clear from frag. 128, 136, 137, 139 ; cf. Hippol. *Ref.* viii. 29 (*D. F. V.*², p. 206). Oath-breaking is taken from Hesiod, *Theog.* 793.

[3] Cf. Xen. *Cyrop.* viii. 7. 17 ff. and A. E. Taylor's remarks on the affinity of this passage with Plato's *Phaedo* (*Varia Socr.* i. 33). The flesh is a 'strange garment ' (frag. 126), not native to the soul.

[4] Compare Pindar's list (*Threnoi*, frag. 133, Christ) : kings, athletes, poets (σοφίᾳ μέγιστοι), who are called 'pure heroes' (ἥρωες ἀγνοί) ; and Plato's nine stages (*Phaedrus*, 248 D).

Now it is chiefly, if not solely, on the ground of this doctrine of immortality, that the *Purifications* have been condemned as inconsistent with the poem *On Nature*, where it is generally held that ' there can be no question of an immortal soul.' [1] We hope to show that there is no inconsistency at all ; but before we can do so, we must turn to the analysis of the physical system. The remaining doctrines contained in the *Purifications* will most conveniently be taken in connection with their counterparts in the theory of nature.

121. *The World Period*

The course of the world, as we expect, is modelled on the cyclic movement of the soul above described. It begins in a state of unity, with all the elements mixed in the ' Sphere ' by Love. Then, as Love streams out of the mass, and Strife pours in from outside, there is a process of separation which terminates, at the lowest point of the circle, in complete segregation of the elements into four regions. The process is then reversed. Love begins to prevail and draws the elements into fusion again, ending in the complete reunion of the Sphere.

The factors in this scheme have already been discussed (p. 63), and we have followed ancient authority [2] in distinguishing the four elements as ' bodily,' while Love and Strife are of that attenuated and fluid consistency which belongs to soul-substance, with the least conceivable degree of corporeality. Empedocles, says Aristotle, identifies Love with the Good ; and Love is both a moving principle, since it draws together, and a material, since it is a part of the mixture. [3] To move is the function of Soul, or God ; but Soul and God can still only be thought of as the finest forms of matter.

The two new elements are invoked to cause motion, which Parmenides had excluded from the real. Love and Strife are, as it were, the two life-forces which once animated matter, but now, as matter solidifies into impenetrable atoms, are squeezed out of it and conceived as subtle and mobile fluids. Strife is

---

[1] Burnet, *E.G.P.*[2], p. 283.

[2] *E.g.* Simpl. *Phys.* 25, 21 : τὰ μὲν σωματικὰ στοιχεῖα ποιεῖ τέτταρα, τὰς δὲ κυρίως ἀρχάς . . . Φιλίαν καὶ Νεῖκος. Cf. Arist. *Met.* A 5 ; Aet. i. 3. 20.

[3] *Met.* λ 10, 1075b 2.

spoken of as 'running out' of the members of the universe, and, in proportion as it does so, 'a soft, immortal stream of blameless Love' pours in to take its place.[1] We need not be surprised at Aristotle's statement [2] that Empedocles' Love is the substrate of the One, in the same sense as the Water of Thales, the Fire of Heracleitus, the Air of Anaximenes. For those earliest philosophers, the primary element was still alive, and consequently self-moving. Empedocles' fluids of Love and Strife are halfway between this conception of an internal life spontaneously moving matter from within, and the purely external and dematerialised motion, by which, in developed Atomism, one piece of matter moves another entirely by a mechanical shock from without. It is as living and self-moving soul-substances that Love and Strife are like the *physis* of the Ionians.

Empedocles' scheme of the cycle of existence, in which worlds pass into being and perish again, is an adaptation of Anaximander's stages of existence, which we have analysed above (p. 8).[3] If we start from the 'Sphere' or Reign of Love, in which all the elements are fused in one mass, it is easy to recognise Anaximander's Limitless Thing, in its primal state, before the distinction of opposites has broken out. At the opposite pole, we have what he called the Reign of *Justice*—all four elements completely separated. In Empedocles, Strife plays the part of *Moira* or *Lachesis* ; [4] only Strife is now no longer a dim, mythical personality, like the moral power inherent in Anaximander's Limitless, but a divine fluid substance doing its work mechanically.

At this point, there is a significant difference between the two systems. Empedocles interpolates the whole of the period of our world's existence between the Reign of Love and the Reign

---

[1] Frag. 35. 12: ὅσσον δ' αἰὲν ὑπεκπροθέοι, τόσον αἰὲν ἐπήιει
ἠπιόφρων Φιλότητος ἀμεμφέος ἄμβροτος ὁρμή.

[2] *Met.* β 1, 996 a 7.

[3] Thus Aristotle brings Anaximander's system and Empedocles' together : *Phys.* a 4, 187 a 20, οἱ δ' ἐκ τοῦ ἑνὸς ἐνούσας τὰς ἐναντιότητας ἐκκρίνεσθαι, ὥσπερ Ἀναξίμανδρός φησι καὶ ὅσοι δ' ἓν καὶ πολλά φασιν εἶναι, ὥσπερ Ἐμπεδοκλῆς καὶ Ἀναξαγόρας· ἐκ τοῦ μείγματος γὰρ καὶ οὗτοι ἐκκρίνουσι τἆλλα. διαφέρουσι δ' ἀλλήλων τῷ τὸν μὲν (Emp.) περίοδον ποιεῖν τούτων, τὸν δ' (Anaxag.) ἅπαξ. . . .

[4] So, in religious representation, the division of the world among the Gods was regarded sometimes as *fated* and determined by drawing of lots, sometimes as the result of *strife* between the Gods (ἔρις).

of Strife. It occupies one half of the circle, in which we pass
from zenith to nadir ; and it is balanced by the opposite half,
in which the movement is upwards from the Reign of Strife back
to the Sphere, causing by the way the existence of another
world, as Love regains the mastery. In Anaximander's scheme
the Reign of Justice came next after the primal state of fusion
and before the existence of individual things. The motive of
Empedocles' rearrangement is clear. To him Strife is an evil
principle ; it causes separation, and, to the mystic, separation
is evil, union is good. Hence, the state of the world in which
Strife triumphs is the lowest depth of evil, not, as it was for
Anaximander, a Reign of Justice. When it is fitted into the
frame of the wheel,[1] it must occupy the lowest point, and the
existence of worlds must fall in the two hemicycles, between the
best state and the worst.

122. *The Hemispheres of Day and Night*

If we form a visual image of this world period, we see a circle
divided by a horizontal diameter into two regions. The upper
one is filled with light radiating from its pole, the lower with
darkness which deepens into utter night at the bottom. Now
this is precisely the picture which, in another connection, gives
us the physical doctrine of the two hemispheres of Day and
Night, which move round the earth in a circle. The diurnal
hemisphere consists of fire ; the nocturnal, of air (the dark
principle) mixed with a little fire.[2] Day and Night are caused
by, or rather consist of, these two hemispheres ; the Sun is only
a reflection of the diurnal fire, focused on the crystalline vault,
and so it travels round with the daylight which causes it. This
physical theory is manifestly a counterpart in actual space of
the wheel of light and darkness, which in the world period is
the wheel of birth and death. As the scattered rays of fire or
light are gathered up into one focus, called the Sun, and then
spread abroad again in the 'backward reflection,'[3] and mixed

---

[1] Cf. the last words of the quotation from Aristotle in note 3, p. 231.

[2] Ps.-Plut. *Strom.* (*D. F. V.*[2], p. 158. 30).

[3] ἀνταύγεια is the technical word.

with darkness, so, in the cosmos, the soft stream of Love is gathered up into the unity of the Sphere, and then, as it is mixed with Strife, diffused and scattered in the opposite hemicycle of the wheel of existence.

When we study the parts played by Fire and Air in the formation of our world, it becomes clear that, of the ' bodily ' elements, Fire is the nearest akin to Love, Air to Strife. Thus, as Love draws things together, so Fire, in defiance of the common representation,[1] is credited with a power of solidifying. The firmament ($o\dot{v}\rho\alpha\nu\acute{o}s$) is solid, consisting of air compacted after the fashion of ice by fire.[2] The astonishing doctrine that fire freezes, can only be explained by this element's close kinship with the attracting force of Love ; and this also accounts for Aristotle's repeated statement that, though Empedocles has four elements, he reduces them to two, opposing fire to all the rest, and treating earth, water, and air as one *physis*.[3] That Air, similarly, is nearest to Strife, follows from the analogy between the two hemispheres of Day (Fire) and Night (Air with a little fire) and the two halves of the world cycle dominated by Love and Strife. There is nothing in the doctrine of the equality of the elements to prevent us from ranging them in a series : Love, Fire, Water and Earth, Air, Strife.

123. *The Sphere and the Reign of Love*

Can we now form a clear picture of the process which is going on at this moment, as our world passes from the Reign of Love to the Reign of Strife ?[4]

---

[1] Arist. *de Gen. et Corr.* 336α 3: ἐπειδὴ γὰρ πέφυκεν, ὥς φασιν, τὸ μὲν θερμὸν διακρίνειν, τὸ δὲ ψυχρὸν συνιστάναι.

[2] Aet. ii. 11. 2 : στερέμνιον εἶναι τὸν οὐρανὸν ἐξ ἀερὸς συμπαγέντος ὑπὸ πυρὸς κρυσταλλοειδῶς. Cf. Aet. ii. 25. 15 : E. ἀέρα συνεστραμμένον . . . πεπηγότα ὑπὸ πυρὸς (τὴν σελήνην). ' Fire in general had a solidifying power ' (Burnet, *E.G.P.*[2], p. 273). Plutarch's identification of fire with *Neikos*, and water with *Philia* (*de prim. frig.* 952 B) appears to be mistaken. The firmament is the shell of the egg (Aet. ii. 31. 4), whose shape Empedocles, following Orphic tradition, attributed to the cosmos.

[3] *De Gen. et Corr.* β 3, 330b 19 (*D.F.V.*[2], p. 159) ; *Met.* A 4, 985α 31.

[4] That our world does fall in this hemicycle, not in the other, I regard as certain. See Burnet, *E.G.P.*[2], p. 270.

The point of departure is the Sphere. We are to conceive the four bodily elements in complete fusion. Outside them is Strife, forming an envelope ' at the outermost limits of the round,' and completely separated from the elements.[1] Where is Love ? It is evidently diffused in equal distribution throughout the whole.[2] If Empedocles had been a complete Atomist, he would have conceived the Sphere as consisting of molecules, each composed of five atoms—of Love, Fire, Water, Earth, Air —Strife alone being absent. But, as it is, we must think of portions, rather than atoms ; and we must remember that Love is not a bodily element, but a soul-substance, and can therefore be conceived as *continuously* diffused throughout the whole mass, not broken up into discontinuous portions like the four primary bodies. If we suppose for a moment the molecular structure, then Love would not be a fifth atom, but the soul pervading and unifying the four bodily portions. Love is also called *Harmonia* ; it is of the same order of things as Heracleitus' Fire-Logos ; that is to say, it is both a fluid and a unifying principle which pervades the elements, as the soul pervades the body and holds it together. The Sphere is the body of God, and Love is the soul which pervades it, and binds it together in the bonds of harmony, as Justice bound the Sphere of Parmenides into indissoluble unity. ' There is no discord or unseemly strife in his limbs ' (frag. 27). ' He was equal on every side and quite limitless ($\dot{a}\pi\epsilon\iota\rho\omega\nu$), a rounded Sphere, rejoicing in his circular solitude ' (frag. 28).

Love in the Sphere is, thus, a thing of the same kind as the harmony-soul of the Pythagoreans, which was both a ratio and a spiritual substance—a combination of notions which Plato

---

[1] Frag. 36. 9, states this very clearly.

[2] I believe this to be the sense of frag. 17. 19 :

$$N\epsilon\hat{\iota}\kappa os \ \tau' \ o\dot{v}\lambda\acute{o}\mu\epsilon\nu o\nu \ \delta\acute{\iota}\chi a \ \tau\hat{\omega}\nu, \ \dot{a}\tau\acute{a}\lambda a\nu\tau o\nu \ \dot{a}\pi\acute{a}\nu\tau\eta\iota,$$
$$\kappa a\grave{\iota} \ \Phi\iota\lambda\acute{o}\tau\eta s \ \dot{\epsilon}\nu \ \tauo\hat{\iota}\sigma\iota\nu, \ \check{\iota}\sigma\eta \ \mu\hat{\eta}\kappa os \ \tau\epsilon \ \pi\lambda\acute{a}\tauos \ \tau\epsilon.$$

The contrasted words $\delta\acute{\iota}\chi a \ \tau\hat{\omega}\nu$ and $\dot{\epsilon}\nu \ \tauo\hat{\iota}\sigma\iota\nu$ are pointless unless these lines describe the Sphere ; and if they do, the description of Love as ' equal in length and breadth ' may mean ' diffused over the whole extent of the Sphere ' ; while $\dot{a}\tau\acute{a}\lambda a\nu\tau o\nu \ \dot{a}\pi\acute{a}\nu\tau\eta\iota$ (*der überall gleich wuchtige*, Diels) I take to mean that Strife envelops the whole mass in a covering that is ' equally balanced all round,' not thicker at any one point than at another. So Parmenides says of his Sphere : $\tau\grave{o} \ \gamma\grave{a}\rho \ o\check{v}\tau\epsilon \ \tau\iota \ \mu\epsilon\hat{\iota}\zeta o\nu \ o\check{v}\tau\epsilon \ \tau\iota \ \beta a\iota\acute{o}\tau\epsilon\rho o\nu \ \pi\epsilon\lambda\acute{\epsilon}\nu a\iota$ $\chi\rho\epsilon\acute{o}\nu \ \dot{\epsilon}\sigma\tau\iota \ \tau\hat{\eta}\iota \ \mathring{\eta} \ \tau\hat{\eta}\iota$ (frag. 8. 44).

showed to be inconsistent, and which puzzled Aristotle. After dismissing the view that the soul can be a 'harmony' in either of two senses—the *combining* (σύνθεσις) or fitting together of separate parts, and the *proportion* (λόγος) of the components of a mixture—Aristotle goes on to say that 'it is equally absurd to regard the soul [1] as the 'proportion of the mixture' (λόγος τῆς μείξεως). For the elements are not mixed in the same proportion in flesh as in bone; so that it will follow that there are many souls, and that too all over the body, if we assume that all the members consist of the elements variously commingled, and that the proportion (λόγος) determining the mixture is a harmony, that is, soul. This is a question we might ask Empedocles, who says that each of the parts is determined by a certain proportion (λόγῳ).[2] Is the soul, then, this proportion, or is it rather something distinct which comes to be in the members? And further, is the mixture caused by Love a random mixture, or a mixture in the right proportion; and if the latter, *is Love the proportion itself or something distinct from the proportion?* ' [3]

The answer, not given by Aristotle, to the last question, is that it is both the proportion or harmony, and also something which Aristotle, but not Empedocles, would regard as 'distinct,' namely, a substance. It is once more the group-soul, the solidarity of a group still conceived, as it had been by primitive man, as a material medium.

In the *Purifications*, God (that is, Love) is further described as 'a sacred mind (φρὴν ἱερή), unutterable, flashing through all the order of things with swift thoughts' (frag. 134)—words which show that this God is, in this respect, identical with the Nous of Anaxagoras. He is also, like the Logos of Heracleitus, the *Law* for all (τὸ πάντων νόμιμον) which 'stretches everywhere through the wide-ruling air and the infinite light of heaven ' (frag. 135).

This primary state of the world has its mythical counterpart

---

[1] Aristotle is of course discussing the *individual* soul.

[2] Arist. *de Anim.* a 5, 410a 1, gives Empedocles' formula for bone, which consists of 2 parts Earth, 2 Water, 4 Fire, ἁρμονίης κόλλησιν ἀρηρότα. At *de Part. Anim.* a 1, 642a 17, he says that this proportion (λόγος) is the *essence* (οὐσία) or *nature* (φύσις) of bone.

[3] *De Anim.* a 4, 408a 13.

in the *Purifications*, which describe the earliest age of man
as the Reign of Aphrodite, the Queen of Love. In that age
Strife was not : ' they had no Ares for a God, nor Kydoimos, no,
nor King Zeus, nor Kronos, nor Poseidon, but Kypris the
Queen' (frag. 128). Her alone they worshipped with rites pure
from the taint of bloodshed, and ' all things were tame and
gentle to man, both beasts and birds, and the flame of lovingkindness burned ' (φιλοφροσύνη δὲ δεδήει, frag. 130).

124. *The breaking up of the Sphere and the Fall of the Soul*

How was this state of bliss broken up ? Here again, we shall
find the religious doctrine coincide with the physical system.
The wheel of Time and Justice cannot stand still; and, as it
turns, ' in the fulness of the alternate time set by the broad oath,
Strife leapt to claim his prerogatives, and waxed mighty in the
limbs of the God, and they all trembled in turn.'[1] As Strife
poured in on all sides into the mass, Love rushed out to meet it.
The bodily elements, too, are swept towards their proper regions,
and from the meeting and mixing of all these streams arise all
the individual things in the world. The elements ' prevail in
turn, as the circle comes round, and pass into one another, waxing
small and great in their appointed turn ; for they alone really
are (ἔστι), but as they run through one another they *become*
(γιγνόνται) men and all the tribes of beasts ' (frag. 26). They
can only be said to ' become,' and not to have an ' abiding life,'
in the sense that ' they grow from many into one, and again are
divided and become many ' ; but ' in so far as, in this perpetual
change, they never cease, in that respect they are for ever immutable in the circle ' (*ibid.*).

Can this doctrine of the becoming of individual things, as a
mixing and separation of portions of the elements, be reconciled
with the religious belief in an immortal, migrating soul ? If not,
we must accept the common view that Empedocles' physical

---

[1] Frag. 30 :   αὐτὰρ ἐπεὶ μέγα Νεῖκος ἐνιμμελέεσσιν ἐθρέφθη
                  ἐς τιμάς τ' ἀνόρουσε τελειομένοιο χρόνοιο,
                  ὅς σφιν ἀμοιβαῖος πλατέος παρ' ἐλήλαται ὅρκου. . . .
    Frag. 31 :   πάντα γὰρ ἐξείης πελεμίζετο γυῖα θεοῖο.
So Plato, *Rep.* 545 D, describing the fall from the perfect form of government to Timarchy, invokes the Muses to say, ὅπως δὴ πρῶτον στάσις ἔμπεσε.

system did not square with his religion. But it will soon appear that there is no discrepancy.

Empedocles uses, once in each poem, a curious phrase which seems to be a cross-reference,[1] hinting that the doctrine of the *Purifications* can be interpreted in physical terms. The appointed moment of 'alternate time,' at which Strife leaps to claim his privileges, is ' *set by a broad oath* ' (πλατέος παρ' ἐλήλαται ὅρκου). After what has been said above (p. 23) about Styx, it is easy to recognise in this oath the Great Oath of the Gods, which secured their privileges in the *dasmos*, and to understand that it is called ' broad ' because it is a barrier or fence (*herkos*.)[2] This broad barrier is actually identical with the enveloping stream of *Neikos*, which enfolded the Sphere during the reign of Love—that chill stream which makes all the limbs of the God shudder when it begins to pour into the mass, just as Styx paralysed the God to whom her water was administered as an ordeal for oath-breaking, 'whenever quarrel and *strife* arose among the immortals.'[3] Neikos, the daemon of strife and division, has for his vehicle the icy stream of Styx. The meeting of the opposed currents of Love and Strife attends the formation of individual existents.

If we turn now to the famous Oracle of Necessity in the *Purifications*, we find that this eternal decree of the Gods is ' *sealed by broad oaths* '—πλατέεσσι κατεσφρηγισμένον ὅρκοις (frag. 115. 2). The oracle decrees the banishment from the Blessed,

---

[1] See p. 225.

[2] Empedocles' ἐλήλαται is reminiscent of Hesiod, *Theog.* 726, τὸν (Τάρταρον) πέρι χάλκεον ἕρκος ἐλήλαται, in the same context with the description of Styx. His term for the elements, ῥιζώματα, comes, through the formula of the Pythagoreans' Great Oath, the tetractys (πηγὴν ἀενάου φύσιος ῥίζωμα τ' ἔχουσαν), from the words which follow those just quoted from the *Theogony* ; ἀμφὶ δέ μιν Νὺξ τριστοιχεὶ κέχυται περὶ δειρήν· αὐτὰρ ὕπερθεν γῆς ῥίζαι πεφύασι καὶ ἀτρυγέτοιο θαλάσσης. (Cf. Olympiod. in Arist. *Meteor.* 28b A : γῆς ἔλεγον (οἱ ἀρχαῖοι) πηγὰς ὥσπερ τινὰς ῥίζας.) Plut. *de Is. et Os.* 381 F : ἡ δὲ καλουμένη τετρακτύς, τὰ ἐξ καὶ τριάκοντα, μέγιστος ἦν ὅρκος . . . καὶ κόσμος ὠνόμασται. For Styx-Horkos associated in Orphic theogony with the heaven-stream, Okeanos, cf. Arist. *Met.* A 3, 983b 27 : εἰσὶ δέ τινες οἳ καὶ τοὺς παμπαλαίους . . . καὶ πρώτους θεολογήσαντας οὕτως (like Thales) οἴονται περὶ τῆς φύσεως ὑπολαβεῖν· Ὠκεανόν τε γὰρ καὶ Τηθὺν ἐποίησαν τῆς γενέσεως πατέρας καὶ τὸν ὅρκον τῶν θεῶν ὕδωρ τὴν καλουμένην ὑπ' αὐτῶν Στύγα τῶν ποιητῶν· τιμιώτατον μὲν γὰρ τὸ πρεσβύτατον· ὅρκος δὲ τὸ τιμιώτατόν ἐστιν.

[3] Hes. *Theog.* 782 : ὁππότ' ἔρις καὶ νεῖκος ἐν ἀθανάτοισιν ὄρηται.

for a great year of thirty thousand seasons, of certain daemons for shedding blood or for oath-breaking.[1] The offence is also described as ' consorting with Strife,' ' putting trust in Strife.' [2] The fall of the individual soul thus means its separation from the original unity of God, the principle of Love and Harmony, and its passing into an impure state, in which it is mixed and tainted with the evil principle of Strife.

Mythically, the Fall of Man may be regarded as the passage from an original state of innocence, through a primal sin, into the troublesome condition of his present life. This myth is given in the description, contained in the *Purifications*, of the breaking up of the Reign of Aphrodite, which was the Golden Age before evil came into man's existence. It is fairly clear that bloodshed was the sin which caused the fall of man, as it was for bloodshed that the daemon is banished by the oracle of Necessity. In those days, we are told, ' the altar did not reek with pure bull's blood, but this was the greatest abomination (μύσος μέγιστον) among men, to eat the goodly limbs after tearing out the life ' (frag. 128).[3] Flesh-eating and the worship of the Gods of Strife, Ares and Kydoimos, were introduced together (frag. 128), and marked the fall of man and the end of the reign of Love. The ' burning flame of lovingkindness ' (frag. 130) was extinguished, and the soul put its trust in Strife.

The exact correspondence between this fall of the soul and the physical theory of the breaking up of the Sphere is now obvious enough. When the Sphere is invaded by the inrushing streams of *Neikos*, all the elements combine to make mortal forms. The four bodily elements compose their bodies; the

---

[1] Cf. Hes. *Theog.* 793 : ὅς κὲν τὴν ἐπίορκον ἀπολλείψας ἐπομόσσῃ
ἀθανάτων . . .
κεῖται νήυτμος τετελεσμένον εἰς ἐνιαυτόν.
The offender is sundered (ἀπομείρεται) from the Gods for a great year of nine ordinary years, and in the tenth he mixes (ἐπιμίσγεται) with them again (801-4).

[2] Frag. 115. 4 and 14:
<Νείκεϊ θ'> ὅς κ' ἐπίορκον ἀμαρτήσας (=ὁμαρτήσας) ἐπομόσσῃ . . .
Νείκει μαινομένῳ πίσυνος.

[3] We seem, by the way, to discern behind this passionate disapproval of the tearing and eating of flesh, besides the condemnation of Olympian sacrifices, a rejection of those primitive Bacchic rites of raw-flesh-eating (ὠμοφαγία) which the Cretan Kouretes had still retained, though they forswore the eating of flesh on other occasions.

two soul-substances compose a fallen, impure soul, in which a portion of Love, now scattered like a fluid broken into drops, is mixed with a portion of Strife. The principle of division has broken up the one all-pervading God, or Soul, of the Sphere into a plurality of daemons, each composed of Love and Strife, of good and evil.[1] Such a daemon can pass from one body to another and go the round of the elements, which all 'loathe' it —for, does it not contain an admixture of loathsome Styx ?[2] It will find no rest till it is purified of this evil principle, and the Love in it is freed from Strife once more, and gathered back into the unity of God. This day will come at the end of our world's existence, when the bodily elements are given over to the rule of Strife, and Love passes out of the mass to form a continuous fluid, enveloping it, as Neikos had done at the opposite pole.

Aristotle's statement that Empedocles makes the individual soul consist of *all* the elements—'for with earth we see earth, etc.'—is not inconsistent with the view we have stated, that the *immortal* part of the soul consists only of Love and Strife. It must be remembered that Aristotle also seems to think of Empedocles' soul as the 'proportion ($\lambda \acute{o} \gamma o \varsigma$) of the mixture,' or the principle of harmony, which for a time holds the body together. In any case, the bodily elements included in the soul's nature during each incarnation will, of course, be dissolved when the body decays. These compose its mortal part, constituting its powers of sense-perception, by which the soul perceives the bodily elements (but not Love and Strife), while it lives in that body. The individuality resides, not in them, but in the mixed portions of Love and Strife, which remain combined so long as the soul is impure, and migrate to other bodies. That

---

[1] Hence Plutarch, *de anim. tranq.* p. 474 B: $\mu \hat{a} \lambda \lambda o \nu$, $\dot{\omega} \varsigma$ 'Εμπεδοκλῆς, διτταί τινες ἕκαστον ἡμῶν γενόμενον παραλαμβάνουσι καὶ κατάρχονται μοῖραι καὶ δαίμονες, *i.e.* a good one and an evil, a portion of Love and a portion of Strife. Porph. *de abst.* iii. 27: εἰ δὲ μή, ἀλλ' ἐντεῦθέν γε τὸ τῆς φύσεως ἡμῶν ἐλάττωμα, ἐντεῦθεν τὸ θρηνούμενον πρὸς τῶν παλαιῶν, ὡς 'τοίων ἔκ τ' ἐρίδων ἔκ τε νείκεων γενόμεσθα,' ὅτι τὸ θεῖον ἀκήρατον καὶ ἐν πᾶσιν ἀβλαβὲς σῴζειν οὐ δυνάμεθα.

[2] Frag. 115. 12: ἄλλος δ' ἐς ἄλλου δέχεται, στυγέουσι δὲ πάντες. Cf. *Ps.-Phokylidea*, 15:

μηδ' ἐπιορκήσῃς μήτ' ἀγνὼς μήτε ἑκοντί·
ψεύδορκον στυγέει θεὸς ἄμβροτος ὅστις ὀμόσσῃ.

there is no contradiction or difficulty in regarding the senses as bodily and mortal, while another part of the soul is unseen and immortal, is clear from Plato's *Phaedo*,[1] where Socrates states, very precisely, just this Orphico-Pythagorean view of soul and body, and draws a clear line between the higher, immortal faculties, which know unseen things, and the senses and desires, which belong to the body and perish with it.   To Empedocles the flesh is an ' alien garment,' and the senses belong to it.[2] That of which it is a garment persists and migrates to other forms, as a weaver wears out many coats.[3]

When we think of the immortal soul as a ratio (λόγος), or proportion of numbers, it is easy to interpret the mixture in it of Love and Strife on Pythagorean lines.   A ratio, or harmony, is a complex held together by a principle of unity.   In so far as it is one, it is bound together by Love ; in so far as it is complex, it contains the principle of plurality, division, disunion, Strife. As Heracleitus says,[4] ' Combinations are wholes and not wholes, drawn together and drawn asunder, consonant and dissonant, one out of all things and all things out of one.'

125. *The consistency of Empedocles*

It appears, then, that there is no more inconsistency in Empedocles' doctrines than was already involved in the conception, which he inherited from the Pythagorean tradition, of the soul as both a ' harmony,' or ratio, and a fluid substance.   This inconsistency, or rather want of distinction, makes no discrepancy between the scientific poem and the religious ; it lies equally behind both.   The two poems show us a religious doctrine, and a translation of it into physical terms, which stands out as extraordinarily ingenious and successful.   We hope that it is also clear that the physical system is simply the cosmology of Anaxi-

---

[1] 63 B ff., especially 65 C–66 A.

[2] Frag. 126 : σαρκῶν ἀλλογνῶτι περιστέλλουσα χιτῶνι.

[3] The illustration used by Kebes in *Phaedo*, 87 C (see Burnet *ad loc.*, who connects it with the Orphic χιτών).   The analogy between Empedocles' soul and the soul as conceived by Chinese Taoism (above, p. 99) is remarkable. The two systems are based on the same fundamental ideas.

[4] Frag. 59 : συνάψιες ὅλα καὶ οὐχ ὅλα, συμφερόμενον διαφερόμενον, συνᾷδον διᾷδον, καὶ ἐκ πάντων ἓν καὶ ἐξ ἑνὸς πάντα.

mander, with such modifications as were dictated by Empedocles' religious beliefs, together with the new notion of elements as 'things,' which Empedocles had taken from Parmenides and turned against its author. Given that notion, it is hardly too much to say that a very acute critic, with a sufficient knowledge of the mystic tradition, and nothing but the *Purifications* to go upon, could have deduced the changes that Empedocles would make in Anaximander's scheme, and reconstructed all the main lines of the new system. So far are we from accepting the view that 'all through this period there was a gulf between men's religious beliefs, if they had any, and their cosmological views.' Empedocles, as we read him, exemplifies, in a most remarkable way, the opposite view, that men's cosmological views were almost entirely dictated by, and deduced from, their religious convictions.

Empedocles is a candid dualist, and consequently annoying to philosophers like Aristotle, who imagine that they have evaded dualism by the fallacies of the 'final cause,' and escaped from mythology when they make 'God' the prime mover. Aristotle[1] complains that Empedocles does not explain the reason of the change which brings Strife back to the possession of his privileges, but only says that 'that is how it is' (οὕτως πέφυκεν), and speaks of the 'fulness of time, fixed by the broad oath,' implying that the change was necessary, but not explaining why. The only reason is that the wheel of Time, Justice, and Destiny must turn and bring in its revenges. If we ask further why this must be, we can hardly expect an answer. It is an oracle of Necessity, or *Moira*; and when modern writers echo Aristotle's complaint, we may fairly ask them how they propose to explain the presence of necessity in the universe, without recourse to mythical representations. To set up 'God' beyond Necessity or Destiny—Zeus above *Moira*—is only to add one more story to a tower of Babel, whose top is already lost in the clouds. The dualist who is content to match God and Destiny, as a pair of equal antagonists, is no more, if no less, mythological; and he does not entangle himself in the difficulties which beset those who have

---

[1] *Met.* β 4, 1000 *b* 12.

to make out that a world, half good and half bad, was designed by pure benevolence united with omnipotence.

The later followers of Empedocles, attacked by Plato in his *Laws*,[1] seem to have fallen into line with the scientific tradition, keeping the four bodily elements of fire, air, earth, and water, and dropping the two soul-substances Love and Strife. They held, accordingly, that the world arose ' by nature and by chance ' (φύσει καὶ τύχῃ), and not ' by art ' or design (τέχνῃ, διὰ νοῦν) which they regarded as a human thing. The four elements they declared to be *physis*, and the soul to be a compound of them, and secondary.[2] Their position was thus, in this respect, identical with the Atomists', and, in their system, Chance (τύχη) holds the place of *Moira*.

126. PLATO : *the Socratic and Mystic dialogues*

The last and greatest attempt to formulate the mystical faith in rational terms was made by Plato. It is impossible, at the end of this essay, to do justice to the Platonic system ; we can only try to indicate how it is related to the two main tendencies we have traced in Greek speculation. Platonism, if we take it to mean principally the theory of Forms or ' Ideas,' will turn out to belong to the mystic tradition. We regard it as another offshoot of Pythagoreanism, another attempt to succeed, where Parmenides had failed, in relating the one God, who is good, to a manifold and imperfect world.

It is now generally agreed that we may distinguish a group of early dialogues, commonly called ' Socratic,' from a later group in which the doctrines characteristic of Orphism and Pythagoreanism for the first time make their appearance.[3] Typical of the Socratic group are the *Apology, Laches, Charmides*, and other minor dialogues, written within ten years after the death of Socrates (399 B.C.). The mystical group, heralded by the *Gorgias*, includes the *Meno, Symposium, Phaedo, Republic, Phaedrus*. It is held that the *Gorgias* was composed shortly

---

[1] 889 B ff. Cf. *D.F. V.*[2], p. 161. 48.

[2] 891 C : πῦρ καὶ ὕδωρ καὶ γῆν καὶ ἀέρα πρῶτα ἡγεῖσθαι τῶν πάντων εἶναι καὶ τὴν φύσιν ὀνομάζειν ταῦτ' αὐτά, ψυχὴν δὲ ἐκ τούτων ὕστερον.

[3] For these questions Hans Raeder, *Platons philosophische Entwickelung*, Leipzig, 1905, should be consulted.

before or after 387 B.C., the year when Plato, at the age of forty, set up his school at the Academy. Before he thus settled at Athens, Plato, who went abroad after the death of Socrates, had almost certainly spent some time with the Megarian Socratics,[1] and also travelled in Sicily, where Pythagorean thought must have survived the dispersion of the communities. We have every reason to connect the change of tone and of doctrine from the Socratic to the mystic group with these opportunities of contact with Pythagoreanism, a type of philosophy which seems to have been little known to the Athens of Plato's youth. The point we seek to bring out is that Plato's development obeys the general rule we have seen at work throughout pre-Socratic philosophy—the rule that the view taken of the 'nature of things' reflects and is determined by beliefs about the nature and destiny of the soul. The theory of Ideas makes its appearance at the same moment with the doctrine of the soul's immortality and divinity; and the whole argument of the *Phaedo* is that the two doctrines stand or fall together.[2] There is therefore a strong *prima facie* case for holding that the Theory of Ideas should be interpreted from the mystic standpoint, and as inspired by the same view of the world and of life and death that gave rise to the systems of Parmenides and Empedocles.

The contrast between the two groups of dialogues comes out strongly, when we compare the *Apology*, Plato's version of Socrates' speech at his trial, with the earlier part of the *Phaedo*, which professes to record Socrates' last conversation with his intimate friends. The comparison involves a problem which has been solved in various ways. Before we state our own solution, the facts must be briefly reviewed. We need only premise that it is extremely difficult to believe that Plato can

---

[1] Hermodorus ap. Diog. L. ii. 106, iii. 6; see Burnet's edition of the *Phaedo*, Oxford, 1911, Introd. I am glad to find myself largely in agreement with the views stated in this valuable introduction, and with the similar views of A. E. Taylor, *Varia Socratica*, i., Oxford 1911. I have long been working towards the conclusion that Plato's system is fundamentally Pythagorean; and I owe to these books much that has helped me to form a clearer opinion.

[2] 76 B: ἴση ἀνάγκη ταῦτά (τὰ εἴδη) τε εἶναι καὶ τὰς ἡμετέρας ψυχὰς πρὶν καὶ ἡμᾶς γεγονέναι, καὶ εἰ μὴ ταῦτα, οὐδὲ τάδε.

have substantially misrepresented what Socrates said on either of these occasions.[1] He was present at the trial, and had ample opportunities of learning what had happened in the prison.

127. *Immortality in the* Apology

The *Apology* has two passages in which Socrates speaks of the nature and significance of death. In the former (p. 29 A), Socrates says that to be afraid of death is the same thing as to think one is wise, when one is not; for it is to suppose that one knows what one does not know. No one knows even so much as whether death may be the greatest of all goods for man, and yet men fear it, as if they knew it to be the greatest of evils. Herein, if anywhere, may lie Socrates' own superiority in wisdom : having no sufficient knowledge about the things in Hades, he does not suppose himself to have any; what he does know, is that it is bad to do wrong and disobey him who is the better, be he God or man. He fears this evil which he knows, rather than that other evil which may possibly be a good.

In his final address after his condemnation (p. 40 c), he says that there is considerable hope that his fate, after all, may be a good one. Death is one of two things. Either it is ' like being nothing ' [2] and having no consciousness of anything ; or it may be, as certain accounts say, a shift, or change of abode, to another place. If it is like a dreamless sleep, that would be a great gain ; for few indeed of our waking days and nights are better and pleasanter than dreamless sleep. If, again, it is like a journey to another country, and the accounts are true which say that all the dead are there, what greater good could there be ? Suppose that, on arriving in Hades, one will be rid of these men who profess to be judges here, and find the true judges, Minos and Rhadamanthus and Aeacus and Triptolemus, and other

---

[1] This point has been brought out with great force by Burnet and Taylor, *opp. citt.* I am, however, inclined to think that in the *Phaedo* Plato would allow himself considerably more freedom than these writers will admit.

[2] οἷον μηδὲν εἶναι. This does not mean sheer annihilation, complete non-existence ; but being a shadow, a cipher, something that does not count ; as when the dying hero in Tragedy says, οὐδέν εἰμ' ἐγώ.

demigods who proved themselves just in their lives.[1] Who, again, would not give much to be in the company of Orpheus, Musaeus, Hesiod, and Homer ? If that is true, Socrates would gladly die many times. The company there would suit him to a marvel; for he would meet others who had been unjustly judged, such as Palamedes and Ajax, and compare his experiences with theirs. Also, he could go on spending his time examining people, to find out who was wise, and who thought he was, and was not. It would be great happiness to question Agamemnon, and Odysseus, and Sisyphus, and countless other men and women. Anyhow, the dead are happier than the living, for, if all that is said be true, they are deathless, and therefore cannot be put to death for practising dialectic !

It will hardly be denied that this passage, with its ironic tone, leaves the impression that Socrates' attitude is agnostic ; but we must remember that Socrates may not have chosen to express his private convictions to such an audience at such a moment. We can accept the *Apology* as a faithful report, without concluding that the totally different attitude towards death taken by the Socrates in the *Phaedo* is not, in the main, historic.

128. *Ideas and Souls in the* Phaedo

The setting of the *Phaedo* marks it as dedicated to the Pythagorean community at Phlius ;[2] and the principal interlocutors, the Thebans, Simmias and Kebes, were alike Socratics and pupils of Philolaus, the Pythagorean who settled at Thebes. Socrates now declares[3] that he dies willingly, because he thinks he will go to the company of good and wise Gods, and perhaps he will find there also dead men who are better than men on earth. Of this last he cannot be certain ; but that he will go to the presence of Gods who are good masters, he is as sure as he can be about any such matter. He has good hope that death is not nothingness, and that, as the ancient accounts say, it is much better for the good than for the bad.

---

[1] It has been pointed out that these demigods may simply be judges among the dead, because they were exceptionally just, without any idea of a 'last judgment' of souls or of a distribution of rewards and punishments.

[2] For details see introductions to Ferrai's and Burnet's editions.

[3] *Phaedo*, 63 B.

Plato seems careful to mark that the discourse, opened by this statement, is a sort of retractation of the *Apology*.[1] It contains a statement of the Pythagorean view of life and death, with which we are already familiar. Plato also indicates that it is to be taken rather as an expression of faith—a thing which is earnestly believed, in its general outlines, to be true—than as a theory which can, as yet, be certainly established by argument. It is a *mythos*, not a *logos*.[2]

The famous sermon is too familiar to be repeated here. What specially concerns us is the analogy between the soul and the true 'natures' or Ideas. The immortal thinking soul, which alone knows reality, is sharply distinguished from the body, with which are associated the lower faculties of sense, emotion, and desire. Death is the complete release of the soul from the infection and impurity of that lower nature ; philosophy is the rehearsal of death, in which the soul retires by herself, shaking off, so far as she can, the senses and lusts of the body, to commune with those invisible and passionless existences, Justice, Beauty, Goodness, and the rest.

The ruling conception of this new *Apology* is the already familiar contrast of the two worlds. There is a supersensible world, to which soul ' by herself' and the objects of true knowledge belong; and there is the sensible world of body, and of visible and tangible things. The world of the body is a prison, or a tomb ; that other world of the soul and of Ideas is the realm of true life and reality, in which all worth resides.

In the course of the arguments that follow, it becomes still clearer that souls and Ideas are things of the same kind. The first two arguments aim at persuading us that the soul exists before birth and after death, and that, before her birth into this world, she not only existed, but had consciousness. The third

---

[1] It begins, 63 B, with the words φέρε δὴ πειραθῶ πιθανώτερον πρὸς ὑμᾶς ἀπολογήσασθαι ἢ πρὸς τοὺς δικαστάς, and ends, 69 E, εἴ τι οὖν ὑμῖν πιθανώτερός εἰμι ἐν τῇ ἀπολογίᾳ ἢ τοῖς 'Αθηναίων δικασταῖς, εὖ ἂν ἔχοι.

[2] This, I believe, is part of the significance of the passage (60 D) about the dream in which Socrates has been warned to 'work at music' (μουσικὴν ποίει καὶ ἐργάζου). Socrates had hitherto taken 'music' to mean philosophy—his own rationalising dialectic ; but now he thinks it may mean literal 'music,' fables not *logoi*. Not being μυθολογικός, he borrows the fables of Aesop and turns them into poetry (61 B). At 61 E he describes the discourse which ollows as μυθολογεῖν. Cf. 70 B, διαμυθολογῶμεν.

tries to dispel Kebes' fear that the soul (which, like other Greeks, he conceives as an extended gaseous substance) may be dissipated, like smoke, when it leaves the body. This argument (p. 77 ff.) may be resumed as follows :

We have to ask, what sort of objects can suffer dissolution, and what cannot ; and to which class soul belongs. Only that which is composite, or consists of pieces that have been put together (τὸ συντεθὲν καὶ σύνθετον ὄν), can be dissolved ; and it is probable that immutable objects like the Ideas are incomposite, and so indissoluble, whereas the particular things, belonging to the groups called after them, are always changing and passing away.

Let us, then, divide things into two classes—the unseen, which never change, and the seen, which are changing perpetually. The body is more 'akin' (συγγενής) to the seen, the soul to the unseen. The soul is invisible ; she is distracted and dazzled by the perception of sense-objects through the bodily faculties ; whereas, when she is withdrawn by herself, she finds rest in contemplating those eternal, pure, immortal objects to which she is akin. Moreover, soul rules over body ; and to rule is the function of that which is divine. Hence, the soul may be expected to be altogether indissoluble, ' or nearly so ' ; for even the body holds together for a long time, and some parts of it are ' practically immortal.' Surely soul, the unseen thing, which goes pure to the good and wise God, cannot be dissolved ; but, if she escapes free from bodily contamination, she reaches ' that which is like herself, divine, immortal, wise,' and becomes, in the mystical sense, *eudaimon*.

129. *Plato's conversion to Pythagoreanism*

How are we to account for the apparent change of view from the *Apology* to the *Phaedo* ? Professors Burnet and Taylor have made out a strong case for believing that both dialogues must be, in the main, historical ; and we have already remarked that there is no difficulty in supposing that Socrates would speak very differently to the judges in the court and to his intimate friends in the prison. The argument points to the conclusion that Socrates was more familiar with Pythagorean ideas than has commonly been supposed ; though it must be noted that none of the positive arguments advanced in the early part of the *Phaedo* is regarded as conclusive, except the argument from *anamnesis*—that all true knowledge is recollection, in this life, of knowledge of the Ideas, acquired by the soul in the other world.[1]

The problem that remains to be faced is this : If Socrates really talked in this way, and discussed the mystic view of immortality as bound up with the theory of Ideas, why is there no trace of this association of doctrines in the earlier Socratic dialogues ? If Plato learnt all this from Socrates, how could he possibly have kept it out of the *Charmides, Laches,* and the rest ?

To this question the most probable answer seems to us to be, that Plato did not learn it from Socrates, but from Pythagorean friends after his master's death. Professor Burnet points out that, though Plato must from his childhood have known Socrates, and heard him talk, we have no ground for supposing that he belonged to the inner circle of Socratics.[2] As a young man, he may have been chiefly interested in the very exciting politics of that troubled time ; and the rationalising, dialectical side of Socrates may have been all he knew. Suppose that this was so, and that after the death of Socrates, when he was twenty-eight, he set himself to defend Socrates' memory from the charge of having corrupted the youth of Athens, by describing the sort of conversations he had witnessed in the porticoes and gymnasia. The subject of these early dialogues is the definition of virtue, or of particular virtues, such as courage and temperance ; the thesis they illustrate is the Socratic doctrine that virtue is knowledge. Knowledge meant clear thinking—both that self-knowledge which refutes the false conceit of wisdom, and the attempt to conceive clearly and isolate in definition the *meaning* of a name like Justice, as distinct from the many things called by that name. There is no hint in these earlier dialogues that such a ' meaning ' (λόγος)

---

[1] See *Phaedo*, 90 E ff., where Socrates admits that he has been arguing as one who has an interest in the conclusion, and not dispassionately, and 91 E, where the *anamnesis* argument alone is reaffirmed as valid.

[2] Burnet, *Phaedo*, 1911, Introd. p. xxvi.

or ' form ' (εἶδος) is regarded as a substantial, existing thing, or as more real than the things called after it, or as in any sense a cause of their existence. Probably Plato, in this first period, thought of it as a secondary and unsubstantial thing, like the Atomist's *eidolon*, or wraith ; and, like other Greeks, imagined the soul as a shadowy phantom of the same kind. The apparently agnostic attitude of Socrates in the *Apology* may well represent Plato's own standpoint at that moment, and all that he then knew of Socrates' beliefs on the subject.

Now, consider the effect upon him of becoming familiar, within a few years of Socrates' death, with those mystic friends of the inner circle who had sympathised with a different side of the master's thought. Hitherto, Plato had known little about the mystics. There was no Pythagorean community at Athens ; Orphism existed there only in a degraded form, which moved Plato to the contempt freely expressed in the *Republic*. It might well be some time before he could whole-heartedly assimilate the new view of Socrates now put before him. He may have been converted at the moment when it flashed upon him that the ' forms ' or ' meanings ' which Socrates had sought, were not unsubstantial wraiths, but the very living natures and indwelling souls of their groups ; when he saw in them the mediators which would take the place of the Pythagorean ' numbers,' and once more fill the gap, left by Parmenides, between the immutable One and the manifold world of sense. It would be very human and natural that the sudden and tremendous illumination of this idea should mark the crisis of his conversion to mysticism, and carry with it the conviction that this, after all, must have been what Socrates was feeling after. His first duty would then be to write dialogues like the *Symposium* and the *Phaedo*, in which Socrates figures as the exponent of the new theory.[1]

130. *Ideas as Soul-substances*

To our minds, the doctrine that souls are like Ideas, and Ideas like souls, is strange and paradoxical. A soul and a con-

---

[1] I would not leave the impression that I hold Socrates to have been either an Orphic or a Pythagorean. I only suggest that Plato, helped by his mystic friends, may have read his new Pythagoreanism back into the thought of Socrates.

cept, such as Beauty or Equality, seem to us to have little in common. Hence we are inclined to assume, as a matter of course, that the distinction must have been equally obvious to Plato, and, proceeding on that assumption, to interpret him as discovering analogies between very different classes of things. This is to reverse the true state of the matter. Plato's task was, not to find resemblances, but to differentiate two kinds of supersensible reality, which had originally been almost or quite indistinguishable. We need only recall the fact that his contemporary, Democritus, explained visual perception by the entrance of ' images ($\epsilon\check{\iota}\delta\omega\lambda a$) which flow off ($\dot{a}\pi o\rho\rho\acute{e}o\nu\tau a$) continually from the objects seen, are of like form ($\dot{o}\mu o\iota\acute{o}\mu o\rho\phi a$) with them, and impinge upon the eye.'[1] Democritus seems to have called these images deikela, ' semblances,' ' appearances ';[2] they were nothing but soul-phantoms or wraiths, reduced, as Atomism demanded, to filmy tissues of atoms. At this stage of thought, images and concepts could still be credited with the properties ascribed to phantoms or souls—objective reality, existence in time, extension and localisation in space, and even bodily properties such as resistance. The task of philosophy was to get concepts clear of these soul-properties. Plato still conceives Ideas as soul-substances, and assigns to them the same properties he now assigns to souls : both alike are immutable, uniform ($\mu o\nu o\epsilon\iota\delta\hat{\eta}$), incomposite, immortal, divine.

131. Two grades of supersensible existence

Further, in his present stage, Plato seems to recognise two grades of supersensible existence : (a) pure, unmixed with body, and (b) impure, mixed with body. Moreover, he seems to think that both Ideas and souls may be on either grade.

(a) The Soul may be withdrawn ' by itself ' ($a\dot{\upsilon}\tau\dot{\eta}$ $\kappa a\theta'$ $a\dot{\upsilon}\tau\acute{\eta}\nu$), and retire to that which is pure, ever-existent, immortal, and unchangeable, and be with this for ever, being akin ($\sigma\upsilon\gamma\gamma\epsilon\nu\acute{\eta}s$)

---

[1] Alex. in Arist. de Sens. p. 56 ; Beare, Greek Theories of Elem. Cognition, p. 30.

[2] Hesych : $\delta\acute{\iota}\kappa\eta\lambda o\nu$—$\phi\acute{a}\sigma\mu a$, $\check{o}\psi\iota s$, $\epsilon\check{\iota}\delta\omega\lambda o\nu$, $\mu\acute{\iota}\mu\eta\mu a$. Cic. ad Fam. xv. 16. 1 : quae ille Gargettius et iam ante Democritus $\epsilon\check{\iota}\delta\omega\lambda a$, hic (Catius Insuber, the Epicurean) spectra nominat. For the religious use of $\delta\acute{\iota}\kappa\eta\lambda o\nu$ see M. P. Nilsson, Der Ursprung der Tragödie, Neue Jahrbücher (1911), xxvii. p. 692,

to it.[1] This retreat into the unseen world means a purification
of soul from the lower and bodily affections. Complete deliverance from these is not attainable till death, when soul is separated
from body, and then only if the soul has been purified in life by
the pursuit of wisdom.

(b) During this mortal life, and even after death, the soul-
substance may be infected and permeated by the bodily.[2] In
life, it is tainted by passions and desires; and, after death, if it
has not departed pure, it remains as a visible ghost, ' wallowing
about graves and tombs, where certain shadowy phantoms of
souls are seen, the *eidola* of those souls which have not been
released in purity, but partake of the visible, and are therefore
seen.'[3] The substance of the soul is, again and again, spoken of
as if it were capable of being ' tainted,' ' mixed,' ' permeated '
with bodily substance. The possibility of its remaining in this
impure state even after death is necessary to account for its
reincarnation; for, if it escaped pure, ' not dragging with it
anything of the body,' there would be no reason why it should
fall back into another mortal form.[4] The language throughout
this part of the *Phaedo* indisputably describes the substance of
the soul as if it were spatially extended and capable of literal
admixture with bodily elements. Every term appropriate to
such a conception is used, and there is not a hint that it is all
mere metaphor. To treat it as such is arbitrary and baseless.

---

[1] *Phaedo,* 79 D.

[2] *Phaedo,* 67 A : μηδὲ ἀναπιμπλώμεθα (infected) τῆς τούτου (τοῦ σώματος)
φύσεως, ἀλλὰ καθαρεύωμεν. 66 B : ἕως ἂν τὸ σῶμα ἔχωμεν καὶ συμπεφυρμένη
ᾖ ἡμῶν ἡ ψυχὴ μετὰ τοιούτου κακοῦ. 80 E : ἐὰν μὲν καθαρὰ ἀπαλλάττηται, μηδὲν
τοῦ σώματος συνεφέλκουσα, ἅτε οὐδὲν κοινωνοῦσα αὐτῷ ἐν τῷ βίῳ ἑκοῦσα εἶναι.
81 B : μεμιασμένη καὶ ἀκάθαρτος τοῦ σώματος. 81 C : διειλημμένη (distended,
permeated) ὑπὸ τοῦ σωματοειδοῦς.

[3] *Phaedo,* 81 D. Compare my interpretation of Empedocles' view of soul
as consisting of an immortal part, composed of the good principle (Love)
tainted during the cycle of reincarnations with an admixture of the evil
principle (Strife), and a mortal part (senses) consisting of the four bodily
elements, p. 239.

[4] *Phaedo,* 81 C. The soul which is ' permeated by the bodily ' and by con-
tinual association (συνουσία) with it has *worked the bodily into its nature or
substance* (ἐνεποίησε σύμφυτον), is weighed down and dragged back into the
visible world by this bodily admixture, which is ἐμβριθές, βαρύ, γεῶδες,
ὁρατόν. Hence, in the *Phaedrus,* 248, the disembodied soul retains the two
lower ' parts,' symbolised by the two horses of the chariot, and by these it
is dragged down again to earth. In these representations, however, strict
consistency is not to be expected.

Now, the Ideas are described in very similar language. They too may exist in transcendental purity, or as embodied, ' present,' in the things which they inform. In the second case, they are what we should call ' instances ' of the Idea—the instances, for example, of Beauty which are somehow ' communicated ' to beautiful things in the world of sense.[1]

(a) As the soul in its pure state is said to be ' by itself ' (αὐτὴ καθ' αὑτήν), steadfast, immutable, divine, and immortal, so in the *Symposium* the Idea, when it is ' by itself ' (αὐτὸ καθ' αὑτὸ) and free from matter, is called uniform, unmixed, pure, divine.[2] The conclusion of the argument at *Phaedo* 80 D states that soul is most like the divine, immortal, intelligible, uniform, indissoluble, unchangeable Idea; while body is like the human, mortal, multiform, unintelligible, dissoluble, and perpetually changing.

(b) The immanent Idea, on the other hand, is described in the same terms as the embodied soul which is permeated with earthly substance. As the soul is ' filled by the body with passions and appetites and fears and all sorts of phantoms and rubbish,' so the Idea, when it is involved in its visible embodiments, is ' infected with human flesh and colours and all sorts of mortal rubbish.'[3]

This comparison shows that the process of differentiating concepts from souls has not yet gone very far in Plato's mind. We believe that, both in the early Socratic period and in these mystical dialogues of his middle life, Ideas and souls are things of the same kind, or barely distinguishable; and that, precisely for that reason, his view of the nature of the Ideas changed simultaneously with his view of the nature of soul, when he was

---

[1] *Euthyd.* 300 E: The many beautiful things are different from Beauty itself (αὐτὸ τὸ καλόν), but a certain beauty (κάλλος τι) is present (πάρεστι) to each of them. *Phaedo*, 100 D: οὐκ ἄλλο τι ποιεῖ αὐτὸ (a beautiful thing) καλὸν ἢ ἡ ἐκείνου τοῦ καλοῦ εἴτε παρουσία εἴτε κοινωνία εἴτε ὅπῃ δὴ καὶ ὅπως προσγενομένη. Throughout the concluding argument, the instance of the Idea *in us* (e.g. τὸ ἐν ἡμῖν μέγεθος, 102 D) is in some sense distinguished from the Idea itself (αὐτὸ τὸ Μέγεθος), which is *in nature* (ἐν τῇ φύσει).

[2] *Symp.* 211: μονοειδές, εἰλικρινές, καθαρὸν, ἄμικτον, θεῖον. See the whole context.

[3] *Phaedo*, 66 C: (soul) ἐρώτων δὲ καὶ ἐπιθυμιῶν καὶ φόβων καὶ εἰδώλων παντοδαπῶν καὶ φλυαρίας ἐμπίμπλησιν ἡμᾶς πολλῆς (τὸ σῶμα). *Symp.* 211 E: (Idea) ἀνάπλεων σαρκῶν τε ἀνθρωπίνων καὶ χρωμάτων καὶ ἄλλης πολλῆς φλυαρίας θνητῆς.

converted to Pythagoreanism. The *Phaedo* announces this conversion as fully accomplished.

According to his new view of the constitution of reality, the ' nature of things '[1] is to be found in these supersensible Ideas, each of which is the centre, and indwelling soul, of a group of objects in the sense-world.

132. *The Idea as Daemon and the nature of ' Participation '*

We have seen how, in the *Phaedo*, the Platonic ' Forms ' or ' Ideas ' are declared to be objects of the same kind with souls. But the Ideas, it must be noted, are not individual souls, but souls of groups, or classes of things, called by their names. They are, in fact, descended from entities of the same order as the daemons described above (Chapter III.)—the impersonal spirits of human groups or natural departments.[2] Justice, for instance, is the one collective soul-idea which is somehow shared in common by all just persons and things. How is this relation to be conceived ? How is it possible for one form or nature to be present in a plurality of things, and yet to remain one ?

---

[1] φύσις in Plato means the World of Ideas ; cf. *Rep.* 597 A : (ἡ κλίνη) ἡ ἐν τῇ φύσει οὖσα, made by God, identical with τὸ εἶδος ὃ δὴ φάμεν εἶναι ὃ ἔστι κλίνη. *Phaedo*, 103 B : τὸ ἐν τῇ φύσει (ἐναντίον) contrasted with τὸ ἐν ἡμῖν. *Parm.* 132 B : τὰ μὲν εἴδη ταῦτα ὥσπερ παραδείγματα ἑστάναι ἐν τῇ φύσει.

[2] See Plato's description of the rule of the *daemons* in the age of Kronos (above, p. 35), each daemon presiding over one kind. The close analogy between Plato's Ideas and the ' species-deities,' of which Tylor, *Prim. Cult.* (1903), ii. p. 243, gives examples, has long been pointed out, especially the Finnish *haltiat* : ' Every object in nature has a " haltia," a guardian deity or genius, a being which was its creator and thenceforth became attached to it. These deities or genii are, however, not bound to each single transitory object, but are free personal beings which have movement, form, body, and soul. Their existence in no wise depends on the existence of the individual objects, for although no object in nature is without its guardian deity, this deity extends to the whole race or species. This ash-tree, this stone, this house has indeed its particular " haltia," yet these same " haltiat " concern themselves with other ash-trees, stones, and houses, of which the individuals may perish, but their presiding genii live on in the species' (p. 245). These *haltiat* are obviously group-souls or daemons arrested in an earlier stage than Plato's Ideas, retaining more soul-properties, which the Ideas have shed on their way towards becoming mere concepts. The obscurity about the relation of the ' species-deity' to the particular instances of it present in members of the group is precisely that which besets the relation of αὐτὸ τὸ Μέγεθος to τὸ ἐν ἡμῖν μέγεθος in Plato's *Phaedo*, 102 D ff.

This is the much-vexed problem of ' participation ' (μέθεξις), which Plato could never solve to his satisfaction.

We understand the problem and its insolubility, when we grasp that this relation called ' participation ' (*methexis*) is, from the first, a mystical, non-rational relation, which defies rational analysis. The Idea is a group-soul, related to its group as a mystery-daemon, like Dionysus, is related to the group of worshippers, his *thiasos*. The worshippers of Dionysus believed that, when they held their orgiastic rites, the one God entered into each and all of them ; each and all became *entheoi* ; they ' partook ' of the one divine nature, which was ' communicated ' to them all, and ' present ' in each. It is thus we must interpret the three terms—*methexis, parousia, koinonia*—by which Plato tries to describe the relation of an Idea to its group. Another term—*mimesis*—has the same significance. *Mimesis* is not ' imitation ' in the sense of an external resemblance : there is no ' likeness ' in this sense between the Idea ' Man ' and a human being, and Plato never could suppose that there was. *Mimesis* has its old sense of ' embodying,' ' representing ': it is like the relation which an actor has to the character he impersonates, only that it is essentially between a *group* and a unity. A better illustration is to be found in a variety of symbols, all of which embody or represent one meaning. This sense of *mimesis* was preserved by the Pythagoreans. Aristotle is exactly right when he says that ' whereas the Pythagoreans say that things exist by " representing " numbers, Plato says it is by " participation " ; he merely changed the name.' [1]

133. *The problem of ' Participation '*

We have seen how the conception of this relation, subsisting between a divine or daemonic being and a group, had been kept alive by the Pythagorean community, which, during its founder's life and after his death, believed itself to be continuously animated and inspired by the master's spirit. We have seen also

[1] Arist. *Met.* a vi. 987 b 9 : κατὰ μέθεξιν γὰρ εἶναι τὰ πολλὰ τῶν συνωνύμων τοῖς εἴδεσιν. τὴν δὲ μέθεξιν τοὔνομα μόνον μετέβαλεν· οἱ μὲν γὰρ Πυθαγόρειοι μιμήσει τὰ ὄντα φασὶν εἶναι τῶν ἀριθμῶν, Πλάτων δὲ μεθέξει. τὴν μέντοι γε μέθεξιν ἢ τὴν μίμησιν ἥτις ἂν εἴη τῶν εἰδῶν ἀφεῖσαν ἐν κοινῷ ζητεῖν.

how, in such cases, the image of the human prophet recedes and gathers about it the glories of miraculous legend. Once more the old story is repeated. Just as the Gods in their day ceased to be functional daemons in close and perpetual relations with their worshippers, and drifted away to Olympus, and finally to the utmost heaven, so Pythagoras had passed from being a marvellous man (δαιμόνιος ἀνήρ, θεῖος ἀνήρ), up the ladder which leads from earth to heaven, to become identified with Apollo himself. The penalty of this Olympian exaltation is always the same : the old sense of intimate communion, based on community of nature, must fade and die. What was once a collective soul, becomes a distinct individual, removed by an impassable gulf from its group.

The same fate awaited the Platonic Idea. The relation called *methexis* will not bear rational analysis. Aristotle, after saying that Plato adopted this relation from the Pythagoreans and merely changed the name, adds that both alike ' left it an open question what on earth this *participation* or *representation* may be.' As regards Plato, the statement is hardly true. Already in the *Phaedo* he has become uncomfortable about it, and declines to commit himself to the terms ' presence ' and ' communion.' [1] Later, in the *Parmenides*, he raises the intellectual difficulties.[2] Parmenides asks whether we are to understand that the whole Idea, or only a part, is present in each thing which ' partakes ' of it. Either alternative is beset with difficulties. The problem cannot be solved, until the Ideas altogether cease to be indwelling group-souls, or daemons, which can impart themselves to a whole group, and yet remain one. Their fate must ultimately be to dry up into mere ' concepts,' or logical objects of thought, immutable still and independent of the subject which knows them, but without life and power. The relation of *methexis* must be reduced to the relation of logical subject to universal predicate. From the point of view of logical theory, this step is an unmitigated gain ; but, although

---

[1] *Phaedo,* 100 D : οὐκ ἄλλο τι ποιεῖ αὐτὸ καλὸν ἢ ἡ ἐκείνου τοῦ Καλοῦ εἴτε παρουσία εἴτε κοινωνία εἴτε ὅπῃ δὴ καὶ ὅπως προσγενομένη (προσαγορευομένη, Wytt.)· οὐ γὰρ ἔτι τοῦτο διισχυρίζομαι, ἀλλ᾽ ὅτι τῷ Καλῷ πάντα τὰ καλὰ [γίγνεται] καλά.

[2] *Parm.* 131.

Plato, as a logician, is irresistibly driven towards it, the mystic in him cries out against it. In the midst of his later and most severely logical work, the protest breaks out : ' Can we ever be made to believe that motion, and life, and soul, and consciousness, are not present in that which is perfectly real ? Can we imagine it as neither alive nor conscious, but, in all its irreproachable solemnity, a senseless, immovable fixture ? ' [1]

The trouble is that, if the Ideas are allowed to cease to be souls, and to become mere concepts, they can no longer be regarded as the *causes*—the only true causes—of the world. The Socrates of the *Phaedo* describes how he has turned his back on all such causes of becoming and perishing as the earlier physicists had alleged, and resorted to one type of explanation for everything. If he is asked, for instance, why a thing is beautiful, he will not say, ' because its colour, or its shape, is so-and-so ' ; his only answer is : ' for no other reason than that it partakes of the Beautiful.' [2]   This is well enough, so long as it means that ' the Beautiful Itself ' is a divine substance, which imparts its nature to all beautiful things, and is somehow ' present ' in them. But, if ' the Beautiful Itself ' is to be a mere universal predicate, and ' partakes of ' is to mean nothing but the subject-predicate relation, what becomes of Socrates' sole and sufficient reason, why things are beautiful ? ' This is beautiful *because* it partakes of the Beautiful ' will now mean exactly the same as ' This is beautiful because it is beautiful ' : ' partakes of ' is a mere synonym of this sense of ' is.' [3]   The Idea is a *cause* no longer.

In the latter part of the *Phaedo*, it is clear that, partly owing to the ambiguity of the word *aitia*, which means ' explanation,' ' reason,' ' ground,' and ' cause ' of existence or of becoming, Plato confuses two very different theories. One is logical, and

---

[1] *Sophist*, 248E : τί δὲ πρὸς Διός ; ὡς ἀληθῶς κίνησιν καὶ ζωὴν καὶ ψυχὴν καὶ φρόνησιν ἢ ῥᾳδίως πεισθησόμεθα τῷ παντελῶς ὄντι μὴ παρεῖναι, μηδὲ ζῆν αὐτὸ μηδὲ φρονεῖν, ἀλλὰ σεμνὸν καὶ ἅγιον, νοῦν οὐκ ἔχον, ἀκίνητον ἑστὸς εἶναι ;

[2] *Phaedo*, 100c.

[3] This obvious difficulty seems to escape those critics of the *Phaedo* who speak as if Plato, when he wrote that dialogue, realised that *methexis* was only a figurative expression for a clearly conceived subject-predicate relation. We must remember that Plato has no words for ' subject ' or ' predicate ' or ' relation.'

states that the *explanation*, or *account*, to be given of the proposition ' this thing is beautiful,' is that there is an Idea, Beautiful, and this thing partakes of it. In modern terminology this is no more than to say : ' Every proposition of the type " x is A " implies that there is a concept, or universal predicate, A, and that x has to it a certain relation.' [1] Taken simply as an analysis of the subject-predicate proposition, this account is unexceptionable ; though it does not hold of the numerical and relational propositions (' one and one are Two,' ' Phaedo is taller than Socrates ') to which Plato also applies it. But that is not all. The logical theory is not distinguished from a metaphysical doctrine, which may be stated thus : ' This beautiful thing *exists* (or begins to exist, $\gamma i\gamma\nu\epsilon\tau a\iota$) for no other reason than that Beauty exists, and this thing partakes (or comes to partake) of its nature.' On this interpretation, the existence of Beauty Itself ($a\dot{v}\tau\dot{o}\ \tau\dot{o}\ \kappa a\lambda\dot{o}\nu$) is asserted to be the *cause* of the existence of all particular beautiful things in the world of sense. The relation called *methexis* is not here the logical relation of subject to predicate in a proposition, but a causal relation. The Idea is to be, somehow, the supersensible *ground* ($a\dot{\iota}\tau\dot{\iota}a$) of the existence of sensible things which become and perish in time. In order to be so, it must impart its nature in some inexplicable way, which can only be described figuratively. It is like an original ($\pi a\rho\dot{a}\delta\epsilon\iota\gamma\mu a$) which casts a copy ($\mu i\mu\eta\mu a$), or likeness ($\epsilon\dot{\iota}\kappa\dot{\omega}\nu$), of itself into a mirror, or some other reflecting medium. The supersensible world is an immutable hierarchy of Ideas, or Types, which throws its image upon the ever-flowing stream of time. Or, it is a heaven of divine souls, which impart themselves to the groups of transitory things that bear their names. The whole conception is manifestly mythical, but it is of the essence of the theory. The logical interpretation is struggling to get clear of the mythical ; the Idea threatens to pass from being an indwelling group-soul to being a mere universal concept, which does not exist at all, and, if it did, could not cause the existence or becoming of particular things.

---

[1] The characteristics of the relation are that it holds only between a ' particular' or thing and a concept ; that it holds *from* the thing to the concept, and not in the reverse sense ; and that every thing has this relation to some concept.

Plato did not realise that he was only making an important discovery in logic ; he thought he was discovering the causes —the sole, true causes—of the existence of the world.

134. *The Olympianisation of the Ideas*

It is curious to observe how the development of the Platonic Ideas corresponds to other developments already described. Originally inherent in their group, they are, at first, partly disengaged from it, and yet remain immanent throughout its extent, and related to it as *causes*. Then, in the second stage, they become completely distinct, and only externally related to their logical extension. The process is like that by which the myth, from being a verbal counterpart of the ritual action, comes to be a generalised representation of it, as it were a universal, detached from the unlimited series of particular celebrations of the rite. It then becomes an ' explanation ' (*aition*), professing to account for the existence and practice of the ritual, just as the Idea is erected into an explanation or account (*logos*) of the things that partake of it. Again, as we have pointed out, the Idea is like the group-soul, at first projected as an ideal (*paradeigma*) of the group, and then becoming a daemon, which is regarded as something partly distinct, and yet the source, or *cause*, of the supernatural powers of the group. Once more the history of rational civilised philosophy repeats the history of pre-rational religious representation.

For, it is in this way, as M. Lévy-Bruhl points out,[1] that ' causes ' were first sought and discovered by primitive man. The process is not one of *associating* two things or events, first conceived as distinct, and then brought into connection as cause and effect. ' We ought not to say, as is often said, that primitive men associate with all objects that strike their senses or imagination, occult forces, magical properties, a sort of soul or vital principle, and that they add animistic beliefs to their perceptions. There is here no association. The mystic properties of persons and things are an integral part of the representation which the primitive man has of them—a representation which, at this

---

[1] *Fonctions mentales*, etc., p. 39.

stage, is an indecomposable whole. Later, at another period of social evolution, what we call the natural phenomenon will tend to become the sole content of the perception, to the exclusion of other elements, which will then take on the aspect of beliefs, and even, finally, of superstitions. But, until this " dissociation " takes place, the perception remains an undifferentiated unity.' We ought never to ask, ' What explanation must the primitive mind give itself of such and such a natural phenomenon ? ' The statement of the problem implies a false hypothesis. There are, for the mentality of the lower societies, no natural phenomena in our sense. For them, the explanation has no need to be sought; it is implicit in the mystical elements of their collective representations. The question that has to be asked is, how the phenomenon, little by little, detached itself from the complex in which it was at first enveloped, so as to be separately apprehended, and how *what was once an integral element in it, became later an ' explanation.'*

The Platonic Ideas seem to owe their existence to a process of *dissociation*, like that which M. Lévy-Bruhl suggests. Their genesis is, accordingly, parallel to the genesis of ' souls,' which we have already described. They emerge from their class, as the daemon or the king emerged from the social group, to be the depositary of its collective consciousness, the externalised and projected vehicle, or source, of its power. Finally, as the group-soul gave place to the individual soul, a corresponding fate is reserved for the Ideas, at the hands of Aristotle. Plato's greatest follower will not shrink from declaring the truth, that the ' Ideas '—these Forms, originally endowed with the attributes of soul—are really nothing but forms. They have no independent existence, no life, no power of causing anything to come into existence.[1] The highest degree of reality will be taken away by Aristotle from that other world of immaterial Ideas, and restored to the world we see around us. To him, the forms, or essences, of individual things will be substances, realities, in the fullest sense.

In proportion as the Ideas cease to be causes and become mere logical concepts, Platonism is threatened with the inevitable

---

[1] *Met.* A 9.

fate of a system which attempts to place the source of life outside and above Nature, in a metaphysical world of immutable reality. When we consider this world of Forms, it turns out to be nothing but a vast scheme of classification (*moirai*), a hierarchy of kinds, broadening downwards from its highest genus to its lowest individual species. It is the characteristic construction of the Intellect, which can divide and analyse, but not create. At the apex is enthroned that very Intellect itself. We call it Reason, God, the Good; but it is idle to pretend that it can create the world. It is as impotent as the Parmenidean One, and for the same reason—its immutable perfection. The hierarchy of forms, by which we seek to link this One to the manifold world of change, is a channel without a stream. Plato, in his final attempt to formulate a cosmology, falls back on the mythical horn of the dilemma, which Parmenides had the courage to avoid. He is forced to attribute to his deified Intellect an impossible impulse of desire. It is the old religious necessity, realised long before by Pherekydes, who said that, when Zeus set about making the world, he changed himself into Eros.[1] This Desire is the mythical Demiurge of the *Timaeus*, who, being good and therefore without jealousy ($\phi\theta\acute{o}\nu o\varsigma$), 'desired that all things should be as like unto himself as possible. This is that most sovereign cause of becoming and of cosmic order, which we shall most surely be right in accepting from men of understanding. For God, desiring that all things should be good, and that, so far as this might be, there should be nothing inferior, having received all that is visible, not in a state of rest, but moving without harmony or measure, brought it from its disorder into order, thinking that this was in all ways better than the other.'[2]

The mythical form of this whole cosmology is not a poetical dress, in which Plato arbitrarily chooses to clothe a perfectly definite and rational scheme, such as modern students set themselves to discover in it. If Plato could have stated it as a

---

[1] Pherek. frag. 3 = Procl. *ad Tim.* 32 c: ὁ Φερεκύδης ἔλεγεν εἰς Ἔρωτα μεταβεβλῆσθαι τὸν Δία μέλλοντα δημιουργεῖν.

[2] Plato, *Timaeus*, 29 E. The language supports the view held by J. Adam that the *Timaeus* gives a picture of a reconstruction of the universe at the beginning of one of the alternating periods, like those of Empedocles and of the *Politicus* myth. Cf. A. E. Taylor, *Plato*, p. 144, London, 1908.

logos, he would have done so, only too gladly ; but he cannot. It is not rational, but mystical—a *mythos* in substance as well as form, and drawn from mythical, mystical sources. There is no tolerable explanation in rational terms. An immutable, passionless Reason may trace the outlines of a scheme of classification, and divide its concepts into duly subordinated genera and species ; but it can do no more. To account for the existence of anything whatever, we have to ascribe to it the unworthy and lower faculty of desire, and give this desire an unworthy and lower object—the existence of an imperfect copy of perfection. But that is the language of religion, not of science.

135. *The Flight of the Philosopher*

When Greek philosophy deified the speculative intellect, it made the supreme effort to work clear of all that was vague and mythical in religion, only to find that the intellect had become a deity and followed the elder Gods of emotional faith to the seventh heaven. In the system of Aristotle (which it is not within our scope to examine in detail), God is sublimated to the topmost pinnacle of abstraction, and conceived as Form without Matter—a pure Thought, cut off from all active or creative energy, for the Ultimate End can have no other end beyond itself. It cannot even think of anything but itself, for no other object is worthy of its attention. It is shut up in unceasing and changeless contemplation of itself. We are asked to believe that this condition is worthy of the names of perfect activity, of life, of blessedness ; and that such a God, though he cannot condescend to move the world in any other way, can move it as being himself the object of love (κινεῖ ὡς ἐρώμενον). God cannot love the world, or send forth his *Logos* into it ; but the world is expected to love him, and all its life is to be caused by desire for this monastic and self-hypnotised abstraction. It may be doubted whether this passion has ever been genuinely felt even by the most intellectual of mystics, much less by the rest of creation. It is only by calling it ' God,' and persuading ourselves that it is alive, and active, and blessed—all which is manifestly mythical—that we can induce the faintest feeling of attraction towards it.

In the system of Aristotle, the two factors of our original complex—the outline, shape, or *eidos* of the *moira*, and the functional force, the behaviour and nature (*physis*) pervading it—fall completely asunder at the two poles of existence. The form has escaped from its content, and the life has passed out of it, by a process analogous to that by which the Olympian Gods shed the functional utility of their daemonic phase, and became idle and impotent forms, floating above a world in which all the processes of life and change go forward without their help. Religion, indeed, left them with individual attributes and capricious wills. But, now that science has left no room in nature for such wills to operate, the divine loses every vestige of desire and power, and is reduced to pure *eidos*—a strengthless *eidolon*.

The philosopher, too, not obscurely aspires to imitate his divine counterpart, and 'follow where all is fled.' At the conclusion of his *Ethics*,[1] Aristotle's ideal for humanity is clearly enough disclosed. Of all moral, practical activities, he argues, 'war and politics are the noblest and on the grandest scale; but even these are incompatible with leisure, and chosen only as a means to some end beyond themselves. The activity of Reason is of higher worth, being speculative, and looking to no further end. It has also a pleasure which is peculiar to it, and enhances its activity. That being so, this activity is self-sufficient; it is free (so far as may be for man) from cares and weariness; it has all the other attributes of felicity. This, then, will be the perfect wellbeing of man.

'Such a life as this, however, is higher than the measure of humanity; not in virtue of his humanity will man lead this life, but in virtue of something divine within him; and, by as much as this something is superior to his composite nature, by so much is its activity superior to the rest of virtue. If, then, Reason is divine in comparison with man, the life of Reason is divine in comparison with human life. We ought not to listen to those who exhort man to keep to man's thoughts,

---

[1] *Eth. Nic. κ* vii. I am not convinced by those interpreters who deny that the wise man, as here described, 'exists as an individual,' and say that he is only 'the formal element (of man's *eudaimonia*) abstracted and personified' (J. A. Stewart, *Notes on the Nicom. Eth.*, vol. ii. p. 443 (1892)).

or a mortal to the thoughts of mortality ; but, so far as may be, to achieve immortality, and do what man may to live according to the highest thing that is in him ; for, though it be little in bulk, in power and worth it is far above all the rest.

' It would seem, too, that this is the true self of every man, since it is the supreme and better part.[1] It will be strange, then, if he should choose not his own life, but some other's. What we said before will be appropriate again here : that what is naturally proper to every creature is the highest and pleasantest for him. And so, to man, this will be the life of Reason, since Reason is, in the highest sense, a man's self. Therefore, this life will also be most blessed.'

The ideal for the individual, then, is to escape from society, as God has escaped from his functional utility in Nature. Man's soul rises, as the daemon had risen, above his social group. He will withdraw, like the Stoic, into autonomous self-sufficiency and Olympian contemplation.

It is only a step further to the mystical trance of neoplatonism, in which thought is swallowed up in the beatific vision of the absolute One, above being and above knowledge, ineffable, unthinkable, no longer even a Reason, but ' beyond Reason ' (ἐπέκεινα νοῦ)—' the escape of the alone to the alone.'[2] In this ecstasy, Thought denies itself; and Philosophy, sinking to the close of her splendid curving flight, folds her wings and drops into the darkness whence she arose —the gloomy Erebus of theurgy and magic.

---

[1] 1178a 2: δόξειε δ' ἂν καὶ εἶναι ἕκαστος τοῦτο, εἴπερ τὸ κύριον καὶ ἄμεινον. I incline to read εἴπερ καὶ κύριον τὸ ἄμεινον, i.e. 'since the better part is also that which makes him in the fullest sense (κυρίως) what he is—his truest self.'

[2] Plot. Enn. VI. ix. 11 : καὶ οὗτος θεῶν καὶ ἀνθρώπων θείων καὶ εὐδαιμόνων βίος, ἀπαλλαγὴ τῶν ἄλλων τῶν τῇδε, βίος ἀνήδονος τῶν τῇδε, φυγὴ μόνου πρὸς μόνον.

INDEX OF CITATIONS

GENERAL INDEX

A priori methods, 126; in treatment of Physis, 137.

ἀδύνατον in Homer, 14.

Agricultural Magic, 167.

Aisa, 120.

Aitia as explanation, 141; ambiguity in Plato, 256; primitively discovered by 'dissociation,' 258.

Anamnesis, 248.

ἀναποδόω, 208.

Anaxagoras, 144; system discussed, 153 ff.

Anaximander, his cosmology, 7 ff.; accepts conception of primary world-order, 19; cosmic structure compared to clan organisation, 62; Limitless as divine, 135; system discussed, 144 ff.; order of Time and Justice, 176; his scheme adapted by Empedocles, 231.

Anaximenes, Air as God, 135; system discussed, 148 ff.

Animism, 101.

ἀνταπόδοσις, 163, 167.

Anthesteria, 165.

Aphrodite in Parmenides, 222.

Apollo, 195; and Pythagoras, 204.

Apology of Socrates, 244.

Aristotle, 'like knows like,' 134; treatment of Plato's Ideas, 259; Form and Matter, 261; ideal for man, 262.

Asha, 172 ff.

Atomism, 137; as goal of Science, 144.
—— of Leukippus, 155 ff.
—— —— like number doctrine, 213.

BLOOD of totem-clan, 57; of group-kin, 87.

Blood-feud, 57.

Blood-kin: differentiated from magical group, 93; collective responsibility, 96.

Blood-soul, 109.

Broad Oath in Empedocles, 237.

Bronze Age (Hesiod), 109.

Buddha, 113, 193.

CALENDARS, succession of, 170.

Callicles, 183.

Causality, at first spatial, 140 ff.; and likeness, 86.

Causes, discovered by 'dissociation,' 258; and explanations, 139 ff.

Chance, 242; world left to, 214.

Chaos, meaning of, 66; in Chinese cosmogony, 99; and Eros, 70; and Poros, 120.

Chronos, 172; of Orphics, 146.

Classification and tribal structure, 57; of tribe, including all Nature, 59; basis of magic, 140; Plato's Ideas as system of, 260.

Collective emotion, 77 ff.; representation defined, 43; responsibility, 57.

Comitium, 53.

Communion in mystical religion, 112.

Conscience, 81.

Contraries: grouped in pairs, 63; separation of, 65; elemental, 116.

Cook, A. B., 32.

Cosmogony: Babylonian, 67; Egyptian, 67; Orphic, 67; Chinese, 67; Pythagorean, 70.

Cosmology of Plato's *Timaeus*, 260.

Cosmos, as political term, 53; basis of Pythagorean ethics, 211.

Crawley, A. E., 109.

DAEMON, rule in Golden Age (Plato), 35; in primitive Greece (Herod.), 37; of house in Pindar, 58; explains hereditary guilt, 58; of Magical Society, 95; of Gens, 96; of natural departments, 96; Good Spirits, 98; reign of (Plato), 98; four types of Greek daemon, 100; blended with hero, 107; of individual, 110; rule in Golden Age, 173; Pythagoras as, 201; in Empedocles, 228 ff.; good and evil genii, 239; and Platonic Idea, 253.

Dasmos, of three sons of Kronos, 15, 17; of the Gods, 21; secured by oath, 22; of seats of worship, 36; cosmic dasmos a late doctrine, 38; of Rhodes, 53; of elements, 116; effected by *lot* or *strife*, 231.

A CATALOG OF SELECTED
DOVER BOOKS
IN ALL FIELDS OF INTEREST

A CATALOG OF SELECTED DOVER
BOOKS IN ALL FIELDS OF INTEREST

CONCERNING THE SPIRITUAL IN ART, Wassily Kandinsky. Pioneering work by father of abstract art. Thoughts on color theory, nature of art. Analysis of earlier masters. 12 illustrations. 80pp. of text. 5⅜ x 8½. 23411-8

ANIMALS: 1,419 Copyright-Free Illustrations of Mammals, Birds, Fish, Insects, etc., Jim Harter (ed.). Clear wood engravings present, in extremely lifelike poses, over 1,000 species of animals. One of the most extensive pictorial sourcebooks of its kind. Captions. Index. 284pp. 9 x 12. 23766-4

CELTIC ART: The Methods of Construction, George Bain. Simple geometric techniques for making Celtic interlacements, spirals, Kells-type initials, animals, humans, etc. Over 500 illustrations. 160pp. 9 x 12. (Available in U.S. only.) 22923-8

AN ATLAS OF ANATOMY FOR ARTISTS, Fritz Schider. Most thorough reference work on art anatomy in the world. Hundreds of illustrations, including selections from works by Vesalius, Leonardo, Goya, Ingres, Michelangelo, others. 593 illustrations. 192pp. 7⅛ x 10¼. 20241-0

CELTIC HAND STROKE-BY-STROKE (Irish Half-Uncial from "The Book of Kells"): An Arthur Baker Calligraphy Manual, Arthur Baker. Complete guide to creating each letter of the alphabet in distinctive Celtic manner. Covers hand position, strokes, pens, inks, paper, more. Illustrated. 48pp. 8¼ x 11. 24336-2

EASY ORIGAMI, John Montroll. Charming collection of 32 projects (hat, cup, pelican, piano, swan, many more) specially designed for the novice origami hobbyist. Clearly illustrated easy-to-follow instructions insure that even beginning papercrafters will achieve successful results. 48pp. 8¼ x 11. 27298-2

THE COMPLETE BOOK OF BIRDHOUSE CONSTRUCTION FOR WOODWORKERS, Scott D. Campbell. Detailed instructions, illustrations, tables. Also data on bird habitat and instinct patterns. Bibliography. 3 tables. 63 illustrations in 15 figures. 48pp. 5¼ x 8½. 24407-5

BLOOMINGDALE'S ILLUSTRATED 1886 CATALOG: Fashions, Dry Goods and Housewares, Bloomingdale Brothers. Famed merchants' extremely rare catalog depicting about 1,700 products: clothing, housewares, firearms, dry goods, jewelry, more. Invaluable for dating, identifying vintage items. Also, copyright-free graphics for artists, designers. Co-published with Henry Ford Museum & Greenfield Village. 160pp. 8¼ x 11. 25780-0

HISTORIC COSTUME IN PICTURES, Braun & Schneider. Over 1,450 costumed figures in clearly detailed engravings–from dawn of civilization to end of 19th century. Captions. Many folk costumes. 256pp. 8⅜ x 11¾. 23150-X

STICKLEY CRAFTSMAN FURNITURE CATALOGS, Gustav Stickley and L. & J. G. Stickley. Beautiful, functional furniture in two authentic catalogs from 1910. 594 illustrations, including 277 photos, show settles, rockers, armchairs, reclining chairs, bookcases, desks, tables. 183pp. 6½ x 9¼.   23838-5

AMERICAN LOCOMOTIVES IN HISTORIC PHOTOGRAPHS: 1858 to 1949, Ron Ziel (ed.). A rare collection of 126 meticulously detailed official photographs, called "builder portraits," of American locomotives that majestically chronicle the rise of steam locomotive power in America. Introduction. Detailed captions. xi+ 129pp. 9 x 12.   27393-8

AMERICA'S LIGHTHOUSES: An Illustrated History, Francis Ross Holland, Jr. Delightfully written, profusely illustrated fact-filled survey of over 200 American light-houses since 1716. History, anecdotes, technological advances, more. 240pp. 8 x 10¾.
25576-X

TOWARDS A NEW ARCHITECTURE, Le Corbusier. Pioneering manifesto by founder of "International School." Technical and aesthetic theories, views of industry, economics, relation of form to function, "mass-production split" and much more. Profusely illustrated. 320pp. 6⅛ x 9¼. (Available in U.S. only.)   25023-7

HOW THE OTHER HALF LIVES, Jacob Riis. Famous journalistic record, exposing poverty and degradation of New York slums around 1900, by major social reformer. 100 striking and influential photographs. 233pp. 10 x 7⅞.   22012-5

FRUIT KEY AND TWIG KEY TO TREES AND SHRUBS, William M. Harlow. One of the handiest and most widely used identification aids. Fruit key covers 120 deciduous and evergreen species; twig key 160 deciduous species. Easily used. Over 300 photographs. 126pp. 5⅜ x 8½.   20511-8

COMMON BIRD SONGS, Dr. Donald J. Borror. Songs of 60 most common U.S. birds: robins, sparrows, cardinals, bluejays, finches, more–arranged in order of increasing complexity. Up to 9 variations of songs of each species.
Cassette and manual 99911-4

ORCHIDS AS HOUSE PLANTS, Rebecca Tyson Northen. Grow cattleyas and many other kinds of orchids–in a window, in a case, or under artificial light. 63 illustrations. 148pp. 5⅜ x 8½.   23261-1

MONSTER MAZES, Dave Phillips. Masterful mazes at four levels of difficulty. Avoid deadly perils and evil creatures to find magical treasures. Solutions for all 32 exciting illustrated puzzles. 48pp. 8¼ x 11.   26005-4

MOZART'S DON GIOVANNI (DOVER OPERA LIBRETTO SERIES), Wolfgang Amadeus Mozart. Introduced and translated by Ellen H. Bleiler. Standard Italian libretto, with complete English translation. Convenient and thoroughly portable–an ideal companion for reading along with a recording or the performance itself. Introduction. List of characters. Plot summary. 121pp. 5¼ x 8½.   24944-1

TECHNICAL MANUAL AND DICTIONARY OF CLASSICAL BALLET, Gail Grant. Defines, explains, comments on steps, movements, poses and concepts. 15-page pictorial section. Basic book for student, viewer. 127pp. 5⅜ x 8½.   21843-0

THE CLARINET AND CLARINET PLAYING, David Pino. Lively, comprehensive work features suggestions about technique, musicianship, and musical interpretation, as well as guidelines for teaching, making your own reeds, and preparing for public performance. Includes an intriguing look at clarinet history. "A godsend," *The Clarinet,* Journal of the International Clarinet Society. Appendixes. 7 illus. 320pp. 5⅜ x 8½. 40270-3

HOLLYWOOD GLAMOR PORTRAITS, John Kobal (ed.). 145 photos from 1926-49. Harlow, Gable, Bogart, Bacall; 94 stars in all. Full background on photographers, technical aspects. 160pp. 8⅜ x 11¼. 23352-9

THE ANNOTATED CASEY AT THE BAT: A Collection of Ballads about the Mighty Casey/Third, Revised Edition, Martin Gardner (ed.). Amusing sequels and parodies of one of America's best-loved poems: Casey's Revenge, Why Casey Whiffed, Casey's Sister at the Bat, others. 256pp. 5⅜ x 8½. 28598-7

THE RAVEN AND OTHER FAVORITE POEMS, Edgar Allan Poe. Over 40 of the author's most memorable poems: "The Bells," "Ulalume," "Israfel," "To Helen," "The Conqueror Worm," "Eldorado," "Annabel Lee," many more. Alphabetic lists of titles and first lines. 64pp. 5$\frac{3}{16}$ x 8¼. 26685-0

PERSONAL MEMOIRS OF U. S. GRANT, Ulysses Simpson Grant. Intelligent, deeply moving firsthand account of Civil War campaigns, considered by many the finest military memoirs ever written. Includes letters, historic photographs, maps and more. 528pp. 6⅛ x 9¼. 28587-1

ANCIENT EGYPTIAN MATERIALS AND INDUSTRIES, A. Lucas and J. Harris. Fascinating, comprehensive, thoroughly documented text describes this ancient civilization's vast resources and the processes that incorporated them in daily life, including the use of animal products, building materials, cosmetics, perfumes and incense, fibers, glazed ware, glass and its manufacture, materials used in the mummification process, and much more. 544pp. 6⅛ x 9¼. (Available in U.S. only.) 40446-3

RUSSIAN STORIES/RUSSKIE RASSKAZY: A Dual-Language Book, edited by Gleb Struve. Twelve tales by such masters as Chekhov, Tolstoy, Dostoevsky, Pushkin, others. Excellent word-for-word English translations on facing pages, plus teaching and study aids, Russian/English vocabulary, biographical/critical introductions, more. 416pp. 5⅜ x 8½. 26244-8

PHILADELPHIA THEN AND NOW: 60 Sites Photographed in the Past and Present, Kenneth Finkel and Susan Oyama. Rare photographs of City Hall, Logan Square, Independence Hall, Betsy Ross House, other landmarks juxtaposed with contemporary views. Captures changing face of historic city. Introduction. Captions. 128pp. 8¼ x 11. 25790-8

AIA ARCHITECTURAL GUIDE TO NASSAU AND SUFFOLK COUNTIES, LONG ISLAND, The American Institute of Architects, Long Island Chapter, and the Society for the Preservation of Long Island Antiquities. Comprehensive, well-researched and generously illustrated volume brings to life over three centuries of Long Island's great architectural heritage. More than 240 photographs with authoritative, extensively detailed captions. 176pp. 8¼ x 11. 26946-9

NORTH AMERICAN INDIAN LIFE: Customs and Traditions of 23 Tribes, Elsie Clews Parsons (ed.). 27 fictionalized essays by noted anthropologists examine religion, customs, government, additional facets of life among the Winnebago, Crow, Zuni, Eskimo, other tribes. 480pp. 6⅛ x 9¼. 27377-6

FRANK LLOYD WRIGHT'S DANA HOUSE, Donald Hoffmann. Pictorial essay of residential masterpiece with over 160 interior and exterior photos, plans, elevations, sketches and studies. 128pp. 9¼ x 10¾. 29120-0

THE MALE AND FEMALE FIGURE IN MOTION: 60 Classic Photographic Sequences, Eadweard Muybridge. 60 true-action photographs of men and women walking, running, climbing, bending, turning, etc., reproduced from rare 19th-century masterpiece. vi + 121pp. 9 x 12. 24745-7

1001 QUESTIONS ANSWERED ABOUT THE SEASHORE, N. J. Berrill and Jacquelyn Berrill. Queries answered about dolphins, sea snails, sponges, starfish, fishes, shore birds, many others. Covers appearance, breeding, growth, feeding, much more. 305pp. 5¼ x 8¼. 23366-9

ATTRACTING BIRDS TO YOUR YARD, William J. Weber. Easy-to-follow guide offers advice on how to attract the greatest diversity of birds: birdhouses, feeders, water and waterers, much more. 96pp. 5³⁄₁₆ x 8¼. 28927-3

MEDICINAL AND OTHER USES OF NORTH AMERICAN PLANTS: A Historical Survey with Special Reference to the Eastern Indian Tribes, Charlotte Erichsen-Brown. Chronological historical citations document 500 years of usage of plants, trees, shrubs native to eastern Canada, northeastern U.S. Also complete identifying information. 343 illustrations. 544pp. 6½ x 9¼. 25951-X

STORYBOOK MAZES, Dave Phillips. 23 stories and mazes on two-page spreads: Wizard of Oz, Treasure Island, Robin Hood, etc. Solutions. 64pp. 8¼ x 11. 23628-5

AMERICAN NEGRO SONGS: 230 Folk Songs and Spirituals, Religious and Secular, John W. Work. This authoritative study traces the African influences of songs sung and played by black Americans at work, in church, and as entertainment. The author discusses the lyric significance of such songs as "Swing Low, Sweet Chariot," "John Henry," and others and offers the words and music for 230 songs. Bibliography. Index of Song Titles. 272pp. 6½ x 9¼. 40271-1

MOVIE-STAR PORTRAITS OF THE FORTIES, John Kobal (ed.). 163 glamor, studio photos of 106 stars of the 1940s: Rita Hayworth, Ava Gardner, Marlon Brando, Clark Gable, many more. 176pp. 8⅜ x 11¼. 23546-7

BENCHLEY LOST AND FOUND, Robert Benchley. Finest humor from early 30s, about pet peeves, child psychologists, post office and others. Mostly unavailable elsewhere. 73 illustrations by Peter Arno and others. 183pp. 5⅜ x 8½. 22410-4

YEKL and THE IMPORTED BRIDEGROOM AND OTHER STORIES OF YIDDISH NEW YORK, Abraham Cahan. Film Hester Street based on *Yekl* (1896). Novel, other stories among first about Jewish immigrants on N.Y.'s East Side. 240pp. 5⅜ x 8½. 22427-9

SELECTED POEMS, Walt Whitman. Generous sampling from *Leaves of Grass*. Twenty-four poems include "I Hear America Singing," "Song of the Open Road," "I Sing the Body Electric," "When Lilacs Last in the Dooryard Bloom'd," "O Captain! My Captain!"—all reprinted from an authoritative edition. Lists of titles and first lines. 128pp. 5³⁄₁₆ x 8¼. 26878-0

THE BEST TALES OF HOFFMANN, E. T. A. Hoffmann. 10 of Hoffmann's most important stories: "Nutcracker and the King of Mice," "The Golden Flowerpot," etc. 458pp. 5⅜ x 8½. 21793-0

FROM FETISH TO GOD IN ANCIENT EGYPT, E. A. Wallis Budge. Rich detailed survey of Egyptian conception of "God" and gods, magic, cult of animals, Osiris, more. Also, superb English translations of hymns and legends. 240 illustrations. 545pp. 5⅜ x 8½. 25803-3

FRENCH STORIES/CONTES FRANÇAIS: A Dual-Language Book, Wallace Fowlie. Ten stories by French masters, Voltaire to Camus: "Micromegas" by Voltaire; "The Atheist's Mass" by Balzac; "Minuet" by de Maupassant; "The Guest" by Camus, six more. Excellent English translations on facing pages. Also French-English vocabulary list, exercises, more. 352pp. 5⅜ x 8½. 26443-2

CHICAGO AT THE TURN OF THE CENTURY IN PHOTOGRAPHS: 122 Historic Views from the Collections of the Chicago Historical Society, Larry A. Viskochil. Rare large-format prints offer detailed views of City Hall, State Street, the Loop, Hull House, Union Station, many other landmarks, circa 1904-1913. Introduction. Captions. Maps. 144pp. 9⅜ x 12¼. 24656-6

OLD BROOKLYN IN EARLY PHOTOGRAPHS, 1865-1929, William Lee Younger. Luna Park, Gravesend race track, construction of Grand Army Plaza, moving of Hotel Brighton, etc. 157 previously unpublished photographs. 165pp. 8⅞ x 11¾. 23587-4

THE MYTHS OF THE NORTH AMERICAN INDIANS, Lewis Spence. Rich anthology of the myths and legends of the Algonquins, Iroquois, Pawnees and Sioux, prefaced by an extensive historical and ethnological commentary. 36 illustrations. 480pp. 5⅜ x 8½. 25967-6

AN ENCYCLOPEDIA OF BATTLES: Accounts of Over 1,560 Battles from 1479 B.C. to the Present, David Eggenberger. Essential details of every major battle in recorded history from the first battle of Megiddo in 1479 B.C. to Grenada in 1984. List of Battle Maps. New Appendix covering the years 1967-1984. Index. 99 illustrations. 544pp. 6½ x 9¼. 24913-1

SAILING ALONE AROUND THE WORLD, Captain Joshua Slocum. First man to sail around the world, alone, in small boat. One of great feats of seamanship told in delightful manner. 67 illustrations. 294pp. 5⅜ x 8½. 20326-3

ANARCHISM AND OTHER ESSAYS, Emma Goldman. Powerful, penetrating, prophetic essays on direct action, role of minorities, prison reform, puritan hypocrisy, violence, etc. 271pp. 5⅜ x 8½. 22484-8

MYTHS OF THE HINDUS AND BUDDHISTS, Ananda K. Coomaraswamy and Sister Nivedita. Great stories of the epics; deeds of Krishna, Shiva, taken from puranas, Vedas, folk tales; etc. 32 illustrations. 400pp. 5⅜ x 8½. 21759-0

THE TRAUMA OF BIRTH, Otto Rank. Rank's controversial thesis that anxiety neurosis is caused by profound psychological trauma which occurs at birth. 256pp. 5⅜ x 8½. 27974-X

A THEOLOGICO-POLITICAL TREATISE, Benedict Spinoza. Also contains unfinished Political Treatise. Great classic on religious liberty, theory of government on common consent. R. Elwes translation. Total of 421pp. 5⅜ x 8½. 20249-6

MY BONDAGE AND MY FREEDOM, Frederick Douglass. Born a slave, Douglass became outspoken force in antislavery movement. The best of Douglass' autobiographies. Graphic description of slave life. 464pp. 5⅜ x 8½.   22457-0

FOLLOWING THE EQUATOR: A Journey Around the World, Mark Twain. Fascinating humorous account of 1897 voyage to Hawaii, Australia, India, New Zealand, etc. Ironic, bemused reports on peoples, customs, climate, flora and fauna, politics, much more. 197 illustrations. 720pp. 5⅜ x 8½.   26113-1

THE PEOPLE CALLED SHAKERS, Edward D. Andrews. Definitive study of Shakers: origins, beliefs, practices, dances, social organization, furniture and crafts, etc. 33 illustrations. 351pp. 5⅜ x 8½.   21081-2

THE MYTHS OF GREECE AND ROME, H. A. Guerber. A classic of mythology, generously illustrated, long prized for its simple, graphic, accurate retelling of the principal myths of Greece and Rome, and for its commentary on their origins and significance. With 64 illustrations by Michelangelo, Raphael, Titian, Rubens, Canova, Bernini and others. 480pp. 5⅜ x 8½.   27584-1

PSYCHOLOGY OF MUSIC, Carl E. Seashore. Classic work discusses music as a medium from psychological viewpoint. Clear treatment of physical acoustics, auditory apparatus, sound perception, development of musical skills, nature of musical feeling, host of other topics. 88 figures. 408pp. 5⅜ x 8½.   21851-1

THE PHILOSOPHY OF HISTORY, Georg W. Hegel. Great classic of Western thought develops concept that history is not chance but rational process, the evolution of freedom. 457pp. 5⅜ x 8½.   20112-0

THE BOOK OF TEA, Kakuzo Okakura. Minor classic of the Orient: entertaining, charming explanation, interpretation of traditional Japanese culture in terms of tea ceremony. 94pp. 5⅜ x 8½.   20070-1

LIFE IN ANCIENT EGYPT, Adolf Erman. Fullest, most thorough, detailed older account with much not in more recent books, domestic life, religion, magic, medicine, commerce, much more. Many illustrations reproduce tomb paintings, carvings, hieroglyphs, etc. 597pp. 5⅜ x 8½.   22632-8

SUNDIALS, Their Theory and Construction, Albert Waugh. Far and away the best, most thorough coverage of ideas, mathematics concerned, types, construction, adjusting anywhere. Simple, nontechnical treatment allows even children to build several of these dials. Over 100 illustrations. 230pp. 5⅜ x 8½.   22947-5

THEORETICAL HYDRODYNAMICS, L. M. Milne-Thomson. Classic exposition of the mathematical theory of fluid motion, applicable to both hydrodynamics and aerodynamics. Over 600 exercises. 768pp. 6⅛ x 9¼.   68970-0

SONGS OF EXPERIENCE: Facsimile Reproduction with 26 Plates in Full Color, William Blake. 26 full-color plates from a rare 1826 edition. Includes "The Tyger," "London," "Holy Thursday," and other poems. Printed text of poems. 48pp. 5¼ x 7.
                                                                                       24636-1

OLD-TIME VIGNETTES IN FULL COLOR, Carol Belanger Grafton (ed.). Over 390 charming, often sentimental illustrations, selected from archives of Victorian graphics—pretty women posing, children playing, food, flowers, kittens and puppies, smiling cherubs, birds and butterflies, much more. All copyright-free. 48pp. 9¼ x 12¼.
                                                                                       27269-9

PERSPECTIVE FOR ARTISTS, Rex Vicat Cole. Depth, perspective of sky and sea, shadows, much more, not usually covered. 391 diagrams, 81 reproductions of drawings and paintings. 279pp. 5⅜ x 8½. 22487-2

DRAWING THE LIVING FIGURE, Joseph Sheppard. Innovative approach to artistic anatomy focuses on specifics of surface anatomy, rather than muscles and bones. Over 170 drawings of live models in front, back and side views, and in widely varying poses. Accompanying diagrams. 177 illustrations. Introduction. Index. 144pp. 8⅜ x11¼. 26723-7

GOTHIC AND OLD ENGLISH ALPHABETS: 100 Complete Fonts, Dan X. Solo. Add power, elegance to posters, signs, other graphics with 100 stunning copyright-free alphabets: Blackstone, Dolbey, Germania, 97 more–including many lower-case, numerals, punctuation marks. 104pp. 8⅛ x 11. 24695-7

HOW TO DO BEADWORK, Mary White. Fundamental book on craft from simple projects to five-bead chains and woven works. 106 illustrations. 142pp. 5⅜ x 8.
20697-1

THE BOOK OF WOOD CARVING, Charles Marshall Sayers. Finest book for beginners discusses fundamentals and offers 34 designs. "Absolutely first rate . . . well thought out and well executed."–E. J. Tangerman. 118pp. 7¾ x 10⅝. 23654-4

ILLUSTRATED CATALOG OF CIVIL WAR MILITARY GOODS: Union Army Weapons, Insignia, Uniform Accessories, and Other Equipment, Schuyler, Hartley, and Graham. Rare, profusely illustrated 1846 catalog includes Union Army uniform and dress regulations, arms and ammunition, coats, insignia, flags, swords, rifles, etc. 226 illustrations. 160pp. 9 x 12. 24939-5

WOMEN'S FASHIONS OF THE EARLY 1900s: An Unabridged Republication of "New York Fashions, 1909," National Cloak & Suit Co. Rare catalog of mail-order fashions documents women's and children's clothing styles shortly after the turn of the century. Captions offer full descriptions, prices. Invaluable resource for fashion, costume historians. Approximately 725 illustrations. 128pp. 8⅜ x 11¼. 27276-1

THE 1912 AND 1915 GUSTAV STICKLEY FURNITURE CATALOGS, Gustav Stickley. With over 200 detailed illustrations and descriptions, these two catalogs are essential reading and reference materials and identification guides for Stickley furniture. Captions cite materials, dimensions and prices. 112pp. 6½ x 9¼. 26676-1

EARLY AMERICAN LOCOMOTIVES, John H. White, Jr. Finest locomotive engravings from early 19th century: historical (1804–74), main-line (after 1870), special, foreign, etc. 147 plates. 142pp. 11⅜ x 8¼. 22772-3

THE TALL SHIPS OF TODAY IN PHOTOGRAPHS, Frank O. Braynard. Lavishly illustrated tribute to nearly 100 majestic contemporary sailing vessels: Amerigo Vespucci, Clearwater, Constitution, Eagle, Mayflower, Sea Cloud, Victory, many more. Authoritative captions provide statistics, background on each ship. 190 black-and-white photographs and illustrations. Introduction. 128pp. 8⅞ x 11¾.
27163-3

LITTLE BOOK OF EARLY AMERICAN CRAFTS AND TRADES, Peter Stockham (ed.). 1807 children's book explains crafts and trades: baker, hatter, cooper, potter, and many others. 23 copperplate illustrations. 140pp. $4\frac{5}{8}$ x 6. 23336-7

VICTORIAN FASHIONS AND COSTUMES FROM HARPER'S BAZAR, 1867–1898, Stella Blum (ed.). Day costumes, evening wear, sports clothes, shoes, hats, other accessories in over 1,000 detailed engravings. 320pp. $9\frac{3}{8}$ x $12\frac{1}{4}$. 22990-4

GUSTAV STICKLEY, THE CRAFTSMAN, Mary Ann Smith. Superb study surveys broad scope of Stickley's achievement, especially in architecture. Design philosophy, rise and fall of the Craftsman empire, descriptions and floor plans for many Craftsman houses, more. 86 black-and-white halftones. 31 line illustrations. Introduction 208pp. $6\frac{1}{2}$ x $9\frac{1}{4}$. 27210-9

THE LONG ISLAND RAIL ROAD IN EARLY PHOTOGRAPHS, Ron Ziel. Over 220 rare photos, informative text document origin (1844) and development of rail service on Long Island. Vintage views of early trains, locomotives, stations, passengers, crews, much more. Captions. $8\frac{7}{8}$ x $11\frac{3}{4}$. 26301-0

VOYAGE OF THE LIBERDADE, Joshua Slocum. Great 19th-century mariner's thrilling, first-hand account of the wreck of his ship off South America, the 35-foot boat he built from the wreckage, and its remarkable voyage home. 128pp. $5\frac{3}{8}$ x $8\frac{1}{2}$. 40022-0

TEN BOOKS ON ARCHITECTURE, Vitruvius. The most important book ever written on architecture. Early Roman aesthetics, technology, classical orders, site selection, all other aspects. Morgan translation. 331pp. $5\frac{3}{8}$ x $8\frac{1}{2}$. 20645-9

THE HUMAN FIGURE IN MOTION, Eadweard Muybridge. More than 4,500 stopped-action photos, in action series, showing undraped men, women, children jumping, lying down, throwing, sitting, wrestling, carrying, etc. 390pp. $7\frac{7}{8}$ x $10\frac{5}{8}$. 20204-6 Clothbd.

TREES OF THE EASTERN AND CENTRAL UNITED STATES AND CANADA, William M. Harlow. Best one-volume guide to 140 trees. Full descriptions, woodlore, range, etc. Over 600 illustrations. Handy size. 288pp. $4\frac{1}{2}$ x $6\frac{3}{8}$. 20395-6

SONGS OF WESTERN BIRDS, Dr. Donald J. Borror. Complete song and call repertoire of 60 western species, including flycatchers, juncoes, cactus wrens, many more–includes fully illustrated booklet. Cassette and manual 99913-0

GROWING AND USING HERBS AND SPICES, Milo Miloradovich. Versatile handbook provides all the information needed for cultivation and use of all the herbs and spices available in North America. 4 illustrations. Index. Glossary. 236pp. $5\frac{3}{8}$ x $8\frac{1}{2}$. 25058-X

BIG BOOK OF MAZES AND LABYRINTHS, Walter Shepherd. 50 mazes and labyrinths in all–classical, solid, ripple, and more–in one great volume. Perfect inexpensive puzzler for clever youngsters. Full solutions. 112pp. $8\frac{1}{8}$ x 11. 22951-3

PIANO TUNING, J. Cree Fischer. Clearest, best book for beginner, amateur. Simple repairs, raising dropped notes, tuning by easy method of flattened fifths. No previous skills needed. 4 illustrations. 201pp. 5⅜ x 8½. 23267-0

HINTS TO SINGERS, Lillian Nordica. Selecting the right teacher, developing confidence, overcoming stage fright, and many other important skills receive thoughtful discussion in this indispensible guide, written by a world-famous diva of four decades' experience. 96pp. 5⅜ x 8½. 40094-8

THE COMPLETE NONSENSE OF EDWARD LEAR, Edward Lear. All nonsense limericks, zany alphabets, Owl and Pussycat, songs, nonsense botany, etc., illustrated by Lear. Total of 320pp. 5⅜ x 8½. (Available in U.S. only.) 20167-8

VICTORIAN PARLOUR POETRY: An Annotated Anthology, Michael R. Turner. 117 gems by Longfellow, Tennyson, Browning, many lesser-known poets. "The Village Blacksmith," "Curfew Must Not Ring Tonight," "Only a Baby Small," dozens more, often difficult to find elsewhere. Index of poets, titles, first lines. xxiii + 325pp. 5⅝ x 8¼. 27044-0

DUBLINERS, James Joyce. Fifteen stories offer vivid, tightly focused observations of the lives of Dublin's poorer classes. At least one, "The Dead," is considered a masterpiece. Reprinted complete and unabridged from standard edition. 160pp. 5³⁄₁₆ x 8¼. 26870-5

GREAT WEIRD TALES: 14 Stories by Lovecraft, Blackwood, Machen and Others, S. T. Joshi (ed.). 14 spellbinding tales, including "The Sin Eater," by Fiona McLeod, "The Eye Above the Mantel," by Frank Belknap Long, as well as renowned works by R. H. Barlow, Lord Dunsany, Arthur Machen, W. C. Morrow and eight other masters of the genre. 256pp. 5⅜ x 8½. (Available in U.S. only.) 40436-6

THE BOOK OF THE SACRED MAGIC OF ABRAMELIN THE MAGE, translated by S. MacGregor Mathers. Medieval manuscript of ceremonial magic. Basic document in Aleister Crowley, Golden Dawn groups. 268pp. 5⅜ x 8½. 23211-5

NEW RUSSIAN-ENGLISH AND ENGLISH-RUSSIAN DICTIONARY, M. A. O'Brien. This is a remarkably handy Russian dictionary, containing a surprising amount of information, including over 70,000 entries. 366pp. 4½ x 6⅛. 20208-9

HISTORIC HOMES OF THE AMERICAN PRESIDENTS, Second, Revised Edition, Irvin Haas. A traveler's guide to American Presidential homes, most open to the public, depicting and describing homes occupied by every American President from George Washington to George Bush. With visiting hours, admission charges, travel routes. 175 photographs. Index. 160pp. 8¼ x 11. 26751-2

NEW YORK IN THE FORTIES, Andreas Feininger. 162 brilliant photographs by the well-known photographer, formerly with *Life* magazine. Commuters, shoppers, Times Square at night, much else from city at its peak. Captions by John von Hartz. 181pp. 9¼ x 10¾. 23585-8

INDIAN SIGN LANGUAGE, William Tomkins. Over 525 signs developed by Sioux and other tribes. Written instructions and diagrams. Also 290 pictographs. 111pp. 6⅛ x 9¼. 22029-X

ANATOMY: A Complete Guide for Artists, Joseph Sheppard. A master of figure drawing shows artists how to render human anatomy convincingly. Over 460 illustrations. 224pp. 8⅜ x 11¼. 27279-6

MEDIEVAL CALLIGRAPHY: Its History and Technique, Marc Drogin. Spirited history, comprehensive instruction manual covers 13 styles (ca. 4th century through 15th). Excellent photographs; directions for duplicating medieval techniques with modern tools. 224pp. 8⅜ x 11¼. 26142-5

DRIED FLOWERS: How to Prepare Them, Sarah Whitlock and Martha Rankin. Complete instructions on how to use silica gel, meal and borax, perlite aggregate, sand and borax, glycerine and water to create attractive permanent flower arrangements. 12 illustrations. 32pp. 5⅜ x 8½. 21802-3

EASY-TO-MAKE BIRD FEEDERS FOR WOODWORKERS, Scott D. Campbell. Detailed, simple-to-use guide for designing, constructing, caring for and using feeders. Text, illustrations for 12 classic and contemporary designs. 96pp. 5⅜ x 8½. 25847-5

SCOTTISH WONDER TALES FROM MYTH AND LEGEND, Donald A. Mackenzie. 16 lively tales tell of giants rumbling down mountainsides, of a magic wand that turns stone pillars into warriors, of gods and goddesses, evil hags, powerful forces and more. 240pp. 5⅜ x 8½. 29677-6

THE HISTORY OF UNDERCLOTHES, C. Willett Cunnington and Phyllis Cunnington. Fascinating, well-documented survey covering six centuries of English undergarments, enhanced with over 100 illustrations: 12th-century laced-up bodice, footed long drawers (1795), 19th-century bustles, 19th-century corsets for men, Victorian "bust improvers," much more. 272pp. 5⅜ x 8¼. 27124-2

ARTS AND CRAFTS FURNITURE: The Complete Brooks Catalog of 1912, Brooks Manufacturing Co. Photos and detailed descriptions of more than 150 now very collectible furniture designs from the Arts and Crafts movement depict davenports, settees, buffets, desks, tables, chairs, bedsteads, dressers and more, all built of solid, quarter-sawed oak. Invaluable for students and enthusiasts of antiques, Americana and the decorative arts. 80pp. 6½ x 9¼. 27471-3

WILBUR AND ORVILLE: A Biography of the Wright Brothers, Fred Howard. Definitive, crisply written study tells the full story of the brothers' lives and work. A vividly written biography, unparalleled in scope and color, that also captures the spirit of an extraordinary era. 560pp. 6⅛ x 9¼. 40297-5

THE ARTS OF THE SAILOR: Knotting, Splicing and Ropework, Hervey Garrett Smith. Indispensable shipboard reference covers tools, basic knots and useful hitches; handsewing and canvas work, more. Over 100 illustrations. Delightful reading for sea lovers. 256pp. 5⅜ x 8½. 26440-8

FRANK LLOYD WRIGHT'S FALLINGWATER: The House and Its History, Second, Revised Edition, Donald Hoffmann. A total revision–both in text and illustrations–of the standard document on Fallingwater, the boldest, most personal architectural statement of Wright's mature years, updated with valuable new material from the recently opened Frank Lloyd Wright Archives. "Fascinating"–*The New York Times*. 116 illustrations. 128pp. 9¼ x 10¾. 27430-6

PHOTOGRAPHIC SKETCHBOOK OF THE CIVIL WAR, Alexander Gardner. 100 photos taken on field during the Civil War. Famous shots of Manassas Harper's Ferry, Lincoln, Richmond, slave pens, etc. 244pp. 10⅝ x 8¼. 22731-6

FIVE ACRES AND INDEPENDENCE, Maurice G. Kains. Great back-to-the-land classic explains basics of self-sufficient farming. The one book to get. 95 illustrations. 397pp. 5⅜ x 8½. 20974-1

SONGS OF EASTERN BIRDS, Dr. Donald J. Borror. Songs and calls of 60 species most common to eastern U.S.: warblers, woodpeckers, flycatchers, thrushes, larks, many more in high-quality recording. Cassette and manual 99912-2

A MODERN HERBAL, Margaret Grieve. Much the fullest, most exact, most useful compilation of herbal material. Gigantic alphabetical encyclopedia, from aconite to zedoary, gives botanical information, medical properties, folklore, economic uses, much else. Indispensable to serious reader. 161 illustrations. 888pp. 6½ x 9¼. 2-vol. set. (Available in U.S. only.) Vol. I: 22798-7
Vol. II: 22799-5

HIDDEN TREASURE MAZE BOOK, Dave Phillips. Solve 34 challenging mazes accompanied by heroic tales of adventure. Evil dragons, people-eating plants, bloodthirsty giants, many more dangerous adversaries lurk at every twist and turn. 34 mazes, stories, solutions. 48pp. 8¼ x 11. 24566-7

LETTERS OF W. A. MOZART, Wolfgang A. Mozart. Remarkable letters show bawdy wit, humor, imagination, musical insights, contemporary musical world; includes some letters from Leopold Mozart. 276pp. 5⅜ x 8½. 22859-2

BASIC PRINCIPLES OF CLASSICAL BALLET, Agrippina Vaganova. Great Russian theoretician, teacher explains methods for teaching classical ballet. 118 illustrations. 175pp. 5⅜ x 8½. 22036-2

THE JUMPING FROG, Mark Twain. Revenge edition. The original story of The Celebrated Jumping Frog of Calaveras County, a hapless French translation, and Twain's hilarious "retranslation" from the French. 12 illustrations. 66pp. 5⅜ x 8½. 22686-7

BEST REMEMBERED POEMS, Martin Gardner (ed.). The 126 poems in this superb collection of 19th- and 20th-century British and American verse range from Shelley's "To a Skylark" to the impassioned "Renascence" of Edna St. Vincent Millay and to Edward Lear's whimsical "The Owl and the Pussycat." 224pp. 5⅜ x 8½. 27165-X

COMPLETE SONNETS, William Shakespeare. Over 150 exquisite poems deal with love, friendship, the tyranny of time, beauty's evanescence, death and other themes in language of remarkable power, precision and beauty. Glossary of archaic terms. 80pp. 5$^{3}/_{16}$ x 8¼. 26686-9

THE BATTLES THAT CHANGED HISTORY, Fletcher Pratt. Eminent historian profiles 16 crucial conflicts, ancient to modern, that changed the course of civilization. 352pp. 5⅜ x 8½. 41129-X

THE WIT AND HUMOR OF OSCAR WILDE, Alvin Redman (ed.). More than 1,000 ripostes, paradoxes, wisecracks: Work is the curse of the drinking classes; I can resist everything except temptation; etc. 258pp. 5⅜ x 8½. 20602-5

SHAKESPEARE LEXICON AND QUOTATION DICTIONARY, Alexander Schmidt. Full definitions, locations, shades of meaning in every word in plays and poems. More than 50,000 exact quotations. 1,485pp. 6½ x 9¼. 2-vol. set.
Vol. 1: 22726-X
Vol. 2: 22727-8

SELECTED POEMS, Emily Dickinson. Over 100 best-known, best-loved poems by one of America's foremost poets, reprinted from authoritative early editions. No comparable edition at this price. Index of first lines. 64pp. 5 3/16 x 8¼. 26466-1

THE INSIDIOUS DR. FU-MANCHU, Sax Rohmer. The first of the popular mystery series introduces a pair of English detectives to their archnemesis, the diabolical Dr. Fu-Manchu. Flavorful atmosphere, fast-paced action, and colorful characters enliven this classic of the genre. 208pp. 5 3/16 x 8¼. 29898-1

THE MALLEUS MALEFICARUM OF KRAMER AND SPRENGER, translated by Montague Summers. Full text of most important witchhunter's "bible," used by both Catholics and Protestants. 278pp. 6⅝ x 10. 22802-9

SPANISH STORIES/CUENTOS ESPAÑOLES: A Dual-Language Book, Angel Flores (ed.). Unique format offers 13 great stories in Spanish by Cervantes, Borges, others. Faithful English translations on facing pages. 352pp. 5⅜ x 8½. 25399-6

GARDEN CITY, LONG ISLAND, IN EARLY PHOTOGRAPHS, 1869–1919, Mildred H. Smith. Handsome treasury of 118 vintage pictures, accompanied by carefully researched captions, document the Garden City Hotel fire (1899), the Vanderbilt Cup Race (1908), the first airmail flight departing from the Nassau Boulevard Aerodrome (1911), and much more. 96pp. 8⅞ x 11¾. 40669-5

OLD QUEENS, N.Y., IN EARLY PHOTOGRAPHS, Vincent F. Seyfried and William Asadorian. Over 160 rare photographs of Maspeth, Jamaica, Jackson Heights, and other areas. Vintage views of DeWitt Clinton mansion, 1939 World's Fair and more. Captions. 192pp. 8⅞ x 11. 26358-4

CAPTURED BY THE INDIANS: 15 Firsthand Accounts, 1750-1870, Frederick Drimmer. Astounding true historical accounts of grisly torture, bloody conflicts, relentless pursuits, miraculous escapes and more, by people who lived to tell the tale. 384pp. 5⅜ x 8½. 24901-8

THE WORLD'S GREAT SPEECHES (Fourth Enlarged Edition), Lewis Copeland, Lawrence W. Lamm, and Stephen J. McKenna. Nearly 300 speeches provide public speakers with a wealth of updated quotes and inspiration–from Pericles' funeral oration and William Jennings Bryan's "Cross of Gold Speech" to Malcolm X's powerful words on the Black Revolution and Earl of Spenser's tribute to his sister, Diana, Princess of Wales. 944pp. 5⅜ x 8⅜. 40903-1

THE BOOK OF THE SWORD, Sir Richard F. Burton. Great Victorian scholar/adventurer's eloquent, erudite history of the "queen of weapons"–from prehistory to early Roman Empire. Evolution and development of early swords, variations (sabre, broadsword, cutlass, scimitar, etc.), much more. 336pp. 6⅛ x 9¼. 25434-8

AUTOBIOGRAPHY: The Story of My Experiments with Truth, Mohandas K. Gandhi. Boyhood, legal studies, purification, the growth of the Satyagraha (nonviolent protest) movement. Critical, inspiring work of the man responsible for the freedom of India. 480pp. 5⅜ x 8½. (Available in U.S. only.) 24593-4

CELTIC MYTHS AND LEGENDS, T. W. Rolleston. Masterful retelling of Irish and Welsh stories and tales. Cuchulain, King Arthur, Deirdre, the Grail, many more. First paperback edition. 58 full-page illustrations. 512pp. 5⅜ x 8½. 26507-2

THE PRINCIPLES OF PSYCHOLOGY, William James. Famous long course complete, unabridged. Stream of thought, time perception, memory, experimental methods; great work decades ahead of its time. 94 figures. 1,391pp. 5⅜ x 8½. 2-vol. set. Vol. I: 20381-6 Vol. II: 20382-4

THE WORLD AS WILL AND REPRESENTATION, Arthur Schopenhauer. Definitive English translation of Schopenhauer's life work, correcting more than 1,000 errors, omissions in earlier translations. Translated by E. F. J. Payne. Total of 1,269pp. 5⅜ x 8½. 2-vol. set. Vol. 1: 21761-2 Vol. 2: 21762-0

MAGIC AND MYSTERY IN TIBET, Madame Alexandra David-Neel. Experiences among lamas, magicians, sages, sorcerers, Bonpa wizards. A true psychic discovery. 32 illustrations. 321pp. 5⅜ x 8½. (Available in U.S. only.) 22682-4

THE EGYPTIAN BOOK OF THE DEAD, E. A. Wallis Budge. Complete reproduction of Ani's papyrus, finest ever found. Full hieroglyphic text, interlinear transliteration, word-for-word translation, smooth translation. 533pp. 6½ x 9¼. 21866-X

MATHEMATICS FOR THE NONMATHEMATICIAN, Morris Kline. Detailed, college-level treatment of mathematics in cultural and historical context, with numerous exercises. Recommended Reading Lists. Tables. Numerous figures. 641pp. 5⅜ x 8½. 24823-2

PROBABILISTIC METHODS IN THE THEORY OF STRUCTURES, Isaac Elishakoff. Well-written introduction covers the elements of the theory of probability from two or more random variables, the reliability of such multivariable structures, the theory of random function, Monte Carlo methods of treating problems incapable of exact solution, and more. Examples. 502pp. 5⅜ x 8½. 40691-1

THE RIME OF THE ANCIENT MARINER, Gustave Doré, S. T. Coleridge. Doré's finest work; 34 plates capture moods, subtleties of poem. Flawless full-size reproductions printed on facing pages with authoritative text of poem. "Beautiful. Simply beautiful."–*Publisher's Weekly.* 77pp. 9¼ x 12. 22305-1

NORTH AMERICAN INDIAN DESIGNS FOR ARTISTS AND CRAFTSPEOPLE, Eva Wilson. Over 360 authentic copyright-free designs adapted from Navajo blankets, Hopi pottery, Sioux buffalo hides, more. Geometrics, symbolic figures, plant and animal motifs, etc. 128pp. 8⅜ x 11. (Not for sale in the United Kingdom.) 25341-4

SCULPTURE: Principles and Practice, Louis Slobodkin. Step-by-step approach to clay, plaster, metals, stone; classical and modern. 253 drawings, photos. 255pp. 8⅛ x 11. 22960-2

THE INFLUENCE OF SEA POWER UPON HISTORY, 1660–1783, A. T. Mahan. Influential classic of naval history and tactics still used as text in war colleges. First paperback edition. 4 maps. 24 battle plans. 640pp. 5⅜ x 8½. 25509-3

THE STORY OF THE TITANIC AS TOLD BY ITS SURVIVORS, Jack Winocour (ed.). What it was really like. Panic, despair, shocking inefficiency, and a little heroism. More thrilling than any fictional account. 26 illustrations. 320pp. 5⅜ x 8½.
20610-6

FAIRY AND FOLK TALES OF THE IRISH PEASANTRY, William Butler Yeats (ed.). Treasury of 64 tales from the twilight world of Celtic myth and legend: "The Soul Cages," "The Kildare Pooka," "King O'Toole and his Goose," many more. Introduction and Notes by W. B. Yeats. 352pp. 5⅜ x 8½.
26941-8

BUDDHIST MAHAYANA TEXTS, E. B. Cowell and others (eds.). Superb, accurate translations of basic documents in Mahayana Buddhism, highly important in history of religions. The Buddha-karita of Asvaghosha, Larger Sukhavativyuha, more. 448pp. 5⅜ x 8½.
25552-2

ONE TWO THREE . . . INFINITY: Facts and Speculations of Science, George Gamow. Great physicist's fascinating, readable overview of contemporary science: number theory, relativity, fourth dimension, entropy, genes, atomic structure, much more. 128 illustrations. Index. 352pp. 5⅜ x 8½.
25664-2

EXPERIMENTATION AND MEASUREMENT, W. J. Youden. Introductory manual explains laws of measurement in simple terms and offers tips for achieving accuracy and minimizing errors. Mathematics of measurement, use of instruments, experimenting with machines. 1994 edition. Foreword. Preface. Introduction. Epilogue. Selected Readings. Glossary. Index. Tables and figures. 128pp. 5⅜ x 8½.   40451-X

DALÍ ON MODERN ART: The Cuckolds of Antiquated Modern Art, Salvador Dalí. Influential painter skewers modern art and its practitioners. Outrageous evaluations of Picasso, Cézanne, Turner, more. 15 renderings of paintings discussed. 44 calligraphic decorations by Dalí. 96pp. 5⅜ x 8½. (Available in U.S. only.)
29220-7

ANTIQUE PLAYING CARDS: A Pictorial History, Henry René D'Allemagne. Over 900 elaborate, decorative images from rare playing cards (14th–20th centuries): Bacchus, death, dancing dogs, hunting scenes, royal coats of arms, players cheating, much more. 96pp. 9¼ x 12¼.
29265-7

MAKING FURNITURE MASTERPIECES: 30 Projects with Measured Drawings, Franklin H. Gottshall. Step-by-step instructions, illustrations for constructing handsome, useful pieces, among them a Sheraton desk, Chippendale chair, Spanish desk, Queen Anne table and a William and Mary dressing mirror. 224pp. 8⅛ x 11¼.
29338-6

THE FOSSIL BOOK: A Record of Prehistoric Life, Patricia V. Rich et al. Profusely illustrated definitive guide covers everything from single-celled organisms and dinosaurs to birds and mammals and the interplay between climate and man. Over 1,500 illustrations. 760pp. 7½ x 10⅛.
29371-8

Paperbound unless otherwise indicated. Available at your book dealer, online at **www.doverpublications.com**, or by writing to Dept. GI, Dover Publications, Inc., 31 East 2nd Street, Mineola, NY 11501. For current price information or for free catalogues (please indicate field of interest), write to Dover Publications or log on to **www.doverpublications.com** and see every Dover book in print. Dover publishes more than 500 books each year on science, elementary and advanced mathematics, biology, music, art, literary history, social sciences, and other areas.